BRITISH CANALS
An Illustrated History

THE CANALS OF THE BRITISH ISLES

EDITED BY CHARLES HADFIELD

British Canals. An illustrated history. By Charles Hadfield
The Canals of Eastern England. By John Boyes and Ronald Russell
The Canals of the East Midlands (including part of London). By Charles Hadfield
The Canals of North West England. By Charles Hadfield and Gordon Biddle
The Canals of the North of Ireland. By W. A. McCutcheon
The Canals of Scotland. By Jean Lindsay
The Canals of the South of Ireland. By V. T. H. and D. R. Delany
The Canals of South and South East England. By Charles Hadfield
The Canals of South Wales and the Border. By Charles Hadfield
The Canals of South West England. By Charles Hadfield
The Canals of the West Midlands. By Charles Hadfield
The Canals of Yorkshire and North East England. By Charles Hadfield
Waterways to Stratford. By Charles Hadfield and John Norris

OTHER BOOKS BY CHARLES HADFIELD

Inland Waterways
Waterways Sights to See
William Jessop, Engineer (with A. W. Skempton)
The Canal Age
Holiday Cruising on Inland Waterways (with Michael Streat)

IN PREPARATION

World Canals. An illustrated history

BRITISH CANALS

An Illustrated History

by
Charles Hadfield

Seventh Edition

DAVID & CHARLES

NEWTON ABBOT   LONDON   NORTH POMFR

British Library Cataloguing in Publication Data

Hadfield, Charles
  British canals.—7th. ed.—(The canals of the British Isles).
  1. Inland navigation—Great Britain—History
  I. Title   II. Series
  386′.0941   HE663
  ISBN 0-7153-8568-2/ (hardback)
        0-7153-8569-0/ (paperback)

1st edition 1950
2nd edition 1959   Reprinted 1962
3rd edition 1966
4th edition 1969   Reprinted 1972
5th edition 1974
6th edition 1979
7th edition 1984

© *Charles Hadfield 1950, 1959, 1962, 1966, 1969, 1972, 1974, 1979, 1984*

...at Britain by
...d, Trowbridge Wilts
...(Publishers) Limited
...rton Abbot Devon

...ed States of America by
...Charles Inc
...Vermont 05053   USA

CONTENTS

	Page
List of Illustrations	7
List of Maps	11
Preface to the Seventh Edition	15

Chapter		Page
I	The Old Days	17
II	Building the Canals	33
III	Life on the Canals	54
IV	The Arteries of the Revolution	81
V	Birmingham, Basingstoke and Pontcysyllte	95
VI	The Canal Mania and the Wars	107
VII	Linking the Seas	132
VIII	Canals and Ports	144
IX	The Golden Years	159
X	The Rivers during the Canal Age	199
XI	War with the Railways	217
XII	The Years of Decline	243
XIII	Time of Hope	259
XIV	The Manchester Ship Canal	282
XV	From Royal Commission to 1948	291
XVI	Transformation Scene	304

Author's Notes and Acknowledgements	337
Sources of Quotations	338
Bibliography	344
Index to the 'Canals of the British Isles' series	349
Index	356

Figure 1 The young Duke of Bridgewater pointing to the Barton aqueduct
that carries his canal from Worsley. Men can be seen towing a flat on the
Mersey & Irwell Navigation below

LIST OF ILLUSTRATIONS

Plates

	Page
A Thames flash-lock	129
Norwich & Lowestoft Navigation share certificate	129
The opening of the Glastonbury Canal	130
Devizes flight of locks on the Kennet & Avon	147
Galton bridge on the Birmingham's summit level	147
A caisson on the Blackhill inclined plane	148
Tub-boats on Trench inclined plane	148
Anderton lift before reconstruction	165
Falkirk tunnel	165
The Paddington packet boat	166
Road, canal and railway at Hebden Bridge in 1845	166
A sailing keel near Doncaster in 1936	183
Steam on the New Junction Canal in 1932	183
Weaver packets in 1957	184
Compartment boats at Castleford	184
Early days at Little Venice	201
Narrow boats and boatpeople	201
Sailing barges at Spalding about 1900	202
Loading sugar beet on the Broads in 1959	202
The *Fairy Queen* on the Forth & Clyde	219
Slateford aqueduct on the Union Canal	219
Loading turf near Tullamore in 1894	220
A scene on the Boyne Navigation in 1894	220
Grange mills on the Grand Canal in 1884	221
The *Countess of Mayo* on the Shannon in 1910	221
A coaster enters the Newry Ship Canal	222
A barge leaves Toomebridge lock on the Lower Bann	222
A horse-drawn pleasure boat on the Llangollen Canal	239
Pleasure cruising on the Ripon Canal early this century	239
Canal children at school	240
The Regent's Park explosion of 1874	240
A Grand Junction steam dredger at work in 1898	257
The Peak Forest Canal is breached	257
The Manchester Ship Canal under construction	258

	Page
Barton swing aqueduct	258
Barges on the Gloucester & Sharpness	275
Cruising on the Shropshire Union	275
A canal boatwoman in her cabin	276

Text Illustrations

Figure		*Page*
1	The young Duke of Bridgewater pointing to the Barton aqueduct	6
2	A stage waggon	18
3	A packhorse train	19
4	Worsley, showing entrances to the colliery canals	31
5	Design for a swing bridge: the tools that built the canals	40
6	Varying profiles of canal construction	42
7	Token issued by John Pinkerton on the Basingstoke Canal	44
8	Puddling a canal	45
9	A share certificate	50
10	Donkeys towing a canal boat	62
11	The inclined plane at Ketley shown on a token	66
12	Boatwoman and baby	73
13	Opening the paddles of a lock	76
14	The early 1820s were disturbed years in Ireland	79
15	A romantic picture of Harecastle tunnel	84
16	Thames & Severn Canal token	90
17	Pontcysyllte aqueduct	104
18	The cast-iron trough of Pontcysyllte aqueduct	105
19	Boats are sold to recover debts	114
20	Early days at Paddington basin	127
21	City Road basin	128
22	Three cross-sections of the Exeter Canal	149
23	Token showing a Tyne keel	158
24	The Lune aqueduct	160
25	Jessop's Rochdale Canal climbs over the Pennines	161
26	The Marple aqueduct	162
27	A cart boat and a tramroad waggon boat	173
28	The two Harecastle tunnels	177
29	A night mixed goods and passenger boat and a swift boat	186

Figure		*Page*
30	A through boat and coach service between Edinburgh and Glasgow	187
31	A passenger boat on the Lancaster Canal	188
32	An Irish through service by boat and coach	189
33	Passenger timetable of 1802 (front)	190
34	Passenger timetable of 1802 (back)	192
35	Seal of the Norwich & Lowestoft Navigation Company	204
36	Tolls on the Trent & Mersey	230–1
37	A gift to railway competition	234
38	An example of heavy price-cutting	237
39	A canal is closed so that a railway may be built	242
40	Pleasure cruising in 1867	255
41	The Church cares for boatmen's souls	263
42	A canal child	266
43	Irlam locks on the Manchester Ship Canal at time of opening	289
44	A canal is restored	321

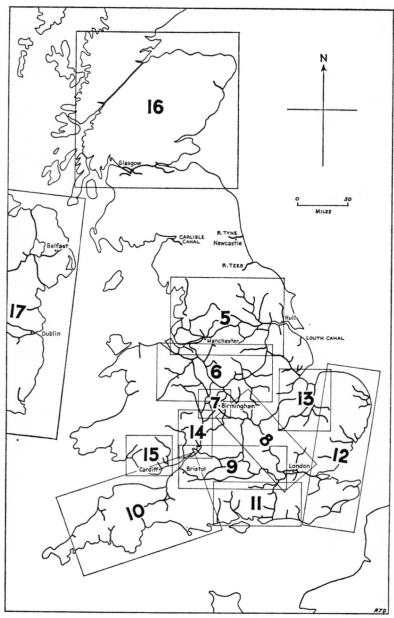

Map 1   Key map to area maps

LIST OF MAPS

Map		Page
1	Key Map to Area Maps*	10
2	Navigable waterways, 1600–60	24
3	Navigable waterways, 1724–7	25
4	The waterway system, 1789	83
5	The canals of Lancashire and Yorkshire	87
6	The North Midlands	97
7	The Birmingham canals and their connections	99
8	The Grand Junction Canal and its connections	110
9	The River Thames and its connections	116
10	The canals of the South-west	122
11	The canals of Southern England	125
12	The waterways of Kent and East Anglia	145
13	The Fenland waterways	168
14	The River Severn and its connections	170
15	The Welsh canals and their tramroad feeders	176
16	The canals of Scotland	181
17	The canals of Ireland	214

* These area maps show the canal system not necessarily at its greatest extent but as it was at the end of the Canal Age, around the 1830s. They are based on the maps published by George Bradshaw in 1830, but a few canals built afterwards have been added.

PREFACE TO THE SEVENTH EDITION

Half a mile from my Devon school there ran the Grand Western Canal. Occasionally a boat laden with stone passed along it, but its main use was for fishing and bathing and for walks along its towpath by courting couples. One day in 1925 I mentioned the canal to a local solicitor, and was told of a box of old papers in his office. There were annual accounts, engineers' reports, Acts of Parliament and shareholders' registers of a hundred or more years before.

So I became interested in the history of one canal, and from the Grand Western set myself to find others. I experienced the delight of discovering for myself a piece of the past and its life, in old documents and maps, and by tramping, clutching an Ordnance map, along towpaths, down lanes and through fields in search of some long disused wharf, lock or inclined plane.

I produced my first article on canal history in 1942, my first (shared) canal book in 1945, and in 1950 the first edition of *British Canals*. Twice rewritten and reset since then, it now appears once more, corrected here and there, its final chapter and that on the Manchester Ship Canal brought up to late 1983, and with a rewritten bibliography. My thanks, going back to 1950, are due to so many who have helped and taught me over the years, that most cannot possibly be named here. I must, however, mention the late David Higham, the literary agent who (with some difficulty) placed the original manuscript, and whose firm still looks after my books, the late John Baker of Phoenix House who published the first two editions, and David Thomas of my old firm of David & Charles who has brought out five more editions as well as a range of my other books. In preparing this new edition I must especially thank Dr Mark Baldwin, whose careful research and checking has enabled it, and Messrs John Collins, R. H. J. Cotton, O. H. Grafton and David Telford of the British Waterways Board, and David L. Hastie of the Manchester Ship Canal Co for their help. Acknowledgement is also due to McKnight Photography for the hardback jacket and paperback cover pictures.

Happily, I have been blessed with a sense that history is continuous, that what is past, what is happening now, and what is likely (or can be influenced) to happen in the future form one pattern. I have therefore been fortunate in being from the 1940s actively associated not only with archivists, librarians, historians, authors and industrial archaeologists, but with very many of those, then and later, active in the British waterways world, whether policy-makers, administrators, canal staff or enthusiasts. Among them, all in their time and fashion remarkable, some now almost forgotten, are Sir Osborne Mance, George Dallas, L. T. C. Rolt, Robert Aickman, Mrs Marshall, Sir Reginald Kerr, Alfred Hayman, C. D. Barwell, Christopher Marsh, Charles Hadlow, Sam Lomas, Jack (and John) James, Eily Gayford, R. H. Wyatt, Sir John Hawton, Lionel Munk, Denys Hutchings, David Hutchings, Sir Frank Price and John Heap —and their successors. Happy is the man who writes history while also living it.

I owe three special debts. One to my wife who, standing at the gas-stove in 1948, approved the first-drafted paragraphs of *British Canals*, and who, unwearied, has encouraged me to produce this seventh edition. One to canals themselves, at first in the British Isles, more recently throughout the Old and New Worlds, which have since 1925 been my companions. Lastly, one to the book itself, once a risk obstinately undertaken, continuingly a friend, a responsibility and a chore, now a milestone in my seventy-fifth year. I owe it affection for the absorption in research and the discipline of writing it has brought me, the waterways it has shown me, the friends I have made and the readers I gave gained during our long relationship.

CHARLES HADFIELD

CHAPTER I

The Old Days

✦✦

On a summer day the motor cruisers rise in Boulter's lock on the surge of water from the gates, till they are released to explore Cliveden Reach and the approach to Cookham. The pleasure craft, and the holiday-makers in them, seem to suit the river, as if it had been dredged and given locks for ease of holidaying. To our fore-fathers, the Thames as seen fifty years ago from the *Prospect of Whitby* at Wapping or the *Grapes* at Limehouse would have seemed more natural. The public houses were sandwiched between ware-houses, while all around craft unloaded. Up and down the river moved ships, sailing barges, or tugs with trains of lighters, seeking at wharves or moorings a place to feed the land with their cargoes.

In medieval times rivers were the veins of the body politic as well as economic. Boundaries between states or shires, they were crossed by fords which became the sites of towns, or by bridges which were often points of battle. Upon rivers the people of that time depended for food, power and transport.

In our day fish are caught in the sea and brought to us by rail and lorry; only the angler still thinks fresh-water fish important. But in earlier times, when sea fish were eaten only by those who lived on the sea coast, when meat was obtainable only for part of the year, and when fasts were frequent and universally practised, river fish played an important part in the national life. Every abbey and great man's house had its fish pond, and across the rivers great and small stretched the fish weirs, usually made of stakes and nets or basket-work. Between the owners of the fisheries and the bargemasters who needed an unimpeded passage continuous war was fought, till the importance of fresh-water fish lessened as the practice of fasting ceased to be universal, as meat became available all the year round, and as the transport of sea fish inland became practicable.

Rivers were also the most important source of power. Every stream had its mills, not only for grinding corn, but for all the other industrial processes of the time, such as fulling cloth or driving the hammers of ironworks. Placed down the bank wherever a head of water could be got, these mills were to be found on the tiny stream that ran through a village, or on the bigger river that was also used for navigation. An artificial cut was made from the river to bring the water at proper height to the water-wheel, and, in order to make sure of a supply of water at all seasons, the mill-owner usually built a weir across the river to hold back the water and so form an artificial reservoir. If the river were navigable, the centre of such a weir was made of planks held upright by cross beams, or dropped into vertical slots, so that they could be removed when it was necessary to pass a barge, or was fitted with a single pair of swinging gates, or one rising vertically. Varieties of these weir openings were called staunches, flash-locks, watergates or half-locks; they did not disappear from the bigger rivers till present times. Their remains can be found on Bottisham Lode, a tributary of the Cam, and elsewhere.

There was seldom a towing path in those days, and the sailing barges that were common craft on rivers were towed by gangs of men, called bow-hauliers, able to ford the side streams and scramble through obstructions better than horses, whenever the sails could not be used. It was not unknown that on their way they damaged the property of gentlemen or farmers, or stole 'Hennes, Geese, Duckes, Piggs, Swannes, Eggs, Woode and all other such Commodytyes'. Going upstream on a river usually undredged, and the

Figure 2   A stage waggon

waters of which were held back as each miller needed to protect the
supplies of his own mill, a barge might go aground, in which case
a man must walk to the next mill above, and bargain with the owner
for a flash—enough water to be released from the weir to raise the
river level and so free the barge. It was written later, but pertinently:

'Barge-masters are frequently obliged to send Ten or Twenty
Miles ahead, and pay extra Fees and Gratuities to obtain a Flash. This
Expence and Loss of Time brings on a considerable Charge to the
Barge-Owner, renders his Arrival at any given Place uncertain, and
gives the Land Carriage the greatest Advantage over that of the
River Navigation.'[1]

When the barge reached the weir itself, there was more bargaining
with the miller, especially in dry weather when water was short,

Figure 3   A packhorse train

before he would consent to open the weir and allow the levels of the
river above and below to equalise sufficiently for the barge to be
hauled up against the flow by a winch. If it were going downstream,
the barge would in the same way need the weir to be opened to allow
it through, and a flash of water to pass it over the shallows below.
Sometimes in the summer the miller would cause bargemasters to

wait for days or even weeks for the water that would take them on their way. The records are full of the quarrels between the two interests: of excessive charges, refusals to give a flash, fights and stratagems. In medieval times, but dying away later, are records of similar efforts to do away with the fish weirs. Taken in all, the obstructions to navigation of the rivers are the most likely origin and recurrent cause of the bad language associated with bargees.

Transport and power are essentials of any economy. If a nation is to grow richer, progress in her agriculture and industry will soon exert pressure upon her sources of power and transport for similar improvements, and if they are not forthcoming, progress will stop. Similarly, innovations in power or transport will give opportunities to industry and agriculture which may be taken, in which case progress is consolidated, or not taken, when the new development will appear to be a financial failure. It is to the gradual correlation of improving transport with increasing industry and agriculture that we can attribute the slow forward movement which became perceptible in Elizabeth's reign, and which later gained speed and, allied to improved means of producing power, became the Industrial Revolution. From a population of four millions in 1600 the people of England increased to over seven millions by 1750. Industry and mining slowly grew in output and variety, but their products could be moved in only three ways, by land, by sea, or by river.

Land carriage has always existed, of course, but before the days of the road engineers of the later eighteenth century roads were so bad that waggons could not always be used, and much was carried on the backs of horses and mules. Except for very short distances, however, the cost of road transport was prohibitively expensive. One horse could draw perhaps two tons on a level road, and from fifty to a hundred tons on a good waterway, according to its size, in each case accompanied by a man and a boy. Road transport was therefore limited to short-distance carriage—for instance, of coal for a few miles round a colliery—or to bring goods to or from a river or the sea.

Round the coasts, the ships of the coasting trade carried many of the goods that nowadays would move by road or rail, though the Thames receives a great deal of Tyne coal as it has been received for hundreds of years, by sea; the names of Seacoal Lane and Newcastle Close (formerly Newcastle Street), off Farringdon Road, remind us of the days when barges used to work up the Fleet river to unload Tyne coal. Up the estuaries the vessels went, to little inland ports on the smaller rivers of East Anglia or to the greater ports such as London on the Thames, Bristol on the Avon, or King's

Lynn on the Great Ouse. At these places goods were transhipped to smaller craft, keels or trows or Western barges, to be taken up river to smaller ports. Such a little port was Bewdley on the Severn, with its warehouses from which the goods landed from the Severn trows were distributed by packhorse and waggon to the countryside of Worcestershire, Staffordshire and Shropshire, and a returning flow was sent down river to the seaports and the West of England. The town was particularly helped in that its own boats were free of the tolls levied by other towns on the river, by a grant of Edward IV after the battle of Tewkesbury to the men of Bewdley, who had helped him. On the other side of England, Cambridge may be instanced. From the earliest times it had been a centre for the distribution of goods brought by water from King's Lynn, and in return it sent corn and produce downstream. The great Stourbridge Fair was maintained largely by waterway trade.

The River Severn was the main water carrier of England. Apart from the traffic that came upstream from the port of Bristol to be distributed from its banks, and that originating from the industries and crafts carried on along its length, such as the saltworks of Droitwich, it carried great quantities of coal from the collieries of Broseley, Benthall and Barr in Shropshire. Out of the two or three hundred thousand tons of coal carried on English rivers at the end of the seventeenth century, one hundred thousand was borne on the Severn to Shrewsbury, Bridgnorth, Bewdley, Worcester, Tewkesbury and Gloucester. The Thames was another distributing and trading river, spreading along its banks the goods and the coal that flowed in to the port of London, and connecting together towns such as Windsor, Reading and Oxford. Other waterways of note were the Trent, the Tyne and the Tees, and in Scotland the Clyde.

The Fen waterways were in a special position. They were indeed the highways of their country, carrying goods from overseas and from coastal ports up the Great Ouse, Nene, Welland and Witham, and sending back the produce of the countryside; bringing into the Fens from the Barnack quarries in Northamptonshire the stone to build the abbeys of Ramsey and Crowland, and the cathedrals of Peterborough, Ely and Lincoln; or carrying passengers and goods on their daily journeys about the Fenland. The fourteenth-century records of Ely:

'. . . show the sacrist and his fellows using the fenland waterways as their normal means of transport; whether it was to synods at Barnwell, or to buy cloth, wax, tallow, lead and other necessaries at Lynn and Boston, or merely to conduct their ordinary day-to-day business at Shippea, Quaveney, Littleport and elsewhere among the fens.'[2]

The period before Elizabeth was one in which legislation was passed mainly to preserve or restore the navigation of rivers already naturally navigable; the period after her reign was taken up much more with attempts to make new navigable rivers. Before Elizabeth the Thames and the Lea, the Yorkshire Ouse, the Kentish Stour and other rivers had been put under the care of corporations or other bodies charged with maintaining the navigation, while Acts had been passed to authorise the removal of fishery and other obstructions from the biggest rivers. Any attempts to improve the navigation had to be made by bodies with powers to compel invasions of the rights of private property. The usual bodies to exercise these powers were either the corporations of cities such as London, Gloucester or York, or the Commissions of Sewers which were set up by an Act of Henry VIII and were concerned primarily with drainage and flood prevention rather than with navigation. They were constituted from the local landowners, with powers to levy a rate upon those whose lands were benefited.

When emphasis fell upon the making navigable of rivers not formerly so, the usual practice was to grant letters patent to one or more people who undertook to make the navigation; for instance, letters were granted in 1634 to Thomas Skipwith to make the Soar navigable. In other cases trustees were appointed, or powers granted to a company. In any of these cases the undertakers (we would now call them entrepreneurs) were given power to collect tolls from all who used the improved navigation, and sometimes the exclusive right to carry goods upon it.

In Elizabeth I's reign the pound-lock was introduced into England, though it was already in use on the Continent; this invention made possible the improvement of river navigation beyond the point to which it could be taken by dredging and the removal of obstructions, and effected so great an economy in the use of water compared with the old flash-lock that a compromise with the millers sometimes became possible. The pound-lock,* used on rivers and canals to alter the level of navigable water, consists of a chamber enclosed within two sets of gates fitted with sluices. A boat enters the chamber to go downstream, the gates are shut, and the water is drained from the chamber through sluices in the lower gates, till the water level inside is equal to that outside. Then the lower gates are opened, and the boat moves into the lower pound. Going upwards, when the boat is to be raised, the lower gates are shut, and the lock chamber is filled with water entering through sluices in the upper

* A pound-lock is so called because it pounds up the water. The levels of canal each side of a lock are called pounds.

gates. If a pound-lock were used, therefore, to pass boats from one level of a river to another, the weirs no longer needed to contain a central movable portion or flash-lock, but could be made continuous. At the same time there was a great saving of water, for whereas a flash given to a barge might cause the lowering of the level of the whole river up to the next weir, by an amount nearly the same as the height of the weir, only a lockful of water was used in passing a boat through a pound-lock.

The first known examples of such pound-locks in Britain were not upon a river, but upon a canal born before its time. John Trew of Glamorgan, an engineer otherwise unknown, built three upon the Exeter Canal between 1564 and 1566. They began also to be built on rivers; seemingly one each on the Lea and the Trent in Elizabeth I's reign, then in the seventeenth century on the Thames between Iffley and Abingdon, the Warwickshire Avon, Wey and elsewhere. They were now included in improvement schemes, as on the Great Ouse, along with the older flash-locks, which continued to be used.

Opposition to navigation improvements came from many quarters. Those interested in road transport naturally disliked a cheaper competitor; landowners along the banks of rivers objected to the introduction of pound-locks because of the danger that their lands might be flooded as a result of raising the water level, or their water-meadows not be flooded because of better flood-control; farmers feared lest the wider areas of trade opened up by improved transport would cause prices to fall, since in times of scarcity corn could by water be obtained from farther away. But the most sustained opposition to particular schemes came from those towns which were distributing centres for goods, and which saw themselves being supplanted. Nottingham, for instance, high up the navigation of the Trent, bitterly opposed the efforts of Derby to make the Derwent navigable, and so cause goods coming up the Trent to pass by Nottingham and go on to Derby without transhipment. Reading opposed the making navigable of the Kennet to Newbury; Liverpool the passage by Mersey and Irwell to Manchester; while York was afraid that if the rivers Aire and Calder were made navigable to Leeds and Wakefield, the textile workers of those parts would be given facilities to compete with its own citizens. Lawyers were therefore engaged, petitions from interested groups sought and members of Parliament approached for their support, as battles took place over navigation Bills.

The first serious attempts to drain the Fens were made in the first decades of the seventeenth century. Towns like Cambridge were afraid lest the navigation of their rivers should be injured. In 1630 an agreement, the Lynn Law, was made with the Duke of Bedford, the chief promoter of the drainage, which provided:

'. . . that the port and haven of King's Lynn shall be preserved,

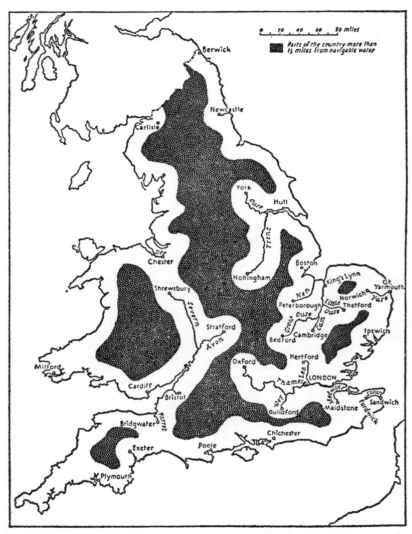

Map 2   Navigable waterways, 1600–60

and the navigation passage and highways, in, upon and about all and every the navigable rivers within the limits of this commission, namely the river of Ouse, Grant, Nean, Welland and Glean, shall be likewise preserved, and no prejudice, annoyance, hurt or hindrance done to them or any of them, by any of the means aforesaid.'[3]

Map 3 Navigable waterways, 1724–7

Though successive regulations to keep a minimum depth in the watercourses for navigation purposes often conflicted with the engineers' wishes to have as little water as practicable in them before possible floods, the rights of navigation were preserved in all legislation for the better drainage of the Fens, in spite of many disputes. Especially were there arguments over Denver sluice, which was considered by the navigation proponents to be the cause of the silting up of the channel below it, till it collapsed early in the eighteenth century.

Thereafter we see three main periods of activity in making rivers navigable. Before the first, from 1662 to 1665, England had about 685 miles of river navigation, including the Thames, Severn, Trent, Yorkshire Ouse and Great Ouse. With the restoration of Charles II in 1660, the nation had turned with relief and energy from the intellectual, religious and military struggles of the Civil War. Of the Acts passed between 1662 and 1665, those covering the Worcestershire Stour and Salwarpe, the Wye and Lugg, Medway, Hampshire Avon, and Itchen are important. On 2 March 1665 the Speaker of the House of Commons told the Lords:

'Cosmographers do agree that this Island is incomparably furnished with pleasant Rivers, like Veins in the Natural Body, which conveys the Blood into all the Parts, whereby the whole is nourished, and made useful; but the Poet tells us, he acts best, *qui miscuit utile dulci*. Therefore we have prepared some Bills for making small Rivers navigable; a Thing that in other Countries hath been more experienced, and hath been found very advantageous; it easeth the People of the great Charge of Land Carriages; preserves the Highways, which are daily worn out with Waggons carrying excessive Burdens; it breeds up a Nursery of Watermen, which, upon Occasion, will prove good Seamen; and with much Facility maintain Intercourse and Communion between Cities and Countries.'[4]

During this Restoration period some canal Bills were introduced, for instance to join Thames to Severn, which failed to pass. An interest in canals was expressed by Sir Robert Southwell when he read a paper to the newly formed Royal Society on the advantages of digging canals from the Midlands to supply London with coal, a point of view which was opposed by John Houghton in his book *Husbandry and Trade*, on the ground that such canals would diminish the sea trade from Newcastle.

In the second period of activity, after the peace of Ryswick and before the War of the Spanish Succession, from 1697 to 1700, Acts were passed for the Tone, the Aire & Calder, the upper Trent, the Lark, the Yorkshire Derwent and other rivers. In the third, from

1719 to 1721, river navigation was caught up in the boom associated with the South Sea Bubble, and there were Acts for the Derbyshire Derwent, Douglas, Weaver, Mersey & Irwell, Bristol Avon and others. The figure of 685 miles of river navigation before 1660 had by 1724 reached 1,160 miles. Apart from the mountainous areas, most of England was now within fifteen miles of a navigable river; goods moved more freely, at less cost, and often in new patterns. Before the Aire and Calder rivers were made navigable, wool finished its journey to the Yorkshire manufacturers from east coast ports, or from Lincolnshire or Leicestershire, by road, while cloth from the Leeds and Wakefield markets was also sent by road to the nearest points on navigable rivers, Knottingley or Rawcliffe on the lower Aire, Selby on the Ouse, or Tadcaster on the Wharfe. York, again, received much of its coal not from the West Riding mines only twenty miles from the city—whence it was brought by road transport —but from Newcastle, by keel down the Tyne, ship to the Humber, and then up the Ouse in lighters to York, a distance of two hundred miles. Sometimes difficult cargoes were handled, as for instance when at Leominster:

'. . . in 1756, the seven Bells were removed from the Tower, and taken to the Wharf on the Lugg at the bottom of Etnam Street (still called Bell Hole in consequence), where they were placed on board a barge and taken down the Lugg and Wye to Chepstow to be recast. The voyage was an adventurous one, for the Lugg Navigation Scheme carried out about that time (by erecting Flood Gates at intervals at a cost of several thousand pounds, instead of building proper Locks) was somewhat of a failure. . . . The Bells were brought back again, with some little difficulty, by water.'[5]

Failures were frequent, indeed, and often three or four groups of undertakers would at different times attempt to make the same river navigable. Many were defeated by opposition from one interest or another, some by the rivers themselves, such as the Worcestershire Stour which destroyed by a flood the work that had been done between 1665 and 1667 to make it navigable to Stourbridge, or the Calder & Hebble, upon which the floods of 1767 and 1768 destroyed the new-built locks. Many plans failed also because of the lack of engineering knowledge at that time. As we shall see, it was the building of canals that largely created the profession of civil engineer by producing a demand big enough to encourage specialists. However, even after well-known engineers with much practical experience were available, the making navigable of rivers was always more difficult than the building of canals, because there were more factors not under the control of the engineer. Such rivers as the

Severn and the Trent were not made properly navigable till the canal age was over. Others like the Swale never were.

Among the rivers which had successfully been made navigable were the Mersey and the Irwell. From Liverpool the River Mersey runs past Runcorn to Warrington and on to a point near Irlam, where it is joined by the River Irwell, upon which Manchester stands. At some time before 1697 the Mersey had been made navigable as far as Warrington, by clearing away the fish-weirs, but it was in 1721 that an Act was passed to authorise a company of undertakers to make the river navigable to Manchester, which:

'. . . will be very beneficial to Trade, advantageous to the Poor, and convenient for the Carriage of Coals, Cannel, Stone, Timber, and other Goods, Wares, and Merchandizes, to and from the Towns and Parts adjacent, and will very much tend to the Imploying and Increase of Watermen and Seamen, and be a Means to preserve the Highways.'[6]

By 1734 the navigation was open, with eight locks between Manchester and Warrington taking flats, sailed if possible, otherwise towed. However, Manchester needed not only trade with Liverpool, but also a supply of coal and three years later, in 1737, the company obtained an Act to make the Worsley Brook navigable, in order that from mines near Worsley coal could be taken down the brook to the Irwell and so to Manchester. The scheme was never carried out for reasons that are not certainly known, but it was, nevertheless, to have important consequences.

The Romans used the Fossdyke from the Witham at Lincoln to the Trent at Torksey as a navigation, but not, it is now thought, the Caerdyke onwards from the Witham to the Nene at Peterborough. Later the Fossdyke was dredged by Bishop Atwater in the reign of Henry I, and was thenceforward used by boats. It is our oldest canal. In the Middle Ages two short canals were built in the twelfth or thirteenth century to carry stone for the building of Rievaulx Abbey in Yorkshire, while about 1490 Sir Andrew Wood is thought to have constructed a short private canal at Largo in Fife.

In more recent times the Exeter Canal was built between 1564 and 1566, and considerably enlarged in 1698–1701; about 1696, Sir Humphrey Mackworth built a short canal from the River Neath to the Melyn lead and copper works. A number of artificial cuts, some several miles long, as on the Wey, the Kennet or the Welland, were also made to shorten or ease the navigation of rivers as part of schemes for improving them. But the first true canal since the Exeter Canal had been reconstructed in 1701 was to be built in the north of Ireland.

The end of fighting between William III and James II saw also the beginning of a drive to build inland navigations as a means of Irish economic development. Several proposals and Bills were considered by the Irish Parliament between 1697 and 1709, for improving the Shannon, Barrow, Boyne and Suir, and for building a canal from Newry to Lough Neagh. None were authorised. In 1715, however, an Act was passed to develop the midland counties of Ireland by drainage works and by making 'navigable and communicable passages for vessels of burthen to pass through'.[7] More far-sighted than practical, this Act (and those of 1721 and 1729 which supplemented it) provided for local commissioners to appoint undertakers for the different works, and to levy tolls: it also foreshadowed the later Grand Canal from Dublin to the Shannon.

Nothing resulted except some work on the River Maigue until in 1729 the small local bodies of commissioners were replaced by four new ones, one for each province. This more centralised approach, and also Dublin merchants' interest in developing coalfields in east Tyrone, combined to get work begun in 1731 on the Newry Canal from Newry to Lough Neagh, by way of which the coalfields could be reached. A third influence was Richard Castle, a French refugee who had studied Continental waterway engineering. He came to Ireland to work for E. L. Pearce, a Dublin architect who, appointed Surveyor General in 1730, was much concerned in executing the 1729 Act.

Engineered at first by Pearce, then by Castle, and after his dismissal in 1736 by Thomas Steers, the Newry Canal was opened in 1742 when 'the "Cope" of Lough Neagh, William Semple Commander'[8] arrived at Dublin, having passed through the canal with a cargo of coal. Eighteen miles long, some 45ft wide and over 5ft deep, with 14 short, wide locks with stone chambers, timber floors and sizeable falls of 12ft to 13½ft, the Newry was a precursor. From the River Blackwater, across Lough Neagh from the Newry, another canal was in 1733 begun towards Coalisland, whence coal was to be brought by road from the Tyrone pits. However, sand, bog and silt from the Blackwater's tributary, the Torrent, held up work, and this 4¾ mile long canal was not to be finished for nearly fifty years. Another waterway, the Lagan Navigation, was begun under an Act of 1753 also to reach Lough Neagh, so that Belfast could share in the hoped-for development. Partly river, partly canal, engineered by Thomas Omer, the line reached Sprucefield near Lisburn in 1765, and stopped. It would not be completed until 1794.

Steers was an astonishing man. Born as long ago as 1672, he built Liverpool's first dock in 1715. He then made the Mersey & Irwell

Navigation and part of the Douglas, and was also concerned with the Weaver, before taking on and completing the Newry Canal. While engaged on this, he began the Salthouse dock at Liverpool in 1738, and in the following year became the town's mayor. Britain's first great navigation engineer, William Steers died, approaching eighty, in 1750. His pupil, Henry Berry, built the first modern canal in England, the Sankey Brook, later called the St Helens Canal. The authorising Act was passed in 1755, nominally to make navigable the little Sankey Brook from the Mersey near Sankey Bridges to St Helens. Henry Berry, however, had probably already decided to build a canal instead. He therefore 'communicated his sentiments to one of the proprietors* who, approving the plan, agreed the work should commence on 5 September 1755, but the project was carefully concealed from the other proprietors, it being apprehended that so novel an undertaking would have met with their opposition'.[9] Most of the canal was opened in 1757, a further portion in 1759, and the whole original line in 1772.

Henry Berry and his backer, John Ashton, must receive their tribute. Yet the credit for creating the heavy transport basis of the Industrial Revolution must go to the third Duke of Bridgewater, for it was his work that found time and place and need correct.

Water and coal made that Revolution. The cotton mills that had been built to exploit the new inventions were driven by water power, and as the mills increased so they spread up the river valleys into the hills of Lancashire and Derbyshire. Industrial towns began to grow on the west, but the sea coal of the Tyne, that was carried to all the rivers and creeks of the east coast, to London and the south coast, was not available to the west. The hearths of Manchester had to be warmed by coal carried on horseback or road waggon from the collieries round; therefore it was expensive and scarce. Wood, the fuel of the village, was not available to the town. In these circumstances the Duke, who had travelled on the Continent and seen canals there which had long been known to engineers and travellers, and who must have been aware of the Sankey Brook already open not far away, decided to build a waterway to carry coal from his collieries. He obtained an Act in 1759 for a canal from Worsley to Salford opposite Manchester and from Worsley to Hollin ferry on the Mersey below the Irwell junction.

It was probably then that the Duke was introduced by his land-agent, John Gilbert, to James Brindley. Forty-three years old, the son of a crofter of the High Peak of Derbyshire, he had been apprenticed to a millwright, which trade covered many crafts other than

* John Ashton of Liverpool, who in 1759 owned 51 of the 120 shares.

Figure 4 Worsley on the Duke of Bridgewater's Canal, showing
entrances to the Duke's underground colliery canals. The boats are
'starvationers'

the building and repair of mill machinery. Brindley, by the care he
took to understand each piece of machinery he saw, became more
efficient than his master. He got a little education, and set up for
himself as a millwright at Leek, in Staffordshire. There he gained a
wide local reputation, and shortly before the Duke employed him
he had been experimenting with steam engines. Because of his knowledge of mills, including the water power that drove them, he obtained employment to survey a possible line for a canal to connect
the rivers Trent and Mersey, which was being promoted by Lord
Anson, Thomas Broade and Earl Gower, the Duke's brother-in-law,
whose agent was John Gilbert's brother. In this way the Duke of

Bridgewater met Brindley, took to the careful, solid millwright, and engaged him to re-survey the line of his canal and to build it under John Gilbert's supervision. Brindley made what he spelt as an 'ochilor servey or a ricconitoring', and he and the Duke decided that the Salford line should be abandoned, and the canal carried over the Irwell on an aqueduct and so into Manchester, probably to make a link with Cheshire easier than it would have been via the Worsley–Hollin ferry canal. A new Act was then obtained to vary the line. In spite of active opposition by the Mersey & Irwell Company, who now realised that the Duke's real object was to get access to Liverpool in competition with themselves, the Duke told Gilbert and Brindley to go ahead.

While the canal was being built, it was a wonder to all. One writer said that when finished, it 'will be the most extraordinary thing in the kingdom, if not in Europe. The boats in some places are to go underground, and in another place over a navigable river, without communicating with its waters. . . .'[10] A year later in 1761, the canal was open to the outskirts of Manchester, and barges were passing over the 200yd long aqueduct 38ft above the Irwell. At Worsley a basin was built at the foot of a sandstone cliff, and from this tunnels ran into the mine, so that coal could be loaded direct into small boats, ancestors of the later narrow boat. Eventually 46 miles of canal on four different levels were tunnelled through the mines, as the Duke's prosperity increased. By 1773 the canal was so successful that Josiah Wedgwood, paying a visit to Worsley, could say:

'We next visited Worsley, which has the appearance of a considerable Seaport town. His Grace has built some hundreds of houses, and is every year adding considerably to their number.'[11]

Coal and water had been brought together, and had been fruitful. The lesson was to be quickly learned. Before we turn away, however, let us share the memories of an old man looking back to his boyhood:

'I remember the delight with which I entered the Duke of Bridgewater's canal boat. . . . I remember his dark brown coat with gold buttons, the handsome rose of black ribbon which ornamented the tie of his hair, his placid but cheerful countenance, his manly and dignified form and carriage—they will never be forgotten. I remember his handsome pleasure boat; I can almost fancy I can still see the Duke, the Lord Gower . . . and Mr. Bradshaw,* standing on the fore end of the vessel on a fine summer evening, enjoying the refreshing breezes excited by quick sailing.'[12]

* The canal superintendent.

CHAPTER II

Building the Canals

THE Duke's canal created the canal age that ended about the year 1840. When it began George II was on the throne, and only thirteen years had passed since Prince Charles had been beaten on Culloden Moor. When it ended, Victoria was Queen. In those eighty years the Industrial Revolution took place.

Before the story of the development in transport that permitted this revolution, I shall try in this and the following chapter to give a composite picture of the birth, growth and adult life of the canals in their prime, and of their circumstances.

The beginnings of canals were essentially local. They were usually projected by men who were manufacturers or mineowners, like the group of pottery manufacturers under the leadership of Josiah Wedgwood who pushed the Trent & Mersey Canal idea past objectors and pessimists to its successful end, the ironmasters who promoted the Glamorganshire, the copper mineowners of Devonshire who built the Tavistock Canal or the coalmasters behind the Barnsley or the Dearne & Dove. Sometimes those living and working in a town to which coal would be brought were the leading promoters, in association with the colliery owners: this was the case with the Shrewsbury, Coventry, Birmingham and many other canals. Sometime the merchants of a small port hoped that canal development in the hinterland would not only develop their town, but expand its export and import trade also: these were the motives behind the promotion of the Chester and the Swansea canals. The arguments put forward in favour of a canal were basically that a waterway would bring raw materials to the factory, carry away the finished products, and supply the people with coal more cheaply than land carriage. Thomas Telford wrote:

'It will be found that Canals are chiefly useful for the following purposes: 1st, For conveying the produce of Mines to the Sea-shore. 2d, Conveying Fuel and Raw Materials to some Manufacturing Towns and Districts, and exporting the Manufactured Goods. 3d, Conveying Groceries and Merchant-goods for the Consumption of the District through which the Canal passes. 4th, Conveying Fuel for Domestic Purposes; Manure for the purposes of Agriculture;

33

transporting the produce of the Districts through which the Canal passes, to the different Markets; and promoting Agricultural Purposes in general.'[1]

In those times, each inland county of Britain was almost self-contained. Industrial works were built where raw materials were found, and sold their finished products in the near neighbourhood. Only along the banks of rivers, and upon the sea coast, was it possible to move products in bulk. Therefore the idea of a canal that would allow trade to be opened up with a different part of the country, or even with a seaport, brought visions of prosperity to manufacturers. The cheapening of raw materials, and the opportunities for the mass production of finished goods given by a widening of the market, filled them with enthusiasm. This prospective widening of the market also received support from the ordinary consumer, since it tended to equalise supplies of coal and foodstuffs. The dangers of famine and the inconveniences of dearth were reduced, while almost every account of the opening of a canal refers to the reduction brought about in the price of coal, and the consequent benefit to the poor.

Since canals were local projects, the money for them had mostly to be raised locally. It was only among men to whom solid advantages were promised that money could be got for a canal that might take many years to build, during which there would be no return unless interest were paid out of capital, and which locked money up in something as static and inconvertible as a waterway. It was local doggedness that finished canals like the Leeds & Liverpool, which took forty-six years to complete, and many others which took ten years or more.

Local capital was supplemented by regional, as in Wales, where one finds ironmasters, merchants, bankers and landed gentry holding shares in a number of enterprises. When Walter Jeffreys of Brecon died in 1815, he held a promissory note (convertible into shares) and seven shares in the Brecknock & Abergavenny Canal; three shares in the Glamorganshire, five in the Swansea, and ten in the Aberdare, as well as five Hay tramroad and two Llanvihangel tramroad shares, both these being connected to a canal. Birmingham and London investors spread their money widely but seldom thickly, and now and then one finds oddities of investment, such as the group of Leicester people who during the canal mania took shares in the Ellesmere and even the Crinan Canal in Scotland.

A good deal of the capital came, as one would expect, from colliery and works owners and merchants, a good deal also from noblemen, landed gentry and the wealthier clergy. Some came from tradesmen and professional men such as doctors and lawyers, while during the canal mania people who were probably in quite a small way of business tried to get rich quick, like the four grocers, two coopers, the innholder, mealman, joiner, mercer and perukemaker of Stratford who all subscribed to the Stratford-upon-Avon Canal.

It would be interesting to study the part the unreformed municipal corporations played in the development of canals; we have noticed them as concerned earlier with river development. Though they seldom took the principal part, as did Exeter in building the Exeter Canal, or Beverley in making Beverley Beck navigable, they sometimes helped to finance surveys, as Liverpool for the Leeds & Liverpool, and often subscribed for shares, as Nottingham for shares in the Nottingham, Chester in the Chester, Carlisle in the Carlisle, or Swansea in the Swansea canals. In such cases the mayor or other representative of the corporation would sit on the committee.

The joint-stock company—that is, the company which is financed by the proceeds of shares sold to the public—goes back in our history beyond the South Sea Bubble of 1720. It was, however, the frenzy of financial speculation in the bubble companies of that time that caused Parliament to pass an Act which made it necessary for any body that intended to act as a corporation to be set up by Act of Parliament. The necessity of getting a private Act each time that a company was formed, with all its trouble and expense, made it likely that few joint-stock companies would be established, though one or two came into existence to make rivers navigable.

When canals began to be built, however, their cost was clearly beyond the resources of all but a few wealthy men and partnerships, and therefore joint-stock companies were necessary. As compulsory powers to buy land, divert streams, cross highways, and do other such things could only be given by Parliament, it was for this reason also necessary to obtain an Act. The number of canal corporations therefore grew rapidly.

Many short branches were built privately without an Act, but few bigger waterways, because of the difficulty of buying land and getting water without compulsory powers. A notable branch built by a canal company without an Act was the Hatherton branch of the Staffordshire & Worcestershire Canal, while among private canals were the Donnington Wood (Duke of Sutherland's) in Shropshire, the Tennant in Wales, and the Torrington in Devon.

The formation of a canal company followed a common sequence of events. First, there was an advertisement in the local newspaper which ran like this one for the Leeds & Liverpool:

'. . . whereas such a navigation would be of great utility to trade, especially in time of war, and more particularly to the counties of York and Lancaster, a meeting would be held at the house of Mr John Day, known by the Sign of the Sun in Bradford aforesaid, on Wednesday, the 2nd. day of July, 1766, at 10 of the clock in the forenoon, to consider of the proper ways and means to effect such navigation, at which meeting the nobility, gentry, and clergy of the said several counties, and all others who think it their duty to interest themselves in a matter of so great importance are requested to attend.'[2]

Then followed the public meeting (often in the assembly room of an inn) when a provisional committee was elected; the subscription for preliminary expenses, the appointment of an engineer to survey and report upon a route and give an estimate of the cost and probable receipts, the further meeting to receive the report, the resolution to apply to Parliament for an Act, the opening of subscription books for shares and the payment of deposits, the organisation of petitions to Parliament in favour of the project, the despatch by river interests, other canal companies, turnpike trustees, landowners, land carriers and anyone else aggrieved of counter petitions, the expensive battle before the Parliamentary committees of Lords and Commons, with a full array of counsel and witnesses, including eminent engineers, the various compromises such as clauses to pay compensation tolls, to limit dividends (on the Derby Canal dividends were limited to 8 per cent, after which money had to go to a reserve balance to reduce tolls), guarantees of another company's dividends (as of the Droitwich and Stourbridge canals by the Worcester & Birmingham), or of turnpike trustees against loss, as the Leicester Navigation had to do, and finally the Act, whereupon:

'. . . on receiving the agreeable news that His Majesty had been at the House of Peers and signed the Bill for making the Navigable Canal from this Town (Birmingham) to Wolverhampton, the Bells were set to ringing, which were continued the whole Day.'[3]

All this cost a great deal of money, and promotion expenses were a serious drain on capital. A contemporary writer says:

'. . . in a much larger proportion of the unproductive concerns, the necessity and utility of these were apparent, and the prospects of the adventurers were good, had not the opposing interests of the Park, and Mill, and Landowners, and of previously existing Navigations, Railways, Roads, etc. interposed in the Legislature, such difficulties, and increased expenses of execution, and in other instances such diminished tolls, exceptions therefrom, or compensation to other concerns, etc., etc., as destroyed these prospects.'[4]

Opposition to canals came from many sources. The landowners

feared lest the waterway should be carried through their fertile low-lying lands, and should drain their water-meadows. They needed to be well compensated also for the inconvenience caused them by a canal that might prevent them from enlarging a park, or which divided part of their property from the rest, and brought with it bargemen who did not always respect the Game Laws.

The local population, while understanding that canals would bring to them cheaply the fuel and the goods they needed, sometimes feared that local produce would be removed from them. Cobbett was the spokesman for this kind of opposition when he wrote of the canal at Cricklade:

'. . . while the poor creatures that raise the wheat and the barley and cheese and the mutton and the beef are living upon potatoes, an accursed canal comes kindly through the parish to convey away the wheat and all the good food to the tax-eaters and their attendants in the Wen.'[5]*

Rural millowners feared loss of water from their streams to the canals, and were supported by the farmers who depended upon the mills for the grinding of their corn, while owners of industrial mills, driven for instance by the Pennine streams, fought bitterly against possible deprivation of their power resources. Road turnpike trustees thought canals would reduce the tolls on their roads, while road carriers saw a loss of livelihood, an argument they backed up with the accusation that a transport monopoly was being created, and that the reduced demand for horses would lead to a smaller demand for oats, and so hit the farmer. The coasting trade saw a reduction in the amount of coal and goods carried by sea, which would now be diverted to the more direct inland navigations, while the existing river or canal interests did all they could to make sure that, if they were affected, they did not suffer, on the one hand by demanding compensation payments for loss of tolls, or the erection of physical bars to conserve their water; on the other by positive inducements, as when the Monmouthshire Canal offered the Brecknock & Abergavenny company £3,000 and ample water if the latter would join its line to the Monmouthshire, rather than build an independent outlet to the River Usk.

All in all, there were some bitter arguments before the Parliamentary committees. This is a specimen, from the speech of the counsel for the Thames Commissioners, opposing a proposed canal (the Hants & Berks Junction) to join the Kennet & Avon Canal at Newbury to the Basingstoke Canal near Old Basing, and so to avoid the passage of the Thames below Reading.

* London.

'Yet even if, which is impossible, water could be procured; and if, which is equally impossible, the repairs [to the Basingstoke Canal] required to an extent little short of beginning *de novo*, could be effected for the sum of ten thousand pounds, instead of ten times ten thousand, where is the money to come from? And what prospect is there of any return for it? Might it not just as well be thrown into the sea; and much better thrown *literally* into the Basingstoke Canal, as in all probability there would not be water enough there to cover it? And what guarantee has this Committee that it ever will be forthcoming? The concern has long been bankrupt; its dividends are, as they have always been, naught. There is but one last lingering trader upon it, and he is on the point of flitting, lest his ruin should be consummated. From what quarter can a single ray of hope be expected to break in upon a scene of such utter desolation? This is not a rational project for improving an eligible line of Canal navigation; but is rather like many of those New World schemes, with unpronounceable names, which are so rife in these days, distinguished by such a fatuous and headlong rage for speculation that, if any one were to start a Mining Company in Utopia, he could presently dispose of the shares at a profit.'[6]

Sometimes the opposition was overwhelmed; sometimes it was persuaded, by conversion of the heart, lining of the pocket or allotment of shares likely to appreciate quickly in value. For instance, a Bristol newspaper remarks of the opponents of the Kennet & Avon Bill:

'Those who went up to London to petition against it, are returned, and are now most laudably employed in pointing out its beneficial effects, and soliciting the assent of all their late demurring neighbours.'[7]

Opposition overcome and the Act obtained, a first general assembly of the shareholders was held. At this a committee and officers were appointed, a clerk, who was probably the local solicitor, to take the minutes, write the important letters and do the legal work, with a full-time assistant paid by the company; an accountant, a treasurer, very likely a banking firm; a principal and a resident engineer, and usually also one or two assistants and a clerk of works. Land was bought and workmen engaged, and then with junketings the first sod was cut. On 26 July 1766, for instance, the population of Burslem and its neighbourhood took the day off to celebrate the beginning of work upon the Trent & Mersey Canal. Everyone, from Lord Gower the Shropshire coalowner to the newest workman, put on his best clothes and gathered beneath the Brownhills. The leaders of the project made speeches. Mr Wedgwood cut the first sod and Mr Brindley, the engineer of the canal, wheeled it away in a barrow. Then:

'. . . a barrel of old Staffordshire ale was broached on the spot; the healths of Earl Gower, Lord Anson, Lord Gray, the county members, the Committee, and other officers were drunk; and Mr Wedgwood was specially thanked, in the name of the whole assembly, for his indefatigable services in this good cause. Succeeding to this were luncheons and dinners at the Leopard and other inns. The masterpotters entertained their friends at home, and regaled the men in the open spaces about the "works". A sheep was roasted whole for the benefit of the poorer potters, and at sunset bonfires were lighted in various parts of the town; a *feu de joie* was fired in front of Mr Wedgwood's house, and within a very large company assembled to partake of the bounteous hospitality which Mrs Wedgwood's skill as a housewife had prepared.'[8]

Then work began. Local brickworks were set up if suitable clay could be found; stone was brought from the quarries, and timber bought. Gangs of men began to dig with picks, shovels and barrows, with occasional mechanical help.* Masons worked on the locks, and for the tunnels shafts were sunk to the right depth from the ground above, and the tunnels dug inwards and outwards. For this work miners were often used, who set their charges of gunpowder by the light of candles, and feared an inrush of water. That which percolated into the workings was drained off, or removed by steam pumps. Ventilation was provided by lighting a fire under a shaft to provide an up-draught, which in turn would cause a down-draught at other shafts.

The skilled workmen who dug the canal navigations—to use the older term—were professionally called cutters or bankers, the unskilled being labourers. The word 'navigator' appears in the 1770s with two meanings, 'canal boatman' and 'canal cutter'. Both meanings persisted, the first only used occasionally, the second common by the 1790s, though not until 1832, according to *The Shorter Oxford English Dictionary*, is it first found shortened to 'navvy'. Some of these cutters were English labourers who had probably left the land because of the enclosure Acts; some were Fenmen, used to digging and embanking drains; some were drawn from the vagrants who had been a poor law problem since the days of Elizabeth, and many

---

* Carne's cutting machine was used on a number of canals, amongst them the Herefordshire & Gloucestershire. An advertisement reads:

'Saturday last was opened near Gloucester Mr Carne's patent machine for expediting the formation of Canals. By this admirable contrivance the labour of removing the earth, which used to require a great number of hands with wheel barrows, is performed with much more expedition by a man and a horse.'[9]

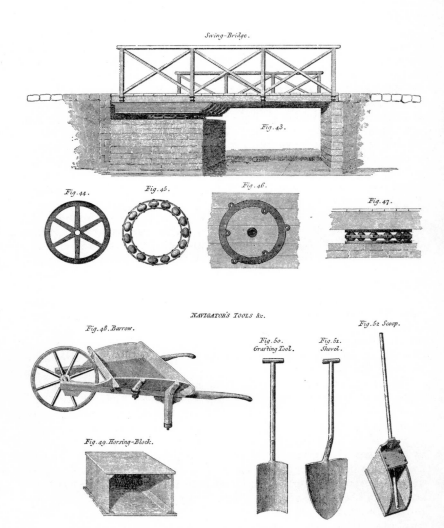

Figure 5 (*Above*) Design for a swing bridge; (*below*) the tools that built the canals. Horsing-blocks were used to support the planks of barrow-runs

were Scottish or Irish. As the construction gangs moved through the countryside they must have brought consternation to the folk of the villages, who had not seen such uproar since the days of the Civil War, and fun to the girls. They were rough men, and local newspapers and books carry stories of robbery and even murder. Here is one account of the navvies working on the improvement of the River Witham under the Act of 1812:

'A dispute arose on a particular Friday between the navvies and a baker named Edmonds, from Wragby, who supplied them with bread; the riot began on the west side of the river, at a public-house with the sign of "The Plough"—they drove the landlord away from the house, took out his barrels, and drank the beer; having taken his sign down, they also took the baker's basket and bread, and, crossing the river, proceeded up to the village of Bardney, one man carrying another cross-legged on his shoulders, the "rider" carrying the captured sign, holding it up in his hands, and being surrounded by a mob armed with their plank-hooks and other tools. They pelted the baker with his bread, and hung his basket on the top of a tree in the village; they then attacked the "Bottle and Glass" public-house —fetched the barrels of beer out of the house, knocked the ends out and drank the ale; Mr Benson, a person who was then the landlord of the "Angel" Inn, to prevent them entering his premises, brought or rolled out his barrels of beer himself, and by this means saved himself and his house.

'During the time they invested the houses in Bardney, the people were so frightened that they gave them anything they asked for; the navvies went about to the inhabitants of the village demanding money and different articles from them, and proclaiming their own prices for provisions for the future; John Edmonds, now living (1881) gave them five shillings.

'The constable of the village was called out, but he alone was of no use, as they would have attacked him at once; he made his escape with difficulty, and was obliged to hide himself in the almshouses; thirteen constables were sent for from Horncastle, they also were useless, and had to go home again—one of them so much injured that he died from the effects afterwards; the cavalry were then sent for, and came as soon as possible . . . with the magistrate, the Rev. Mr Mouncey, of Gautby, who read the Riot Act. The rioters (several of whom secreted themselves) were immediately surrounded by the cavalry, who drove them up together and examined them, afterwards they filled three carts and a waggon with the rioters, whom they carried away with them to Horncastle and Spilsby; in due course these disturbers were prosecuted and imprisoned.'[10]

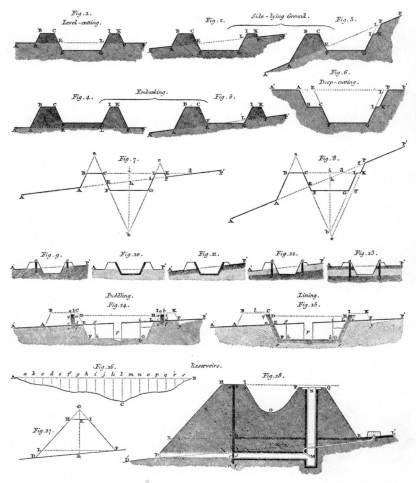

Figure 6 Varying profiles of canal construction. The towpath is on the left in all the examples

They had some excuse, for often they were not even paid their 2s (10p) to 3s (15p) a day in cash each week. Those working on the Kennet & Avon in 1797, for instance, were paid in twenty-one-day notes, which they then had to find someone to cash for them at a discount, while in 1804 the tunnellers and cutters working directly for the canal company on the Grand Junction at Blisworth were paid monthly. A doctor was occasionally retained to look after them when they were injured or ill, as on the Liskeard & Looe Union; more often the men paid into a fund, as on the Peak Forest, to which the company also subscribed, and from which sickness payments were made.

There were more intellectual moments in their lives, such as that recorded by the Committee of the Gloucester & Berkeley Canal:

'Ordered, That Mr Wheeler pay the workmen who found the Coins £1-1-0 and that he count them over and deliver them to Mr Cheston, who has kindly offered to decypher them, and give his opinion of their value.'[11]

But many references to them by the engineers ran like this:

'Richᵈ Jones . . . not in the work at 2 o'clock P.M. nor had been in the work this day. All his men a Drinking except 3 men in the Big Tunnel.'[12]

And now and then a few lines appeared in the local newspaper:

'Early on Saturday Morning last, a little beyond Winson Green, in the Birmingham Canal Navigation, the Earth fell suddenly in and killed John Lester, one of the Workmen, occasioned, it is thought, by the heavy Rains on Friday Evening.'[13]

Just as later most of the railways were built by great contractors like Brassey, so were some of the canals. The extensive Pinkerton family worked on canals and navigations as widely spread as the Selby, Driffield, Barnsley, Erewash, Birmingham & Fazeley, Gloucester & Berkeley, Kidwelly & Llanelly and Basingstoke canals. Their name is perpetuated upon the One Shilling token issued to workmen on the Basingstoke. Edward (later Sir Edward) Banks, himself or through the firm of Joliffe & Banks, built parts of the Leeds & Liverpool, Lancaster, Ulverston, Ashton-under-Lyne and Huddersfield Canals, and also the Goole Canal of the Aire & Calder. Hugh McIntosh worked on the Croydon and Grand Western extension, and rebuilt much of the Aire & Calder. Most of the earlier canals, however, were built by local contractors, many of them leaders of groups of workmen formed for this purpose, and they often undertook quite small sections. A few were built by direct labour, or finished by this means after the contractors had withdrawn. In charge of construction was a clerk of works, or resident engineer, with his subordinates, while over him was the principal engineer who had laid out the line and was generally responsible for the work, though he might have charge of building half a dozen major canals at the same time. The resident engineer in turn employed overlookers, for, as Robert Whitworth told the Ashby Canal shareholders in 1794,

Figure 7   Token issued by John Pinkerton to .the workmen on the Basingstoke Canal. The Pinkerton family were contractors for many canals in England and Wales

'neither puddlers or masons ought to be left to themselves, even one Day, in some particular situations',[14] and also checkers to count the men employed by the contractors, in order that 'subsist' money could then be advanced by the company to the contractors until the work was periodically measured up and a progress payment made. Cutting went on to the accompaniment of bickerings with the contractors over payments on account and accusations of bad work, and with the men over demands for rises in pay or losses of tools.

It was in the canal age that the profession of the civil engineer came to birth. The great names were men of many origins, who because of their ability had become expert in the new problems: Brindley learned his trade as a millwright; Telford was a working mason; Rennie a mechanically minded farmer's son; Smeaton the son of an attorney; Outram of a 'gentleman'; Jessop of a foreman shipwright. Others learned from these. Robert Whitworth senior and Thomas Dadford senior had been Brindley's assistants, and in turn fathered engineers, while Hugh Henshall was his brother-in-law. Jessop had been Smeaton's pupil. Others again began life as contractors, like Thomas Sheasby.

We must remember that at the time most of the canals were surveyed the first Ordnance map had not been issued. That did not appear until 1 January 1801, and it was not till 1844 that all the country south of a line from Hull to Preston had been mapped. No previous detailed survey of England had ever been made, and the engineer was therefore dependent upon probably inaccurate local maps and the special survey he himself carried out, and which was afterwards published for the encouragement of prospective subscribers. The engineers found themselves in most difficulty with geology. Even a careful survey, including trials of the ground over which the canal was to pass, or through which tunnels were to be made, often failed to detect formations that were difficult to cope with, and not all surveys were careful. Many were sketchy, with the result that the engineer encountered construction difficulties that ran up the expenses.

Some engineers took on too much. Brindley early on found himself with half a dozen big schemes on his hands at once. He handled them by delegating as much responsibility as possible to his assistants whom he installed as resident engineers on the Birmingham, Stafford-

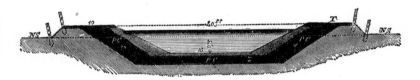

Figure 8 Puddling a canal. In porous ground the bed is given 18in of puddle below, and 3ft at the sides; in retentive soil, puddle is only needed at each side to prevent lateral leakage that would weaken the banks

shire & Worcestershire, Coventry and Oxford canals, while he himself gave most of his time to the Duke's canal and the Trent & Mersey. This view of his responsibilities did not commend itself to the businessmen of the Birmingham Canal, who observed[15] 'that Mr. Brindley hath frequently passed by, and sometimes come into Town, without giving them an opportunity of meeting to confer with him upon the progress of the undertaking'. They expressed 'their dissatisfaction at not being able to see him at such times'. A few months later the Coventry proprietors summarily dismissed him. All the same, he probably died of overwork added to his diabetes and the nephritis he contracted at Ipstones while surveying for the Caldon branch of the Trent & Mersey.

Brindley was primarily a builder of narrow boat canals: of all he worked on, only the Bridgewater and the Droitwich took barges, in

each case from a neighbouring river. Of his assistants, trained by
having responsibility thrust upon them, Thomas Dadford senior
(and later his sons) and Samuel Simcock of the Oxford and Birmingham canals were also mainly narrow canal builders. A third, Robert
Whitworth, did much of his best work on broad canals: the Thames
& Severn, Leeds & Liverpool summit level, Forth & Clyde and
Ashby-de-la-Zouch.

Two other groups were more in the European tradition of bigger
waterways. One was headed by John Smeaton, who had travelled
abroad before basing himself in Yorkshire. He himself built much
of the Calder & Hebble and the Forth & Clyde, and had as pupil
William Jessop, England's greatest builder of big waterways. Among
them were much of the Aire & Calder of his time; the Barnsley,
Rochdale, Trent Navigation, Nottingham, Cromford and Grand
Junction canals. He only built one narrow canal, the Ellesmere, and
then by accident, for when he was engaged the promoters intended
it to be broad. Smeaton's and Jessop's school can reasonably claim
John Rennie, builder of two great broad canals, the Lancaster and
the Kennet & Avon, the two William Crosleys, first-class working
engineers, and later George Leather, who made the Goole Canal and
created the modern Aire & Calder. Telford, too, owed much to the
Smeaton tradition. His first major canal work was as Jessop's resident engineer for many years on the Ellesmere; his second with
Jessop to create, and alone to execute, the great Caledonian, and
finally, paralleling in the midlands what Leather was doing in Yorkshire, to build the narrow Birmingham main line and the Birmingham
& Liverpool Junction (now the Shropshire Union main line).

An Irish group was also in the European tradition. English
engineers worked in Ireland, notably Steers, Jessop, Rennie and
Chapman, but Ireland also had her own school: Richard Castle of
French, Davis Ducart of Italian, and Thomas Omer of Dutch de-
scent; John Killaly, greatest of them all, John Brownrigg and
Richard Evans.

One is struck by the engineering skill and resourcefulness that
built Britain's canals. No tunnel of any size, other than mining
tunnels, had ever been built in Britain before Brindley built
the Harecastle, over one and a half miles long. Aqueducts, embankments, cuttings, locks, inclined planes, canal lifts, all were designed
and built as the need for them arose. To us they seem small enough
feats compared to the achievements of modern engineering, but to
contemporaries they were sources of wonder. Josiah Wedgwood
wrote of the flight of locks on the Duke of Bridgewater's Canal at
Runcorn:

'I was quite astonish'd at the vastness of the plan and the greatness of stile in the execution. The Walls of the Locks are truly admirable, both for strength and beauty of workmanship. The front Lock next the sea (for such it seems when the Tide is in) in particular, whose walls are compos'd of vast stones from 1 to 12 Tons weight, & yet by the excellent machinery made use of, some of which is still left standing, they had as perfect command of these huge masses of Rock as a common bricklayer of the brick in his hands. In short, to behold Ten of these Locks all at a view, with their Gates, Acqeducts, Cisterns, Sluices, bridges, &c. &c., the whole seems to be the work of the Titans, rather than the production of our Pigmy race of beings. . . .'[16]

The engineer was riding from one end to the other of the line under construction, living in inns, working out his problems by candlelight, and now and then getting involved in unpleasantness. When the engineer of the Leeds & Liverpool found it necessary to dismiss a contractor, the committee wrote:

'. . . in confirmation that the Committee approve the steps you have taken they have signed their names hereto and desire you will exert yourself in the best manner you are able, and keep up your spirits, and you will be supported in every proper measure, and that no sinister, envious, or ilnatural insinuations will be listened to.'[17]

The general assembly of proprietors was meeting once or twice a year to hear reports on progress, and sometimes to dine at the company's expense. (The meeting of the Gloucester & Berkeley proprietors at the end of 1795 cost £20.42½.) Usually the Act provided that a certain number of shares had to be present in person or by proxy if a valid meeting was to be held, and meetings that had to be adjourned for lack of attendance were not uncommon. Affairs were managed by an executive committee, under which there might be one or more working committees to superintend construction; the Oxford Canal had three of these district committees.

On the executive committee the chairman or other moving spirit was keeping an eye on the engineer and the spending of money, and was handling the negotiations for the purchase of land. Land buying was always a difficulty. The procedure was that the land was first valued by professional valuers employed by the company; if the landowner did not accept the valuation, the chairman or someone from the company tried to reach agreement. In case of failure, the dispute was then referred to a body of commissioners named in the Act, who were usually all the landowners of the county who had a certain income per annum from it, a quorum of whom had power to judge. Since landowners tended to favour landowners, the scales were weighted against the canal companies, and the obstructive usually got their price. It was therefore often the case that the land for a canal cost more than the estimates allowed for. There was a further appeal from the commissioners to a jury, which was seldom used. In one case on the Leeds & Liverpool in Yorkshire, however, the jury reduced the values put on land by the commissioners. Most land was bought at about thirty years' purchase, with special compensation when the line of canal cut house from farm, or farm from road, which was increased when a great estate was affected: the Grand Junction paid £5,000 to Lord Clarendon for the right to pass through Grove Park, and another large sum to Lord Essex to pass through Cassiobury Park.

Now and then distinguished visitors arrived to view the work. King George III and his Queen saw the Thames & Severn Canal and the Sapperton tunnel a year before it was opened, and:

'. . . expressed the most decided astonishment at a work of such magnitude, expence, and general utility, being conducted by private persons.'[18]

Canal shares were usually in denominations of £100. A deposit was payable when the shares were first subscribed, and then, as the canal was built, calls of so many pounds a share were made upon the shareholders till the full amount had been paid. The getting of the cash for these calls was not always easy. Even if everything was going well, the shareholder always liked to hold on to his money as long as possible in order to earn the interest; for this reason payment of interest out of capital was usually made on the calls paid up while work was in progress. If the canal were in difficulties, and it was clear that it would cost more and therefore earn less on its capital than had been intended, the shareholder was even more reluctant to pay the calls, and often preferred to forfeit his shares or risk a lawsuit rather than put more money into a hopeless enterprise. Partly paid forfeited shares were auctioned, or even given to anyone who would undertake to pay further calls. On the other hand, the canal committees in such cases did everything they could to wheedle extra money out of the shareholders, for instance, by sending their clerk to call personally on nervous proprietors. Many canals got into difficulties because of the clause in their Acts authorising them to pay interest on capital during construction. If this were paid in cash, it drained away the resources needed for building; if in bonds, it created a debt that hampered the company afterwards.

Canal committees naturally turned for temporary accommodation to their banks, and found, as others have done, that bankers took a more gloomy view of the future than they did themselves. In April

1797 the Kennet & Avon's bankers refused to advance more money against unpaid calls 'on account of the pressure of the times',[19] but relented after making conditions which included slowing down expenditure on construction to the tempo of the calls made. In 1796 the Peak Forest committee, faced with an overdraft of £4,000, themselves guaranteed £1,000 of this sum and £4,000 more to complete the summit level and the tramroad at Marple which preceded the locks, and in 1803 there was the curious case of the Glamorganshire Bank which made the Swansea Canal a loan on condition of being appointed its treasurers, the loan only to run its full term on condition that the bank retained the appointment. Finally, there was always the danger of bank failure or embarrassment, particularly awkward if members of the canal committee were also partners in the bank. In 1816 Thomas Eyton was a member of the Shropshire Canal committee, and the Rev J. Rocke was treasurer, when the bank of Eyton, Rocke & Eyton in Shrewsbury 'for a short time suspended Business and have not yet resumed it'.[20] The company changed over to that of Reynolds, Charlton & Shakeshaft in Wellington, in which Joseph Reynolds, also a member of the committee, was a partner.

The original Act of Parliament always provided for the raising of an additional amount—usually one-third as much again—should the original capital have proved insufficient to finish the canal. This amount could be raised in a number of different ways. On the one hand, calls beyond the nominal amount of each share could be made on the original shares, or fresh shares could be issued. If the latter, they might have to be auctioned or issued at a discount in order to induce people to take them up. On the other hand, some form of preference could be given to those who came to the rescue of the concern, either by the issue of preference shares (a form of share found more often in the later railway promotions) or by bonds, convertible or not, annuities, promissory notes or mortgages either of the tolls of the canal, or of the waterway and tolls together. If the canal were later a success, the payment of interest on these prior charges, and later the repayment of the capital sums, only delayed the coming of dividends on the ordinary shares; but in some cases the existence of the prior charges extinguished all hope for the ordinary shareholders, for these canals never succeeded in paying off their debts.

An instance of the removal of prior charges was the Thames & Severn. By 1808 this concern had accumulated a debt of £193,892.50, made up of arrears of interest of £76,767.50, and a principal debt of £117,125. Since the company was not earning enough to pay the current interest on the debt, financial reconstruction was essential,

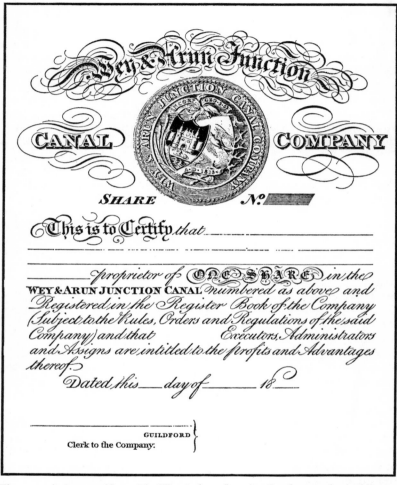

Figure 9   A share certificate. The Wey & Arun Junction Canal was authorised in 1813

and eventually the debt-holders agreed to a scheme by which the old shareholders gained a hope—and later the actuality—of dividends. The resources of the company in spare land and property were turned into cash, and at the same time a new class of 'red' share was created to stand alongside the old or 'black' shares. Each £100 of debt was then exchanged for a £100 red share and £21 in cash. The red shares were entitled to a preferential dividend of 1½ per cent. After that had been paid the black shares received 1½ per cent, and any balance was equally divided between the two classes of share. There were a few occasions on which such a balance was in fact divided. By this method the whole debt was extinguished.

We are so used today to government aid to industry that we may forget it has a long history. In 1784 the government lent £50,000 to the Forth & Clyde Canal company, and in 1799 lent £25,000 to the Crinan Canal proprietors out of the repayments. In 1817 the Poor Employment Act set up Exchequer Bill Loan Commissioners with power to lend money to concerns that would employ the poor, especially unskilled labourers, in order to relieve the unemployment that had followed the end of the Napoleonic Wars. Loans could be made for ten years. A number of canals were helped in this way: some, like the Gloucester & Berkeley and the Regent's, were successes, and the money without which the waterway would never have been finished was repaid. Some, like the Portsmouth & Arundel, were not; this company was unable to repay any of the £40,000 it had been lent, though fortunately the sum had been guaranteed by the Earl of Egremont.

At last the projected canal would be completed (unless like the Salisbury & Southampton or the Dorset & Somerset, it was never finished, because the money that could possibly be raised was not enough to overcome all the difficulties of finishing the line). Financial troubles would be forgotten; the water would be let in, boats bought, toll and lock-keepers and accounting staff appointed and security bonds arranged, and plans made for the opening day.

The opening of a canal was an occasion for considerable jollification. Sometimes verse contributed, as when Elizabeth Davies, who kept a lollipop shop in Wind Street, Neath, wrote a song of nineteen verses, of which two are given here, to commemorate the opening of the Neath & Swansea Junction (usually called the Tennant) Canal:

'O! could I make verses with humour and wit,
George Tennant, Esquire's great genius to fit;
From morn until even, I would sit down and tell,
And sing in the praise of Neath Junction Canal.

*   *   *

'I hope when he's dead and laid in his grave,
His soul will in heaven be eternally saved;
It will then be recorded for ages to tell,
Who was the great founder of Neath Junction Canal.'[21]

The following contemporary account from a newspaper describes the opening in 1824 of the Thames & Medway Canal, the ill-fated venture which was built to connect the Thames at Gravesend with the Medway at Strood opposite Rochester, and whose tunnel, $2\frac{1}{4}$ miles long, the second longest canal tunnel built in Britain, is now used by railway passengers travelling from Strood to Higham:

'There were four barges occupied by the company; and there was a fifth barge, preceding such four barges, occupied with musicians. In the first of the Company's barges were—Sir C. Flower, R. Sutton, Esq., the Rev. Mr Owen, and several other Directors, &c. Previously to starting, Sir C. Flower stood up by the flag-staff, and exclaimed Success and prosperity to the Thames and Medway canal, with three times three. These were given with considerable effect. The most gratifying part of the view, however, was the entrance into the tunnel.

'Above the Higham entrance immense crowds of persons were assembled, Ladies, Naval and Military Officers; and Sir Charles Flower again gave the signal for huzzas, which were answered by the surrounding spectators. At the entrance of the Tunnel, the light of Frindsbury Arch at the end could be distinctly seen; and the effect was very curious. The towing-path was thronged with spectators, and the Canal-workers carried lighted torches. . . .

'The barges, which occasionally paused in the tunnel, were about forty minutes in passing through it. On passing through Frindsbury outlet, there is a capacious basin, which forms the terminations of this canal. Around this basin there were great crowds of persons and several of His Majesty's boats, with Officers on board; amongst them was Admiral Sir J. Moorsom. The Officers greeted the company on their coming out of the tunnel most cordially, giving the signal for huzzas, and the band struck up "Rule Britannia". The Officers and others joined the procession on the landing, and proceeded to the Crown Inn, Rochester. It is gratifying to be able to state, that the whole procession proceeded most orderly and agreeably, and not the slightest accident occurred.

'The party proceeded to the Crown Inn, Rochester, where a very handsome dinner (two guinea tickets) was provided, to which the company, to the amount of upwards of one hundred persons, sat down soon after five o'clock. As proof of the excellence of the Dinner, it may be mentioned, that besides the usual wines, there were Burgundy, Champagne, Claret, &c. and there was a delightful dessert. R. Sutton Esq. was in the Chair. On his right was Sir G. Hoste, in his regimentals; and on his left was Sir C. Flower. There were several Naval and Military Officers in their uniform present, and they were seated at the upper table.

'The cloth having been removed, three professional singers residing in Rochester performed *Non Nobis Domine.*

'The toasts of "The King—The Duke of York, and the rest of the Royal Family—and The Duke of Clarence and the Navy".

'Sir C. Flower then rose, and gave the health of their worthy Chairman. He would not pronounce that Gentleman's praises—what they had that day seen was his best eulogium—(Loud applause). But for him the work was not likely ever to have been completed. He, therefore, gave "the health of their worthy Chairman, Mr Sutton" (Applause).

'Mr Sutton returned his acknowledgements; and he afterwards spoke of the magnitude of the work which had been accomplished. There had been united two of the most valuable rivers in the kingdom, and two of the richest rivers of the world, and the importance of the work, he thought, could not well be too highly appreciated. The value of the works they could all understand. If any person's property or comforts had been disturbed, it was a subject of lamentation; and he could state that, if ample remuneration had not already been made, the Company would be happy to make the completest compensation. He trusted that the great work, besides being of use to the commerce of the country, would be of particular value to the ancient city of Rochester; and he trusted that the time was not far distant when the port of Rochester would be declared a free port—(Applause)—and that it might have warehouses for the bonding of goods. (Hear, hear!)—The result, he trusted, would be prosperous; and he could assure them with great truth, when he contemplated the immense work that had been accomplished, he considered that the happiest day of his life (Loud applause).

'Several other toasts followed, and amongst the vocal performances was "The Meeting of the Waters". At ten o'clock the company separated.

'After the procession the workmen, to the amount of between two and three hundred, had a dinner at the Canal Tavern, &c.'[22]

CHAPTER III

Life on the Canals

++++++++++++++++++++++++++++++++++++++✦++++++++++++++++++++++++++++++++++++++

THE opening of a canal often had an astonishing effect upon the development of the towns with which it was associated. In the case of Stourport, the town was indeed created by the trade that followed the cutting of the Staffordshire & Worcestershire Canal. Again, the Lancaster Canal ended its northerly course at Kendal, and a local historian writes as follows:

'. . . the spirit of improvement fully manifested itself in 1818 and 1819. The date of the new town may, we conceive, truly be placed here, at the time of the opening of the Lancaster and Kendal canal. This event gave an impulse to the public spirit of the inhabitants, and formed the commencement of a new era in the history of Kendal. . . . The old Miller's Close Bridge, which had stood since 1743, and was very narrow, and ill adapted to be the general medium of intercourse with the canal, was now thrown down, and wholly rebuilt on a wider scale. The large warehouses and other buildings at the canal harbour, were all erected at this time; Kent Lane (which before was very steep, and so narrow that two carts could scarcely pass) was thrown open, and the ascent considerably diminished; Long Pool was widened; Gandy Street erected; Kent Terrace and Castle Crescent were built shortly after. The Union Building Society commenced operations about this time; and indeed on every side, numerous habitations were superadded to the town . . . in a very short time, the town assumed a new and modern appearance—so very different that any person having been absent a few years, could scarcely have identified it.'[1]

In some places the canal company owned a good deal of land, and when trade caused this to be developed, a large income accrued from rents. This was, for instance, the case with the Grand Junction Canal, which owned much land in Paddington.

Certainly along the line of canal and at the basins great changes took place. Along the line factories were built and wharves provided for them, often on side cuts. At the basins warehouses were built, and coal-wharves, sheds, cranes, and weigh-houses provided. In Coventry the coal-wharves lay below the boats, so that coal could be unloaded direct into carts. Offices were provided for the clerks, often in a specially built eighteenth-century house that still stands to remind us of those days, as does Canal House at Oxford beside Nuffield college that occupies the site of the former canal basin. Along the line of the waterway and at the basins public houses were named the *Canal*, the *Navigation Inn* or the *Wharf*, or more specifically the *Grand Junction Arms*, the *Calder and Hebble* or the *Grosvenor Basin*,* as earlier they had been called the *Pack Horse* or the *Row Barge*.

The administration of a canal was never easy in the days before telephones and telegrams, or even the penny post. In the canal office, usually in a main town, were the agent or superintendent, the accountant and chief toll-collector, and the resident clerk, each with a staff, while the engineer had his own house. Strung out along the line were toll-collectors, who usually had to give security bonds for their honesty, wharfingers, lock-keepers, on the bigger canals assistant engineers in charge of portions of the route, lengthsmen or bank rangers, and maintenance craftsmen such as carpenters and masons, the least of whom was the mole catcher. When the company did its own carrying, and employed craft and crews, there was also a carrying manager to seek traffic and supervise the boatmen.

The shareholders would now meet twice a year to hear a financial statement and declare a dividend, which, unlike present practice, was usually only paid through a bank on application personally or by agent, and was therefore advertised in the local press. At the earlier of these two meetings in the year the managing committee would be elected.

This committee was the real governing body of the canal, and met as often as it was needed, probably monthly on a big canal, three or four times a year on a small one. It had about fifteen members, drawn from the more influential shareholders. Occasionally it was constituted regionally, as on the Kennet & Avon, where a number of seats were allotted to each of the three districts into which the canal was divided. Occasionally, also, as with the Swansea Canal, it consisted of all the shareholders with five or more shares, a system which should have led to inefficiency, but in that case did not. The quorum for committee meetings was low—three on the Peak Forest, five on the Glamorganshire—for attendances were often poor. The members therefore usually received an attendance payment to compensate for the distances they had to travel, and sometimes a free meal as well, 'Beer and a genteel Dessert to be included'.[2] Meetings were either

* The first in Praed Street, Paddington, the second at Salterhebble near Halifax, the third, a reminder of the old Grosvenor Canal, at the side of Victoria Station in London when this book was first published.

at the company's office or at the local inn, while once a year the committee probably made a boat trip to inspect their property.

When the canal was a big concern, and could afford to pay permanent officials well, business was carried on efficiently. Trouble occurred with concerns too small to pay good salaries. Much of the administrative responsibility then fell upon the managing committee, which often consisted of country gentlemen and professional men without the time or inclination to undertake it. The company's fortunes then depended upon the chairman, still more upon the clerk. He was usually a solicitor from a local and established firm, who might put much more work into the canal company than his salary justified, to please his clients among the shareholders and out of his own conscientiousness. If both were energetic, business went well. If not, it went ill. Energy in chairmen was helped by the large shareholdings they usually had, and often by annual honoraria from the shareholders, or occasional gifts of silver plate. One or two were paid regular salaries, and gave much of their time to the work: for instance, the Grand Junction had for many years a paid chairman of its managing committee.

In the bigger concerns the difficulties of the managing committees were of other kinds. Their administration was good, but their policies, being of such great importance to the economic life of their areas, were targets for constant criticism both from inside and outside their number. An example of an inside criticism which reads with a modern air comes from the Birmingham Canal in 1769:

'That upon examining into the Particulars of a Misunderstanding which happened in the Committee between Messrs. Garbett and Bentley, it appeared, that Mr Garbett did not intend to insinuate Mr Bentley's having wilfully mispent any of the Company's Money, but always thought he did his best; and (taking the whole of Mr Bentley's Conduct into Consideration) that the Public were under Obligations to him. It likewise appeared that Mr Garbett did frequently *request for the Poor* to be supplied with Coal, *in Preference to any Person whatsoever*, and that there is no Reason to say, he ever did make a Point for the Brass Work to receive the constant Supply of Three Tons per Day: But there are many Reasons to believe that *Mr Garbett did exert himself* for Coal being Sold at *no more* than 4d. per Cwt. at the present, and *cheaper as soon as it was possible*, and that he never did desire any from the Wharf, either for his own Works or Dwelling House.'[3]

The size of canals varied greatly, due to the essentially local characteristics of each project. In width they can be grouped roughly into ship, broad, narrow and tub-boat canals, as long as it is understood that no clear line can be drawn between one class and another.

The early ship canals such as the Caledonian, the Gloucester & Berkeley or the Exeter, were of course small compared to the Manchester Ship Canal of a later day. The sizes of locks at time of opening were on the Caledonian 170ft × 38ft, the Gloucester & Berkeley 163ft × 38ft, the Exeter 128ft × 26ft 8in. On the Manchester Ship Canal the large locks are 600ft × 65ft.

The broad canals, such as the Kennet & Avon, Leeds & Liverpool, Rochdale, Bridgewater or Forth & Clyde, could take vessels from 55ft to some 80ft long, and from 12ft to 21ft wide, carrying from 50 to about a hundred tons. Many of them, like the Droitwich, Sir John Ramsden's, Stroudwater, Erewash and the lower part of the Chesterfield Canal, were branches of river navigations, and were built broad to take river craft.

Three main routes were built broad: from Forth to Clyde; from Liverpool across the Pennines by the Leeds & Liverpool or the Rochdale to Hull; and from Bristol to London by the Thames & Severn or the Kennet & Avon. Two others failed. In 1793 and 1794 the Grand Junction company, planning a waterway that at one end joined the Thames, and having an engineer William Jessop, experienced on the Aire & Calder and the Trent, decided to build a broad canal from London to Braunston near Rugby, and the Ashby followed suit. Pressure was now put by the Grand Junction upon the Oxford, Coventry and Trent & Mersey to widen also, so that, by building a short link from the head of the Ashby Canal across the Trent to the Trent & Mersey, a broad canal would be obtained from London to Manchester and Liverpool. The Coventry and the Oxford stalled: the Trent & Mersey opposed. The Ashby and the Chester (broad) canal shareholders, helped by Sir Nigel Gresley, a colliery owner of Newcastle under Lyme, and some dissident pottery manufacturers, then in 1796 promoted a new broad canal, the Commercial, to join the Ashby to the Chester canals by way of Uttoxeter, Hanley and Newcastle, to achieve the same object once the Coventry and Oxford had widened from Braunston to Marston. This scheme failed also; no further serious attempt was ever made to build a broad line from London to Manchester and Liverpool, and future development was thereby stultified.

There was also a vision of a broad canal from Exeter to London, first by way of the Grand Western to Taunton, the proposed Bristol & Taunton and Bristol–Cirencester canals, the Thames & Severn, the Thames Navigation, the broadened Oxford to Hampton Gay, and the proposed London & Western or Hampton Gay Canal to

London; later from Bristol by the Kennet & Avon. The former route is shown on a map issued about 1792 by the supporters of the Hampton Gay Canal; of the latter a pamphleteer of 1811 said:

'It should be observed here, that it is proposed to make the Canal from Bristol to Taunton of the same dimensions as the Kennet & Avon Canal and the Grand Western Canal: so that barges of fifty tons burthen may be laden at Exeter, and proceed to London (a distance of upwards of 200 miles) without shifting their cargoes.'[4]

However, the cohesive forces necessary to carry out such co-ordinated plans were not strong enough.

Most English midland canals were built to narrow dimensions, to take narrow boats 70–72ft long, and about 6ft 10in wide, carrying some 25–30 tons. In Wales, the important canals took boats 60–65ft long and about 9ft wide. No true narrow-boat canals were built in Ireland, though one, the far from successful Ulster Canal, could only take craft 11ft 6in wide. Brindley and his assistants engineered the early narrow canals of the midlands. When he came to plan them, he by-passed experience in Yorkshire and Lancashire, and chose a boat size probably based on the Worsley coal-carrying mine boats. Such canals were cheaper—though not much cheaper—to build, and economical of water. But the Industrial Revolution was quickly to catch up with what they could do, and then leave them aside.

The tub-boat canals had very small boats carrying about five tons, and often had inclined planes—that is, railways up and down which boats were drawn by one method or another—instead of locks. There were two groups of these canals, which were suited to hilly country: one in west Somerset, Devon and Cornwall, the other in Shropshire, and also a single canal, the Kidwelly & Llanelly, in Wales.

The boats that were used varied as greatly. On the river navigations sailing boats were the commonest—trows and barges on the Severn, flats on the Mersey and the Weaver, keels on the Tyne and in Yorkshire, wherries in Norfolk, lighters in the Fens, Western barges on the Thames, Medway barges on that river. These all differed in size and build, but the following will serve for examples. The trow was nearly flat bottomed, was 16–20ft wide, and some 100ft long, carrying from 40–80 or more tons according to the depth of the river, with a main and topmast perhaps 80ft high, sometimes a mizzen mast, and square sails. The barge (sometimes called a frigate) was a good deal smaller, and carried 20–40 tons. The Tyne keels were some 42ft long and 19ft broad; those of Yorkshire were about 54ft long, 14ft broad, and carried 80 tons and upwards. Horse-drawn barges were also used on river navigations—those of the Kennet were 109ft long and 17ft wide.

On the broad canals horse-drawn barges or river sailing barges were used; on the narrow canals were monkey boats, each of the size to fit the locks on the canal on which it was used. Most long-distance haulage on the midland canals within the Manchester–Stourport–London–Nottingham cross was done on narrow boats, since they could be worked singly through narrow locks and in pairs through broad. Tub-boat canals had small boats carrying a few tons, often operated in trains. Those on the Bude Canal were fitted with wheels on the bottom, so that they could run on the rails of the inclined planes.

The first barge made of iron, *The Trial*, was built by John Wilkinson the ironmaster and launched on the River Severn at Coalbrookdale on 9 July 1787. 'It answers all my expectations,' he wrote, and 'it has convinced the unbelievers, who were 999 in a thousand.' After *The Trial*, some iron narrow boats were built: Eric Svedenstierna saw several at Wilkinson's Bilston works in 1803. But wood remained the usual building material until much later.

Experiments were made with steam boats on inland waterways before the end of the eighteenth century. From 1818, however, passenger and goods-carrying steam packets multiplied, especially on the Yorkshire Ouse, Trent, Mersey and Thames. In 1826, a steam tug began to work regularly through Islington tunnel on the Regent's Canal, and experimental cargo carriers to appear on the canals, like the stern paddle-wheeler which arrived at Birmingham from London in 1826 carrying 20 tons. In 1831, the Aire & Calder put a steam paddle tug on their Goole–Leeds run, and thenceforward extended steam working rapidly. Tugs followed on other waterways, like the Caledonian and the Norwich & Lowestoft, but it was not until after the middle of the century that steam canal boats were much developed for cargo carrying. Never, indeed, did they replace the horse; that had to wait for diesels.

The canal company provided public wharves in charge of a wharfinger, the crane, weighing machine, warehouses and stables being enclosed by a wall and gates. Other warehouses built by the company might be let to permanent tenants, either local traders or one or more carrying concerns like Pickfords, and specialised buildings like salt-houses, iron, flour and cheese warehouses, were put up when they were needed. A company would also maintain wharves on other waterways than its own, at which goods intended for its line would be collected. Private wharves and warehouses, either on the line of the waterway or on private branches, were built by other users.

Towing on the river navigations was usually by gangs of men, a practice that continued well into the nineteenth century. On the

Severn, Telford, writing at the turn of the eighteenth century, referred to 'the present barbarous and expensive custom of performing this slave-like office by men'.[5] A witness giving evidence on the Severn Towing Path Bill of 1803 said that about 150 men were employed upon this work on the twenty-four miles from Bewdley to Coalbrookdale. The cost of towing this distance was 3s (15p) per man, each of whom was reckoned to pull three tons. He estimated that one horse could do the work of six men, at a third less cost. Within the next ten years a horse towing path was made upwards to Shrewsbury and downwards to Gloucester. On the upper Medway, however, this bow-hauling (said to be so called from the bows of rope attached to the towing line, on which the men pulled) continued till about 1838. Sometimes these river towpaths were made by separate towing-path companies, as on the Severn or the Wye; a separate public body, as on the Great Ouse from Denver Sluice to King's Lynn, or privately, with access allowed upon payment to the landowner, as on the Stour, where haling rents, as they were called, were paid for many years to Abram Constable, the brother of the painter. Sailing was commonly employed as an alternative to towing when it was practicable, in Yorkshire, in East Anglia where many rivers had no towing paths, on the Medway, the Weaver and the Severn. Nowadays, of course, motor barges or tugs are used on rivers, often to tow or push other craft.

On canals, also, towing by men was an occasional practice in the early days, for instance on the Trent & Mersey and the Stroudwater. Usually, however, horse towing was the method from the beginning. When boats going in opposite directions met, the empty boat dropped its towline under the laden boat or, if both were laden, the outer under the inner. The overtaking of one moving boat by another was usually prohibited in by-laws, and their speed laid down as between 2 and 3mph. A few later and improved canals, such as Telford's reconstruction of part of the Birmingham Canal, had towpaths on both sides.

Horses usually drew one boat. But when steam and later diesel craft came in, one boat often towed another. A narrow-boat motor, for instance, towed a butty. In such cases the butty or towed boat had to be worked through a single lock by its crew. Until very recently the push-towed barges of the Sheffield and South Yorkshire were still being bow-hauled by men through the small locks above Doncaster.

In tunnels, however, which seldom had a towpath in order to save expense in construction, the boats were legged through by the boatmen or by special leggers lying on their backs on boards pro-

jecting from the boats, and pushing with their feet against the sides
or roof. They were recommended to 'strap themselves to a short
Cord affix'd to the Boat to prevent their being drown'd'.[6] Here is
a contemporary in 1858 describing a night passage of Islington tunnel in the narrow boat *Stourport*:

'A couple of strong thick boards . . . are hooked on to places
formed on each side of the barge, near the head . . . On these two
narrow, insecure platforms, the two venturesome boatmen lie on
their backs, holding on by grasping the board underneath, and with
their legs, up to the waist, hanging over the water. . . . the operation
consists in moving the *Stourport* through the black tunnel, by a
measured side-step against the slimy, glistening walls; the right foot
is first planted in a half-slanting direction, and the left foot is constantly brought over with a sweep to take the vacated place, until
the right can recover its footing . . . the four stout legs, and its
four heavily hobnailed boots . . . make a full echoing sound upon
the walls like the measured clapping of hands.'[7]

On the Grand Junction in 1825 there was a complaint of 'the
nuisance arising from the notoriously bad characters of the persons
who frequent the neighbourhood of the Tunnels upon the plea of
assisting Boats through them',[8] and it seems that later at Blisworth
at any rate leggers were licensed, and carried an identifying arm-
plate. Occasionally also boats were shafted or poled through, or a
fixed or power-driven endless chain was used.

Probably the first tunnel to be built with a towpath through it
was either Armitage* on the Trent & Mersey Canal or Cookley
on the Staffordshire & Worcestershire. Later, longer tunnels were
built with towpaths, such as Berwick on the Shrewsbury Canal,
which had a path on wooden bearers over the water, or the second
Harecastle. Some tunnels built still later had a path on each side, like
Newbold on the Oxford Canal or Netherton on the Birmingham.
Where a tunnel had no path through it, a horse path ran over the top.
Beside Sapperton tunnel on the Thames & Severn there stands
Tunnel House, a public house where the men in charge of the horses
paused while the leggers did their work.

There are some instances of bridges without towpaths through
the arches. In these cases the towrope had to be cast off at each
bridge and the horse and trailing line taken across the road. On
the Stratford-upon-Avon Canal and part of the Staffordshire &
Worcestershire the bridges, instead of towpaths under, had a slot
in the centre of the arch to take the towrope.

The commonest means of towing was the horse, though donkeys

* Now opened out.

were used in pairs on some canals, and mules occasionally. A writer upon the Birmingham Canal in 1783 shows that the occupant of the towpath did not always enjoy the work.

'The boats . . . are each drawn by something like the skeleton of a horse, covered with skin: whether he subsists upon the scent of the water, is a doubt; but whether his life is a scene of affliction, is

Figure 10   Donkeys towing a canal boat

not; for the unfeeling driver has no employment but to whip him from one end of the canal to the other. While the teams practised the turnpike road, the lash was divided among five unfortunate animals, but now the whole wrath of the driver falls upon one.'[9]

This was, of course, long before the date of the first Act to prevent cruelty to horses (1823), or of the foundation of the Royal Society for the Prevention of Cruelty to Animals (1824).

When a towpath changes sides on a canal, a bridge, for this reason called a turnover bridge, is provided to carry the path across, often so designed that the towline need not be cast off while the horse changed sides. On rivers, however, there was often nothing so convenient. Horses might be ferried over by a special boat, or by the boat they were towing, as on the River Stour in Suffolk, upon which short piers were provided for the horse to use to and from the boat that carried him over.

The towing was usually done by the animals belonging to the

carrier who owned the boat. Sometimes, however, as on the Tennant Canal and, from 1847, on the Regent's, towing was a responsibility of the owners of the canal, who provided their own horses and added a charge for the service to the toll. On waterways taking coastal or seagoing craft, it was often done by independents—in Yorkshire called horse marines, elsewhere trackers—who waited at places like Goole, Weston Point or Sharpness for incoming craft, and then bargained with the captains for the services of themselves and their animals. In the midlands, steering firms existed that would hire boats, horses and men as needed.

Stables were provided at wharves by canal companies and carriers, these latter also providing them at their own depots. Canalside pubs, too, had stable accommodation, for boats tended to moor at night where stables could be found. In England, animals were never stabled on the boats, as on American canals.

Stoppages or delays caused by floods, ice, repairs or shortage of water were recurrent hindrances to the passage of boats, and had great effect when canal traffic had to compete with the regularity, even more than the speed, of delivery offered by the railways. There was little to be done about floods, except to build the canal itself above the flood meadows where it ran near a river, or, if it was a river navigation, to build special flood locks or flood gates to control the water levels inside the lock cuts.

Ice boats, usually short, wide and built of iron, with a high rail down the centre which men could hold, helped to keep traffic moving during frosts, unless the broken ice blocked the locks. When ice formed thickly, a team of farm horses was hired to pull such a boat, and men to rock it as it crashed its way forward. In London Mr C. Gatti had a contract with the Regent's company to buy their ice, which was stored in a special ice-well near Hampstead Road lock.

Stoppages for repairs to lock gates, or the puddling of the bed, always took a week or two each year, and if different canals on a through route closed their waterways at different times, delays to goods could be very serious. It was for this reason that neighbouring groups of canals usually arranged to stop at the same time.

Maintenance consisted mainly of tunnel, lock and bridge repairs on the one hand, and dredging on the other, laboriously done by manual labour using a spoon dredger or similar device until the power of steam was called in. In 1808 the Grand Junction's engineer ordered from Bridgnorth a 4hp engine to be put on a boat and used to drive a pump, having seen there 'a Steam Engine invented by Mr Trevethick on a very simple construction'.[10] The Stroudwater had a steam dredger in 1815, and by the 1820s they were becoming usual.

Water shortage became more and more serious as the traffic carried in the canal age continued to increase, and as the concurrent expansion of big towns caused competition for water supplies. To counteract the effects of leakage, of evaporation, and of the transfer of water from the higher to the lower levels as the locks were worked, a constant accession of supply to the higher levels was needed. This came either from side streams entering the canal, or from some big source of supply such as a reservoir, itself fed by streams.

The Acts under which canals were built specified exactly the streams that could be tapped and the other water that could be taken. At a time when so much of industry depended upon water power, millowners naturally opposed the building of canals that might draw off their water during times of drought, and only gave way if their supplies were protected by the building of special reservoirs, or if they were compensated for water taken, or in some cases if their mills were bought by the canal company. The supply of the summit or top level was often a matter of difficulty, especially when the canal crossed a watershed and was therefore by definition out of reach of large supplies. Reservoirs were built wherever possible—the Tring reservoirs on the Grand Union are a familiar example—or the summit level was deepened to provide an additional supply, as on the Cromford Canal. In other cases water was pumped to the summit level. The great well that supplied the Thames & Severn can still be seen near the Foss Way at Thames Head. The Worcester & Birmingham Canal was so strongly opposed by the millowners that the Bill was twice thrown out, until the company agreed to pump water up 425ft from the Severn. Luckily for the proprietors, however, it was found practicable to build reservoirs at the summit level. It was to this canal that the enabling Act of Parliament* specifically reserved the water from any springs in the bed of the canal, and such rainwater as fell on its surface! The Wisbech Canal was entirely dependent for its water upon supplies which could enter from the River Nene at spring tides. The canal was sometimes hardly navigable just before this water was admitted. Water which had anyway to be pumped from collieries was sometimes an important source of supply, as in the Birmingham area.

Measures were also taken to economise the use of water at the locks, by making boats pass the locks alternately up and down, so making one lockful do for two boats, by using locks with more than one set of gates or pairs of locks of different sizes, thereby using

* 31 Geo III, c 59, s 9.

the minimum of water necessary to pass small craft, or by building side ponds. A side pond was a basin alongside the lock, into which was run not quite half of the water from an emptying lock, instead of into the lower pound of the canal. When the lock had next to be filled, the first part of its contents came from the side pond and not from the upper pound. Thus one lockful of water passed two boats. Such ponds can often be seen, as on the Buckby flight of the Grand Union. A variation of this practice, said to have been first introduced by James Morgan, the engineer of the Regent's Canal, was to build pairs of locks, one for up and one for down traffic, so that as far as possible one could act as a side pond for the other. Another practice was to build stop gates where two canals joined: for example, where the Dearne & Dove Canal joined the Barnsley Canal; or even a physical bar, as at Worcester Bar where the Worcester & Birmingham joined the Birmingham, to prevent loss of water from the better supplied waterway to the other. Lastly, water was sometimes pumped back from a lower to a higher level, as on the Birmingham Canal Navigations or the Tinsley flight of the Sheffield Canal.

The design of locks remained more or less the same from Brindley days to the twentieth century. Now we have power-worked paddles and gates on the bigger canals, while a single hydraulic pattern is appearing on the smaller. There were some early experiments with alternatives to hand-operated paddle gear, such as the compressed-air type that the Peak Forest company seems to have tried. Early locks, however, did not have the usual iron or masonry protection to the sill, nor did boats carry a stem fender, for many byelaws enjoin the boatman to use a piece of wood to prevent the boat striking the sill. Damage to locks was the reason given for prohibiting the double-ended boat, with a detachable rudder hung on projecting eyes at each end.

Not all early locks had a railed walkway over the gates, or a bridge, to enable the boatman to get quickly from one side to the other. When keel captains asked the Driffield Navigation commissioners to provide a safer passage over the gates, they minuted in 1841: 'it was ordered that some little repairs to the tops of the Gates should be made without putting up a Rail which would make the passage over too much of a thoroughfare for persons not concerned on the Navigation, which the Commissioners think they ought not to do.'[11]

Many of the most bitter quarrels and lasting enmities between canal companies arose from water questions. The Staffordshire & Worcestershire were continually preoccupied with efforts to buy cheaply from the Birmingham company the water coming down the

Wolverhampton locks, with buying further supplies from the Wyrley
& Essington, which was blessed with a superfluity, and with selling
dearly what was needed by the Birmingham & Liverpool Junction.

In very hilly country the inclined plane and the canal lift were both
used to save water by making the building of locks unnecessary.
There is now no boat-carrying inclined plane working in Britain on
a canal, but at one time there were over twenty, on the Bude,

Figure 11   The inclined plane at Ketley shown on a token

Torrington, Chard, Grand Western, Kidwelly & Llanelly, Shrewsbury, Shropshire, Donnington Wood, Grand Junction and Monkland canals, and a visit to the site of one of them is always interesting.
The first in the British Isles, built by Davis Ducart on the Tyrone
(Ducart's) Canal, worked intermittently between 1777 and 1787.
England's first was built in 1788 by William Reynolds upon the
private Ketley Canal in Shropshire, and a contemporary description
of it, by Telford, is representative:

'Instead of descending in the usual way, by locks [he], continued
to bring the canal forward to an abrupt part of the bank, the
skirts of which terminated on a level with the iron-works. At the top
of this bank he built a small lock, and from the bottom of the lock,
and down the face of the bank, he constructed an inclined plane with
a double iron railway. He then erected an upright frame of timber,
in which, across the lock, was fixed a large wooden barrel; round this
barrel a rope was passed, and was fixed to a movable frame; this last
frame was formed of a size sufficient to receive a canal boat, and the
bottom upon which the boat rested, was preserved in nearly an
horizontal position, by having two large wheels before and two small
ones behind, varying as much in the diameters as the inclined plane
varied from an horizontal plane. This frame was placed in the lock,
the loaded boat was also brought from the upper canal into the

lock, the lock gates were shut, and on the water being drawn from the lock into a side pond, the boat settled upon the horizontal wooden frame, and as the bottom of the lock was formed with nearly the same declivity as the inclined plane, upon the lower gates being opened, the frame with the boat passed down the iron railway, on the inclined plane, into the lower canal, which had been formed on a level with the Ketley iron-works, being a fall of 73 feet. . . . A double railway having been laid upon the inclined plane, the loaded boat in passing down, brought up another boat containing a load nearly equal to one-third part of that which passed down. The velocities of the boats were regulated by brake acting upon a large wheel placed upon the axis on which the ropes connected with the carriage, were coiled.'[12]

This plane was counterbalanced, the loaded boat bringing up an empty or partly loaded one, a system that was only practicable when the predominant traffic carried was downwards; otherwise a steam engine was used if coal was cheap, and hydraulic power if it was not. Most of the Westcountry planes had waterwheels fed by a stream, but another and somewhat unreliable hydraulic method was used on the Hobbacott Down plane of the Bude Canal, the biggest of all, with a vertical rise of 225ft. A Victorian engineer, Vernon-Harcourt, described the method:

'The barges are drawn up in trains, and are to some extent counterpoised by the descending trains of barges. . . . The water power is supplied . . . by two large tubs ascending and descending alternately in two wells, the tub at the top of its well being filled with water, and in its descent drawing the barges up the incline. When the tub full of water reaches the bottom of the well, the water is emptied through a flap-door in the bottom of the tub; and the empty tub in the other well, having been drawn up its well by the descending tub, is at the top ready to be filled with water in its turn.'[13]

The canal lift, or balance lock, as it was sometimes called, though invented in Britain, was not successfully used until James Green installed seven of them on the Grand Western Canal's Taunton extension that was opened in 1838. Previously two inventors, Edward Rowland and Exuperius Pickering, had built in 1796, probably near Ruabon, an experimental lift for use on the Ellesmere Canal. It used the float principle, whereby a caisson holding the boat rode up and down on a float in a well which could be filled with water or emptied as necessary. It was never used, but the principle is that of some modern Continental lifts like that at Henrichenburg. Working in a different way, one with a 46ft lift had been built by Robert Weldon in 1798 on the Somersetshire Coal Canal, but it had been a failure, and had been replaced first by an inclined plane and then by a flight of locks. Another, designed by James Fussell of Mells, was successfully demonstrated on the Dorset & Somerset Canal, but could not be proved because the canal was never used. A fourth, with a 12ft lift, was built at Tardebigge on the Worcester & Birmingham in 1808. Like Weldon's, this was large enough to take a narrow boat. But though it worked satisfactorily on trials, Rennie advised that it would prove unreliable, and the company therefore decided to build locks. A fifth was designed by Colonel (later Sir William) Congreve and built at Camden Town on the Regent's Canal in 1814. It failed to work successfully, and was abandoned in 1816 without having been used.

A lift usually consisted of a caisson or tank into which the canal boat was floated, and of cables which ran over wheels at the top of the lift either to counterbalance weights, or to another caisson. Chains under each caisson, which coiled or uncoiled as they moved in relation to each other, kept the caissons in balance. In order to raise a boat from one level to another, water was added to the upper caisson, either until the caisson to be lifted began to move upwards, in which case the movement was controlled by a brake, or nearly to that point, the final impetus being given by manual or mechanical power. A lift could have one or two independently operated caissons, or two which balanced each other. The seven lifts on the Grand Western Canal, with rises varying from $12\frac{1}{2}$–42ft, were counterbalanced, one 8 ton boat being raised while another was lowered. These worked successfully for thirty years. Subsequently, in 1875, the Anderton lift connecting the Weaver Navigation with the Trent & Mersey Canal, and capable of lifting two full-sized narrow boats, was built, and still exists. Its caissons, once counterbalanced, are now independently operated. The Anderton was the prototype of canal lifts still used on the Continent and in Canada; the earlier of these were indeed built by its designer, Edwin Clark.

After all precautions had been taken, however, shortage of water, especially in the summer, was a perennial trouble on canals and river navigations. It meant that smaller cargoes than possible were carried, thereby increasing overhead costs, and that boats ran aground unnecessarily and had to be lightened, to everyone's annoyance and loss. This state of things became increasingly serious. Some industrial canals, especially those round Birmingham, had the advantage that they could draw most of their water from supplies pumped from colliery workings. Others built more and larger reservoirs, or installed machinery to pump upwards from streams or from their own lower levels.

Water was often sold to canalside works, but in the early days of steam engines, when it seems to have been considered that they consumed no water, this clause was inserted in the Birmingham Canal's Act of 1783:

'And whereas sundry Improvements have lately been made upon Steam or Fire Engines . . . And Whereas such Engines will consume considerable Quantities of Coal, and by the tonnage thereupon promote the Interest of the Navigation, as well as that of the Manufactories of Birmingham, if erected in its Neighbourhood; but as such Machines can only be erected where cold Water can be obtained to condense the Steam which is necessary to the working of them; and as such Water can be taken from the Navigation without Prejudice thereto, because such Machines, when properly constructed, do not waste or destroy any Water, but may be made to return to the Navigation a Quantity of warm Water equal to the cold Water which they drew from it . . . be it therefore enacted. . . . That it may be lawful . . . to draw from the said Canal such Quantities of Water as shall be sufficient to supply the said Engines . . .'[14]

Today canals supply water for industrial or agricultural purposes, much of it being returned for re-use; the resulting revenue helps their maintenance costs. We owe to them also the preservation of parts of our cities, for during the World War II they were in many towns the principal source of emergency water supply for the National Fire Service. Indeed, they still form an emergency reserve.

The revenue of canal companies chiefly arose from tolls charged at the rate of so many pence per ton per mile carried, as distinct from the freight charges of the carriers. Milestones were set up along the towpaths so that these point-to-point tolls could be accurately calculated. Charges were lowest for bulk commodities such as coal, culm (slack for lime-burning) and limestone, higher for more valuable bulk cargoes such as iron ore, and higher still for finished goods like iron-castings, and for groceries and general merchandise. In the case of coal, it was the usual practice to allow 21cwt or more to the ton, to cover transfer losses and theft.

The maximum tolls that could be charged upon each class of goods were laid down in the company Act, and could not be increased without further Parliamentary authority. The tendency was, however, the other way, as increasing trade, together with the competition of road transport, the coasting trade, and later railways, worked to reduce tolls. In addition, there was always pressure from the industrialists on one canal to get tolls lowered, in order that they might compete better with factories or mines served by other canals.

Small transport concerns, often very dependent upon a few businesses for their livelihood, found it difficult to resist such pressures.

Changes of toll within the Parliamentary limits had to be confirmed by shareholders' meetings, either those held regularly once or twice a year, or others specially called. In a few early cases the commissioners, whose usual function was to arbitrate in land valuation cases, or the magistrates in Quarter Sessions, had power to vary tolls.

Companies were not allowed to discriminate between users by giving special tolls, nor to charge more on one part of the line than another, till the Canal Tolls Act of 1845 gave power to vary tolls. Trade was encouraged by the giving of long credit: three months was usual, and with railway competition it tended to become longer.

The giving of drawbacks was a common practice. These were subsidies in the form of a partial refund of tolls, paid to those who shipped goods for long distances. They were usually given to encourage the development of markets for coal on other canals than that of the company granting them. The Ashby Canal, for instance, gave a drawback on all Moira, Gresley and Swadlincote coal carried the length of the canal and on to the Coventry; this drawback enabled these collieries, and especially Moira, to build up good distant sales, among them to Oxford colleges. Canal companies often competed briskly with one another in this way on the fringes of their territories, sometimes also carrying out raids far into each other's heartlands.

In order to reach the compromises with opponents that would get them their Acts, canal companies often had to hamper themselves with clauses allowing certain goods to move without payment of toll, a factor that acted to their detriment when they came to compete with railways which were not similarly handicapped. For instance, on the Chesterfield Canal hay and corn in the straw going to be stacked had to be carried toll-free for five miles; materials for the repair of parish roads, and manures for lands which had been cut by the canal, were carried toll-free provided no locks were passed. On the Derby Canal up to 5,000 tons of coal a year had to be carried toll-free to Derby for the use of the poor, a method of relieving the poor rates of the town at the expense of the company. Apart from tolls, some companies reaped a harvest from compensation payments. These arose when a new canal was projected that might cause trade to be diverted from existing navigations. In such cases the opposition of the old proprietors was only withdrawn when the new company had agreed to compensate them for any loss of trade. These payments became a widespread and restrictive network over the waterway system. For example, the Act for the Ashby-de-la-Zouch Canal (1794) provided that the Coventry Canal should collect 5d. a ton on all goods, with certain exceptions, passing to or from the Ashby Canal to or from the Coventry, Oxford or Grand Junction Canals, and should have power to place its own toll-houses, stop-bars and collectors on the Ashby Canal in order to collect the payments.

The tolls payable were calculated upon a written note declaring the type, weight, origin and destination of the cargo, presented by the carrier and endorsed by the toll-collector. If the latter had any reason to suspect the accuracy of the declaration—and he often did—then he made his own check of the tonnage the boat was carrying. This was found out by gauging. Each boat when it first came upon a canal was taken to a dock, where its draught when empty and when carrying various loads was found. Figures were then marked on the boat's side in four or six places, being either cut into the wood or cast on a metal plate.

Some canals had weighing machines instead of docks. These substantial structures had a cradle on to which a boat was floated. The water was then let out, and the boat weighed empty for record purposes. That figure known, it was simple to detect an overweight cargo by sending the boat to be weighed: indeed, the machine's existence was usually deterrent enough. Weighing machines were installed on a number of waterways, among them at North Road lock, Cardiff, on the Glamorganshire Canal, Midford on the Somersetshire Coal Canal, and Brimscombe on the Thames & Severn. That from Cardiff is now at the Waterways Museum, Stoke Bruerne.

An improved method of gauging was introduced about 1810. Instead of the figures showing different immersion depths for different loads being marked on the boat's side, they were entered in books which were kept at the toll-houses. The actual depth at which a boat was floating at any given time was found by using a hollow tube, with a rest to fit on the gunwale, which was put into the water beside the boat at four or six places. Inside the tube was a rod marked in feet and inches, which rose as the tube sank and showed the freeboard in inches. The average of the readings was then compared with the figures in the company's book for the boat concerned, and the tonnage read off.

Most waterways insisted that boats coming on to their water from another canal should be gauged by their officers, a rule less onerous in fact than appearance because most boats worked along well-defined routes. About 1798, however, eight canal and river companies in the Trent area joined in common gauging arrangements, the printed record books of which provide us nowadays with an exact picture of the boats used at the time in that area.

River and canal companies were hardly ever either empowered to put, or prohibited from putting, boats on their own or neighbouring waterways and carrying goods, so long as there was fair competition with other carriers. Many did carry from the beginning, like the Aire & Calder or the Mersey & Irwell. Others did intermittently, usually buying barges and running them until independent traders appeared, and then selling them. Others again organised carrying firms, nominally separate by being run by groups of canal shareholders, as the Trent & Mersey company originally did with its carrying counterpart, Hugh Henshall & Co.

It is probable that, as competition increased after the Napoleonic Wars had ended, canal companies who also ran carrying craft realised that they could in practice vary tolls in their own favour by adjusting freight charges, and that this led to complaints. The Ellesmere & Chester company at that time sought special authority to carry, an authority made general in 1845 by the Canal Carriers' Act. Many companies, however, remained toll-takers only to the end upon waterways that were open to all users. Today we still have a mixed system, the British Waterways Board's fleets operating side by side with private carriers.

Many canal and navigation companies ran businesses in some of the commodities they carried. The Upper Medway company traded in coal so successfully that they had a virtual monopoly for a century, and were also for a time in timber and iron. The Brecknock & Abergavenny went in for trading in coal, and thought of acquiring a colliery; later they transferred their trading interests to the nominally independent Brecon Boat Company. One or two companies actually ran or leased collieries. Many again owned lime-kilns, but the Peak Forest was exceptional. This company owned a number of kilns and rented others, and also worked large limestone quarries. They used very modern ways of encouraging the greater use of limestone, such as paying part of the cost of new kilns built within a time-limit, if their limestone only was used; subsidising publications on the uses of lime; making bulk contracts for sales which included toll, freight and the cost of the stone in one price, and offering loads at special rates so that turnpike trustees could experiment with it for road building.

Much canal carrying was done by private carrying companies or partnerships. These could be of any size, some running two or three boats, some twenty or more. They paid their men by the ton carried and not by weekly wages. Some men worked part-time as boatmen, others full-time, but for different employers. The most famous firm during the canal age was Pickfords, originally road waggon proprietors, whose activities appear widely in the 1790s and who leased warehouses and wharves and owned many boats 'which travel night and day, and arrive in London whith as much

Figure 12 Boatwoman and baby

punctuality from the midland and some of the most distant parts of the kingdom, as the waggons do.'[15] The canals felt the loss severely when, in the 1840s, Pickfords ceased to carry by canal, and went over to the railways.

There were of course many other firms, some general carriers, some specialising in fly-boat (express) work. There were, again, trading firms owning their own boats, or hiring them, and carrying their own raw materials or finished products, as on the Swansea Canal, where there were hardly any independent traders. Lastly, there were the small men, each owning a boat or two, and plying for hire as does a tramp steamer. There were never many of them on the narrow canals, but a few of the 'Number Ones' survived to our own times. There were probably more in Yorkshire, where the individually owned keel fitted well into the way carrying was organised on such navigations as the Don and the Calder & Hebble. Here the navigation company accepted goods even though it did not possess its own boats: instead, it contracted with carriers, individual owners and partnerships alike, to do the work for them.

If one should ask what manner of men these were, part of the answer is on a blue-printed earthenware plate that was made between 1800 and 1820. In the centre is a canalside scene, with the following verse below, and round the edge are the names on ribbons:

'Pickford, Beach, and Snell's, are jolly Lads, & true ones:
Kenworthy, & Worthington's, You'll likewise find true blue ones:
Wakeman, Green & Ames, amiss you'll never find Sirs,
Holt's, Crocket & Salkeld's, will sail fast as the wind Sirs.
True harted & jolly ones you'll find with Heath & Crawley,
Sturland's Henshall's, Alkin's too, can likewise use their mauley
So likewise can the Boatmen all, & drink their can of flip Sirs,
Thay'll drink there grog, & toast their lass, & then thay'll
Crack their whip Sirs.'[16]

Those who work on the waterways today are inheritors of a craft, with detailed and interesting traditions. It has sometimes been suggested that the canal boatmen and boatwomen had a special origin, for example, that they were gypsies. One sees no reason to accept such a suggestion, or to assume that they were recruited in ways other than those normally used to draw men to the new industrial areas of the late eighteenth and early nineteenth centuries. Many doubtless came from river and coastal craft to the canals; many had probably been locally employed navvies, who took to the waterways they had built; many came from canalside towns and villages, places where the building, loading and passing of boats was a familiar thing. Among these must have been small farmers, men with horses and carts who found good employment carting for local contractors building the canal, and who then probably took to the boats because they already possessed horses.

During the canal age boats seem in the main to have been worked by men and boys only, the usual bye-laws demanding two men to each boat, or at least a man and a stout boy, the latter to lead the horse. A Stourbridge Canal bye-law of 1789, however, demanded two men and a boy for any boat passing a lock. Let us not forget the boys: they were numerous and hard-worked. Wages were relatively good, the profits of carrying were reasonable, and boatmen earned enough money to keep their families in cottages ashore. It used to be thought there were few family boats before railway competition. It is now known that family narrow boats were quite common by the 1810s. Partly this use of family instead of paid help was the result

of competition between carrier and carrier, route and route: partly
of the housing shortage after the Napoleonic Wars; partly because,
as the length of canal journeys increased with the system's growth,
so a man was likely to see less and less of a wife and family ashore.
The coming of railways encouraged what was already taking place,
until by the time of George Smith, the canal reformer of the 1870s,
the family boat was common on narrow canals, though fly-boats
were always worked by men only. Under quite different circumstances, many of the sailing keels that traded along the Yorkshire navigations were also family boats, certainly from early in the nineteenth
century.

Time's pressure on the boatmen, toll-keepers and lock-keepers
slowly increased through the canal age. It was a consequence of the
increased development of the transport system that took place more
especially after the end of the Napoleonic Wars, though symptoms
of it had appeared earlier: for instance, some fly-boats began running
in the 1790s. We can see the process at work on the Staffordshire &
Worcestershire, which moved over the years from a near-monopoly
to a very competitive transport position. Before 1816 the normal
hours for boats to pass the locks were 5am to 9pm on moonlit
nights, and 6am to 8pm otherwise. In that year express or fly-boats
were put on, which paid an annual licence fee to be allowed to pass
the locks at any time. In 1820 the hours were extended to 4am to
10pm during the summer, and soon afterwards boats were allowed
to pass at any hour if they paid a small extra charge for each trip.
Finally, from 1830 the locks were open day and night for all boats,
the lock-keepers being paid a little extra: for instance, in February
1832 the man at Stourport lock got 14s (70p) a week and 4s (20p)
night wages. One sympathises with William Bagnall when the committee minuted in the same year 'That the Bed in the Nighthouse
at Heywood be taken away and that our Clerk do warn William
Bagnall to be more vigilant in his Duty and not permit any Boat to
pass without his knowledge.'[17] Separate day and night men were
afterwards employed at the busy points on the canal.

A sign of this increasing pressure of business was the passing in
1840 of the Constables Act, empowering canal and river authorities
to appoint their own police, though it does not seem that many
companies did so.

Early boats had no cabins—these began to appear in the 1790s.
However, as journeys lengthened, crews often slept ashore in the
canalside inns while their horses occupied the inn stables, or in
friends' houses.

In the early days boat people were recruited from outside, but in time boys became men, and there grew up a largely self-perpetuating boating community, increasingly separated from the population it served. Then slowly the situation reversed: as carrying contracted, the younger people left the boats to begin other lives with better prospects.

The life of the waterways has always had its hazards. Men, women and children have now and then fallen into a lock, been crushed by a boat, or slipped into the canal in the darkness. Boat horses were drowned, or burnt in their stables. Of accidents to the boats themselves I have chosen two, one normal enough, the other fortunately exceptional.

Figure 13   Opening the paddles of a lock

The Basingstoke company reported in 1802:

'. . . one of the Company's Barges, the *Baxter*, encountered a sudden and violent Storm, about the Nine Elms, as she was going up the Thames, loaded with Grocery and Merchandize, which rendered her totally unmanageable, and she must have sunk in the Middle of the River, but for the assistance of a large Sailing Vessel which kept her floating till she gat near the Shore, when she went to the Bottom and was soon filled with Water. . . . At the same Time another loaded

Barge, the Property of a Mr Jones, also going up the River, sunk, after she had been hauled close to the Shore; and Three other Vessels, of different Descriptions, were seen to go down about the same Time. . . . While the Committee express their Concern at so heavy a Disaster, they are happy in being able to assure the Proprietors, after an attentive Examination of all the Circumstances, they have abundant Evidence that the Accident did not happen through any Error or Misconduct of the Bargemen or Servants. . . .'[18]

In 1874 the *Illustrated London News* carried an account of the famous Regent's Park explosion. The following is an extract:

'An extraordinary accident, which happened yesterday week at five o'clock in the morning, cost the loss of several lives, much damage to houses and furniture, and a vast alarm to the north-western suburbs of London. This was the blowing up of a barge laden with petroleum and gunpowder for blasting, which was one of a train drawn by a steam-tug along the Regent's Canal. . . . The train of six light barges, of which the first was a steamer, left the wharf in the City-road about three o'clock that morning. Next after the steamer, the Ready, was the fly-boat Jane, whose steerer or captain was named Boswell. Next to her was the Dee, the steerer Edwards; and next came the unfortunate Tilbury, whose steerer was Charles Baxton, of Loughborough, in Leicestershire. The Jane "had a little gunpowder on board". The Tilbury's lading is thus described by the official report: "The cargo consisted chiefly of sugar and other miscellaneous articles, such as nuts, straw-boards, coffee, and some two or three barrels of petroleum, and about five tons of gunpowder.". . . Three or four minutes before five o'clock, this train of barges was passing under the bridge at North Gate, Regent's Park. . . . On board the ill-fated Tilbury were the steersman, Charles Baxton, who was about thirty-five years of age; William Taylor, a labourer, of twenty-five; another man and a boy. The Tilbury was directly under the bridge when by some means yet unexplained, the powder caught fire and the whole was blown up. The men on board this barge were killed, and the barge was shattered to pieces, while one of the other barges was sunk. A column of thick smoke and a great blaze of fire followed the explosion. The bridge was entirely destroyed; several of the neighbouring houses were half-ruined, their roofs and walls being greatly injured; and in hundreds of other houses, a mile east or west of the place, the windows were broken, and many fragile articles of furniture. . . . The noise and shock were perceived in every quarter of London, and in many instances ten or twelve miles away, both on the north and the south side of the Thames. . . . Women and children rushed out of the houses, screaming for help, some in their night-dresses, others wrapped in blankets, and were not easily pacified by those of cooler mind whom they met. People soon hastened up from every quarter of town. The police, the Fire Brigade, and a detachment of Horse Guards (Blue) from Albany Barracks, presently arrived and kept order, while the task of saving what remained and searching for the lost was actively begun.'[19]

The boat people in the past had few friends and many enemies. The presence of this perpetually moving population was not welcome to those who lived near waterways, and new canal projects were sometimes opposed for fear of the damage that might be done by them to property, or the poaching that might result. The owners of boats also complained of them for pilfering, bartering coal from cargoes for food and drink, dumping coal in rivers to lighten barges, and incidentally to warm the riverside villagers who dredged it, and spending money in public houses that had been given them to pay tolls, while their good service and hard, laborious work remained unrecorded.

Another hard-working class of people deserves to be mentioned, the lock and toll-keepers. On the canals, lock-keepers were given a house as well as their wages, and often a coal allowance (to remove temptation) and perhaps one for candles. They might be asked to do some gauging and toll-collecting on traffic loading near their locks, to inspect tonnage bills, to help pass the boats, and to trim hedges or break ice. They were expected not to leave their posts, unlike Eynon Bowen on the Swansea Canal, who was fined in 1818 because 'A great part of his time is taken up in farming and other concerns'.[20] Some companies provided 'an upper Waistcoat and a Badge thereupon to distinguish them from other persons . . .'.[21] The toll-keepers had, of course, to be honest in accounting for receipts (they were usually covered by security bonds) and for making sure that boats were properly gauged and that their waybills were in order. They also had to refrain from trading with the boatmen or borrowing money from them.

When these men were old, they were usually given a small pension. One thinks kindly of the committee of the Staffordshire & Worcestershire, whose records reveal a long tradition of good works, for minuting in 1823: 'John Buttery . . . being incapable of attending to his Situation owing to Old Age. Ordered that he be replaced, and that an annual pension be allowed him . . . and until a Successor be appointed, Ordered that our Clerk write to Crowley and Company requiring them to give notice to their Boatmen not to molest or insult John Buttery in his passing their Boats along the Canal.'[22]

They had to be strong characters, for their work was lonely and

FELONY

AND

Reward.

WHEREAS on the Night of *Tuesday* the 13th instant, the Hatches of a Boat lying in the Docks at MULLINGAR were forced open, and the TOOLS belonging to four Ship Carpenters taken away; and on the Night of *Wednesday* the 25th instant, Boat No. 49, lying in the Docks upon the BROADSTONE LEVEL, DUBLIN, was attacked by a number of Persons, when they tied the Men belonging thereto, and carried away the TOOLS of six Ship Carpenters that had been working at said Boat. They also made use of expressions threatening destruction to any Carpenter that would work under certain Wages; and that they would destroy the Property of any individual that would not give the prescribed Wages for the Repairs of their Boats. A WRITTEN NOTICE to the foregoing effect was left in the Boat at Mullingar.

NOW the COURT OF DIRECTORS of the NEW ROYAL CANAL COMPANY, for the purpose of preventing the continuance of such an illegal Combination, do hereby offer

A REWARD OF

Fifty Pounds

for the discovery, and prosecution to conviction, of the Person or Persons who were concerned in the carrying away the said Tools, or in the writing or publishing of the Felonious Threats aforesaid, or

A Reward of Ten Pounds

shall be given to any Person giving private Information, which may lead to the conviction of such Offender, or Offenders, as aforesaid, or of any Person who shall, in consequence of said Notice, conspire to carry into effect the Threats therein contained, or commit any Outrage on the Person or Property of any Trader on the Royal Canal, or any Person in his Employment.

By Order of the Court of Directors,

SAMUEL DRAPER,
Secretary.

ROYAL CANAL HOUSE,
30th July, 1821.

Figure 14 The early 1820s were very disturbed years in Ireland. The Royal Canal suffered even more than the Grand Canal from 'combinations' among boatmen, malicious breaches of the banks, and attacks on boats

responsible. Here, to end this chapter, are two pictures of their lives; the first concerns a Thames lock-keeper.

'Tedding^n Lock 28/3/1818

'. . . It has been always Customary with me to rise at dawn of day because in general ye Barges move from Richmond then & often do before if the Moon shines till day & this was the Case on y^e 20th early. I rose at just past 4 & was Employed in the Office arranging some small matters before y^e Craft came when I heard a Man's Voice calling. I open'd one of the Shutters & saw a Man standing about $\frac{1}{2}$ Way between my Window & the lower Gate, and he Pointed with his hand and said here's a Trow coming. I had no doubt in my own mind but that the Trow was very near, & as the Wind blew hard & right into the Pound it was highly necessary the Gates should be opened & ready. I now took my hat & was going out but the Ins^t I open'd the Door a Stout Fellow rushed in & seized me by the throat. While we were struggling in came 2 More & one of them had something in his hand resembling $\frac{1}{2}$ a Sack. I was thrown with Violence over a Chair and we both came rolling to y^e Ground & I then felt one of them cover my head & press it so close down that I really began to fear they meant to suffocate me. . . . They then took my Keys from my Coat pocket by rolling me over, and having broke every Lock and Emtied every small Box of Mrs S in the next room they all ran out leaving me locked in & in darkness. By their bad discourse I must (think) them Bargemen of lowest Class. I had about 11 or 12 Single Pound Notes & full six Pounds Silver & ye most part Sm^l Silver & 4 or 5 shillings in Copper. I do indeed much fear that this is only ye beginning, for which ever Lock Receives much value it will be a Temptation to such Villains to make an attempt at ye end of ye Week. . . .

. . . Richd Savory.'[23]

On the Regent's Canal in London in 1830 the 'Eastern division of the Canal, was almost constantly the scene of the most disgraceful Riots. Such were the lawless set that frequented the Canal (to hunt Ducks, Swim Dogs, etc.) that a party of the Police were in constant pay, and absolutely necessary to protect the Lock-keepers from personal harm; but this did not always succeed, for on several occasions, Lock-keepers have been so severely treated, in defending the Company's property from damage, that in some cases they were several months in recovering from the Injuries they received.'[24]

CHAPTER IV

The Arteries of the Revolution

So immediate was the success of the Duke of Bridgewater's canal from Worsley towards Manchester, which had been opened in 1761, that he went back to Parliament during the following year for authority to continue to the Mersey near Runcorn, so that his coal might go to Liverpool without using the Mersey & Irwell.

This was a much more ambitious plan. That the duke had put it forward in the light of his experience with the Worsley canal, and was employing Brindley as resident engineer to build it, were pointers to the future that were not lost upon businessmen, among them Josiah Wedgwood of the Potteries and his partner Thomas Bentley, and the salt manufacturers of Cheshire dependent upon the River Weaver.

Men's minds were used to rivers being navigable, and it was a logical development, though a startling one when it came, that rivers could be joined together, so that goods could travel from the sea at either end to any intermediate point, and from any point to either river mouth. Many such schemes had been suggested in the past—for instance, the junction of the rivers Thames and Severn by way of the Bristol Avon proposed by Mathew in the seventeenth century—but now they suddenly seemed practicable. Such an arrangement to link Trent and Mersey would suit Wedgwood excellently, for at present his raw material came mostly by sea from Cornwall and Devon to the Mersey, by barge up the Weaver to Winsford bridge, and then by packhorse to the Potteries. Now his raw material could be brought from the Mersey to his doorstep, and his products be carried away in either direction as far as Liverpool or Hull.

The upper section of the Trent had already been made navigable to Burton-on-Trent under an Act of 1699. When, therefore, Wedgwood and his associates proposed to make a canal, at first called the Grand Trunk and later the Trent & Mersey, from Wilden Ferry below Burton to the Mersey, there was heavy opposition by river interests. The Burton (upper Trent) Navigation maintained that the canal should end at Burton rather than fourteen miles lower down at

81

Wilden Ferry, while the Weaver Navigation, that had so far carried all the salt and part of the pottery trade, tried to get the western end of the proposed canal connected to its own river. The promoters of the new scheme were anxious to obtain efficiency of transport by avoiding any commitments to the old navigations, as they were called, which compelled them to join their canal to unimproved waterways or be charged monopoly rates. The opposition of the rivers was so active that at one stage the Cheshire gentlemen who supported the case of the River Weaver surveyed the route for an alternative canal to the Trent by way of Stafford, and fought the Trent & Mersey Canal Bill right to the Parliamentary Committee. Indeed, the owners of the Burton Navigation continued their opposition until their activity ended in 1805.

To get the Duke's support, an agreement was reached by which he would build the portion of the Trent & Mersey Canal from Preston Brook to Runcorn, altering his own line from Manchester to Runcorn to join the new canal. The plans for the Trent & Mersey Canal led enterprising men to envisage a connection between it, at Great Haywood in Staffordshire, and the River Severn at what is now Stourport, but was then a hamlet. Both groups of promoters employed Brindley as engineer, and both obtained their Acts on the same day of the same year, 1766.

These great projects, the Trent & Mersey, 93⅛ miles long and with an authorised capital of £150,000, and the Staffordshire & Worcestershire, 46⅛ miles long, with £100,000 of capital, were worthy of Brindley's capacities. The Bridgewater Canal had been built level from Worsley to Manchester, and was being continued on the same level to Runcorn, where it would fall to the Mersey by a flight of ten locks; but the locks had not yet been built, and his experience was in fact limited to the construction of level line, to the embankments and aqueduct at Barton, and the tunnels at Worsley, made under John Gilbert's supervision. Yet he did not fear to plan four aqueducts and 43 locks on the Staffordshire & Worcestershire, or 75 locks, the 2,880yd long Harecastle tunnel, and several other tunnels on the Trent & Mersey. In spite of many difficulties, the Staffordshire & Worcestershire was completed in 1772 (the year of Brindley's death), and the Trent & Mersey in 1777.

Once the line of the Trent & Mersey had been decided, it was likely that men would seek to join it to the Thames. The effort began in 1768, when an Act was obtained for the Coventry Canal, mainly to supply Coventry with coal from mines along the line, but joined to the Trent & Mersey at Fradley near Lichfield. Brindley was again the engineer, but the initial capital of £50,000 was found only to be

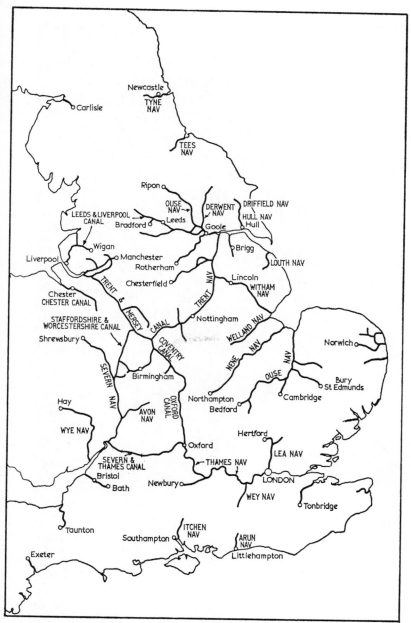

Map 4 The waterway system, 1789

Figure 15　A romantic picture of Harecastle tunnel, published in 1785. Nothing shown is even approximately correct

enough to complete half of the line, from Coventry to Atherstone. The proprietors could not find additional money, and for ten years the completed portion remained isolated. Meanwhile, the year after the Coventry Act had been passed, a proposal was authorised for a canal from the River Thames at Oxford to join the Coventry Canal at Longford near Coventry, also to be constructed by Brindley. By 1778 the 63¾ miles of canal between Longford and Banbury were open, and it was therefore of importance to the proprietors of the Oxford Canal that they should induce the Coventry to complete its line.

Meanwhile waterways had come to Birmingham. In the same year that the Coventry had obtained its Act, 1768, the Birmingham Canal was authorised, from the Staffordshire & Worcestershire at Autherley to the town of Birmingham, and was completed in 1772. This was the first canal to be built as a tributary to one of the new artificial rivers; it became the prototype of many more industrial canals of the same type. In contrast, the same year of 1768 saw the authorisation of an artificial tributary to a natural river, the Droitwich Canal, from the Severn to that town. This canal was made of large size to take the river craft, whereas the Trent & Mersey, Staffordshire & Worcestershire, Coventry, Oxford, and Birmingham canals had all been planned with narrow locks.

In 1781 and 1782 the Oxford, Coventry and Trent & Mersey companies supported a project for a canal from the coalmines round Wednesbury to join the Coventry Canal near Fazeley, whence the coal could be taken north or south. The promoters and their supporters met at Coleshill in 1782 and agreed that the Oxford Canal should be completed from Banbury to Oxford, and the Coventry from Atherstone to Fazeley, while the Trent & Mersey and the Birmingham & Fazeley, as it was called, would each finish half of the Fazeley–Fradley section. The Birmingham Canal company now became very worried lest they should lose their monopoly position in the coal-carrying trade of the Birmingham area, and organised a nominally separate company (which was amalgamated with its parent in 1784) to build from their canal at Farmer's Bridge, Birmingham, to Fazeley, so that Wednesbury coal would not by-pass their line. After a terrific Parliamentary battle, the Birmingham Canal group won, and the new canal was authorised in 1783. They took over the Coleshill agreement, and started construction. In 1790, after some recalcitrance by the rather faint-hearted Coventry company, the whole Birmingham–Fazeley–Fradley–Coventry–Oxford line was finished. So was completed the last link in the interconnection of the four great rivers of Trent, Mersey, Severn and Thames. Brindley did not live to see it, however, for he died in 1772.

That the traffic had only been waiting for the communication is shown by the tolls and weighing charges combined taken by the Oxford company:

Year	£
1789–90	10,697
1792–3	17,970
1795–6	25,880

In the same year of 1766 that saw the authorisation of the Trent & Mersey and the Staffordshire & Worcestershire the Forth & Clyde Canal was projected with John Smeaton as engineer, and two years later its tributary the Monkland Canal. Since the Forth & Clyde was in concept a sea-to-sea canal it will be described in Chapter VII.

Two chains still waited to be thrown across England from river to river; in the north a connection between the Mersey on the west and the Aire & Calder Navigation in Yorkshire that gave access to the Humber; in the south a junction between the Bristol Channel and the Thames by way of the Severn or the Bristol Avon.

The first Act to make navigable the Aire to Leeds and its tributary the Calder to Wakefield had been passed in 1699, as a result of efforts by the mayor and several aldermen of Leeds, and some gentlemen of Wakefield. Under it locks were built and a depth of 3½ft obtained. The northern link between the Aire at Leeds and the Mersey at Liverpool was first planned and in 1766 surveyed by the Yorkshire engineer John Longbothom. It was re-surveyed, and most of it approved, by Brindley and his assistant Robert Whitworth, and in 1770 an Act was obtained, the authorised capital being £260,000. The planned line of this Leeds & Liverpool Canal was 108¾ miles long. This was built on the Yorkshire side, but on the Lancashire it ran north of the present line by Whalley and the Ribble valley, then south of Preston and by Leyland to Newburgh and the present line to Liverpool. In the list of staff appears the name of Joseph Priestley as accountant. He soon became superintendent, and served the company till 1817, when he died, aged seventy-seven. His monument, embellished with emblems of surveying and canal operation, is in Bradford cathedral. It was another Joseph Priestley, perhaps his son, who in 1831 published the best contemporary account of the canals and navigable rivers of Britain.

The coal of the Wigan neighbourhood had in the past been distributed by taking it down the River Douglas, finally made navigable to Tarleton on the Ribble in 1742, whence it was carried by coasting vessels to the Mersey or further, especially to Ireland. One of the

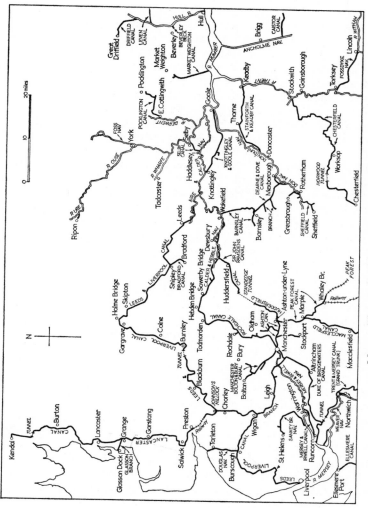

Map 5 The canals of Lancashire and Yorkshire

first Acts of the new Leeds & Liverpool company was to buy a controlling interest in the Douglas Navigation. Later the two concerns were amalgamated.

Before building began there had been controversy between the promoters in Yorkshire, whose interest was in a direct and cheap communication with Liverpool, and those in Lancashire, who wanted a less direct line that would include more Lancashire towns. The Yorkshire promoters, led by the appropriately named John Hustler, carried the day, and the Act was obtained for the shorter line.

John Longbothom began construction. By 1774 28 miles on the Lancashire side had been opened from Liverpool to Newburgh, whence there was access to Wigan by the Douglas, and three years later 30 miles on the Yorkshire side had been completed from Leeds, where the canal joined the Aire & Calder Navigation, to Gargrave. While the Lancashire part was building, however, a group of dissident Lancashire promoters who had withdrawn from the Leeds & Liverpool company had promoted a canal from Wigan to Liverpool, saying that the route by the Douglas to Newburgh and thence by the Leeds & Liverpool was too roundabout and uncertain. Their Bill was defeated in 1772, and by 1779 an all-canal line had been opened from Wigan to Liverpool. Two years later the Rufford branch from Burscough to the Ribble, to by-pass most of the Douglas, was completed.

Meanwhile, a moment for choosing life or death had come to the Aire & Calder, for in 1772 a newly promoted company supported unofficially by many concerned with the Leeds & Liverpool had introduced a Bill to build a canal from Leeds to Selby on the Ouse, so by-passing the Aire & Calder completely. The latter defeated the Bill, and itself then built a shorter canal from the Aire at Haddlesey to Selby, the present Selby Canal, so avoiding the difficult passage of the lower Aire. Other side cuts to improve the river passage were also begun as part of a modernisation programme.

Work had stopped, however, on the Leeds & Liverpool for lack of money. The War of American Independence was being fought, and for thirteen years nothing was done. The completed portions were of value, however, for that in Yorkshire joined Bradford (by the Bradford Canal) and Gargrave above Skipton to Leeds and the Aire & Calder Navigation, while that in Lancashire carried rapidly increasing quantities of coal from Wigan. By 1785 nearly 4 per cent was being earned on the capital so far expended.

In 1790 work began again at the Gargrave end, with Robert Whitworth as engineer, though his estimate of the money needed to finish the canal sufficed only for 14 miles to Barrowford, including

Foulridge tunnel. Meanwhile, the growth of new manufacturing districts had made the company decide that a short route between east and west was less important than a route that passed through these areas. The line was therefore altered to run by Burnley, Church and Blackburn to Johnson's Hillock, and work proceeded as the debts of the company grew. The branch canal from Newburgh to Wigan now became part of the main line, while the Lancaster Canal, authorised in 1792, was used for 11 miles of the route in Lancashire, from Johnson's Hillock to Wigan top lock. At last, in 1816, forty-six years after the canal had been authorised, it was completed by making the last portion below Blackburn. It had cost some £800,000 and had grown in length to 127¼ miles. Though designed for through carriage, its revenue came principally from the separate trade of the two ends, from Burnley, Blackburn and the other cotton towns and from Wigan down to Liverpool and from the highlands of York-shire to Leeds and the Aire & Calder. In 1820 the Leeds & Liverpool was linked by the Leigh branch to the Bridgewater Canal and so to Manchester, but, though it ran to Liverpool, it had no physical connection with the Mersey till 1846. Ironically, although the Leeds & Liverpool was by over twenty years the first trans-Pennine canal to be begun, it was the last of three to be finished: another broad canal, the Rochdale, from the Bridgewater at Manchester to the Calder & Hebble at Sowerby Bridge, was authorised in 1794 and opened in 1804, while the narrow Huddersfield Canal, also authorised in 1794, was finished in 1811 through the 5,456yd long Standedge tunnel.

The idea of joining Severn to Thames is at least as old as the reign of Elizabeth I. The first practical step was taken in 1730, when an Act was obtained to make navigable the River Stroudwater from the Severn to the town of Stroud. The owners of the many mills on the river were so strong in opposition, however (they even inserted a clause in the Act that no boat was to pass between 14 August and 15 October without the consent of the majority of the millowners), that nothing was done. A second Act was passed in 1759. It is of interest for the extraordinary scheme it produced. In order to over-come the objections of the millowners it was proposed to make the river navigable without locks. Below each mill a cut was to be made towards the river above the mill, the two waterways being separated by a 12ft bank. On this bank a double crane was to be fitted. The boats themselves were to carry six to eight boxes of cargo, each hold-ing one ton of goods, which were then to be lifted from one boat to another by the crane at each bank. A crane with two jibs was pro-vided so that boxes could be interchanged without setting them down. John Kemmett and the other projectors did about half the work (and offered also to make the Calder and the upper Don navigable in the same way) and then gave up, presumably for lack of money.

In 1774 plans were made for a canal, which the promoters attempted to build under the powers given in former Acts to improve the river. After some work had been done they were stopped by injunction, and a new Act had to be got in 1776. The canal was opened in 1779, big enough to take Severn trows. It was 8 miles long and had 12 locks.

The building of the Stroudwater Canal encouraged action to join Severn to Thames. An Act was passed in 1783, Whitworth was engaged as engineer with Josiah Clowes under him, and the Thames & Severn Canal was opened in 1789. It was 30¼ miles long, counting the branch to Cirencester, and ran from the Stroudwater at Wallbridge (Stroud) to the Thames at Inglesham above Lechlade. It included Sapperton tunnel, over two miles long, the third longest canal tunnel in Britain.

The Thames & Severn started life with three handicaps: disordered finance as a result of loose administration while it was building; a summit level through the Great Oolite that throughout its long life lost up to three million gallons of water a day in leakage and which was in any case short of water; and the bad state of the navigation of the upper River Thames. These causes persisted,

Figure 16 Thames & Severn Canal token. On the left is a Severn trow, on the right the Coates entrance to Sapperton tunnel

though the finances were reorganised. The canal was never more than a part-success, and for most of its life to 1927 a failure.

It was otherwise with the second of the three canals built to join the Bristol Channel to the Thames. The proposal to link the River Kennet at Newbury with the River Avon at Bath grew out of a proposal of 1788 to extend the Kennet navigation from Newbury by a canal to Hungerford, but got its impetus from the canal mania of 1792, and was authorised as the Kennet & Avon Canal in 1794.

The project was on a grand scale, for a broad canal 57 miles long, to include a great flight of 29 locks at Devizes. John Rennie was engineer. The first part of the line, from Newbury to Hungerford, was opened in 1798 with:

'. . . a barge freighted with a wrought Portland stone staircase, for J. Pearce, esq., of Chilton Lodge, a large quantity of deals, and nine chaldron of sea coal, in the whole amounting to 40 tons.'[1]

Troubles were many, and as early as 1800, 450 out of the 3,500 issued shares of £120 had been forfeited for non-payment of calls upon them, due to the nervousness of shareholders. The lack of proper survey before work was begun caused much extra expense, and it was not until 1810 that the line was completed, at a cost of £980,000. Yet, spurred on by their enthusiastic chairman, Charles Dundas, the shareholders, who already had a controlling interest in the Avon, went on to buy the Kennet Navigation for £70,000 cash and £1,500 a year, and made plans for expansions and through routes on a grand scale. For instance, some Kennet & Avon proprietors took up shares in the Grand Western Canal of Devon, seeing it as part of a through route from Exeter to London.

The Kennet & Avon was a successful canal. Its dividends were small, for the cost of upkeep was high; but in its prime it carried 341,878 tons of goods in a year (1838–9), against the 60,894 of the Thames & Severn for the same year. Sold to the Great Western Railway while still a going concern, it is now being restored for pleasure craft use, while its two competitors are broken down and empty.

The Wilts & Berks was a narrow canal, planned not as a through waterway from Bristol to London, but as a carrier of coal to the agricultural areas of the Vale of White Horse. (Before Tom Brown began his schooldays he often wanted to board a Wilts & Berks boat). It was built under an Act of 1795 from Semington on the Kennet & Avon to Abingdon on the River Thames, by way of Swindon (not then of course a big town) and with branches to Calne, Chippenham and Wantage. Its history was that of many agricultural canals, though its high cost of £255,000 was not. Moderately used till railway competition (it carried 62,899 tons in 1838), it afterwards slowly declined, and as we shall see, passed through several hands before final closure in 1914. Yet it had a few years of exciting life.

Begun after the Kennet & Avon, it was finished first. Into the minds of its promoters there entered in 1809 the fancy of beating both the Kennet & Avon, in trouble over its 29 locks at Devizes, and the Thames Navigation, the only outlet for the traffic of the Thames & Severn Canal, grounded in its own shallows between Lechlade and Oxford. They forgot that the Wilts & Berks was a narrow and shallow canal, longer than the Kennet & Avon, and they made a bid for the through traffic between Bristol, London and the midlands. First they planned a short connecting link to the Thames & Severn, to take traffic from that canal at Latton and carry it by Swindon and the Wilts & Berks to Abingdon, so by-passing the upper Thames. This link was in fact built as the North Wilts, and opened in 1819. To avoid the navigation difficulties of the lower Thames, second only to those of the upper river, they then proposed a cut from Abingdon across country to join the Grand Junction. There was to be another from Wootton Bassett direct to Bristol to cut out the Kennet & Avon west of Semington and also the Avon, and yet another canal from Abingdon to the Stratford-upon-Avon Canal to attract Birmingham and midlands trade.

It was a gloriously grandiose plan, but narrow boats and a winding line were not serious competitors to a broad canal on a through route, like the Kennet & Avon, though for some years from 1809, and after the opening of the Kennet & Avon, fly-boats (express goods boats) were operated between London and Bristol via Abingdon. The North Wilts did help the Thames & Severn quite considerably by providing a route that avoided the upper Thames, but it made no great change in the condition of its parent, the Wilts & Berks, which subsided once again into bringing coal from the Somersetshire Coal Canal (a branch of the Kennet & Avon) to the Vale, and carrying away agricultural produce. These three canals completed the circuit of Britain, by Mersey, Trent, Thames, Severn and Mersey again. But in time they fall outside the first period of canal building to which the others belong.

Meanwhile, two arteries were being built in Ireland to supplement Steers's old Newry Canal, which Thomas Omer, an engineer of Dutch descent, had by 1769 extended by a small ship canal taking craft of 120 tons.

The first, the Lagan Navigation from Belfast to Lough Neagh, was begun by Thomas Omer in 1756. He had built the river section upwards to near Lisburn by 1765, but there work stopped, partly because money was short, partly because of doubts whether it was sensible to continue a river navigation so liable to floods as the Lagan. After Robert Whitworth had put up alternative ideas for continuing by canal, a company took over from the old commissioners, Richard Owen from the Leeds & Liverpool was engaged as engineer, and work began again in 1782. The whole line was opened to Lough Neagh on the first day of 1794, 25¾ miles long with 27 locks, each 62ft by 14ft 6in, very similar in size to those of Owen's former canal. Owen's works included the four-arched Spencer's Bridge aqueduct, and the Union three-lock staircase at Sprucefield above Lisburn.

The second was the Grand Canal, the line from Dublin to the Shannon, and its major branch the Barrow. The idea of opening up the centre of Ireland had been behind the Act of 1715. In 1751, the Corporation for Promoting and Carrying on an Inland Navigation in Ireland was set up by the Irish Parliament to amalgamate the four bodies of provincial commissioners established in 1729. The Corporation appointed the existing commissioners, and put impetus behind waterway building. An Act of 1772 enabled the commissioners to transfer works to private interests. However, the Corporation was dissolved in 1787, having spent some £850,000, and separate bodies of commissioners for different waterways were substituted. Within ten years of their first establishment, the Corporation had initiated work on the Shannon in 1755, the Grand Canal in 1756 and the Barrow and Boyne in 1759.

The Grand Canal was to be 79 miles long without branches, reaching the Shannon at Shannon Harbour above Banagher. The chosen line was surveyed by Thomas Omer, and work begun on a large scale, Omer's first lock being 136ft long, able to take a 175 ton barge. Not long afterwards, the city of Dublin decided to draw water for town use from the canal, now to serve a double purpose. But canal work went on very slowly, until after about 20 miles had been built, it stopped in 1768 before a series of inquiries as to why so much had been spent and so little achieved.

Eventually a company was formed to take the work over, and complete it on a reduced scale. John Smeaton was now asked to advise on what needed to be done, but, busy as he was on the Forth & Clyde Canal, he declined. However, in 1773 he came over, bringing his pupil William Jessop. The latter spent some time with John Trail, who had worked mainly as Dublin's water supply engineer, and supported by Smeaton, recommended the canal should be continued on a smaller scale. This was agreed, and construction went on with Trail, William Chapman and other engineers as residents and Jessop as consultant. The first twelve miles were opened to traffic in 1779, the Bog of Allen was crossed in the 1790s, and at last in 1805, after John Killaly had been engineer since 1798, the whole canal was finished with its 41 locks 70ft by 13ft 7½in, two months after Jessop's Grand Junction in England.

Its major offshoot, mainly river navigation, partly canal, the Barrow, had been begun by Thomas Omer in 1759. It went on very slowly indeed until, after a report by William Chapman thirty years later, a company was also formed in 1790. Under it, Chapman rebuilt some of the old work and created new, and early in the new century, with government help, the navigation was finished, nearly 42 miles long from the Grand's Barrow branch to Athy (itself 28½ miles long, and opened in 1791) to the tideway of the Barrow at St Mullins.

In 1759, Thomas Omer also began work on the lower Boyne from Drogheda to Slane, mostly by building a lateral canal. Though £75,000 had been spent, the section to Slane was seemingly unfinished and semi-derelict when the corporation was abolished in 1787. A River Boyne Company took over in 1790, and by 1800 had extended the line to Navan, 19 miles from Drogheda with 20 broad locks. About a mile of a proposed extension upwards to Trim was also cut before work ended.

Back in England, after the authorisation of the Leeds & Liverpool in 1770, three tributary canals were built, the little Bradford to link that town with the Leeds & Liverpool, the Chester from the mouth of the Dee through Chester to Nantwich, and the great Chesterfield Canal to run from that town through the mining area near it to the River Trent at Stockwith.

Then came a long period of consolidation, lasting from 1774 to 1788. Capital and labour were being fully employed upon the great routes that crossed the British Isles; the war of American Independence was being fought and lost; and men were watching to see whether this new method of transport would be a financial success. If so, it was clear that speculative gentlemen would take a hand. How successful it was we can see from the takings upon the Duke of Bridgewater's Canal, which in 1791 amounted to £61,143.

CHAPTER V

Birmingham, Basingstoke and Pontcysyllte

The first period of canal development in England saw the authorisation of waterways linking Mersey with Severn and Trent, and Mersey with Aire and Calder, together with some tributaries. Sixteen years elapsed between the Act for the Chester Canal in 1772 and those for the Andover and the Cromford canals in 1789—the harbingers of the canal mania. In this period the few canals that were authorised fall into three groups, the only exceptions being the Erewash, a tributary canal of the Trent, and a number of small privately owned and built navigations from Cornwall to Yorkshire. The first group consists of the Stroudwater and Thames & Severn canals, already described, which together were the first link between Severn & Thames. The other groups consisted on the one hand of a number of canals in the Birmingham area, and on the other of a new kind of waterway, the Basingstoke, the first of the agricultural canals.

The original Birmingham Canal that had been authorised in 1768 and opened in 1772 not only brought coal to Birmingham from pits along its line, and goods from the Staffordshire and Worcestershire, and so from the whole canal system built at that time; it carried coal away from the fields round Wednesbury, and sent it towards the Severn to compete with that from Shropshire. Before it was built, a historian of Birmingham, Hutton, says that coal brought by land cost 13s (65p) a ton, and that it was common to see a train of waggons for miles, to the great destruction of the road, and the annoyance of travellers. Its construction brought down the price to 7s (35p) while its profits raised the value of its £140 shares to £420 by 1782, for which year a dividend of 15 per cent was paid. 'It is happy for the world', Hutton says, 'that public interest is grafted upon private, and that both flourish together.'

In 1776 there began the process that ended in giving Birmingham its present network of canals. Two companies were formed, and obtained their Acts on the same day. One, the Stourbridge Canal, was to spend £38,000 on making a cut from the town of Stourbridge to the Staffs & Worcs Canal at Stourton, together with two branches, one being to Black Delph in the direction of Dudley. The other, the Dudley Canal, was to spend £9,700 to build from Dudley itself to join the Stourbridge Canal at Black Delph. The two navigations combined enabled coal to be carried from the mining district around Dudley to the Severn in competition with that taken on the Birmingham Canal to Autherley Junction,* and sent down the Staffs & Worcs.

The Birmingham Canal was, however, very prosperous, and we have seen how it fought and won a battle to build an extension to Fazeley under its own control which provided outlets for coal from the Wednesbury area to the east as well as to the west.

It was in 1785 that the Dudley Canal proprietors applied for and were granted an Act to connect their canal with the Birmingham at Tipton by means of the proposed Dudley tunnel. In this way a shorter line was made possible between Birmingham and the Severn than that by Autherley. The tunnel was not completed, however, before a new navigation was promoted also to connect the Black Country with the Severn. This was the Worcester & Birmingham, the promoters of which went to Parliament with a proposal for a direct line from Birmingham to the Severn at Worcester. Since this line gave the new company a decided advantage over the Staffs & Worcs for Birmingham traffic, including egress to a more easily navigable part of the River Severn, that company strongly opposed the Bill, which was, however, carried in 1791. The Birmingham Canal had also opposed the new venture as tending to divert Birmingham–Severn trade from their line, and its proprietors were able to get inserted in the Worcester & Birmingham Act a clause that no physical junction was to be made between the two canals, ostensibly to conserve their water, so that traffic originating on the Birmingham would have to go by way of Autherley to the Severn, or at least by Tipton, if it were not to be transhipped. This Worcester Bar, as it was called, between the two canals at Birmingham was not pierced till 1815.

The Dudley proprietors at once saw their opportunity to gain traffic from the Birmingham as a result of the physical bar: they applied for an Act to authorise a junction between their canal and the Worcester & Birmingham at Selly Oak. The Birmingham Canal owners now saw that traffic for the south would be able to pass from Tipton down the Dudley and along the new branch to Selly

---

* The junction of the Birmingham Canal with the Staffs & Worcs is now called Aldersley, and the neighbouring junction of the Staffs & Worcs with the Shropshire Union main line (formerly the Birmingham & Liverpool Junction) is called Autherley. In the old days both were sometimes called Autherley.

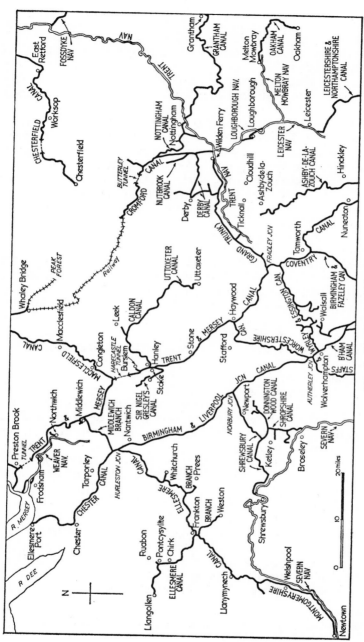

Map 6 The North Midlands

Oak, thus avoiding the Birmingham altogether, and coal from Netherton, instead of passing through the Dudley tunnel to the Birmingham, would pass along the new branch. They strongly opposed the Dudley Canal plan, and offered to connect their canal to the Netherton coalmines, but were defeated, in spite of their cry that:

'A parallel Canal, as this [to Selly Oak] certainly is, goes to the almost total Destruction of the Coal Trade on the present Birmingham Canal, and the Coals which ought from their Locality to be brought to the Birmingham Market, may be conveyed into Worcestershire, Gloucestershire, &c. without any equivalent Advantage or Prospect of any to the Inhabitants of Birmingham.'[1] The Dudley extension to Selly Oak through the Lappal tunnel* was built, and opened in 1798.

Another event displeasing to the Birmingham company was the opening of the first part of the Stratford-upon-Avon Canal in 1802 from a junction with the Worcester & Birmingham at King's Norton not far from Selly Oak, to Kingswood, where it joined the recently built Warwick & Birmingham, by which there was access to London. This meant that coal and iron traffic from the Stourbridge, Dudley and Netherton districts, and also from Coalbrookdale on the Severn and from Stourport and other places on the Staffs & Worcs, had good water access to London without using the Birmingham Canal.

While the rivalry with the Dudley was going on, the Birmingham's proprietors were increasing the capacity of their original line by lowering the old summit level at Smethwick by eliminating three locks at each end, duplicating those that remained, and making a cutting that was 46ft deep at one point. Later, in 1827, the old summit was completely removed by substituting a cutting now running up to 71ft deep. There was indeed trade for everyone then, though in time the character of the traffic changed as the coal areas around Wednesbury and Bilston became exhausted. Ironworks tended therefore to move to new coalfields, and to be replaced by engineering works.

The Birmingham Canal company followed a careful financing policy. As the prosperity of this early canal rapidly increased, so the owners of the original five hundred shares found themselves possessed of a valuable property bringing in an increasing income, which they did not wish to share with anyone. They therefore

* From 1841, boats were helped to pass, first one way and then the other, through this tunnel, the fourth longest in Britain (3,795yd), by pumping water into or out of the canal at one end of the tunnel, and so creating a current.

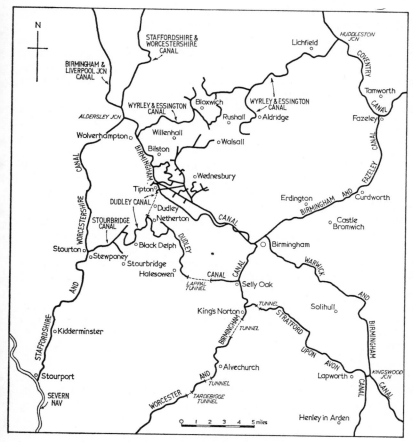

Map 7 The Birmingham canals and their connections

borrowed money for the many extensions made before 1800, and piled up a considerable debt, in spite of which the company paid £34 per £140 share as dividend in 1800. In 1810–11, when the dividend had become £42, the company doubled the capital to 1,000 shares by a bonus issue to existing shareholders, doubled it again to 2,000 in 1820, to 4,000 in 1824, and to 8,000 in 1836, in which year the dividend stood at £6 5s (£6.25) per share, equivalent to £100 per original £140 share. Yet this wealthy company had in 1835 the enormous debt of £568,000, which the company decided completely to liquidate by charging £71 of debt to each share, the owner of which was then expected to produce that amount in cash. If he did not, the interest on it was deducted from his dividends. Most of the debt was in fact liquidated in this way.

The Birmingham system of canals continued to grow and throw out branches, till in 1898 the waterways then included in the group had a length of 159 miles. The system lies on a plateau at three main levels, the Wolverhampton at 473ft, the Birmingham at 453ft, and the Walsall at 408ft. These levels are connected to each other and to the lower levels that join the waterways leading to the plateau by flights of narrow locks. These connecting waterways have all to climb to the plateau by further flights of locks, for instance, the thirty locks at Tardebigge which lift the Worcester & Birmingham Canal 217ft. The Birmingham system had 216 locks in its 159 miles of narrow canal when the whole system was navigable, and it still forms the centre of the narrow canal system of England.

While this great extension of canal building was taking place in the growing industrial area around Birmingham, the prosperous landowners of the south had been considering a canal that was not to carry fuel, raw materials or finished goods to or from factories or large towns, but was to open up the countryside and enable the latest agricultural methods to be used on poor land. Suggested as early as 1769, the Basingstoke Canal obtained its Act in 1778, though owing to the War of American Independence and the national stresses that accompanied it, work was not begun till the war was over.

This line, 37½ miles long as constructed, from the town of Basingstoke to the River Wey near its mouth at Weybridge, was partly intended to form a route for goods to pass to and from Salisbury, Bristol and the west by road transport, instead of the existing water passage from London up the Thames to Reading and thence along the Kennet to Newbury. (The Kennet & Avon Canal had not been built at that time.) It was because it feared this diversion of traffic that the town of Reading protested against the proposal.

This hoped for change of route to the west was not, however, the principal reason for promoting the canal:

'The mutual carriage of goods to and from the capital will be of great importance, and the west country manufactures will find from hence an easy and cheap conveyance. An object of still greater importance is the likelihood of this canal being the means of promoting the cultivation of the extensive barren grounds before-mentioned [Bagshot and other adjacent heaths], thro' a great part of which it must necessarily pass, after having been first conducted through a country full of chalk, from whence that manure is now carried in large quantities, at the expence of one shilling per waggon load per mile; whereas by the canal it will cost but one penny a ton for the same distance; and the boats will return laden with peat and peat-ashes (the last are esteemed an excellent manure for saint-foin, clover, etc.) to the mutual benefit of cultivation, and the emolument of the proprietors.'[2]

The value of water carriage in enabling manure—to use the old word—to be applied by farmers to their land has hardly been given its right importance in the history of that revolution in agricultural methods that went on in Britain at the same time as the Industrial Revolution. To obtain lime, or sometimes sea-sand, for their land in the days before made-up roads in country districts was difficult and expensive,

'So that those farmers who had spirit enough (and really some degree of enterprise as well as perseverance in this case was necessary) to purchase artificial manure, were obliged to have recourse to that slow and tedious mode of fetching it in bags on horseback. The mode alluded to, was for farmers living ten or twelve miles distant from the lime-kiln to send out four pack-horses . . . with a servant and a saddle-horse, four days in a week, and from this exertion and parade, he received home no more than 24 double Winchester bushels of lime, a quantity . . . little more than sufficient to manure half an acre of land.'[3]

When waterways became available, limestone was quarried at convenient points, and carried on canal boats to the kilns to be found at many an old wharf, before the lime was passed to the farmer. In the westcountry, sea-sand (rich in calcium carbonate) was used instead, and the Bude Canal was planned and built principally to carry such sand from Bude harbour into the interior of Devon and Cornwall. In good years the canal, fully opened in 1825, carried over 50,000 tons of it.

The Basingstoke Canal was a financial failure, the surface reasons for which are easy to see. Estimated at £86,000, with a further £40,000 of capital authorised if necessary, over £150,000 was spent to get the waterway open in 1794. Part of this excessive cost was due to the usual but occasionally fatal permission given in most canal Acts, to pay interest out of capital while the canal was under construction. In this case a debt was created of over £55,000 for interest, which deprived the company of the power to raise enough additional capital to finish the canal. In the end, by scrapes, loans and a bank overdraft, the canal was opened, and a weary effort began to pay off the bonds.

Though a revenue of £7,783pa had been estimated in 1797, this figure was never approached, the highest known being £5,416 in

1838–9. The balances available for debt reduction were never great, and to the end of its days the company continued to pay off the bonds, without reaching the stage when it could contemplate a dividend, however small, upon its original share capital. It is clear that the canal was of considerable benefit to the agriculture of the district through which it passed, and to the town of Basingstoke. The building of the Kennet & Avon Canal, however, ended its hopes of carrying through traffic destined for the west, goods for Portsmouth and Southampton left it as soon as the end of the Napoleonic Wars made the coasting trade safe again, and the gleam of hope given by the Hants & Berks Junction Canal proposal to join the Basingstoke to the Kennet & Avon was extinguished by the Bills' failures in 1824 and 1826. Tonnages averaged about 20,000 tons a year, against 30,700 tons a year estimated in 1797, till the canal slowly died of railway competition, though several attempts were made to revive it, some of them distinctly ludicrous, some definitely fraudulent.

Having glanced at a system of industrial canals that were successful and an agricultural waterway that was a failure, it may be interesting to pass to a group that was promoted to carry goods in one direction, and ended by carrying them in quite another.

What the Forth Bridge is to the railway enthusiast, or the Holyhead road to the road man, Pontcysyllte is to the canal lover. This great aqueduct, created by William Jessop and Thomas Telford, built by Telford and opened in 1805, is 1,007ft long, with nineteen arches, and carries a canal 121ft above the River Dee. The piers were built solid for 70ft and then hollow, and on them was laid a cast-iron trough 11ft 10in wide, with a towpath carried over part of it on iron pillars.

An iron trough instead of a puddled channel enabled a much lighter construction to be built than would otherwise have been needed. The first iron trough aqueduct to be completed was a small single-span one for the Derby Canal, for which Benjamin Outram was engineer, in February 1796. A month later, the much bigger one at Longdon-on-Tern on the Shrewsbury Canal was put into service: it was built by Telford, but may have been an ironmaster's idea. Pontcysyllte was a monument with Standedge tunnel, the Duke of Bridgewater's underground canal system, Ketley inclined plane and the Grand Western canal lifts, to the enterprise of canal proprietors and engineers; it was also a monument to a complete change of mind on the part of a canal company.

The story of the Chester and Ellesmere Canals, that later became part of the Shropshire Union system, begins in 1772, when an Act was obtained for the Chester Canal, to run from the Dee at Chester to Nantwich and Middlewich to join the Trent & Mersey. This project was the first thoroughly unsuccessful canal. About £71,000 was spent to build the canal as far as Nantwich, which it reached in 1779. The connection to Middlewich was not made for fifty years, because the Trent & Mersey company discouraged a junction of the two canals that might result in traffic passing to the sea by way of the rivers Dee or Weaver. So unsuccessful was the canal that it became semi-derelict, a state which had to be remedied when a change came in its prospects.

In the 1790s two schemes were promoted to link Chester on the Dee with Shrewsbury on the Severn: one (which became the Ellesmere Canal), for a line from Chester by way of Wrexham to the west of the Dee, the other from the Chester Canal seven miles from the city, to run to the east of the river, with a branch to Llangollen. The former line was chosen in spite of its engineering difficulties, and in 1793 the Ellesmere Canal obtained its Act.

The plan was to link the three rivers, Severn, Dee and Mersey, by a canal from Netherpool on the Mersey (now called Ellesmere Port) across the Wirral peninsula to Chester, and thence by way of Wrexham, Chirk, Ellesmere, Frankton, and Weston to Shrewsbury on the Severn. Branches were proposed to bring coal, lime and slate to the farmers, and also one to Llanymynech, whence the Montgomeryshire Canal, whose Act was obtained in the following year, was to carry the waterway on past Welshpool to Newtown in Montgomeryshire. The intention was to serve the North Wales industrial area near Wrexham and distribute its products, and to open up the country both by bringing fuel and manure, and also commodities carried up the three rivers from farther afield.

The proprietors began with the Wirral line, which was built as a broad canal to take barges from the rivers Dee and Mersey and from the Bridgewater Canal, and which carried enough goods and passengers to pay its way soon after it was opened in 1795.

They also began cutting in the middle of their line, from Chirk to Weston, together with the branch to Llanymynech, while putting in hand the expensive Chirk and Pontcysyllte aqueducts, and the difficult work between the two. It was planned that coal from the Ruabon collieries, near Pontcysyllte, would be carried south towards Montgomeryshire, whence the boats would return with limestone from Llanymynech for the kilns at Weston, the lime then being distributed over the countryside. In addition, it was hoped that Weston would be near enough to Shrewsbury to act as a focal point for traffic

that would go the rest of the way by road till the remainder of the
line should be built.

A new line for the canal between Pontcysyllte and Chester was
authorised by an Act of 1796, but 2⅓ miles of its Ffrwd branch near
Wrexham were all that was built. By 1800 the opening of new
collieries offered Chester cheaper coal than the canal could bring.
A less expensive way for the sections already built or building to

Figure 17   Pontcysyllte aqueduct on the Ellesmere (now the Llangollen) Canal

reach Chester was therefore decided upon. The line was now taken
from Frankton to the Chester Canal at Hurleston near Nantwich,
with short branches to Whitchurch and Ellesmere, and a longer one
meant to run to Prees Higher Heath, but which only got to Quina

Brook. This work, accomplished in 1805, provided a waterway from the Mersey and Dee to Weston quite different from that originally intended.

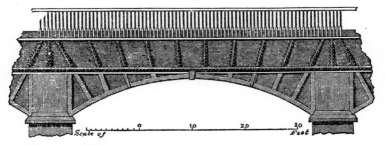

Figure 18   Side view of the cast-iron trough of Pontcysyllte aqueduct

Though the original main line by way of Pontcysyllte had been abandoned, the aqueducts at Chirk and Pontcysyllte were proceeded with, even though they lay on what was now a branch. It was evidently thought that the coal to be carried from the Ruabon collieries made the works worth while. Indeed, when the great aqueduct was finished, a basin and lines of tramroad were built at its far end to handle the coal and other products of Ruabon. The water supply feeder from Llantisilio past Llangollen was also made navigable to provide additional traffic.

The aqueduct was opened with ceremony, still carrying on one of its piers the cast-iron plate from the masonry aqueduct that was begun before the iron trough design at a higher level took its place, with the inscription:

The Nobility and Gentry of
The adjacent Counties,
Having united their efforts with
The great commercial interests of this Country
In creating an intercourse and union between
ENGLAND AND NORTH WALES,
By a navigable communication of the three Rivers
SEVERN, DEE, AND MERSEY,
For the mutual benefit of Agriculture and Trade,
Caused the first stone of this Aqueduct of
PONTCYSYLTE,
To be laid on the 25th day of July, 1795,
When Richard Myddelton, of Chirk, Esq. M.P.

One of the original patrons of the
ELLESMERE CANAL,
Was Lord of this Manor,
And in the Reign of our Sovereign
GEORGE THE THIRD,
When the equity of the Laws, and
The security of Property,
Promoted the general welfare of the Nation;
While the Arts and Sciences flourished
By his Patronage, and
The conduct of civil life was improved
By his example.
The navigation over this Aqueduct
was opened 26th November, 1805.

By 1805 over £450,000 had been spent, and the company had
come to an end of its resources. Thenceforward there was a lull in
its activity, till in 1813 an Act was passed to amalgamate the two
companies, each Chester share being reckoned as one-fourth of a
share in the united navigation, and till in 1827 an Act was passed
which at last allowed a junction to be made near Middlewich with
the Trent & Mersey (it was opened in 1833), so connecting the
Ellesmere & Chester to the main canal network. The previous year,
1826, had seen a new canal authorised, to be called the Birmingham
& Liverpool Junction, to shorten the distance and reduce the lockage
between the Mersey and Autherley to 66¼ miles and 45 locks instead
of 80¾ miles and 75 locks by way of the Trent & Mersey. The new
canal ran from the old Chester Canal at Nantwich to the Staffs &
Worcs near Autherley, and was opened in 1835.

The period from 1772 to 1827 therefore saw the full range of
possibilities of the Chester and the Ellesmere canals. The old Chester,
the greatest failure of the pre-war period, ended as an essential link
in the best main line between Birmingham and the Mersey, while the
Ellesmere, which had begun as a north to south canal from the
Mersey via Chester to Shrewsbury, turned its main line east and west
and ran from Hurleston near Nantwich to Llanymynech.

CHAPTER VI

The Canal Mania and the Wars

THE first period of canal expansion had ended in 1778, with the opening of the Selby Canal from the old Aire & Calder line to the Yorkshire Ouse; a year earlier the Trent & Mersey had been completed: the year before that the Bridgewater to the Mersey at Runcorn. But the effects of canals built and building upon the national economy were delayed. At the time when results might have been looked for, the difficulties of the American War, and then the period of national gloom that followed it, a time when England regarded herself as down and out, a nation with a past but no future, did not encourage the men of enterprise. Gradually the feeling of despair gave way to one of tolerability and then to optimism. Trade was improving, and even the French Revolution could not disguise the prosperity that was resulting from cheap transport of coal and commodities. Men turned their minds once again to expansion, a tendency helped by the men of money, who saw in the solid prosperity of the older canals a means to tempt money out of the pockets of the incautious, and by the engineers who, like John Longbothom, put advertisements in newspapers that read:

'The survey of canals by the piece, or examining them by the day. His terms by day are Three Guineas per day, exclusive of expenses. He has men, good surveyors and levellers, very capable of taking the survey of canals, which he charges as common surveyors, and staffholders, exclusive of expenses.'[1]

The boom began in 1790, and was dead by 1797: it reached its peak in Britain in late 1792 and the early part of 1793, and was reflected in the legislation of 1793 and 1794. The following table shows its legislative progress.

Year	No of new canals authorised	Capital authorised
1789	2	£131,000
1790	1	£90,000
1791	7	£743,000
1792	7	£1,056,100
1793	20	£2,824,700

Year	No of new canals authorised	Capital authorised
1794	10	£2,037,900
1795	4	£395,000
1796	3	£585,000
1797	1	£18,000

The cause of the boom within the canal world lay first in the prosperity of the earlier waterways. Everyone thought he knew how profitable was the Duke of Bridgewater's Canal, but the Birmingham paid over 23 per cent for 1789, and others like the Trent & Mersey and the Staffordshire & Worcestershire were very solid businesses. Second, perhaps, in the opening of the Thames & Severn Canal in 1789, which gave a water route of a sort between the midlands and London, and between Bristol and London, and the completion in 1790 of a shorter line from Birmingham to London via Fazeley and Oxford. Lastly, one may think, in the interest taken by businessmen generally. In Birmingham and the Potteries, men like Boulton and Wedgwood had long supported canals, but in 1788 the Darbys and the Reynoldses of Coalbrookdale promoted the Shropshire Canal; in 1789 the great Sir Richard Arkwright took a leading part in putting forward the Cromford Canal; and in 1790 Richard Crawshay of Cyfarthfa joined with lesser ironmasters to seek an Act for the Glamorganshire Canal. Profitability, expansion, and the support of big business: clearly the landowner, the clergyman and the tradesman could all put their money into canals.

All over the country the canal mania took hold and raged, so much so that at Leicester and Birmingham special 'Navigation Share Offices' were set up. Because they wanted to keep a good thing to themselves, promoters tended to hold subscription meetings quietly, and because they did so, wherever a meeting was held, hopeful speculators rushed to the place seeking to put down deposits on shares they could immediately sell at a profit, in one case only to find that the supposed canal meeting was really a hunt dinner.

Let us follow the mania in the columns of a single rural newspaper, the *British Chronicle* of Hereford, far from the country's industrial heart. In 1789 there was to the north of Hereford no canal at all; none of any size in South Wales; none to the west; and in the direction of England nothing nearer than Droitwich. Small barges carrying about 20 tons each brought coal and other goods up the Wye to the city, when there was enough water in the river. There were no locks on it, and no horse towing path.

In 1790 the Glamorganshire Canal had been authorised, not very far away, and in 1791 two nearer home, that from Hereford to Gloucester with £105,000 of capital, and that from Kington and Leominster to Stourport with £190,000, both born out of the need to bring coal to the towns and villages and to carry away their goods and produce. These two appeared often in the paper's columns, but soon news from farther away came in. In May 1791 it was reported that £60,000 had been subscribed in an hour for a canal from Manchester to Rochdale; in June that the Forth & Clyde Canal was open; in September that a meeting had been held at Ellesmere to consider a canal from the Severn to the Dee; in November that the capital of £40,000 for the Grantham Canal had been raised at a single meeting; in December, nearer home, that £51,000 had been subscribed to the Monmouthshire Canal from Newport to Pontypool and Crumlin.

By early 1792 the columns were filling up with canal news: the Gloucester & Berkeley ship canal project was going ahead; so were the Leominster, the Monmouthshire, and the Lancaster canals, to the last of which £170,000 had been subscribed at one meeting; and a canal from Birmingham to London. In July, appositely for author and publisher, John Phillips's *General History of Inland Navigation* was published, the first book about British canals as a whole, and one that must have opened many people's eyes to the possibilities of water transport. By August an extension of the Monmouthshire Canal was being considered—the Brecknock & Abergavenny—and in September the newspaper published a list of canal shares which were standing at a premium. Though not complete, it whetted the appetite:

Canals completed		*Canals projected*	
Birmingham	£1,170 prem	Grand Junction	£350 prem
Staffs & Worcs	£700 prem	Leicester	£155 prem
Coventry	£350 prem	Melton Mowbray	£55 prem
Stourbridge	£350 prem	Worcs & Birmingham	£25 prem
Oxford	£50 prem		

On 19 September the paper reported that 'last Saturday's *Gazette* gives notice of applications . . . for no fewer than twenty-five Navigable Cuts and Canals, many of them of immense extent. . . .' By November and December the paper was full of canal news, which then died away before the onset of the wave of merchant and banking bankruptcies of early 1793. For instance, on 13 March 1793, the newspaper recorded that 'In consequence of the temporary suspension of business of the Monmouthshire bank at Chepstow, the premium on Monmouthshire Canal shares has dropped from near 100 per cent by

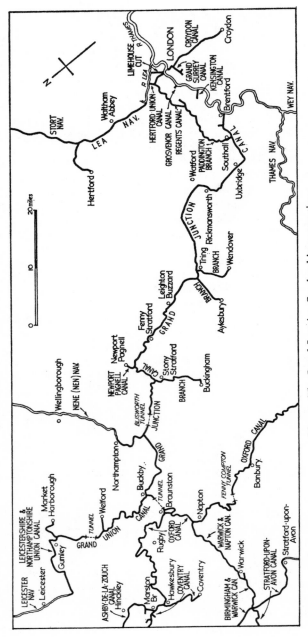

Map 8   The Grand Junction Canal and its connections

25 per cent in the course of last week.' Many people who had borrowed to cover their liabilities for shares must have been caught, and after their experiences many more must have looked a little cynically on a news-item that appeared in October:

'U.S.A. CANALS'

'A plan is proposed for insulating the whole of the United States of America; the expense, 4 millions of dollars. It will give a water-communication between every city, without going to the sea. Engineers are already employed on the surveys.'

Three local canal schemes had been born in the mania, and were wound up during 1793. A canal from Brecon to Hay and Whitney quietly died, and one from Abergavenny to Hereford was turned down by a meeting of landowners. (Twenty years later horse tramroads were to be built over the general routes of both.) A third, from the Leominster Canal to the Montgomeryshire Canal near Welshpool via Ludlow and Bishop's Castle, was seen to be too expensive, and was dropped.

So much for Hereford. The following extract from an account of what happened round Bristol helps to bring the canal mania to life:

'The "canal mania" of 1792, though productive of less important results than the railway mania of 1845, was in many respects a counterpart of that memorable delirium. On the 20th November a meeting to promote the construction of a canal from Bristol to Gloucester was held in the Guildhall, when the scheme was enthusiastically supported by influential persons, and a very large sum was subscribed by those present, who struggled violently with each other in their rush to the subscription book. A few days later, a Somerset paper announced that a meeting would be held at Wells to promote a canal from Bristol to Taunton. The design had been formed in this city [Bristol], but the promoters strove to keep it a secret, and bought up all the newspapers containing the advertisement. The news nevertheless leaked out on the evening before the intended gathering, and a host of speculators set off to secure shares in the undertaking, some arriving only to find that the subscription list was full. The third meeting was at Devizes, on the 12th December. Only one day's notice was given of this movement, which was to promote a canal from Bristol to Southampton and London, but the news rapidly spread, and thousands of intending subscribers rushed to the little town, where the proposed capital was offered several times over. The "race to Devizes" on the part of Bristolians, who had hired or bought up at absurd prices all the old hacks that could be found, and plunged along the miry roads through a long wintry night, was attended with many comic incidents. A legion of schemes followed, Bristol being the proposed terminus of canals to all parts of the country, and some of the projected waterways running in close proximity to each other. A pamphlet published in 1795, narrating the story of the mania, states that the passion of speculation spread like an epidemical disease through the city, every man believing that he would gain thousands by his adventures. The shares which were at 50 premium to-day were expected to rise to 60 tomorrow and to 100 in a week.'[2]

All over the country waterways had been projected, and sufficient money raised to pay an engineer for a survey, however hurried. Many were never embodied in a Bill, and fewer still were authorised by an Act. Those that passed the sieve were mostly solid schemes which, though they probably cost much more than their projectors had foreseen, and took much longer to build, in the end were successes. Such were the Neath and Manchester, Bolton & Bury Canals authorised in 1791, the Lancaster, Nottingham, Monmouthshire or Ashton-under-Lyne in 1792, the Grand Junction, Shrewsbury, Barnsley or Dearne & Dove in 1793, or the Swansea or Rochdale canals in 1794. More of them, while useful, were only moderately profitable: the Worcester & Birmingham (1791), Wyrley & Essington (1792), Stratford-upon-Avon or Ellesmere (1793), Peak Forest, Huddersfield or Ashby (1794). Six were failures. The Herefordshire & Gloucestershire took from 1791 to 1845 to reach Hereford from Gloucester, the Grand Western, the Leominster and the Foss never completed their lines; the Salisbury & Southampton and the Dorset & Somerset were abandoned during construction. None of these, except the Foss, ever paid a dividend during their working lives.

The immediate consequence of the mania was that a great deal of canal building all started at the same time, many companies sharing engineers and competing for cutters. In September 1793 Denys Rolle wrote: 'From the Immense Numbers of Canals now coming on and the not only absence of a Multitude of the Labouring Class abroad in the War but the vast suppos'd Diminution that there will arise from the destruction in it, a great scarcity of Hands for the Cultivation will be found at the End. . . .'[3] He goes on to say that some Irish already work in harvesting and canal cutting, and he proposes that more should be encouraged to come over. This scarcity of hands must indeed have been felt the following year, for the Peak Forest committee decided in July 1794 to start cutting 'so soon as the Corn Harvest shall be got in'.[4]

Out of the mania came a harvest of useful hard-working waterways, essential to the continued growth of the Industrial Revolution, of which the Barnsley and the Dearne & Dove may serve as examples. Promoted as rivals, the Barnsley, a client of the Aire & Calder, the Dearne & Dove of the Don, met at a junction lock outside Barnsley, whence the Barnsley Canal's line extended upwards to the edge of the especially valuable Silkstone coalfield. Their Acts passed on the same 1793 day, both opened in 1804. Within fifteen years each was carrying over 100,000 tons of coal, besides stone and timber for building houses and mills, iron and corn. This last, coming from the fields of Lincolnshire and East Anglia by sea or by the Trent, was carried along the canals the opposite way to the coal, to feed the people of Barnsley and the coalfield.

Because so much Irish canal money came from public funds, the canal mania hardly touched Ireland, except perhaps in the promotion of the Royal Canal from Dublin to the upper Shannon. Promoted by a private company in 1789, but with borrowed state money, costs soon outran estimates. Even with a government grant of £96,856, the company could not complete its line, and in 1813, with nearly a million spent, the Directors-General of Inland Navigation took over. They finished the line in 1817, and then handed the canal to a New Royal Canal Company, in which shareholders got £40 stock for each £100 they held in the old company. The Royal had cost over £1,400,000 for its 90 miles from Dublin to Cloondara on the Shannon. With its written-down capital, the company could pay dividends up to 2 per cent until the railways came. In 1836, 88,334 tons were carried, and in 1837, 46,450 passengers.

Another factor in transport began to affect canals projected at this time. Now that the financial crisis had dried up available capital, and the rise in prices had caused many canals under construction to cost more than had been estimated, engineers began to find that many of the branches or extensions already planned were unnecessary. Instead they proposed tramroads.

The use of waggons running upon rails is as old in this country as the reign of Queen Elizabeth I. Later they were employed to bring coal from the collieries of the north-east to the staithes of the Tyne, and from the Shropshire collieries to the Severn. It was natural therefore that horse tramroads, which for two hundred years had been used as feeders to rivers, should be used also as feeders to canals.

These tramroads* first had wooden rails; later the wood was

* See *The Evolution of Railways*, by Charles E. Lee, 2nd ed, 1943, *Stone Blocks and Iron Rails*, by Bertram Baxter, 1966, and *Early Wooden Railways* by M. J. T. Lewis, 1971. In this book I use the word tramroad to include all types of horse-drawn line, whatever the pattern of rail.

covered with a strip of iron, the waggon wheels being flanged, and later still iron edge-rails were used. Then John Curr, followed by Benjamin Outram, introduced the plateway, which instead of rails used L-shaped iron plates about three feet long. The sleeper was a rough cube of granite with a hole in the centre; this was filled with an oak plug, into which a spike to hold the plate was driven. The

Royal Canal.

The Court of Directors of the New Royal Canal Company hereby give Notice, that they

Will Sell by Auction,

On TUESDAY, the 24th of SEPTEMBER Instant,

At the Fourth Lock upon the Royal Canal,

The Under-mentioned Boats,

For the demands they have against them, if the same are not paid to their Collector, at the BROADSTONE, previous to the said Day:

BOAT No. 28, *Morris*, Owner.

BOAT No. 70, *Owner not ascertained.*   BOAT No. 507, *Blanchfield*, Owner.

Also a CARAVAN that has been run only a short time, several Lots of Old Timber, and other Materials.—Sale to commence at Twelve o'Clock.

WILLIAM COLE, Auctioneer,
No. 2, Lower Ormond-quay.

ROYAL CANAL HOUSE,
Broadstone, 16th September, 1822.

Figure 19   From time to time boats whose owners had failed to pay tolls were seized and sold

waggon wheels were flangeless, being held in position by the flanges on the inner sides of the plates. These plateways became very popular, and Outram, his assistant and successor John Hodgkinson, and other engineers laid several hundred miles of them. They also converted many of the older railways to plateways between the early 1790s and about 1830, after which these tramroads began to give way to the conventional railway as we know it, with edge-rails and the flange on the wheel. Some plateways continued in use well into the present century.

These horse tramroads constituted an adjunct to canals whose importance has not perhaps been fully understood, for they enabled canal branches to be built which as waterways would have been uneconomic. For instance, the Act for the Ashby-de-la-Zouch Canal in 1794 authorised a canal from a junction with the Coventry Canal at Marston bridge to Ashby, with branches to the limeworks at Ticknall and Cloudhill, a total of 43 miles with a great deal of lockage. In fact, the canal was only cut for 30 miles to Moira, the branches being built by Outram as plateways joining the canal at Willersley.

The tramroads extending from the two arms of the Monmouthshire Canal were an outstanding example of such development. In the 1830s a considerable mileage of tramroads ran up the valleys, much of it owned by the canal company. Some of these were in turn connected to another tramroad system depending from the Brecknock & Abergavenny Canal and extending as far as Hereford. Tramroads were also widely developed elsewhere in South Wales, near Coalbrookdale in connection with the tub-boat canals in the area, in Derbyshire (notably the plateways owned by the Peak Forest and Derby canal companies), and in the north, especially near the rivers Tyne and Wear.

In 1797 Telford the engineer wrote a chapter in Plymley's *General View of the Agriculture of Shropshire*, in which he advocated the construction of a number of canals, and of branches to existing canals. In 1800 he wrote a supplement, in which he said:

'Since the year 1797, when the above account of the inland navigation of the country of Salop was made out, another mode of conveyance has frequently been adopted in this country to a considerable extent; I mean that of forming roads with iron rails laid along them, upon which the articles are conveyed on waggons, containing from six to thirty cwt.; experience has now convinced us, that in countries whose surfaces are rugged, or where it is difficult to obtain water for lockage, where the weight of the articles of produce is great in comparison with their bulk, and when they are mostly to be conveyed from a higher to a lower level—that in those cases, iron railways are in general preferable to a canal navigation. . . . Upon the whole, this useful contrivance may be varied so as to suit the surface of many different countries, at a comparatively moderate expense. It may be constructed in a much more expeditious manner than navigable canals; it may be introduced into many districts where canals are wholly inapplicable; and in case of any change in the working of the

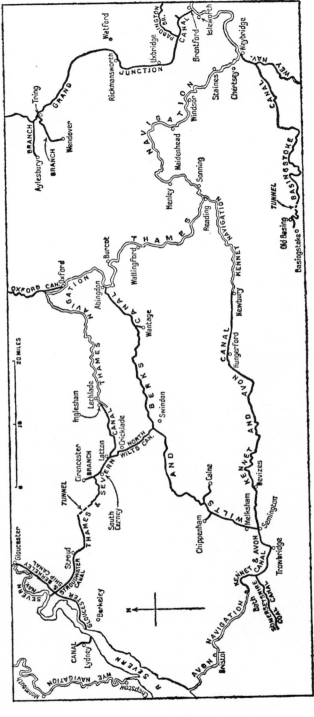

Map 9   The River Thames and its connections

mines or manufactures, the rails may be taken up and put down again, in a new situation, at a moderate expense.'[5]

Tramroads could be double-track or single with passing places. The usual load for the four-wheeled waggons was two tons, a number—called a gang or train—being pulled by each horse. When the lines could be worked by gravity, as often happened on the Tyne, in Wales, or in the Somerset coalfield, a train of half a dozen or more waggons was run by its own weight to the canal side, a boy applying the brake, and a horse being tied to the last waggon or riding in it to pull back the empty train.

Outram tried to put rafts on the Somersetshire Coal Canal, which would take such tramroad waggons without it being necessary to shift their contents, but the difficulties on the one hand of getting the waggons on to the rafts, and on the other of navigating the rafts when a wind was blowing, were too great. Waggon-boats were, however, later successfully used on the Don Navigation in Yorkshire, and on the Forth & Clyde Canal to carry waggons from the Monkland & Kirkintilloch Railroad.

Tramroads were also used to connect portions of canal. The flight of sixteen locks at Marple on the Peak Forest Canal, and the tunnel at Blisworth on the Grand Junction, took so long to construct that temporary tramroads were built to enable through trade to begin. In the case of the Lancaster Canal, the difficulties of fulfilling the original intention of carrying the waterway over the Ribble estuary were so great that the two parts of the canal were permanently connected by a tramroad.

Sometimes these tramroads were built and owned by canal companies: the Brecknock & Abergavenny, remarkable for having completed and worked a tramroad before having cut a yard of canal, the Monmouthshire, Peak Forest, Trent & Mersey and others were important tramroad owners. Sometimes they were built by independent companies, as the Surrey Iron Railway or the Oystermouth, or by companies having many common shareholders with a neighbouring canal, as the Hay Railway. Sometimes they were privately owned by the proprietors of the collieries or works they served, as the Hills of Blaenavon or Crawshay Bailey of Nantyglo owned lines from their works to the canals.

Many canal Acts gave the companies power to make tramroad branches, usually to a distance of from four to eight miles from the canal. If on application by an owner of a mine or works within the specified distance the canal company refused to make a tramroad, then the powers of construction were transferred to the applicant. Some canal companies, like the Swansea, steadfastly refused to make

tramroads, and left them to the businessmen; others like the Monmouthshire built many. These clauses were inserted in order to
avoid the system of way-leaves in force on the Tyne and Wear, where
railway owners had to make a payment to the landowner for everything that passed over his land. In the Chesterfield Canal Act, instead
of tramroads, power was given to make toll-free roads up to one
mile long, and in other Acts the power to make 'stone-roads' was
alternative to that to make tramroads. It must not be forgotten that
many roads were general-purpose feeders to canals throughout the
country, and that canal companies spent much time complaining to
the town and country local authorities that such feeder roads were
inadequate or badly maintained.

When the canals were built, the takings of turnpike trustees of
roads that ran parallel with canals fell sharply: for instance, those of
the Loughborough–Leicester road fell from £1,800 in 1792 to £1,162
in 1802, after the Leicester Navigation had been opened in 1794. Not
till 1830 did the takings again equal the earlier figure, and then it was
due to the increase of passenger traffic. On the other hand, roads
which from their situation were natural feeders to canals gained in
revenue: the tolls of the Hinckley road in Leicestershire rose from
£602 in 1792 to £888 in 1802 for this reason. Roads that suffered
from canal competition had two consolations, that the removal of
heavy traffic saved road trustees a great deal in upkeep costs, while
the waterway was useful to carry roadstone, usually toll-free unless
canal water was short, to the nearest part of the road.*

The outbreak of the French Revolutionary War in 1793, at a time
when industrial and transport expansion had been taking place
throughout the country, and the financial crisis of that year, put a
brake on developments. Though men thought that the revolutionary
armies would quickly be defeated by the combination of power
brought against them, they feared that the revolutionary spirit itself
might cross the Channel. Enterprise was damped down, and thoughts
turned to the practical problems of the war, and to coping with the
steady rise in prices that was one of its consequences.

A number of canals that had been begun in the mania soon found
themselves with lines uncompleted and capital exhausted owing to
rising prices, at a time when money was difficult to borrow.

In 1797 the Kennet & Avon said: 'the distress of the times during
the last year . . . has increased the pressure on your committee for
money to carry on the work, and also the difficulty of obtaining it',[6]
and in 1798: 'not only the rise of labour and the increased price of

---

* See *A Leicestershire Road*, by Percy Russell, 1934, for much interesting detailed
information on this subject.

almost every article employed on the Works, have occasioned a considerable excess beyond the original estimate, but a variety of particulars . . .',[7] while in 1800, 450 of the Kennet & Avon's shares were forfeited because the owners either would not or could not pay further calls upon them. In the north, the Huddersfield Canal's shareholders were being told that 'from the bankruptcy of several of the proprietors of shares . . . the deaths of other proprietors insolvent, and . . . several of the proprietors having left the kingdom, it is become impossible to procure payment of the whole of the money subscribed.'[8]

Five of the problems raised by the war especially affected the canals. The success of the French privateers that lay in wait in the Channel and round the coasts meant that the coasting trade could no longer be relied upon. Therefore men began to consider how much of this trade could be diverted to the inland navigations. In 1800, for instance, there met a House of Commons Committee on the Coal Trade, to find out whether coal could be brought by inland waterway or road transport to London in adequate quantities, should the Tyne colliers be unable to make the sea passage. There was support for schemes that would provide alternative routes to those by sea. Plans were canvassed for a canal from London to Portsmouth, and for a connection between the Basingstoke, now acting as a carrier of Portsmouth and Southampton trade, and the River Itchen. Schemes for a canal across Somerset or Devon were pursued because they would enable traffic to get to the south coast from Wales without having to pass round Land's End and risk the privateers that waited there and along the south coast, and projects between Tyne and Solway Firth so that troops could be moved more quickly should the French attack Ireland or the east coast. The great state enterprise of the Caledonian Canal was begun, partly to enable warships to cross quickly from one side of Britain to the other.

The second problem was that of possible invasion. The government itself built the Royal Military Canal from Shorncliffe to Winchelsea along the south-eastern coast. It was designed originally to serve the double purpose of a barrier to an invading army, and a means of moving troops and stores quickly along the stretch of coast most threatened by the enemy.

Some canal companies, or their workpeople, thought they might be affected. In July 1797 the committee of the Grand Junction received from their employees a letter sent to them by way of the Marquis of Buckingham:

'We, the underwritten, being the Engineer, Inspectors, Foremen, Hagmasters, and Workingmen, employed on the works of the Grand

Junction Canal, highly sensible of the blessings of our free Constitution, and truly loyal to our King, think ourselves called upon, as Englishmen, to stand forth in support of our Laws and Property, and that of our Honourable Employers; and do therefore associate, under the following Rules and Articles, which we request our worthy Engineer, Mr Barnes, to transmit in our names, and on our behalf, to the Marquis of Buckingham, Lord Lieutenant of the County of Buckingham, with our loyal request that he will lay it before the King, with our firmest assurances that we will spill the last drop of our blood, in the cause of Old England, against all Foreign and Domestic Enemies.'[9]

Later, in October 1803, the committee of the Basingstoke recorded in their minutes the following:

'Several of the London Proprietors having called upon the Committee, recommending, that after the Example of other corporate Bodies, the Company should offer such Assistance, as they may be able to give to Government, towards transporting Baggage, or Stores up or down the Canal, and the consent of Mr George Smith and the Rest of the Bargemasters, having been obtained, a Letter was written by the Direction of the Committee, and taken by the Chairman and Mr Baker, to Lord Hobart, offering Ten of the Basingstoke Canal Barges, in Case of Invasion, or the Appearance of the Enemy on the Coast, to transport Stores, free of Expence, from London to any Part of the Canal, which Lord Hobart assured them would be gratefully received by Government.'[10]

Pickfords, who were at that time both canal and road carriers, also offered to the government in the same year the use of 400 horses, 50 waggons, and 28 boats.

The third problem was that of obtaining quicker transport about the country for troops and stores, and now for the first time the usefulness of canals to speed up movement became clear to the authorities. On 18 June 1798 the Grand Junction company issued a notice to its men that a considerable body of troops were to embark at Blisworth for Liverpool, and that the locks and canal were to be kept clear for the urgent movement of fifteen boats on each of two days. Another example is taken from *The Times* of 19 December 1806:

'The first division of the troops that are to proceed by the Paddington Canal* for Liverpool, and thence by transports for Dublin, will leave Paddington to-day, and will be followed by others to-morrow and Sunday. By this mode of conveyance the men will be only seven days in reaching Liverpool, and with comparatively little fatigue, as

* The Grand Junction which ended at Paddington Basin, London.

it would take them above fourteen days to march that distance. Relays of fresh horses for the canal boats have been ordered to be in readiness at all the stages.' Indeed, when invasion threatened, a central fortified citadel was built at Weedon, on a short branch from the Grand Junction Canal, to which king and cabinet could move from London if necessary. The branch canal was provided with portcullises against water penetration of the defences.

The fourth problem was presented by high prices, especially of food. This situation led in time to a rise in wages, but there was a time lag which caused distress. For instance, on 1 September 1800, the Town Clerk of Nottingham drafted a letter to the Duke of Portland, then Home Secretary, in which he said:

'. . . riot has been occasioned by the Difficulty of obtaining Flour & the Price at which the small Quantity that could be procured was obtained. . . . They seemed Disposed to plunder the Warehouses & some Boats laden with Corn but were prevented except in the first moment of their unexpected appearance near the Canal.'[11]

Nervousness of what the working-class might do if it ceased to 'stand forth in support of our Laws and Property, and that of our Honourable Employers', also showed itself. The same James Barnes, the engineer who had been the bearer of the loyal sentiments of the Grand Junction's employees in 1797, was in 1801 faced with a strike for higher wages by the men working on the Wolverton embankment. The Grand Junction committee told him 'to discharge at all risque these offenders, and to use his utmost endeavours to bring them to Justice, and to call on the Magistracy and Yeomanry of this County to repress and punish all acts of Outrage and Violence and an illegal conspiracy or combination for increase of wages'.[12]

The fifth problem was that of increasing output from the homeland. This was achieved under the inducement that rising prices gave to producers, and led to many kinds of new enterprises. The story of the Tavistock Canal is one of them.

Today Britain produces hardly any copper, but in the early part of the nineteenth century Devonshire and Cornwall mined 25 per cent of the world's supply. The war brought steeply rising prices for the ore, but the output from Wheal Crowndale near Tavistock in Devon was limited by the difficulty of getting it to the River Tamar, whence it could be taken to Devonport to be put on board the coasting ships. In 1803, therefore, a meeting was held on 16 March in the Tavistock Guildhall to consider connecting Tavistock with the navigable portion of the River Tamar at Morwellham quay by:

'. . . a CANAL to be taken up from the *River Tavy*, near the *Abbey Bridge*, in *Tavistock*, and carried from thence to *Lumburn Valley*, from

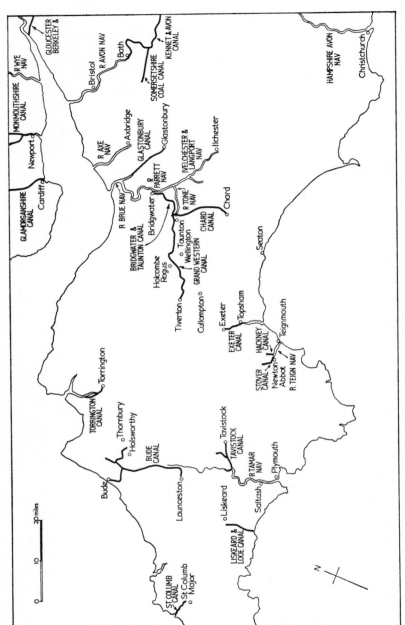

Map 10   The canals of the South-west

thence by an *Embankment* across that Valley, and a TUNNEL through MORWELL-DOWN, and a BRANCH or SIDE-CUT to the *Slate-Quarries*, at MILL HILL.'[13]

An estimate of £40,000 was made and an Act obtained.

The proprietors were men of enterprise and imagination, for their canal swam with oddities. Though only four miles long, one and a half miles lay through a tunnel. At the far end of this tunnel was a drop of 237ft to the level of the Tamar, and:

'. . . after duly weighing the merits of various plans . . . the Committee . . . adopted that of an inclined Plane, furnished with iron railways, on which carriages fitted to transport boxes which may contain ores, coals, lime, etc., are made to ascend and descend by the application of a machine driven by water supplied from the canal.'[14]

The water in the canal was deliberately given a current flowing downwards to the plane from the intake on the River Tavy at Tavistock. On its way it drove the mining machinery, carried the boats filled with ore down through the tunnel, and finally finished its usefulness by working the wheel of the inclined plane.

The canal company obtained from the Duke of Bedford, owner of the surrounding land, the right to mine any copper or other mineral found in the course of making the canal, and copper was indeed struck soon after the tunnel was begun. This lode became Wheal Crebor, and until 1828 the mine was managed in conjunction with the canal. The mining profits of £5,462 for 1813 from Wheal Crebor shows how high were the industrial rewards of war.

It took thirteen years to cut the tunnel. We may indeed agree with the report of the canal committee for 1816, which says:

'The Tavistock Tunnel will be a lasting monument of the patience of those who executed and of the spirit and enterprise of the Proprietors who supported the work and who have so steadily pursued their object through the disheartening circumstances which have of late attended all mining pursuits.'[15]

The canal was opened on 24 June 1817, but the boom in copper caused by the war had given way to a depressed state of trade that never fully passed away, and which led in the third quarter of the century to the disappearance of the Devonshire copper industry, though the metal is still mined in Cornwall in conjunction with tin. The canal had cost some £62,000, but it seldom returned to its owners more than £600 a year in net profit. Yet for forty years it carried about 17,000 tons of goods a year in its 8 ton boats (it was only 16ft wide at top and 3ft deep), merchandise for the town of Tavistock up against the stream, and copper ore, limestone, slate and granite downwards to the Tamar.

At last the competition of the South Devon & Tavistock Railway and the decline of the mines proved too much for the little enterprise, which was sold to the Duke of Bedford in 1873 for £3,200. Yet today it is not useless, for the water that once drove the engines of Wheal Crowndale and Wheal Crebor now provides the power for a hydro-electric plant beside Morwellham quay. The tunnel, still in use, is still 'a lasting monument of the patience of those who executed and of the spirit and enterprise of the Proprietors who supported the work'.

Meanwhile the Act of Union with Ireland of 1800 had made the United Kingdom responsible for most Irish waterway expenditure, undertaken as this was for development reasons or to provide employment. Just before, Directors-General of Inland Navigation had been appointed, with power to take over all Irish waterways not under private companies, whether administered by local commissioners (now abolished) under the 1787 Act or not, and to make grants to enable company-owned canals to be finished.

Except for the great Caledonian Canal, nearly all the new waterways authorised between 1800 and the end of the war in 1815 were in connection with the Grand Junction line that joined the midlands to London by a more direct route from Braunston on the Oxford Canal than the old one by way of the city of Oxford and the Thames, or else were in the neighbourhood of London.

The Grand Junction Canal had been authorised in 1793 with a capital of £600,000. The Duke of Grafton, the Earl of Clarendon, the Earl of Essex and Earl Spencer were on its Board, and the Marquis of Buckingham was its strong supporter. Later, when the Commons became more important in relation to private Bills, there were fewer peers and more members of Parliament on its managing committee —five, for instance, in 1812. This political influence, supported as it was by the considerable connections the committee members had with shareholders in other canal companies, was a grievance to those who got in the way of the Grand Junction company.

William Praed, who, after having been a partner in the Cornish Bank at Truro, had in 1803 started Praed & Co in London, was chairman,* William Jessop was chief and James Barnes resident engineer. The canal, 93½ miles long, ran from the Oxford Canal at Braunston by way of Braunston and Blisworth tunnels to Wolverton, Leighton Buzzard, Tring and King's Langley to the Thames at Brentford, and was finished in 1800 except for the tunnel, 1¾ miles long, at Blisworth. The first attempt at this tunnel failed, and Outram then built a double-track tramroad over the hill to make a temporary link

* Praed Street, Paddington, is named after him.

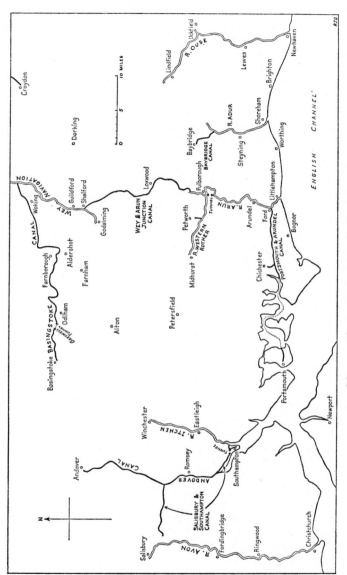

Map 11 The canals of southern England

between the two parts of the canal, and enable it to carry through traffic. The second tunnel was then begun, and opened on 25 March 1805. Branches were built before that date to Stony Stratford and on to Buckingham; to the military depot at Weedon; to Wendover; and to Newport Pagnell by an independent company. Later, further branches were made to Aylesbury and Northampton.

The opening of the Grand Junction gave the Birmingham–London waterway route its final form. This line, say from Newhall basin, Birmingham, to Brentford, was originally completed in 1789 by way of the Birmingham and Staffs & Worcs canals, the Severn, the Stroudwater and Thames & Severn canals, and the Thames. This roundabout route of 269½ miles was superseded within a few months, in 1790, by that via Fazeley and Oxford to the Thames, which reduced the distance to 227½ miles. This was itself spectacularly reduced to 138½ miles in 1800, on the one hand by the opening of the Grand Junction, and on the other by the substitution of the Warwick & Birmingham and Warwick & Napton canals for the line by way of Fazeley and Hawkesbury. The Oxford Canal, now reduced to a five-mile link in this through line from Napton to Braunston, was compensated for its loss of tonnage and did not suffer, but the Coventry temporarily lost some of its trade, and its shares fell from £400 to £350. By 1825, however, it had far more than recouped itself by its rapidly growing coal trade, and its shares in that year stood at £1,230. Finally, in 1801, a branch from Bull's Bridge on the main Grand Junction line was opened to Paddington basin, and the last river section in what was now an all-canal route into London disappeared. In turn this branch was in 1820 connected by the Regent's Canal, authorised in 1812, with the Thames at Limehouse.

Other developments were taking place round the upper end of the Grand Junction. In the time of the mania the Leicestershire & Northamptonshire Union Canal had been projected to link Leicester, itself connected to the Trent through the Loughborough and Leicester Navigations, with the Nene at Northampton. Building began from the Leicester end, and in 1797 was completed to Debdale wharf, seventeen miles out of the proposed forty-four. There the project rested for a time, apart from the building of a branch to Market Harborough in 1809. The construction of the Grand Junction reanimated the project, and eventually it was decided to join the uncompleted Leicestershire & Northamptonshire to that canal at Buckby wharf (Norton Junction) by means of a new company's line, the Grand Union,* authorised in 1810, which had been promoted partly

---

* Not to be confused with the Grand Union Canal formed in 1929 to amalgamate the Regent's, Grand Junction and other canal companies.

by Leicester interests and partly by the Grand Junction. This canal was opened in 1814, and a connection thereby made between London and the Trent, though its two flights of narrow locks at Watford and Foxton prevented the development of through wide boat services.

Figure 20   Early days at Paddington basin, terminus of the Grand Junction Canal. A passenger packet boat is seen leaving

A plateway from the Grand Junction to Northampton had been built in 1805, and when this was replaced in 1815 by a canal branch, the Nene was joined to the other two, and the original object of the canal line from Leicester partially (because of the Grand Union's narrow locks) attained.

Around London were authorised the Grand Surrey (1801), planned to run from the Thames at Rotherhithe to Mitcham, but which did not get farther than Camberwell, the Croydon from Rotherhithe to Croydon, the Thames & Medway from Gravesend to Frindsbury opposite Rochester, the Isle of Dogs Canal, built by the City of London and designed to shorten the passage round the Isle of Dogs from Limehouse to Blackwall, and the Wey & Arun Junction, to create a through communication from the Thames to the south coast at Littlehampton. In addition to these canals, the Surrey Iron Railway from Wandsworth to Croydon, and its extension, the Croydon, Merstham & Godstone, which was only partly built, were parts of the same development of communications round the rapidly growing city of London.

One last enterprise falls within the scope of this chapter. Though the main rivers of England had by this time been joined together, the only connection of the canal system with the network of Fenland waterways that served the combined purposes of drainage and navigation was the tramroad, later the canal, that joined the Grand Junction to Northampton. One suggestion for a link was the Stamford Junction Canal, proposed by J. Jepson Oddy (who fought a local election on it, and published a book in 1810) to link the Nene and

Figure 21   City Road basin in London on the Regent's Canal

the Witham with the Welland at Stamford, and the Welland with the Oakham Canal. This agricultural canal had been opened about 1803, an extension of the Melton Mowbray or Wreak Navigation, itself a branch off the Leicester Navigation. A second suggestion about the same time proposed a Market Harborough–Stamford link.

But it was another scheme that got as far as an Act of Parliament. As early as 1778 Whitworth, acting on the orders of the Common Council of the City of London, surveyed a line of junction between the River Stort, which through the Lea was joined with the Thames at Bow Creek near Blackwall, and the Cam near Cambridge. The plan was revived during the war, and an Act obtained in 1812 for a canal, the London & Cambridge Junction, to run from the Stort near Bishop's Stortford to the Cam near Clayhithe Sluice, with a

Page 129, Plate I (*above*) Lifting the paddles of a flash-lock on the Thames; (*below*) a share certificate

branch to Whaddon, the line to be 28¼ miles long. The authorised capital was £870,000, but it was enacted that £425,250 should be raised before work began. For this the times were not propitious, and in 1814 permission was granted for part only of the line to be built, from the Cam to Saffron Walden, with the branch to Whaddon. This also did not materialise, and the last of the great river connections, between Thames and Great Ouse by way of the Cam, was never made.

CHAPTER VII

Linking the Seas

+++++++++++++++++++++++++++++++++++++◆++++++++++++++++++++++++++++++++++++

Two notable areas in Britain where canals to link the seas have occupied men's energies are Scotland and Somerset–Devon. In the first area canals were built, in the second no plan succeeded.

Among the consequences of the Forty-Five were that the government naturally sought to break up a clan system that had given strength to rebellion, and also to create a network of good roads through the Highlands that would make them less inaccessible. The two together tended to transform the old feeling of the Highland chieftain that he was most important when he had the greatest number of retainers into a newer one that he was most important when he was wealthiest. He therefore turned to money making. His land went down to sheep, and there was no longer a place for the old peasant economy. At the same time the building of the new roads gave Highlanders news of easier lives to be led to the south or over the seas in America, and the means to get there.

Many important men were dismayed by these tendencies, and in various ways sought to develop the Highlands so that new methods of earning their living could be offered to the inhabitants. Among these men was John Knox, a Scotsman who had made his money in England, and who, when retired, used it to further the prosperity of the north. He saw that the promotion of fisheries and manufactures, which he and others had suggested, depended upon improved transport. In a book published in 1784, and writing of the proposed establishment of Highland fisheries, he said:

'The inhabitants of these neglected shores, unable to avail themselves of the bounty which their seas afford, have lived in penury amidst the sources of affluence. I shall therefore specify such measures as seem most conducive to the purposes of general utility in the full establishment of a populous thriving colony. The first object which presents itself is the opening shorter communications between the Atlantic and the British Sea; the advantages of which are so obvious that they may be considered the groundwork of all succeeding improvements, not only in the Highlands but over Scotland in general.'[1]

He named three, from Fort William to Inverness, from Loch Fyne to the Atlantic, and from Forth to Clyde. 'The three canals here recommended would', he said, 'open up a circumnavigation within the heart of the kingdom to the unspeakable benefit of commerce and the fisheries.'

All three canals had been suggested, and in fact surveyed, before he wrote; one, the Forth & Clyde, partly built. He well summed up the needs of Scotland, however, and had much influence upon the course of events which in time gave her all three of the sea-to-sea canals he advocated. They are now called the Caledonian, the Crinan, and the Forth & Clyde canals.

A glance at the map of the Highlands shows the Great Glen, that astonishing rift across the country from Loch Linnhe north-east to Inverness. With a sea loch at either end, and with four lochs in its length, the Great Glen seemed made for a canal that would save ships the great dangers of passing round the north of Scotland. The natural difficulties of a passage in the days of sail from one side of Great Britain to the other, both for merchant ships and fishing vessels, were a good argument for the building of a canal. The Napoleonic wars, that made the passage through the English Channel hazardous from privateers and which drove ships everywhere to keep close to the land, added immediacy to the argument. Yet none could pretend that the project was one attractive to the commercial man. The costs were likely to be great, and the returns too little known. For this reason, and because the policy of providing public works was then being pressed upon the Government as a means for preventing wholesale emigration from the Highlands, Telford was sent by the Treasury to report upon the cost and practicability of such a canal.

He reported in 1802, in favour of a ship canal. Government agreed, and appointed commissioners. Jessop was called in, and the two engineers then re-surveyed the line, Jessop alone signing the final estimate. Soon afterwards the proposed dimensions were enlarged to take 32-gun frigates. Jessop did working drawings, and cutting began as a canal 20ft deep with 23 locks that would run from sea to sea through the Great Glen, connecting lochs Lochy, Oich, Ness and Dochfour and cost over £500,000. Jessop as senior engineer worked upon it with Telford until 1812, not long before his death.

Hopes were great. An excitable contemporary chronicler of canals, writing in the same year, and remembering what water transport had done for Wales, said:

'Undoubtedly in digging this canal veins of minerals will be found that will incite artists and manufacturers to flock to a place where land can be had at a cheap rate, and will induce the land owners to give pecuniary assistance where wanted to forward undertakings, by

which the riches of the bowels of the mountains may produce ten
or twenty-fold returns, eight or ten times a year. The mountains in
Wales continued unexplored, barren, and useless for ages, but are
now found to contain lead, iron, copper, coals, marble, &c. &c. in
the greatest plenty, and some hundreds of people are employed, and
whole villages built to accommodate them on a spot which a very
few years ago was an uninhabited waste.'[2]

The Caledonian Canal was unlucky. For Telford it was a comparative failure; for the State a perpetual drain of money; for the
inhabitants of the Highlands something of a white elephant. When it
was opened in 1822 it was unfinished, and would not take the bigger
ships from which Telford had expected much of its trade, and when,
deepened and reconstructed, though even now not of the depth of
20ft that had been planned, it was reopened in 1847, the age of steam
had come, and the best argument for the existence of the canal had
ceased to be valid.

During 1804 an organisation was built up, staff recruited, the line
laid out, materials ordered, and work begun inwards from the sea-
locks. Given the problems offered by size, terrain and climate, it was
bound to be slow. The canal cost over £900,000 before, unfinished,
it was opened at the insistence of a government annoyed by continuing expense and public criticism. Estimating had indeed been
good, but war had caused a heavy rise in the prices of labour and
supplies. There were also construction troubles, the worst in the
middle district, Fort Augustus to Loch Lochy, the last to be built.
By the time work seriously started here in 1817, John Simpson, who
had been in charge of construction, had died in 1816, and Matthew
Davidson, another of the engineers, had only a year to live. Deprived
of these two highly experienced men from Pontcysyllte days, and
with heavy pressure from above to open as soon as possible, work
went too fast; there were slips in the Laggan cutting, and the side
wall of the bottom lock at Fort Augustus fell in.

On 24 October 1822, two years after Telford had ceased to be
engineer, the canal was opened, with 12ft of water in the cuts and
15ft in the locks, enough only for fishing boats and small ships.
However, this did not spoil the opening ceremony. Vessels passed
through the canal carrying the commissioners and local notables,
and the *Inverness Courier* reported that:

'The termination of the voyage was marked by a grand salute from
the Fort, whilst the Inhabitants of Fort William demonstrated their
joy by kindling a large bonfire. A plentiful supply of whisky, given
by the gentlemen of Fort William, did not in the least tend to damp
the ardour of the populace. At half past seven o'clock 67 gentlemen,

the guests of Mr Grant sat down, in the hall of the Mason Lodge, to a handsome and plentiful dinner.'

It was. The reporter tells with decreasing accuracy of the thirty-nine toasts that were drunk and the more than thirty-nine speeches that were made (including one of which he frankly says: 'Corrimony returned thanks in a speech of considerable length, of which we regret we cannot give even an outline', and ends:

'At 12 o'clock the party broke up; but some of the gentlemen still remained, and, with genuine Highland spirit, prolonged the festivities of this memorable evening.'[3]

Apart from lack of water and a number of mishaps and accidents, partly due to the premature opening, the working of sailing ships through the lochs turned out to be difficult. There was no towing path along their sides, and the Great Glen made a funnel for wind which, if it were adverse, could and did hold ships up for weeks, thus preventing a saving in time over the route through the Pentland Firth. On the canal sections there was a horse towage service charged at 5s (25p) a day, Corpach to Loch Lochy and Clachnaharry to Loch Ness being each reckoned one day's towage.

After nearly twenty years of inefficient operation, the commissioners asked James Walker to report upon the canal. In 1839 he pointed out that the traffic passing was probably only about $2\frac{1}{2}$ per cent of that rounding the north of Scotland; and reported that in his view the canal should be completed, deepened to 17ft, and provided with steam tugs to pass sailing ships through. Then began three years of reports and select committees, at the end of which the government decided it was better to complete than to abandon the canal. In 1842, therefore, it was agreed to go ahead; the work was done, and the canal reopened in 1847 to take craft up to 500 tons, at an additional cost of £228,000. Since then it has continued in use: in earlier years its toll receipts usually balanced its maintenance costs, but seldom provided anything towards major repairs. More recently, even its maintenance has required subsidy.

During World War I there was a time, in 1918, when traffic on the canal was really heavy, and when those who foresaw its value in war were justified. Mines and sinkers were brought from America to Corpach at the western end of the canal, transhipped into 100 ton lighters, and passed through the canal to Muirtown basin near Inverness, where at U.S. Naval Base 18, they were assembled before being taken out into the North Sea to form part of the Northern Barrage, the minefield that was planned to stretch from the Orkneys to the coast of Norway, and to cut off German submarines from the Atlantic.

In 1920 the long and onerous task of the commissioners came to an end, and the management of the canal passed to the Ministry of Transport. Discussion went on upon the possibility of constructing a much larger ship canal which would have a lower summit level and so avoid most of the lockage on the old canal, including the eight locks at Banavie known as Neptune's Staircase that acted as a bottleneck to traffic. During a time of economy, however, such a proposal had no chance of success. During World War II the canal again found a period of activity. With nationalisation it passed to the British Transport Commission and later to the British Waterways Board. It still takes small ships (larger ones at the Corpach or western end) and fishing craft, but also now an increasing number of yachts in transit and of locally based motor cruisers.

The second of John Knox's proposals was for a canal from Loch Fyne to the Atlantic. The great peninsula of Kintyre blocks off the direct route to the north, and it was to cut through it, and so save vessels 85 miles of voyage and the passage of the Mull of Kintyre, that the Crinan Canal was projected. It was considered partly as a continuation of the Forth & Clyde Canal, so that vessels proceeding from the west coast of Scotland to the east coast or vice versa could make use of both navigations, but partly also as a means of helping the prosperity of the western coasts and isles by making them more accessible to the Glasgow market.

Ten years before the State had agreed to build the Caledonian Canal, the projectors of the Crinan put out their prospectus. Their scheme was much smaller—the estimate was £63,628—and it is clear that it was put forward with philanthropic rather than commercial reasons in the front of the promoters' minds.

'While the extensive prospects of the present existing trade of the kingdom, passing through the Crinan canal, and the natural increase which may be expected from a greater facility of communication, hold out a probable return for the money to be expended in making and maintaining it, the inestimable benefit which must arise therefrom to the inhabitants of the Western Coasts and Islands of Scotland, are extremely interesting to a benevolent mind, and may alone be an inducement to many to subscribe without an anxious regard to future profit.'

They go on manfully to say:

'An indolent dependence on the aid of Government, to public works, in this part of the kingdom, is often the bane of carrying on great improvements, and it is right, on all occasions, to endeavour to excite the spirit of the country to depend upon its own exertions.[4]'

Rennie, the engineer, revised the estimate to £107,512 for a canal now to be 15ft and not 12ft deep. An Act was obtained in 1793, and a capital of £150,000 was authorised. Philanthropy in fact raised £98,000. In order to open the canal the proprietors had to borrow £25,000 from the Treasury, to whom the canal was mortgaged. It was opened in 1801, but owing to shortage of money, unfinished at the western end, where a shallow and awkward channel remained to damage and discourage ships. Because the canal was built as economically as possible it also had inadequate depth (10ft), and a very short summit level of only 1,114yd, approached by four locks on one side and five on the other. The expense of cutting through this short summit would have simplified the navigation of the canal.

The waterway was always in financial difficulties; money was lent by the Treasury on several occasions to pay for repairs and in 1817 the management was vested in the commissioners of the Caledonian Canal. Thirty-one years later, in 1848, it was formally transferred to the State, and put under the commissioners, who retained control until superseded by the Ministry of Transport in 1920, and later by the British Transport Commission and the British Waterways Board. Yachts, motor cruisers and fishing boats, are now the principal users.

The third, and most successful in its time, of the sea-to-sea canals of Scotland was the Forth & Clyde Canal. To join the seas with a waterway across the narrow isthmus between the two firths was so obvious a proposal that it had many times been made, for instance by Defoe in his *Tour* (1724-6), when he wrote:

'. . . it would take up a Volume by itself, to lay down the several advantages to the Trade of Scotland, that would immediately occur by such a Navigation, and then to give a true Survey of the Ground, the Easiness of its being perform'd, and the probable Charge of it, all which might be done. But it is too much to undertake here, it must lye till Posterity, by the rising Greatness of their Commerce, shall not only feel the Want of it, but find themselves able for the Performance.'[5]

Some forty years after Defoe wrote, commerce felt the need for such a waterway. Posterity, however, divided itself into two groups. On the one hand were those interested in the general prosperity of Scotland: these were headed by the Board of Trustees for the Encouragement of Fisheries, Manufactures and Improvements in Scotland, a public body with government funds to spend upon the promotion of Scottish trade and supported by Edinburgh interests; they wanted a sea-to-sea canal that would link the trade of the western and eastern coasts, and would be of size enough to take coasting vessels. On the other hand were the merchants of Glasgow. It was to their interest that trade should not pass through Glasgow, but be centred in it, and they therefore supported a barge canal that would bring to their city the trade of the east coast, and of Europe that looked towards the east coast.

The trustees asked John Smeaton for a survey. He reported in 1764, offering two routes, the first roughly as the canal was later to be built, the second by way of Loch Lomond. The first, 5ft deep, he estimated at £74,000. Glasgow interests then got Robert Mackell and James Watt of steam-kettle fame to bring Smeaton's line nearer Glasgow and, with depth reduced to 4ft, the plan reached Parliament in 1767. Meanwhile the supporters of a 'great canal' had been holding meetings as far away as Perth and Aberdeen, and succeeded in obtaining subscriptions of over £100,000. The original Bill was withdrawn, whereupon the disgusted Watt wrote to his wife:

'I think I shall not long to have anything to do with the House of Commons again—I never saw so many wrong-headed people on all sides gathered together. . . . I believe *the Deevil* has possession of them.'[6]

Smeaton reported on a canal 7ft deep, to cost £147,337. Some supporters wanted 10ft depth to take sloops, but the 7ft proposal went through in 1768, the Act authorising £200,000 of capital. Smeaton with Mackell as resident engineer, began work that year; by 1775 the canal, built from the Forth end, had reached Stockingfield, 3 miles from Glasgow. Two years later, most of the Glasgow branch was opened. That city had got what it wanted, a canal to the eastern coast, but the through sea-to-sea communication was still lacking. It was when affairs were in this state that John Knox wrote his book, and advocated the completion of the line as one of his three canals to improve Scottish trade. In 1784, however, £50,000 was advanced to the company by the Government, and work began again, now with Robert Whitworth as engineer. At last, in July 1790, the canal was fully opened, 35 miles long, with 40 locks and Whitworth's 4 arched Kelvin aqueduct. Thenceforward, the company became more and more prosperous. Receipts rose from some £8,000 a year to £50,000. The construction of the Monkland and later of the Edinburgh & Glasgow Union Canal to join it brought additional traffic, and it flourished until the opening of the Newcastle & Carlisle Railway, and later of the Edinburgh & Glasgow, reduced its receipts. The Forth & Clyde Canal was finally bought by the Caledonian Railway in 1867, largely because the company coveted its harbour at Grangemouth, and continued to decline in usefulness, tonnage carried falling from 3,022,583 in 1868 to 817,836 in 1908, 27,571 in 1942, and 14,839 in 1953. It closed at the beginning of 1963.

In its day, however, it was a giant. We may particularly remember it because upon its waters, in 1789, Symington tried out the second of his steam paddle boats, and, as he records, 'in presence of hundreds of spectators, who lined the banks of the canal, the boat glided along, propelled at the rate of five miles an hour'.

This experiment interested Lord Dundas, the governor of the canal company, and later Symington was employed by him to prepare a new engine to be fitted to a hull specially built as a tug, called the *Charlotte Dundas*, and to drive a stern paddle-wheel. Trials were held from January 1801, and in March 1803 the boat pulled two laden barges from lock 20 to Glasgow in 9¼ hours. Though the trials had been successful, the proprietors decided not to use her owing to the damage that might be caused to the banks by the wash; so the *Charlotte Dundas* was beached in a creek off the canal, till her hull broke up from the weather and souvenir hunters. It was to be very many years before steam craft regularly used the canal.

From time to time a mid-Scotland ship canal has been proposed, and after World War I a special association actively promoted it. In 1930, and again in 1946, government committees reported upon the project, in both cases adversely. The latter estimated that the cost of a sea-level canal 32ft deep might be some £109 millions, excluding interest upon construction, and were doubtful whether such a canal would cover its maintenance costs, while its strategic importance would be relatively small.

We could pause here to study the three trans-Pennine canals that were built, all variations on the Humber–Mersey route, and to wonder whether a modern transport policy might not seriously consider a new one to link the Aire & Calder and the Manchester Ship Canal. A fourth line also, from the Tyne to the Solway Firth and Maryport, was proposed from the time of the canal mania for forty years, but built in small part only as the Carlisle Canal from the Firth to that city. Instead, however, let us look at one less known sea-to-sea scheme that formerly took the imagination of Englishmen.

Of all the capes in England, men in the little sailing ships of the coasting trade before the days of steam feared Land's End the most, both for its rocks and its contrary winds. So from the earliest times of canal building plans were made to cut a waterway across Somerset, Devon or Cornwall to avoid the dangers and shorten the time of the voyage. The coal exporters and merchants of South Wales wanted to sell more goods along the south coast of England and in London, while the landowners and merchants of the South-west stood to gain by cheap goods brought by waterway to their harbours and countryside.

Two ways of sending goods across the peninsula of the South-west

were suggested; by barge canal, which would have meant their transhipment into ships at each end of the canal; and by ship canal.

There were many plans for a barge canal, from 1769 when Whitworth under Brindley's supervision, first surveyed two routes, one
from the River Exe to Taunton, whence barges would use the Tone
Navigation to Bridgwater, where they would enter another canal to
go via Glastonbury and Axbridge to Uphill near Bristol, the other
from Seaton across Devon to the River Parrett at Langport. Two of
the many that were planned were partially built. Both were products
of the canal mania.

The Grand Western Canal was intended to run from Topsham to
Taunton in Somerset, whence traffic could work to Bridgwater by
way of the navigable rivers Tone and Parrett. It was to be 46 miles
long, including branches to Cullompton and Tiverton, and its total
cost was estimated at £166,724. The Act for its construction was
passed in 1796, but by then the prices of goods and the wages of labour
were rising because of the war, and the whole venture looked to the
proprietors too risky. So the plan was laid aside till better times.

It was thought in 1809 that these had come, and plans for building
the canal were brought out of storage. Several engineers, Robert
Whitworth, John Longbothom and William Jessop among them, had
made surveys, but John Rennie's had been the final one, and he
was therefore engaged to superintend construction. The proprietors
allowed for costs exceeding the original estimate by 50 per cent as a
result of increased prices, and a start was made upon the original plan
of a barge canal.

Two disastrous mistakes were made at the start. The proprietors
decided, for the sake of the carriage in stone, over-estimated at
£10,000 a year from the Burlescombe quarries to Tiverton, to start
the work of cutting not at one end or other of the canal, but in the
middle. Work was therefore begun on the Tiverton branch and on
part of the main line, a length of 11 miles. If construction had been
begun from the Taunton or the Topsham end, there would have
been a trade in coal as soon as the first few miles of the canal were
open, while the materials used for construction and those which had
to be removed could have been easily and cheaply carried.

The second mistake was made by Rennie, who decided to improve
upon the original plan by lowering the summit level at Holcombe
Rogus 16ft in order to save lockage upon the main line and the Tiverton branch, and to save the cost of a reservoir by using the Lowd-
wells springs. He did, but at the expense of much heavy and difficult
cutting and embanking. The next three years were spent in happy
optimism by the local committee who represented the shareholders,

and in a struggle against physical obstacles by the engineer. At last, in 1812, the short section was open for traffic. Without a lock, it had cost £244,505 for 11 miles, or more than the estimate of 1793 for the whole 46 miles of the canal with its branches. Coal had to be brought by road from Taunton to the end of the canal at Holcombe Rogus, and thence to Tiverton by water, while the stone traffic for which the section had been first constructed never yielded £1,000 in any one year.

The proprietors of this self-contained section of a sea-to-sea canal that they could not afford to finish licked their wounds, and resisted the blandishments of engineers who wanted to complete the canal at trifling cost. James Green, an Exeter engineer who had done competent work on the Exeter, Bude and Torrington canals, and had even been called over to Wales to advise on the Kidwelly & Llanelly Canal, in the end made a proposal that sounded workable. He suggested that the canal should be completed to Taunton on a smaller scale, in order that it should obtain the benefits of connection with the newly built Bridgwater & Taunton Canal, and so with a seaport. He estimated the cost at £61,324, a figure just within the remaining resources of the committee.

On the Bude Canal inclined planes had been successfully used instead of locks; he therefore suggested that the new section should have no locks, but instead an inclined plane at Wellisford and seven vertical lifts.

Green convinced the management committee, and work began. Unfortunately for his reputation, Green not only failed to make the inclined plane work by the hydraulic power for which it was designed, so that a steam engine had to be installed, but he was so confident of the design of his lifts* that he went ahead with construction before he had made the necessary practical experiments. Too late he found difficulty in equalising the levels of water in the two pounds of the canal and the two caissons, so that the stop gates could be raised and the boats pass easily in and out of the lifts. He cured the trouble in time, and at his own expense, but the delay in opening the canal cost the proprietors their last capital. To get traffic started the committee were forced not only to raise an additional subscription amongst themselves, but to borrow from their own superintendent.

The extension was opened in 1838, and a modest prosperity set in for the Grand Western Canal, till the railway came a few years later. But no further word was heard of extending it to Topsham to join the English to the Bristol Channel.

The second project begun but not completed was the Dorset &

* See p 68.

Somerset, 49 miles long, planned from beside the Dorset Stour to join the Kennet & Avon Canal near Bath, whence traffic could work down the Avon to Bristol. Like the Grand Western, the Dorset & Somerset obtained its Act in 1796. Like the Grand Western again, the proprietors chose to start work on a 9 mile long branch in the middle of their line, in order to carry coal to Frome from the collieries at Nettlebridge. A lift was built for them near Mells that worked on trials and others were begun, but by 1803 their ready money was exhausted and 1¾ miles of the branch remained to be cut. Shareholders, frightened at rising costs, failed to pay further calls on the shares, no one would take up promissory notes, and work stopped. It never began again, and today it is difficult to trace this canal that never carried traffic.

The principal ship canal project was surveyed by Thomas Telford and James Green along the same general line as many previous proposals, including one by Rennie in 1811 for a small ship canal to take 120 ton vessels. It was planned now to carry ships of 200 tons along a line 44½ miles in length from Stolford near Bridgwater to Beer near Seaton. There were to be 60 locks, and harbours at each end of the line. It was estimated that 1,095,527 tons of goods would pass through the canal each year, and that receipts, including harbour dues, would be £210,847 from the through traffic alone. Of the proposed capital of £1,750,000, the sum of £1,518,000 was actually promised, and a Bill went before Parliament for the English & Bristol Channels Ship Canal, and was passed in 1825. Soon after the passing of the Act, however, a slump set in. In 1828 the committee reported sadly:

'The severe shock ... which was given to public confidence shortly after the passing of the Act, and the consequent aversion to almost every speculative activity, have not failed to affect the Ship Canal, so as to render it highly improbable that so large a capital as £1,750,000 will now be raised for the accomplishment of this object.'[7]

The idea of cutting a waterway through the peninsula has attracted enthusiasts up to this century, and some dozen proposals have been made. One of the most charmingly optimistic was that of Mr Hern of Cardiff in 1922. He suggested that a canal should be built to carry ships of 15,000 tons, costing £37,000,000. Among the arguments he used is that:

'A Feature of attraction, and I think a source of considerable profit to the canal whichever route it follows, will be the pleasure traffic which will pass through beautiful country having near its banks many places of historic and other interest, providing for tourists a pleasant and useful journey, appealing more to many people than trains and motor chars-a-banc or even motor cars, to places of rest and beauty in South Devon, such as Torquay, Teignmouth, etc., and to the delightful neighbourhood of Bournemouth, Southampton, and the Isle of Wight.'[8]

In fact the project of a ship canal ceased to offer utility at all commensurate with the cost as soon as steam replaced wind as a motive power. Whereas sailing ships might spend days or even weeks waiting for the wind that would take them round Cape Wrath or Land's End, and often came to grief from the tides of the Pentland Firth or the rocks of Scilly, steam power made such voyages both regular and safe. The saving of time and insurance premiums was therefore not enough to make it worth the while of the shipowner to pay the dues of the Caledonian Canal or the proposed English & Bristol Channels Ship Canal. For that reason the one lost money, and the other was never built.

CHAPTER VIII

Canals and Ports

APART from the sea-to-sea canals, we can envisage the waterway system of Britain as a network of canals and rivers joining together the principal towns, and linking sources of raw materials with industrial areas. Some of the traffic on it was purely internal, originating at one point and being carried to another. Much, however, had either arrived at a port by coasting or foreign-trading vessel, or was destined for shipment from a port. This trade passed to and from the ports at the edges of the web, where the navigable waterways ended and tidal water began. Many of these ports, like Bristol on the Avon or London on the Thames, had been distribution centres where goods were transhipped either into river barges or road waggons, before the days of canals; the coming of artificial waterways had merely increased their commercial importance. Others, like Goole on the Aire & Calder or Ellesmere Port on the Shropshire Union, were creations of the canal age.

Some of these rivers, like the Severn, had always been difficult navigations in their tidal stretches. Some were quite suitable for small craft, but had to be dredged and possibly embanked in places to take the larger ships that were coming into use, especially after the introduction of steamships. Such rivers were the Thames, the Tyne, the Tees and the Wear. Some, especially in the Fenlands, silted up so much that extensive training works had to be carried out, as on the Great Ouse to King's Lynn, or an artificial cut provided in place of an unusable river channel, as on the Nene below Wisbech. The object of these training works was to narrow and straighten a river channel in order to increase the speed of the current, and so its scouring effect on the river bed. In one case, Bristol, William Jessop cut a new channel for the river, the old one being cut off by locks and turned into a floating harbour. In other cases nothing was done, and the little ports, like Hedon on the Humber, that once flourished became no longer accessible. It sometimes proved impossible to preserve or improve the navigation of a river channel, and therefore to prevent trade deserting a port upon it, a canal was cut from the sea to the town to take the place of the river navigation. Now and then a town near the sea, but without a harbour, decided to turn itself into a port

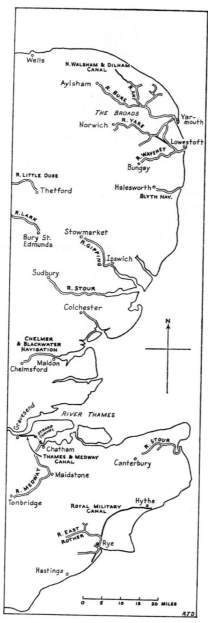

Map 12 The waterways of Kent and East Anglia

by building a canal to salt water. We may take as examples of canals built to avoid a river navigation the Exeter Canal and the Gloucester & Berkeley; of one planned to make a port out of a town not on the sea or a navigable river, the Ulverston.

The Exeter and the Gloucester & Berkeley canals are similar in that both ports suffered from a difficult river; they differ in that the Exeter led only to the city, while the Gloucester & Berkeley not only made Gloucester a port of import for the country round it, but also a place of transhipment into river barges and canal boats, which then went up the Severn into the midland inland waterway system, or by way of the Stroudwater and Thames & Severn canals towards Oxford or the Vale of White Horse.

The story of the Exeter Canal goes back to the reign of Edward I in the thirteenth century. Until about that time, the River Exe had been tidal to Exeter, and small craft used to ascend the river to the city. Then Isabella de Fortibus, Countess of Devon, built a weir across the river—Countess Wear is still well known—and the earls of Devon followed her lead with other weirs, at the same time building a quay at Topsham, near the mouth of the Exe, where goods for Exeter had to be landed and pay the earl's dues. Though the citizens won lawsuits, the earls maintained the weirs.

Therefore, in 1563 the citizens of Exeter, exasperated by three hundred years of obstructions in the river, engaged John Trew of Glamorgan as engineer of a barge canal to run from a point below Countess Wear alongside the Exe to the city, where it would rejoin the river. Here a wharf would be built, fitted with a crane. The canal that Trew built was a very small affair, only 3ft deep, 16ft wide and 1¾ miles long, but it had three locks upon it, probably with vertically rising gates, which were the first pound-locks upon any British navigation. It was, and is, a municipal affair, and a tribute to the public spirit of the city.

Although Trew had promised to build a canal that was accessible at all states of the tide, he did not in fact do so, and therefore by 1677 it had been carried farther down river to Topsham, and in 1701 enlarged to 10ft depth and 50ft breadth, dimensions sufficient for coasting craft and small deep-sea ships.

There followed a time when many canal schemes were discussed in the South-west, and it looked as if the port of Exeter would become, like Gloucester later, the focal point of canals running to Crediton, Okehampton, North Devon and Cornwall. They came to nothing. It seemed to the corporation that their canal must be improved, both in the interests of the city itself and to attract capital to canals that might be connected with it.

Page 147, Plate III (above) The 29 locks and their side-ponds on the Devizes flight on the Kennet & Avon Canal early in this century; (below) Galton bridge on the rebuilt summit level of the Birmingham Canal Navigations' main line

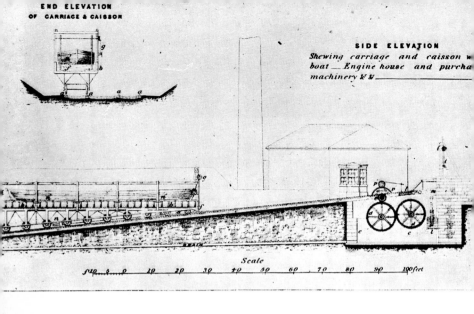

Scale
510 5 0 10 20 30 40 50 60 70 80 90 100 feet

Page 148, Plate IV (*above*) A longitudinal 20 wheeled caisson on Blackhill inclined plan
Monkland Canal. The plane was opened in 1850; (*below*) tub-boats being carried on Tren
inclined plane on the Shrewsbury Canal

James Green was called in, and between 1820 and 1827 he completely reconstructed the canal, making it 15ft deep, and carrying the entrance 2 miles farther down the estuary to Turf, where 12ft of water was available on all tides. The canal could take vessels of 400 tons, but by now Exeter's most important business, the export

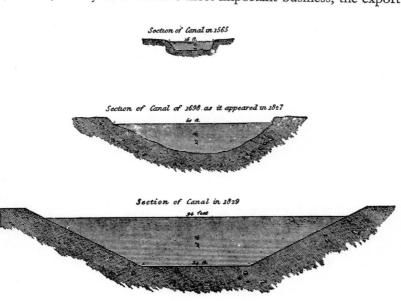

Figure 22   Three cross-sections of the Exeter Canal

of woollen goods, had ceased, and nothing comparable had taken its place. However, the corporation supported an early railway Act of 1832 for a line from the canal basin at Exeter to Crediton, and when action failed, agreed with the Bristol & Exeter Railway that its line should come to the basin.

Then two great changes took place. On the one hand, the corporation changed its mind about the terminus of the railway, which in fact ended at Red Cow (St. David's), and it was not till 1867 that the basin had railway communication by a branch line near St Thomas's. On the other hand, the coming of steamships made the canal's dimensions inadequate. Competition from railways, instead of the co-operation that might have been possible, and the falling off of traffic caused the tolls received to fall below the interest charges on the money that had been borrowed to reconstruct the canal. The creditors then took over the canal, and it did not revert to the city until 1883, when the corporation were empowered to use much of their property to redeem the canal bonds at one-quarter of their value. The canal is too small to make Exeter an important port, and its main traffic is some 50,000 tons a year of sludge carried by the MV *Countess Wear*. The basin, no longer commercially used, now displays part of the Exeter Maritime Museum's collection.

A ship canal from Berkeley Pill on the Severn to Gloucester was planned in order that shipping bound for Gloucester could avoid the difficult and dangerous passage of the river between those points, and that the transhipment of goods from ships to barges or vice versa should take place in the basin at Gloucester, into which craft could pass from the river by means of a lock. The Act for this canal was passed in 1793: two years later, John Phillips wrote in his *History of Inland Navigation*:

'This undertaking for its magnitude and accommodations, deserves to be considered as of the first importance; its magnitude is intended for the passage of vessels of more than three hundred tons burthen; and its accommodations to commerce, by uniting the city of Gloucester, by an easy and certain water carriage with the port of Bristol, and from thence with all the world, may justly be deemed an object of great magnitude to trade. The whole of this scheme evinces an extent of idea, known only in a free country; and an ardour of enterprise, which none but an industrious and commercial people could endure. . . .'[1]

When he wrote that last sentence, John Phillips spoke more truly than he knew. The ardour of enterprise of the proprietors of the Gloucester & Berkeley Canal carried them to success through great difficulties. It was thirty-four years after they obtained their Act before the canal was opened, and, because they had had to borrow heavily from the Government and to mortgage their property in return, it was seventy-eight years before the descendants of the men who first subscribed for shares were in full control of their property. They would, however, be rewarded by current plans to enlarge the canal to take 2500 dwt vessels, with 1500 dwt on to Worcester.

The threads of many happenings made familiar in the stories of other canals which were under construction during the canal mania meet in the history of this, the biggest canal at the time of its inception that had been promoted in Great Britain. In the minute-book is recorded the effort to introduce mechanical canal cutting by the use of Carne's machine, which was in use on the neighbouring Herefordshire & Gloucestershire, and the eventual construction of a machine by a local inventor and proprietor that failed to work; the immediate attendance upon the committee of a gentleman from Bristol to ask if they would discuss a plan to build a barge canal from Bristol to their own; the letter from Boulton & Watt saying they could not have immediate delivery of a steam engine for pumping water out of the channel during cutting, because of the great demand for steam engines; the agreement with the Herefordshire & Gloucestershire not to attract each other's workmen; the insistence by landowners upon written authority for all surveyors coming on to their lands, and upon compensation for all damage; and trouble with workmen, engineers, estimates, surveys and contractors.

Relations with the workmen started off well, the committee recording:

'It being understood, that it is customary, at the commencement of every Canal, to allow some liquor to the Workmen, and Mr Edson having reported that the number of Workmen now employed are fifty—

Ordered, That he do give one shilling, to each of those men . . .'[2]

Trouble with engineers was chronic, until just before the canal was opened, when the family of Clegram moved in, the father as engineer and the son as clerk, and remained as fixtures, till in 1885 the son, now engineer, retired and was given a seat on the board. The usual practice was followed of appointing a 'Chief and Principal Engineer', in this case Robert Mylne, at a yearly retainer of £350 and travelling expenses, and a resident engineer. During the mania the few canal engineers with reputations took on far more work than they could carefully deal with. Mylne was not, in fact, one of them, but rather, as engineer of London's New River Company, an expert on water provision and supply, as well as being an excellent architect. He was, however, as busy as the others, and so, like most of them, he seldom visited the site unless a crisis occurred, and depended upon the reports of the resident engineer for the material upon which to give advice. At the same time the number of canals simultaneously under construction made it difficult for canal committees to engage competent resident engineers; yet if they were incompetent, the damage was done before the chief engineer heard about it.

The first resident engineer on the Gloucester & Berkeley was Dennis Edson, engaged at 200 guineas a year, who lasted only nine months before he was dismissed. Twenty years earlier he had been dismissed from the Chester Canal, and seven years later he was to be again so from the Grand Surrey, so it was not a unique experience. Already the committee were in difficulties as a result, for they took on the twenty-six-year-old James Dadford, who at any rate was one of a competent engineering family, and wrote anxiously to Mylne:

'. . . and they are so very anxious to have doubts removed, that much embarrass them, and as they conceive very much affect their future operations, that they cannot be satisfied, but by your personal attendance, which they trust you will not defer longer than next week.'[3]

Eventually the company's affairs reached such a state that a proprietor wrote to the committee, saying that he thought Mylne was to do everything, the resident engineer merely carrying out instructions, instead of which:

'. . . but a small quantity of his personal attendance has been *necessarily occupied* by the Works, and since our engagement with Mr Dadford, scarcely any. . . . As for the Idea which in the Days of our ignorance was broached, with some success, that an Engineer may render us sufficient services, by *thinking* and *contriving* for us, while *sitting at his ease in London*: I will not suppose any member of the Committee is *now* amused by it, or that it is necessary for me to endeavour to *do it away*.'[4]

Mylne came down to face the committee, and agreed in future to accept payment by the day, at four guineas and travelling expenses.

From this it may be understood that the company was in trouble. The original plan had been for a canal 17¾ miles long, 70ft broad at top (or water level), and 18ft deep, estimated by Mylne to cost £121,330, to cover which the Act authorised £140,000, and a further £60,000 if necessary. Work began in 1794 at the Gloucester end, in excavating the dock and cutting down towards Berkeley. By 1799 available cash had run out, and the canal had only been cut to Hardwicke, about 5½ miles from Gloucester. Confidence had almost gone, and the efforts the committee made to interest their shareholders in putting up further money were in vain, either for a narrow canal to continue to the junction with the Stroudwater Canal, which would open trade through the Thames & Severn, or to change the final junction with the Severn from Berkeley Pill to Hock Crib, which was nearer but less convenient. The shareholders, like those of so many other canals of the mania who had been caught by the effects of the war and the results of inefficiency and over-optimism, refused to budge, and the partly finished canal lay useless. Dadford was given notice: there was nothing for him to do.

The committee spent the next twenty years alternating bursts of enthusiasm with long spells of inactivity, in trying to decide where to end the canal (they finally chose Sharpness Point, rather than Berkeley Pill or Hock Crib) and to raise the necessary money, at one time even by a lottery scheme that was turned down personally by William Pitt.

It was the Government that in the end helped the canal proprietors to restart. The passing of the Poor Employment Act in 1817, and the setting up of the Exchequer Bill Loan Commissioners, have already been referred to. The commissioners had power to lend money for works that would employ the unemployed poor, and the canal committee obtained from them a loan of £65,000 towards the £120,000 that, it was now estimated, would be necessary to finish the canal. Telford inspected the canal on behalf of the commissioners, and pronounced it a good risk.

So work began again, fertilised by government money, and the Duke of Gloucester came down to lay the foundation stone of the docks at Sharpness, while three hogsheads of ale were drunk by the workmen. The sad history of the canal was compensated by the magniloquence of the inscription:

'To extend the advantages of commerce into the Interior of the Kingdom, and to facilitate the Intercourse with Foreign Countries, the Gloucester and Berkeley Canal Company projected this work. The approbation of the most illustrious and dignified Personages of the realm sanctioned the undertaking; and the countenance of His Royal Highness William Frederick Duke of Gloucester, assisted by the noble House of Berkeley, was particularly evinced in graciously condescending to lay the first stone of this Harbour, the fifteenth day of July, 1818. Long may it remain unmoved, a Monument of national enterprise, a benefit to the proprietors, and a secure Harbour for the commerce of the World.'[5]

John Upton, who had been taken on as clerk and became engineer *de facto* in 1815, and who had almost at once written a pamphlet in which he had set right the mistakes of his predecessors, reverted to clerk six months after the resumption of work, and soon afterwards resigned when an inquiry brought to light that materials for the works had been supplied by him as seller to himself as engineer. John Woodhouse succeeded him, and was in turn dismissed for the similar offence of allowing his son to supply unsuitable stone only a year later. To trouble with the engineers was added trouble with the contractors, one of whom went bankrupt, and at the end of 1820 the committee confessed to the proprietors that with only the junction to the Stroudwater Canal finished and the rest of the works part-built, £120,000 was still needed, that they could not pay the interest and repayments of principal due to the Exchequer Bill Loan Commissioners under their agreement, and that the commissioners were going to take over the canal as mortgagees unless money was raised to pay them. Meanwhile all work had stopped.

Now began a frantic search for money, which ended in the raising of some £60,000 in preference shares, and the loan of a further

£60,000, later increased to £95,000, by the commissioners, who now administered the funds of the company jointly with the committee. Civil Service control in this case led to a great increase in efficiency. A new contractor was appointed; Captain Nicholls became chairman—he was later to become Sir George Nicholls, a commissioner of the Poor Law and chairman of the Birmingham Canal Navigations; warehouses were built; the completion of the canal was pressed on; till on 19 April 1827 the wearied committee recorded:

'Resolved, the two Boats, Band and Colour be provided for the use of the Committee on the 26th. inst., and that Mr. Dowling be applied to, to provide a public Ordinary to be paid for, at the individual expence of Gentlemen who may be disposed to attend on the occasion.'[6]

We may note the Treasury flavour of the last lines!

The canal was open, in a flurry of settling debts to contractors, arranging for market passenger boats, dealing with the now numerous applications from traders to erect warehouses or wharves, looking for more water supplies, and making terms with the organisation of trackers, the men who hauled the sailing ships along the waterway until a regular service of tugs was introduced about 1862. It was the greatest canal in Britain, deeper (18ft) than the Caledonian at that time, and took ships carrying 600 tons of cargo. Trade increased: 2,360 vessels used the port in 1827, 4,272 in 1828, 5,199 in 1829, and 7,981 in 1830, but an unpleasant letter arrived from the commissioners saying that they did not think it expedient any longer to control the affairs of the company, and that they would therefore take steps to dispose of the concern for the recovery of the debt due to the public, unless the company could suggest an arrangement for its early liquidation.

Indeed, it was nearly twenty years later before the company was free from periodical threats to sell them up, by raising the money to repay the commissioners, partly by the creation of first preference shares, and partly by borrowing from an insurance company. The canal had altogether cost £444,000. The mortgage to the insurance company was not finally repaid till 1871, when the committee's report triumphantly reads:

'. . . this Company became free from the restrictions of the mortgages originally imposed by the Government, and received the whole of their title deeds into their own possession.'[7]

Thenceforward the policy of the company was made up of three strands, which met in the 1870s. The first was co-operation with railways.

It is so natural to think of railways as competitors of canals—as indeed they proved—that it is not at once realised that canals such as the Gloucester & Berkeley, being primarily ports, had much more to gain through good railway connections to their docks than to lose by rail competition along their route. This applied especially to ports having a foreign trade, for the general result of the coming of railways was to increase foreign and decrease coastwise trade. As far back as 1806, three years before the Gloucester & Cheltenham Tramroad got its Act, the committee of the Gloucester & Berkeley told its promoters that they would agree to the rails being laid to their basin at Gloucester (where they remained till 1862). In 1843 they gave permission to the Birmingham & Gloucester Railway to lay its rails to the docks, and by 1862 the railway connections to the Gloucester basins were complete.

The company was also anxious to build up a coal export trade, at first from Gloucester, later from Sharpness Docks. For this reason every encouragement was given by the proprietors to a company formed to build a Severn railway bridge near Sharpness, and so to bring Welsh and Forest of Dean coal. When the bridge company got into difficulties the Gloucester & Berkeley subscribed a considerable amount to its capital. The bridge was opened in 1879.

The second strand of policy was the promotion of inland waterways. It must be remembered that Gloucester was a terminal port in respect of the country round it; it was also a place of transhipment of cargoes from seagoing craft to river lighters going up the Severn to Worcester, to barges working through the Thames & Severn Canal to the Thames, or to narrow boats bound either for the Wilts & Berks, by way of the Thames & Severn, or for the Staffs & Worcs (from Stourport), or the Worcester & Birmingham (from Worcester).

The Gloucester & Berkeley company took an interest in a number of schemes. It opposed the improvement of the Severn by various proposed private navigation companies, nominally in the cause of a free river, in fact because it feared that the improvement of the navigation would cost more in tolls to craft on the river than the added facilities were worth, and so would discourage traffic. When the Severn Commissioners were set up as a public body, however, the canal company supported them financially.

Its interest extended beyond the Severn. The Staffs & Worcs Canal was a prosperous concern that maintained its independence of railways without difficulty. The Worcester & Birmingham, however, was not, since on the one hand, it had an expensive line to keep up, while on the other it suffered severely from railway competition. As early as 1858 a proposal came before Parliament for the lease of this canal to the Oxford, Worcester & Wolverhampton Railway.

It was opposed and defeated. Thenceforward the Worcester & Birmingham was the prize for two sets of chess-players: the railway interests on the one hand, and the waterways on the other, on the whole led by the Gloucester & Berkeley. Though the Worcester & Birmingham passed into the hands of a receiver in 1868, the game lasted till 1874, when the Gloucester & Berkeley leased it, together with the Droitwich and the Droitwich Junction, both these having formerly been leased to the Worcester & Birmingham. The canal company now possessed two separated waterways, one a ship canal and one a part-narrow, part-broad boat canal, that were connected by the Severn in which they were financially interested, and that gave them a through water route to Birmingham.

The Gloucester & Berkeley company started well by giving its new acquisitions a thorough overhaul and dredging. In the case of the Droitwich 73,000 tons of mud were removed, according to the engineer 'the accumulation, I should think, of the last half century'. Yet in no year did their new purchase earn enough to pay what it was costing the parent company in interest on mortgage debt taken over and in payments to shareholders guaranteed under the terms of the lease; by the end of the century tolls received were hardly balancing maintenance costs.

The company also did its best to keep open the canals towards the Thames. In 1897 it successfully opposed the abandonment of the Wilts & Berks by its owners, while it became a stockholder in the Thames & Severn Canal Trust that took over the waterway from the Great Western Railway, and ran it until funds gave out, when it passed to the Gloucestershire County Council, who kept it open until 1927.

The two threads of co-operation with the railways and encouragement of waterways were twisted with a third, the improvement of the port at Gloucester and the harbour at Sharpness. New basins were built at the former, and many developments took place as warehouses and wharves were constructed. At Sharpness, a port which had been built for sailing ships and could not take the bigger steamers, and which therefore had been suffering heavy competition from the newer steamer docks at Swansea, Cardiff, Newport and Avonmouth, a larger harbour and entrance lock were opened in 1874, and steamers carrying over 1,000 tons of cargo navigated the canal. There followed a three-years rate-cutting war with Avonmouth to attract the Bristol Channel trade, ended in 1882 by an agreement, and a resumption of the preference dividends that had been cut off during the rate war. From that time to the present the canal has continued to serve Gloucester, and now looks hopefully forward to enlargement.

Ulverston in Lancashire was a town from which the estuary of the River Leven had receded. In 1793, therefore, an Act was obtained to make a small ship canal of about a mile and a quarter from the river to the town. On 23 August 1793 all Ulverston was delirious with joy as the inhabitants went in a procession headed by two fiddles and bagpipes to see the first sod cut by Lt-Col Sunderland, the company's chairman.

The canal was opened in November 1796. It was a substantial affair, 15ft deep and 66ft wide at water level, and provided with two large basins. It was used largely for the export of iron and copper ores and slate, and the import of coal, timber and the merchandise needed in the town and its district. At first its trade was small: in 1798 ninety-four vessels entered the canal, the tonnage being 4,704. By 1821 the number of vessels had become 259 and the tonnage 13,960. From 1829 to 1844 the number of vessels each year entering the canal averaged 531 and the tonnage 35,009. Then came two years of great activity as ships entered with materials for the building of the Furness Railway. When that line was opened in 1846 trade at once fell away, to 388 ships and 25,220 tonnage in 1849. Thenceforward it declined, until in 1862 the Furness Railway Company bought it. Since the authorised capital was £7,000, to which must be added the cost of subsequent works such as the pier and a weir, and the railway paid £22,005 for it, the proprietors were probably not out of pocket. It was abandoned in 1945.

This short account of a short canal does show the economic importance to its neighbourhood even of such a minor work as the Ulverston Canal. Later in the nineteenth century a plan for a greater inland port was put forward and successfully carried out by a larger town than Ulverston. Since it deserves a chapter to itself, the story of the Manchester Ship Canal is told later in this book.

Finally, one freak deserves a mention; the Grand Surrey Canal, which began as a canal and became an extended dock. The canal grew out of various proposals among others for a waterway from Deptford to Kingston, with branches to Epsom and Croydon, but the Act of 1801 under which it was authorised was for a canal from the River Thames at Rotherhithe, through Peckham, Camberwell and Kennington to Mitcham. The engineer, Ralph Dodd, got to work at once, and in 1801 cutting began on the Rotherhithe section. In April 1802 he was dismissed, and thereafter the company became less and less interested in extending the canal, which was slowly cut past the junction at New Cross with the Croydon Canal (opened in 1809) to Camberwell, together with a later branch to Peckham, while the entrance lock into the Thames was opened in 1807. At Camber-

well and Peckham the canal remained, while the company developed
as a dock concern, though for a long time not a prosperous one,
mainly owing to the competition of other docks.

Figure 23   Token showing a Tyne keel

The use of the Grand Surrey as an inland waterway really ended in
1836, when the through traffic that passed over it to and from the
Croydon Canal ceased when that canal was sold to a railway company. Thenceforward the wharves that had sprung up along it must
be thought of as extensions to its docks. In 1855 the company became the Grand Surrey Docks & Canal Co, and was authorised to
build the Albion Dock. In 1864 it amalgamated with the Commercial
Docks Co, which had bought the old Greenland and other docks,
and the combined company became the owner of the Surrey Commercial docks system. Soon afterwards the canal was connected to
the Greenland dock. In 1908 the canal, together with the docks, was
transferred to the Port of London Authority. At the end of January
1971 the whole canal was closed, a minor casualty in the ending of
the long service to London of the whole Surrey Commercial docks
system.

CHAPTER IX

The Golden Years

+++++++++++++++++++++++++++++++++++++++◆+++++++++++++++++++++++++++++++++++++++

The slump that followed the Napoleonic War affected all waterways, but especially those which had gained abnormal traffic during the war as a result of the danger from privateers that had faced the coastal trade. The Basingstoke committee welcomed the return of peace with the remark:

'That from the facilities afforded in peace to the conveyance of goods by sea, some considerable injury must be sustained by the Canal . . .'[1]

The pattern of the waterways of the British Isles was now approaching its final complexity. We have examined in detail some of the groups of which it was made up, such as the arterial canals connecting together the great rivers and the network round Birmingham. Other groups had been formed, and it is at these that we must now look if we are to get a reasonable picture of the waterway system as a whole.

First, then, the two that had grown up largely during the war, and were by the end of it almost complete, in Lancashire and Yorkshire. On the Lancashire side the great Leeds & Liverpool, not yet finished, curved through Blackburn, Burnley and Colne on its way to Yorkshire. Part of its route was over the Lancaster. This broad canal began at Wigan and ran north through Preston and Lancaster, then over Rennie's great Lune aqueduct and through Hincaster tunnel to Kendal in Westmorland. It was completed in 1819. The Lancaster was an oddity, because it was broken in the middle by a 5 mile long tramroad that crossed the valley of the Ribble just south of Preston. This tramroad, with the double transhipment of goods that it entailed, was an obstacle to through traffic greater than its value. It was last used throughout in January 1862, after which the canal was broken into two pieces.

From Manchester there ran out a spray of canals, climbing into the valleys where factories were still driven by water power. One author maintains that even in 1831 half the cotton mills in Britain were on the banks of the Goyt or the Etherow. The Rochdale Canal left the Bridgewater Canal and climbed past Oldham to the valley of the River Roch. It gave a branch to Rochdale (and later one to Heywood) and then crossed from Lancashire into Yorkshire without a summit tunnel to end at Sowerby Bridge, where it joined the Calder & Hebble Navigation that itself connected with the Aire & Calder system. To the south ran the narrow-boat Ashton-under-Lyne Canal (connected to the Rochdale and so to the Bridgewater) to Ashton, where it joined

Figure 24   Rennie's aqueduct over the Lune on the Lancaster Canal

the Huddersfield, also narrow, that once again climbed over the Pennines into Yorkshire, this time by way of the great Standedge tunnel, the longest tunnel (then 5,456yd, now 5,698yd) at the highest point (637ft) of any artificial waterway in Britain. It ended at Huddersfield, where it was connected to the Calder & Hebble Navigation by the small but vital privately owned canal known as Sir John Ramsden's or the Huddersfield Broad Canal. It also connected at Dukinfield with the Peak Forest Canal that passed over the great Marple aqueduct, and then climbed the valley of the Goyt to Whaley Bridge, where it joined the Cromford & High Peak Railway, which ran across the high lands to the Cromford Canal. This railway with its many inclined planes had been envisaged as part of a through canal-rail line from London via Leicester and the Cromford Canal to Manchester, but it never became so, though it served by its threat of competition to keep rates down between the Trent and Manchester on the competing Trent & Mersey and Macclesfield Canal routes. Near Whaley Bridge was another terminus of the Peak Forest Canal at Bugsworth (now Buxworth), whence a tramroad owned by the canal company ran up to limestone quarries beyond Chapel-en-le-Frith.

Although the Leeds & Liverpool had been the first begun of the three Pennine canals, and though it was first over the summit, it was the last to be completed, in 1816. The Rochdale Canal provided the first through connection when it opened in 1804, followed by the Huddersfield in 1811 after the long struggle to complete its great tunnel at Standedge. Of the three, the Rochdale was the greatest carrier of trans-Pennine traffic. The Leeds and Liverpool flourished more on highly developed local traffic on each side of its summit, while the Huddersfield's traffic was far less than either.

Figure 25   Jessop's Rochdale Canal climbs over the Pennines

North out of Manchester ran the Manchester, Bolton & Bury, west the Bridgewater Canal to Runcorn for Liverpool, north-west the Worsley branch that was now connected to the Leeds & Liverpool by the Leigh branch of that canal, while to Liverpool there was also available the old but efficient river route of the Mersey & Irwell Navigation. The Rochdale was connected to the Bridgewater Canal, but not to the Mersey & Irwell Navigation, and towards the end of

the canal period a new waterway, the Manchester & Salford Junction, was built to make the junction. From Marple on the Peak Forest was to run the Macclesfield Canal, not then built, down past that town to join the Trent & Mersey to the west of Harecastle tunnel, and to shorten the distance between points on that canal and Manchester at the cost of additional lockage.

Though rivers played a small part in the waterway system of Lancashire, in Yorkshire they were the basis of the network, canals or river cuts being used to improve the river navigations. The base line lay west to east. From Leeds ran one branch of the Aire & Calder Navigation, and from Wakefield another; they joined at Castleford, and then used the Aire and the Selby Canal to reach the Yorkshire Ouse at Selby, whence there was access to the Humber and Hull. This old but flourishing navigation had not yet been rebuilt, nor a new canal yet cut from Ferrybridge to Goole. From Selby there was access up the Ouse to York and on suitable tides up the Wharfe to Tadcaster. Beyond York lay the Linton Lock Navigation and then, on its continuation the Ure, the Ripon Canal terminating at that city. North of the Humber estuary, the navigable River Hull led to Beverley, Leven and Driffield, all on branch canals.

To the south, the Stainforth & Keadby Canal ran from the Trent at Keadby into the busy River Don, passing by Doncaster and Rotherham to Tinsley, whence a canal climbing to Sheffield was opened in 1819. The older route for Don traffic by the Dutch River to Goole and the Ouse was now little used, most going instead by Keadby. From Swinton on the Don, the Dearne & Dove Canal ran past coal- and iron-carrying branches to Elsecar and Worsbrough to a stop-lock junction with the Barnsley Canal, coming down from the Silkstone coalfield on its way to the Calder at Wakefield. On the Trent there was access by Stockwith to the Chesterfield Canal, and at Torksey passage might be made from the Trent through the Fossdyke to the Witham Navigation and so to the Wash at Boston.

A third group to be considered were those canals cut especially to carry coal or iron to the nearest artery or to the sea. These waterways usually had no town at their inmost end, but terminated at an ironworks or a colliery. Their construction made a great contribution to the output of the two raw materials upon which the Industrial Revolution leant more and more heavily as it progressed into the nineteenth century. Isolated examples, such as the Monkland near Glasgow and the Somersetshire Coal Canal that connected with the Kennet & Avon not far from Bath, were constructed in many parts of the country, but there were in addition three notable groups: the Welsh canals, the Derbyshire group and the Shropshire group.

A few small private canals existed in Wales before 1790, but the important canals of South Wales were all built in the few years after that date to transport coal, limestone, copper ore and other industrial raw materials up and down the valleys, and to carry away iron and industrial products to the ports. The Swansea Canal from above Ystradgynlais to Swansea, the Neath from Glynneath to Neath and on to Giant's Grave, the Glamorganshire from Merthyr Tydfil to Cardiff, the Monmouthshire with its two branches, one from Crumlin and one from above Pontypool to Newport, the Brecknock & Abergavenny from the mines and ironworks near Gilwern to Brecon, were all open by 1800.

After 1800 three important additions were made to the existing Welsh canals: the Brecknock & Abergavenny was joined in 1812 to the Monmouthshire Canal at Pontymoile: the Aberdare Canal was completed in 1812 from near that town to join the Glamorganshire; and the Tennant Canal, the biggest private canal made except for the Duke of Bridgewater's, was finished.

The Tennant enterprise grew remarkably. It began as a small private canal that Edward Elton had built from a colliery at Glan-y-wern to the River Neath at Redjacket, and opened in 1790. It was taken over in 1818 by George Tennant, and part of it used to make a canal joining the River Tawe below Swansea to the River Neath at Redjacket, and intended to offer coal coming down the Neath Canal a better shipping place on the Tawe than it had at Giant's Grave. It did not serve the purpose. Tennant then extended it upwards past Neath Abbey and Neath itself to join the Neath Canal at Aberdulais, and at the Swansea end built new wharves at what was now called Port Tennant. This was the canal whose opening Elizabeth Davies so eloquently commemorated in her verses.* It was completed in 1824.

There was one other canal which intended importance but failed to achieve it, the Kidwelly & Llanelly, with a line to Pembrey New Harbour or Burry Port, and another up the Gwendraeth valley to Cwmmawr, with three inclined planes built by James Green, only two of which were brought into use.

The main valley canals, the Swansea, Neath, Glamorganshire and Monmouthshire, were heavily locked: the Swansea fell 213ft by 36 locks in 16 miles, the Neath 157ft by 19 locks in 13 miles, the Glamorganshire 542ft by 50 locks in 25 miles, and the Monmouthshire 337ft by 31 locks in 9 miles from its Pontymoile branch that connected with the Brecknock & Abergavenny Canal, and practically all loaded traffic was one way. There was less difficulty with water supply, however, and almost no tunnelling.

* See pp 51–2.

Page 165, Plate V (above) Anderton vertical lift connecting the Weaver with the Trent & Mersey Canal, before reconstruction in 1908. On each side are salt shoots; (below) Falkirk tunnel on the Edinburgh & Glasgow Union Canal

Page 166, Plate VI (*above*) Hazards of a trip on the Paddington packet boat on the Grand
Junction Canal; (*below*) road, canal and railway near Hebden Bridge on the Rochdale Canal in
1845

These canals and the smaller private waterways that joined them, served by a network of horse tramroads, were profitable to their proprietors as well as being of great industrial value and the foundation of their respective ports. Before they were built, the products of the South Wales iron industry had been carried on horseback or muleback over the mountains to points where they could be loaded into waggons to be taken to the ports. How the waterways made possible the growth of the industry can be seen from the following figures of iron carried on two of the canals:

Year	Glamorganshire tons	Monmouthshire tons
1807	—	23,019
1817	39,497	43,407
1827	84,946	91,618
1837	124,810	144,277

Before the Glamorganshire was completed in 1798, Cardiff had a population of about one thousand. By 1841 its population was more than ten thousand, and its exports had increased many times. Representative figures for iron have been given: those for coal are:

Year	Glamorganshire tons	Monmouthshire tons
1819	34,606	—
1829	83,729	471,675
1839	211,214	484,993

Secondly, there were a group of canals in the Erewash valley, running north from the Trent near Nottingham. These comprised the Erewash Canal and its continuation the Cromford, with the Nutbrook as a tributary of the Erewash. From this central line offshoots led on the one side to Nottingham (the Nottingham Canal) and on the other to Derby (the Derby Canal), so that the coal, iron, limestone, paving-stones and other goods coming down the main line could be diverted to either of these towns or to places beyond them on other connecting navigations, or could pass into the Trent to go down river as far as Gainsborough (for shipping by sea) and Torksey (for Lincoln), or across it into the Loughborough Navigation and so to Leicester and the south. In 1808, 269,456 tons of coal were carried on the Cromford, Erewash and Nottingham Canals and this figure grew steadily till railway times.

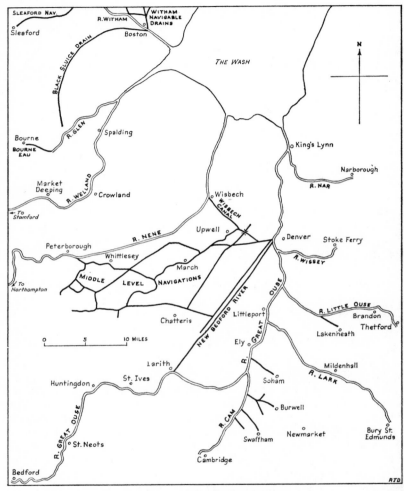

Map 13   The Fenland waterways

The third group comprised the Shropshire tub-boat canals. The Shropshire coalfield was, as we saw, one of the first to use river transport. Iron had been smelted in the district with charcoal since at least the first half of the seventeenth century, but when Abraham Darby first learned to smelt iron with coke at Coalbrookdale, he laid the foundation of a tight little industrial pocket of collieries and iron-works. The country was so hilly, however, that to build ordinary canals was out of the question. William Reynolds of Ketley, one of the works in the Coalbrookdale group, provided the answer when he introduced the inclined plane at Ketley.

The earliest canal in the area, the Donnington Wood (or Duke of Sutherland's Tub-boat) Canal, had been built about 1765 from col-lieries at Donnington Wood to Pave Lane near Newport by Earl Gower, the Duke of Bridgewater's brother-in-law, and the two Gilberts, Thomas and John. But William Reynolds's little Ketley Canal led to the formation of the Shropshire Canal Company to build 8 miles of canal from the Donnington Wood Canal past the Ketley Canal to the Severn at Coalport, with a branch to Coalbrookdale, and three inclined planes. This canal carried the industrial output of the area to the river where it was transferred to river craft. Later, the Shrewsbury Canal was built to carry coal more easily from Donning-ton to Shrewsbury. It also had an inclined plane, at Trench. Lastly, a plane was built on a branch of the Donnington Wood Canal which had previously had a vertical lift for the cargo, though not for the boats.

These canals were small in size, and cheap to construct. Their little tub-boats holding 5–8 tons each were navigated in trains between the planes, and the cost of operation was low. It was not until 1835 that this self-contained tub-boat system was connected to the main canal network by means of the Newport branch of the Birmingham & Liverpool Junction. The Shrewsbury Canal was then converted for narrow boat use, though only for those even narrower than usual. Cargoes from the rest of the system had to be transhipped to the narrow boats at Trench wharf below the plane there.

It would be fascinating to the student to trace out in detail the new patterns of trade that this wide and interlacing system of rivers and canals brought about, but it would demand of the reader more know-ledge of economic history, and more interest in it, than can reason-ably be asked of him in a book that is not written for specialists. Let us give a glance to the coal trade, however, in order to get some idea of what happened in some way to every raw material and finished commodity, and of the repercussions upon the manufacturers, their men, and the towns in which their work was done.

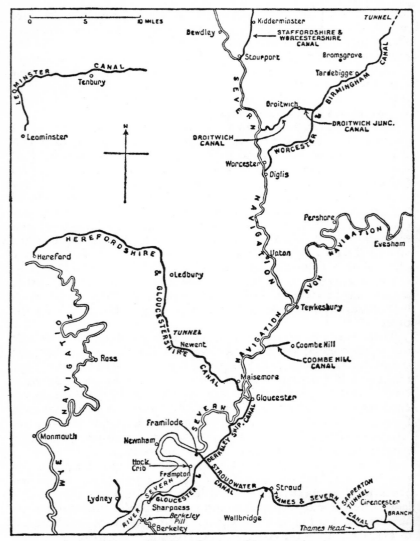

Map 14   The River Severn and its connections

Before the canals, coal went by sea from the north-east coast to those towns accessible to the little coasting vessels. This sea-coal came up the Thames to London, and up the many rivers of the east coast into the heart of Yorkshire, Lincolnshire and East Anglia. Land coal was supplied by road transport only in the neighbourhood of the collieries, for its cost of carriage rose steeply as the distance increased, whether in waggons or on horseback. Only where there was a river to help the distribution, as the Severn helped that of Shropshire, did land coal go far afield. There were therefore parts of the country that found it difficult to get coal at all, except at a prohibitive price.

The motive of cheap coal was a great one in the history of canal development and, after the waterways were built, land coal or sea coal was transported by water everywhere south of Lancashire or Yorkshire, except to parts of North Wales. Yorkshire coal went east by the Aire & Calder or the Don, till it met the sea coal in from the Humber, though Yorkshire coal also went south along the coast. Wigan coal also crossed the Pennines, as well as going south to Liverpool and west on its old route down the Douglas Navigation on its way to Ireland. Welsh coal came down the valleys by canal, and was then shipped to Bristol and the South-west; Forest of Dean coal went to Gloucester and Cheltenham, and through the Thames & Severn as far east as Oxford; Somerset coal by way of the Kennet & Avon and the Wilts & Berks also moved east till at Reading it met the sea coal coming up the Thames, or at Abingdon or Oxford Leicestershire or Warwickshire coal from the Oxford Canal. Within the midlands the coal of that area competed freely, Leicestershire mainly against Derbyshire, Staffordshire against Warwickshire, and pressed down the Grand Junction towards London. By main canals or branches from them, such country places as Buckingham, Newport Pagnell, Oakham and Ledbury found themselves supplied with fuel for domestic and industrial use, while the great manufacturing towns had a constant supply, not dependent upon the output of a single colliery, and at a cheaper price, which naturally drew coal-using industries to the canal side.

In Ireland, the Grand Canal from Dublin to the Shannon had been opened in 1805, the Barrow navigation to St Mullins fifteen years before. The Royal from Dublin to the upper Shannon was almost finished as the war ended. To the north, the first canal to Lough Neagh, the Newry, had been supplemented by a second, the Lagan from Belfast, completed in 1794. From the lough the $4\frac{3}{8}$ mile long Coalisland Canal had been built from the Blackwater river, though by 1787, when it had opened, the earlier Ducart's tub-boat canal with its three primitive inclines had closed. On the north coast, the Strabane Canal, 4 miles long from that town to the River Foyle, had been opened in 1796.

In Scotland, coal from the Monkland or the Forth & Clyde went by boat to Glasgow and then by ship from Bowling or Grangemouth up and down the coast: before long it would be going by canal to Edinburgh also.

Such was the canal system at the end of the Napoleonic Wars. Peace brought a slump; both men and horses that had been employed in purposes of war returned to the works of peace, and helped to compete with the navigations by taking to transport over the improved roads of the time. Henceforward road transport was a serious competitor for the trade in merchandise and groceries which, while small in volume compared with that in raw materials, earned high tolls and was the support of the fly-boats. Prices fell as unemployment rose. The years from 1815, when Waterloo brought peace at last, to 1822 when the coming boom made men willing to venture capital, were times when little was done to expand the canal system, and when competition for the existing business was keen. In 1822 the Basingstoke committee wrote:

'As an instance of the extreme to which the competition among Waggon-masters has been carried, the Committee beg leave to state that one hundred weight of goods is conveyed from London to Farnham by land, for one shilling and sixpence, which by the Canal, the same quantity must cost one shilling and threepence, and where the difference is so slight, it may be readily imagined the land carriage will be preferred, for its rapidity.

'In ordinary times, the expense of conveyance on land was about three times as much as by water. . . .'[2]

Of the biggest projects of this period, the Aire & Calder's Ferrybridge and Goole Canal will be described in Chapter X. The Edinburgh & Glasgow Union was authorised in 1817 with a capital of £290,000 to connect Edinburgh with the Forth & Clyde Canal near Falkirk by a line 30 miles long, all on one level except for the flight of locks that brought the canal down 110ft to the Forth & Clyde. This project, however, only fell into the post-war period by accident. It had first been reported on in 1793, and from that time, with a pause during the mid-period of the war, pamphlets for or against one or another suggested course for it had poured out.

A second was the Portsmouth & Arundel, the unluckiest of all canals. In 1813 an Act had been obtained for the Wey & Arun Junction, by means of which goods could be brought from London up the Thames to Weybridge, through the Wey river and the Wey & Arun

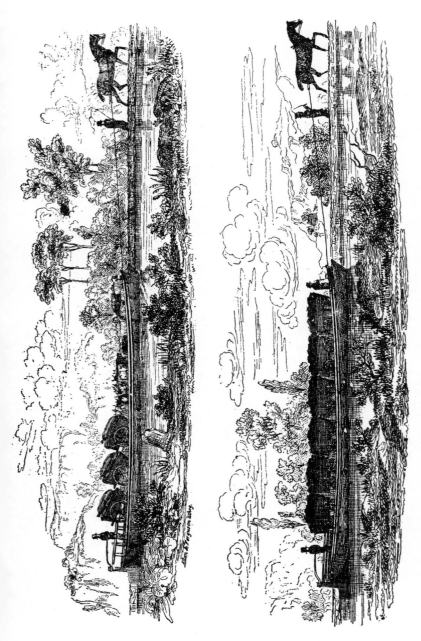

Figure 27 Forth & Clyde Canal (*above*) a boat to carry loaded carts; (*below*) one to carry loaded tramroad waggons

Junction Canal to the River Arun, by which they could be taken to
Arundel and Littlehampton. It was probably because this new means
of communication with London was coming into existence that the
Portsmouth & Arundel was planned to connect those towns, and
so give a through water communication with London. It was proposed to make a canal from Ford on the Arun to Chichester harbour.
Thence a channel was to be dredged round Thorney and Hayling
islands and across Langstone harbour to Portsea Island. Thence a
canal was to be cut across the peninsula to Portsmouth.

Before the canal was finished an agreement for tolls on traffic
worked through the Portsmouth & Arundel, the Arun, and the Wey
& Arun Junction, was made, and this last canal altered its waterway
so that the same barges could be used for the through passage. The
Portsmouth section of the canal was opened in September 1822, and
the whole canal in May 1823. A certain amount of through traffic
resulted, but on 3 December 1824 an indignant meeting at the Beneficial Society's Hall in Portsmouth called attention to the fact that
sea-water from the canal on the island was getting into the springs
and wells from which the people who lived near the waterway got
their drinking water. Three weeks later the proprietors at their meeting stated that compensation had been given in certain cases, and
others were being considered, but that the company 'were not to be
dictated to by any set of individuals, however respectable'.

The company survived, and made efforts to build up the through
trade, which, however, languished and died. So did the Portsmouth
& Arundel Canal. The Portsea portion had hardly been used at all,
and about 1855 the rest of the canal followed it, except for the short
branch from Chichester to Chichester harbour, which had been built
on a larger scale. The company was finally wound up under an order
of 1888.

The third of the new projects was the Bude Canal. Authorised in
1819, it was planned to run from Bude on the north coast of Cornwall
to Thornbury, with a branch to Launceston, and various other
branches, with a total length of almost forty-six miles. The intention
of the promoters was to build a tub-boat canal to carry sea-sand into
the interior, to be used as a fertiliser. It was therefore planned on the
model of the Shropshire Canal, without locks except on the entrance
section, and with six inclined planes, the biggest of which, at Hobbacott Down, was 225ft high and 907ft long. The boats, to carry some
4 tons each, had wheels permanently fixed beneath them, in order
that they could run directly on to the rails of the inclined planes.
Because coal was expensive in Cornwall, the planes were worked
hydraulically, five by water-wheel, and that at Hobbacott Down by

the bucket-in-the-well system, supplemented by a steam engine on the numerous occasions when one of the bucket-chains broke.

By 1826 35 miles of the canal had been built at a cost of about £118,000. It carried some 50,000 tons of sea-sand a year for many years, but not until much later did it declare a dividend for its shareholders. It was finally all closed in 1891 except for a length at Bude, after which the Bude–Stratton Urban District Council took over the reservoir at Tamar Lake and part of the canal as a means of water supply. One of its wheeled tub-boats is in the Exeter Maritime Museum.

During the prosperity of 1824 three ship canal projects were before the public. The proposal for an English & Bristol Channels Ship Canal was sufficiently well thought of to obtain an Act of Parliament, but went no further; that for a waterway from the estuary of the Dee to Manchester was speculative and not solidly supported. It was, however, the ancestor of the Manchester Ship Canal, and is referred to in the story of that enterprise. The most ambitious scheme of all, for a ship canal from London to Portsmouth on a far bigger scale than the existing waterway, and with a capital of £5 millions, never seriously caught the public imagination, and was overwhelmed by the succeeding slump. A fourth scheme which fell into this period, the Norwich & Lowestoft Ship Canal, was in fact a plan of river development, and is described in the following chapter.

In 1825 the first public railway to be successfully operated by locomotive engines was opened between Stockton and Darlington. Originally a canal had been projected, but the proposal had then been changed to a railway. As we have seen, horse railways and tramroads were not a new idea. Starting as coal lines to feed the Tyne and the Severn, they had been extensively constructed to feed canals. Later, in the 1820s, more ambitious lines were planned and built, notably the 33 mile long Cromford & High Peak Railway which was authorised in 1825 (after the Stockton & Darlington was open) as a horse-operated line, and opened in 1831, and the Stratford & Moreton, completed in 1826 as a branch of the Stratford-upon-Avon Canal, while extensive mineral lines such as the Sirhowy had existed for many years in the Welsh coal and iron districts.

In all, some two dozen railways had been authorised by special Act of Parliament before 1824, as well as the many lines sanctioned in canal Acts or built privately. In the years 1824 and 1825, however, there was a tremendous outburst of speculative activity in railways, usually for locomotive routes; in those years most of the great lines of the next decade, such as the Great Western and the London &

Birmingham, were first projected. In all, proposals for some sixty railways in the British Isles were put forward at this time, and a number were authorised by Act of Parliament. A second outburst followed in 1830.

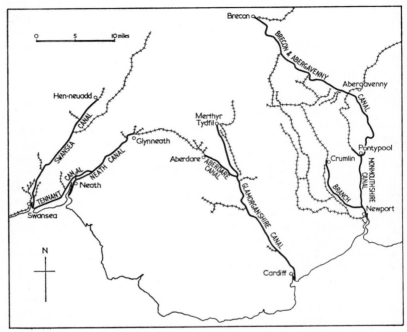

Map 15   The Welsh canals and their tramroad feeders

The use of locomotives on the Stockton & Darlington marks for us the virtual beginning of railway history. To contemporaries, however, this was an interesting development that increased the utility of railways, but did not alter the general view of the public, that railways were essentially feeders to waterways, useful in hilly country where the making of canals was impossibly expensive, or over country where the expected traffic was light. Later public opinion was to swing to the opposite extreme, that waterways had no longer any part to play in the future of transport. Such a state of things justified the prevision of the old Duke of Bridgewater when he alledgedly said of canals: 'They will last my time, but I see mischief in those damned tramroads.'

The extension of the railway idea, and the faster operation of railways that followed the introduction of locomotives, was one cause of an increase in the efficiency and enterprise of the waterways.

A symptom of this was an effort at improvement. The Harecastle tunnel on the Trent & Mersey Canal was doubled in 1827, the new

Figure 28   The two Harecastle tunnels: Telford's on the left, Brindley's original bore on the right

tunnel, 16ft high and 14ft wide, having taken only three years to build, whereas the first tunnel, 12ft high and 9¼ft wide, had taken eleven years, so greatly had engineering technique improved in the meantime. In other cases, the distance between two points was lessened, in order to save time and wages now that competition fiercer than that between water and road transport was dawning. It is noticeable that whereas the early canals carried out Brindley's principle of following as far as possible the contour of the ground, and sacrificed shortness to ease and cheapness of construction and to water conservation owing to the absence of locks, the later ones, such as the Birmingham & Liverpool Junction, were made as straight as possible, even at the expense of considerable cutting and embanking to maintain the level. A notable example of the straightening of a contour canal was the Oxford, which between 1829 and 1834 was shortened from 91 to 77½ miles.

The Birmingham & Liverpool Junction (now the Shropshire

Union main line) was a 'modern' narrow canal. Authorised in 1826 and opened in 1835, engineered by Telford and Cubitt, it was intended to shorten the distance between Ellesmere Port on the Mersey and Birmingham and to provide a waterway less obstructed by tunnels and locks. It was expensive to build, for it completely deserted the contours, and drove across country from the end of the old Chester Canal at Nantwich on embankments and through cuttings to a junction with the Staffs & Worcs at Autherley. After using half a mile of that canal, boats from Ellesmere Port passed into the Birmingham Canal, which itself had been recently reconstructed by Telford.

Efforts were then made to extend the new model right through to London, by building a canal from a point on the Stratford-upon-Avon accessible from Birmingham to Highgate with a minimum of lockage. But by 1835 when the Birmingham & Liverpool Junction was opened and the extension was being advocated, it was no longer possible to raise large sums to build new canals. Railways were the thing. Even the more modest Central Union proposal, to improve the London–Birmingham route by a cut from the Worcester & Birmingham to the Warwick & Birmingham, and another from that canal to the Coventry, was not seriously supported, though it would have reduced the number of locks between Birmingham and Braunston from 54 to 17 by avoiding the heavy lockage down to and up from the Avon valley at Warwick.

In Ireland, too, a great through canal line was thought of, to link Belfast and Newry with the Shannon. Connected as these cities already were with Lough Neagh, the new line required a canal from the Blackwater river at the far side of the lough to the River Finn giving upon upper Lough Erne, and another from that lough to the Shannon at Leitrim above Carrick-on-Shannon.

In 1825 the Ulster Canal Company was empowered to build the first of these links, from the Blackwater to the Finn. Much of the money was found not by shareholders but by the Exchequer Bill Loan Commissioners, whose engineer, Telford, worked with John Killaly on construction. Between them they made the serious mistake of building the locks to take craft of the same length as those on the Newry or the Lagan canals, but 3ft narrower, 11ft 6in against 14ft 6in. Therefore only specially built craft could navigate it. Finished in 1841 at a cost of £231,000, over half of it public money, 45⅝ miles long with 26 locks, the Ulster was hardly being used twenty years later.

Meanwhile the second link in the through route, the Ballinamore & Ballyconnell Canal from upper Lough Erne to the Shannon, stimulated by the completion of the Ulster but with the additional aim of improving drainage, was begun in 1846. This time with 16 locks taking craft 82ft by 16ft 6in, the new canal was built by the Board of Works and opened in 1858, the navigation works having cost some £229,000. Traffic was negligible, but nevertheless the Board, now also the owners of the Ulster, closed that canal in 1865 and spent £22,000 on improving it, though without widening the locks. It was reopened in 1873, by which time the Ballinamore & Ballyconnell in turn was almost impassable. The through line was therefore never achieved in practice. If it had been, it is improbable that much traffic would have appeared on such an unlikely route.

There had also been a change in Irish waterway organisation. The Directors-General of Inland Navigation, who on the whole had done well, were replaced in 1831 by a new Board of Public Works to oversee all government works. In 1839, however, the Shannon was given its own commissioners, though in 1852 the navigation reverted to the Board, who still have charge of it.

We must now return to the period just before the railway age. It was at this time that the running of fly-boats became important, though from the early days of canals a certain number of these express boats, running to a timetable, using relays of horses and double crews, carrying merchandise and parcels, setting down and picking up at wharves along the line with priority over all other traffic and permission to work all through the night had been run. They were usually light boats, carrying less cargo than their slower brethren. These rules adopted by the Kennet & Avon Canal in 1840 for the operation of fly-boats will show the conditions under which they worked, and the surprisingly good service they gave:

'The following Resolutions relative to the passage of Fly Boats from Bath to Reading and vice versa are recommended for adoption:

'1st. That Boats not exceeding 15 Tons Tonnage will be allowed to trade on the Canal between Reading and Bath.

'2nd. No Boat will be allowed to pass with the construction of which the Engineer shall not be satisfied.

'3rd. Each single Boat shall be charged 3£ per day. When two Boats shall pass together each Boat will be charged £2-15-0 only.

'4th. In case there shall be more than 15 Tons in one Boat, the same shall be liable to all the Charges and penalties imposed by the Company for false entries.

'5th. In consideration of and to participate in the above terms, the parties must engage to start one Boat at least every day from Bath and from Reading whether having a complete Cargo or not, to deliver goods from Bristol to London and Vice Versa in 36 hours,* unavoid-

* This means 36 hours from Bath to Reading, not for the whole distance from Bristol to London.

able stoppages excepted, the Boats to have every facility granted for their passage.'[3]

At the same time as an increased use of fly-boats, experiments were tried with such craft as the boats for carrying loaded carts and loaded tramroad waggons that were put on the Forth & Clyde Canal in order to save transhipment costs.

It was during this period also that passenger-carrying on canals reached its peak. Few nowadays know that passenger services were ever run on British canals, until the modern trip and hotel boats revived for pleasure travel what had once been provided as an ordinary means of transport. Yet it had been a common practice even on the old river navigations—for instance, the River Wey Act of 1651 laid down a maximum fare for passengers from Guildford to London. Soon after canals were first built passengers were carried on them, and this business grew until in the 1820s and 1830s it became very large on certain waterways. In 1773 Josiah Wedgwood wrote:

'From Warrington to Manchester the Duke has set up two passage boats, one carries passengers at a shilling each. The other is divided into three rooms, & the rates are 2/6 p head for the best room, 10d., and 12d., and it is the pleasantest and cheapest mode of travelling you can conceive . . .'[4]

while a year later the Leeds & Liverpool Canal Company enacted:

'That every person passing in any boat between Wigan and Liverpool, or any other part of the line, shall pay for every two miles or under, one half-penny; each passenger to be allowed fourteen pounds weight of luggage; and in case any boatman shall neglect to give a just account of the number of passengers he shall at any time carry on his boat, with the distance each passenger shall have passed, he shall forfeit the sum of ten shillings.'[5]

Again, in 1783, the Forth & Clyde Company put on their canal two track boats that carried both goods and passengers, which were described a few years later by a local poet, James Maxwell:

'For here a cabin in each end is found,
 That doth with all conveniences abound.
 One in the head, for ladies nine or ten,
 Another in the stern, for gentlemen,
 With fires and tables, seats to sit at ease;
 They may regale themselves with what they please.
 For all utensils here are at command,
 To eat and drink whate'er they have at hand.'[6]

In Scotland passenger-carrying reached a high degree of efficiency.
On the Forth & Clyde itself, and later on the Edinburgh & Glasgow
Union that connected with it, regular services were provided both
by the company's own boats and by others, though in England the

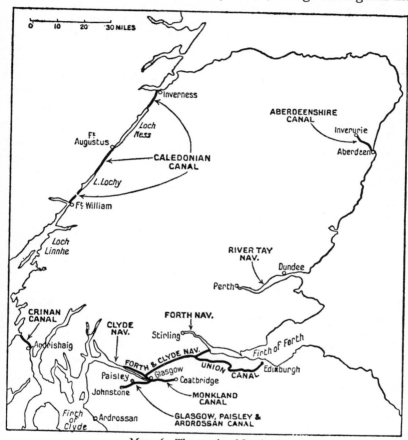

Map 16   The canals of Scotland

usual practice was to allow private carriers to operate passenger
services, the canal company merely taking tolls.

These mixed Forth & Clyde boats carried about 5,000 passengers
a year, and encouraged the company to put on a daily service for
passengers only in 1809. Each boat had cabin and steerage accommodation, the cabin being provided with newspapers, books and

games. Meals and drinks were also obtainable on board. These boats did the 25 miles between Glasgow and Lock 16 (Falkirk) in 5½ hours, later reduced to 3 hours. They were pulled by two horses, the second ridden, which were changed every 2 miles at the stables still to be seen alongside the canal, but now converted to houses.

Passengers found the boats cleaner and more comfortable than the stage coaches, and the numbers carried on the Forth & Clyde Canal rose from 44,000 in 1812 to nearly 200,000 in 1836. In 1831 sleepers were put on between Glasgow and Edinburgh which made the journey of 56 miles in under 11 hours, and a handbill of 1841 shows that four passenger boats a day were then leaving Glasgow, with through bookings by canal or canal and coach together to Edinburgh, Stirling, Alloa, Falkirk, Perth and Kirkaldy.

The achievement of the Glasgow, Paisley & Ardrossan Canal is even more striking. This narrow waterway had originally been planned to run from Glasgow through Paisley to the sea at Ardrossan, and it obtained its Act in 1806. Funds ran out when it had reached Johnstone beyond Paisley in 1811, and eventually it was completed by a railway.

Before 1830 the passengers carried on it between Paisley and Glasgow, a distance of 8 miles, did not exceed 30,000 a year. William Houston, who had money in the company, determined to build up the traffic, by the use of fast light boats of special design carrying 80–90 passengers, and by charging about ¾d a mile. The boats were built of thin iron sheets, with fabric cabin covering over supports. They were some 70ft long, 6ft wide, weighed only 33cwt and drew 19¼in when fully loaded. He had the following results:

Year ending 30 Sept	Passengers carried	No of boats each day each way
1831	79,455	4
1832	148,516	7
1833	240,062	9
1834	307,275	12
1835	373,290	12

In this last year Houston cut his fares for the 8 miles from 9d to 6d cabin and from 6d to 4d steerage, and still further increased his trade, until his long white boats and scarlet-jacketed postilions became well known. Other canal companies heard of William Houston's boats and ordered similar ones, or bought them second-hand: we find them on the Don, the Lancaster and Carlisle canals, the Bridgewater, the Grand Canal of Ireland, and even the Kennet & Avon.

Page 183, Plate VII (*above*) A sailing keel on the Sheffield & South Yorkshire Navigation near Doncaster in 1936; (*below*) steam on the New Junction Canal in 1932

Page 184, Plate VIII (above) Steam packets at Northwich on the Weaver Navigation in 1957; (below) a train of empty compartment boats at Castleford. Note the false bow in front of the tug as the train is running empty, and the way the leading boat has been cocked up to lessen drag

A writer of 1835 says of these Scottish canals:

'If any one had stated five years ago, that by improvements, in the build of Canal Passage Boats, a speed of ten miles per hour would be regularly maintained on Canal routes; and that the charges to passengers, carried at this speed, would be the same as at the previous slow speed, of four or five miles per hour; that in one small district of Scotland alone, distances amounting in all to nine hundred miles each day . . . should be performed by these improved light Boats at the above speed . . . the assertion would have been received with unlimited ridicule. Yet such is now the case.'[7]

When railway competition came, prices were cut, until both canal and railway were carrying passengers from Paisley to Glasgow for 2d. Then, in 1843, the canal company gave up passenger and parcel carrying in return for an annual payment, and its horses and boats were sold.

In England there are records of passenger carrying on many canals. The Lancaster Canal, for instance, in 1802 was advertising trips from Lancaster to Preston, saying:

'. . . for safety, economy and comfort no other mode of conveyance could be so eligible; for there the timid might be at ease and the most delicate mind without fear.'[8]

A daily service between Kendal and Preston was operated from 1820 with boats that covered the 57 miles in 14 hours, tea, coffee and refreshments being served on board. In 1833 an express boat was introduced to compete with the stage coaches, which cut the time from Kendal to Preston to 7¼ hours. In the first 6 months 14,000 passengers were carried. Passenger boats did not finally leave the canal until 1846.

Regular services were operated on such waterways as the Bridgewater, Mersey & Irwell, Leeds & Liverpool, Aire & Calder and Yorkshire Ouse; for shorter periods on the Birmingham, the Chester, the Ellesmere and the Grand Junction, while on others market boats were run, as on the Gloucester & Berkeley and the Derby Canal, upon which:

'. . . a market-boat, decked over, with seats, and a fire-place, for the accommodation of passengers, starts from Swarkestone every Friday morning, to carry market-people to Derby, at 6d. each; which again leaves Derby at 4 o'clock for Swarkestone.'[9]

The oddest collection of passengers was perhaps that reported in the *Derby Mercury* for 19 April 1826: 'On Saturday last arrived in this town by canal, a fine Lama, a Kangaroo, a Ram with four horns, and a female Goat with two young kids, remarkably handsome animals, as a present from Lord Byron to a Gentleman whose residence is in

Figure 20 Forth & Clyde Canal: (above) a night mixed goods and passenger boat; (below) a swift passenger boat

this neighbourhood, all of which had been picked up in the course of the voyage of the *Blonde* to the Sandwich Islands in the autumn of 1824.'

In Ireland, the Grand Canal Company maintained long-lived pas-

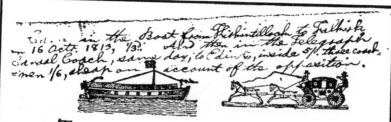

Cd . . . in the Boat from Rithintilloch to Fulkirk on 16 Octr. 1813, 1/3. And then in the Telegraph Canal Coach, same day, to Edinr., inside 5/. three coach-=men 1/6, cheap on account of its opposition.

THE FORTH and CLYDE CANAL BASKET COACH and PASSAGE BOAT, the Cheapest, Safest, and most Comfortable Travelling of any Conveyance between Edinburgh and Glasgow.

In consequence of opposition and reduction of Fares (by which the Public will be benefited) the FORTH and CLYDE CANAL COACH COMPANY have resolved to *reduce the Fares* of this so justly favourite Coach, as low as any other on the Road—have, therefore, in the mean time, fixed the Fares as under :—

Insides, Edinburgh, to the Boat...........................7s.	}	*Fares by the Boat.*	
Basket, as good as Inside.:..................................6s.	}	Best Cabin......4s.	
Outside, or Top...4s.	}	Second Cabin...2s.	

Making this Conveyance between Edinburgh and Glasgow only half the Expence of any other.

On MONDAY the 11th instant, a NEW COACH will start from Stirling at Twelve o'Clock, for the Conveyance of Passengers to Glasgow by the Boat, and Edinburgh by the Forth and Clyde Canal Coach, and from Edinburgh and Glasgow to Stirling, by the same Conveyance.

The Forth and Clyde Canal Coach leaves M·GIE's, No. 5, Shakespeare Square, and LECKIE's, No. 2, Prince's Street, Edinburgh, every lawful Morning, at Half-past Eight o'Clock, where Tickets are to be had ; and at the Duty House, opposite the Register Office; at the End of the North Bridge; also; at Mr BELL's Coach Office, opposite the Tron Church, High Street. And in Glasgow, at the Forth and Clyde Canal Passage Boat and Coach Office, No. 635, Argyll Street; or at Mr ROBERTSON's, Commercial Inn, near the Tontine; and of Mr STEWART, the Master of the Charlotte Passage Boat, who sells Tickets for this Coach only, and from whom the Passengers receive the utmost civility and attention. The Boat that takes the Passengers for Edinburgh, leaves Port-Dundas at Eight o'Clock every lawful Morning.

October 3d, 1813.

Printed by W. TAIT, Journal Office, G.... . :

Ր-Ձ-Ѡ

Figure 30   A through boat and coach service between Edinburgh and Glasgow

senger services between Dublin and the Shannon, later Ballinasloe, and to the Barrow, and enterprisingly built fine hotels also, though these proved less successful than the boats. First put on in 1780 between Dublin and Sallins, packet-boat services were extended and then curtailed, until they ended with the year 1852. The importance

given to packet-boats shows in this rule for lock-keepers made by the
Royal Canal Company in 1813:

'If a Lock-Keeper has not his Upper-Chamber full, and his Gates
open to receive the Packet-Boat the moment she arrives on her

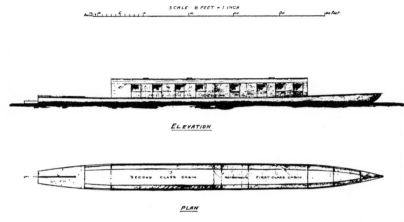

Figure 31   A passenger boat on the Lancaster Canal, of the light type first introduced
on the Glasgow, Paisley & Ardrossan Canal

Passage to Dublin, he shall be liable to a Fine of Two Shillings & Six
Pence.'

Here is a description of Irish canal travelling from one of Charles
Lever's novels:

'Little, does he know, who voyages in a canal boat, dragged along
some three miles and a half per hour, ignominiously at the tails of
two ambling hackneys, what pride, pomp, and circumstances, await
him at the first town he enters . . . suddenly the loud bray of the
horn breaks upon his ears—the sound is re-echoed from a distance—
the far-off tinkle of a bell is borne along the water, and he sees before
him, as if conjured up by some magician's wand, the roofs and
chimneys of a little village. Meanwhile, the excitement about him
increases; the deck is lumbered with hampers and boxes, and parcels—
the note of departure to many a cloaked and freize-coated passenger
has rung . . . the large brass bell at the stern of the boat is thundering
away with its clanging sound; the banks are crowded with people;
and as if to favour the melo-dramatic magic of the scene, the track-
rope is cast off, the weary posters trot away towards their stable, and
the stately barge floats on, to its destined haven, without the aid of
any visible influence.'[10]

GRAND CANAL.

Cheap Travelling,

Between DUBLIN and ATHLONE, by TULLAMORE,

Commencing on Friday, the 15th day of November, 1811.

FARE.

Boat, between Dublin and Tullamore, 45 Miles.			Coach, between Tullamore and Athlone, 19 Miles.			Total.	
	s.	*d.*		*s.*	*d.*	*s.*	*d.*
First Cabin,	13	0	Inside,	5	0	18	0
Second Cabin,	8	8	Outside,	3	4	12	0

Coach Fare, from Tullamore to Clara, Inside, - 1s. 8d.—Outside, 1s. 8d.
Ditto, - - - to Moate, - - 3s. 4d.— - 2s. 1d.

LUGGAGE allowed in Coach——Inside, 40lb.—Outside, 20lb.

Extra Luggage to be paid for, at the rate of one penny per lb.

A Passage-Boat departs from Dublin, every morning, at seven o'clock; and arrives in Tullamore, at ten minutes after eight o'clock, in the evening;—and another Boat departs from Dublin, every afternoon, at two o'clock, and arrives in Tullamore, at half after three o'clock, next morning.—And a COACH, capable of conveying six inside and ten outside Passengers, departs from the Company's Hotel at Tullamore, every morning, at five o'clock; and, passing through the towns of Clara and Moate, arrives at half after nine o'clock, at Mr. JOHN GARTY's Hotel, in *Athlone.*

NOTE.—Under this arrangement, a passenger, leaving Dublin in the Boat, at two o'clock in the evening, will arrive in Athlone, about nine o'clock next morning.

The Coach departs, from Athlone, every afternoon, at half after two o'clock, and, passing through Moate and Clara, arrives at seven o'clock, in the evening, at Tullamore Hotel: whence a Boat proceeds, at half after nine o'clock, for Dublin; where it arrives at twenty minutes after eleven o'clock, next morning:—and, another Boat proceeds from Tullamore, every morning, at seven o'clock, and arrives in Dublin at ten minutes after eight o'clock in the evening.

N. B. No charge made in the Boat for any child, under the age of one year; and only half price charged for the passage and ordinary of any child between that age and seven years.

Breakfast, Dinner, and Supper, provided in the Boats, as usual.

Small parcels carried in the Boat and Coach, between Dublin and Athlone, at moderate rates.

Seats for the Coach, from Tullamore to Athlone, may be engaged from the Boat-Masters on the Passage; and Seats from Athlone to Tullamore to be engaged at Mr. JOHN GARTY's Hotel, in *Athlone.*

By Order,

15th November, 1811. .   DANIEL BAGOT, *Sec.*

DUBLIN: PRINTED BY WILLIAM PORTER, GRAFTON-STREET, *Printer and Stationer to the Grand Canal Company.*

Figure 32   A through service by boat and coach. The Grand Canal Company always aimed at offsetting direct coach competition

THE ELLESMERE CANAL PACKET

WILL SAIL FROM

SAMUEL ACKERLEY'S,

THE ELLESMERE CANAL TAVERN,

TOWER-WHARF, CHESTER,

AS FOLLOWS:—1802.

January.			*February.*			*March.*			*April.*			*May.*			*June.*		
Days.	H.	M.	Days.	H.	M.	Days.	H.	M.	Days.	H.	M.	Days.	H.	M.	Days.	H.	M.
F 1	6	0	M 1	6	30	M 1	6	0	Th 1	7	0	S 1	7	0	Tu 1	8*	10
S 2	6	15	● 2	7	0	Tu 2	6	20	● 2	7	40	● 2	7	30	W 2	9*	0
Su 3	6	50	W 3	7	50	W 3	7	0	S 3	8	20	M 3	8	0	Th 3	9*	30
● 4	7	40	Th 4	8	40	● 4	7	40	Su 4	8	50	Tu 4	8	40	F 4	10*	10
Tu 5	8	30	F 5	9	20	F 5	8	20	M 5	9	30	W 5	9	20	S 5	10	50
W 6	9	0	S 6	10	0	S 6	9	0	Tu 6	10	0	Th 6	9	40	Su 6	11*	20
Th 7	9	50	Su 7	10	50	Su 7	9	30	W 7	10	50	F 7	10	0			
F 8	10	30	M 8	11	30	M 8	10	20	Th 8	11	30	S 8	11	30	☽ 8	1	10
S 9	11	20	☽ 9	12	0	Tu 9	11	0	F 9	12	20	☽ 9	12	30	9	2	0
☽ 10	12	20	W 10	1	0	W 10	11	40	☽ 10	1	20	M 10	1	30	Th 10	3	0
M 11	1	0	Th 11	1	30	☽ 11	12	30	Su 11	2	20	Tu 11	2	30	F 11	3	30
Tu 12	1	30	F 12	2	10	F 12	1	30	M 12	3	0	W 12	3	0	S 12	5	40
W 13	2	0	S 13	6	0	S 13	2	0	Tu 13	6	0	Th 13	5	40	Su 13	6*	0
Th 14	dontgo		Su 14	6	15	Su 14	5	30	W 14	6	15	F 14	6	15	M 14	6*	40
F 15	6	0	M 15	6	40	M 15	6	0	Th 15	6	40	S 15	6	50	○ 15	7*	20
S 16	6	20	Tu 16	7	30	Tu 16	6	20	F 16	7	10	Su 16	7	10	W 16	8*	0
Su 17	7	0	○ 17	8	0	W 17	7	0	S 17	7	40	○ 17	7	50	Th 17	8*	30
○ 18	7	40	Th 18	8	30	Th 18	7	40	○ 18	8	10	Tu 18	8	20	F 18	9*	0
Tu 19	8	20	F 19	9	0	○ 19	8	20	M 19	8	50	W 19	9	0	S 19	10	0
W 20	9	0	S 20	9	30	S 20	8	40	Tu 20	9	10	Th 20	9	30	Su 20	11*	0
Th 21	9	30	Su 21	10	0	Su 21	9	0	W 21	9	50	F 21	10	10	M 21	12	0
F 22	10	0	M 22	10	30	M 22	9	40	Th 22	10	20	S 22	11	0	☾ 22	1	0
S 23	10	30	Tu 23	11	0	Tu 23	10	0	F 23	11	0	Su 23	12	0	W 23	2	0
Su 24	11	0	W 24	11	30	W 24	10	40	S 24	12	0	☾ 24	1	0	Th 24	3	0
M 25	11	30	☾ 25	12	20	Th 25	11	20	☾ 25	1	0	Tu 25	2	0	F 25	3	30
Tu 26	12	20	F 26	1	10	☾ 26	12	0	M 26	2	0	W 26	3	0	S 26	5	40
☾ 27	1	0	S 27	2	0	S 27	1	0	Tu 27	3	0	Th 27	3	30	Su 27	6*	0
Th 28	2	0	Su 28	dontgo		Su 28	2	0	W 28	6	0	F 28	6	0	M 28	6*	40
F 29	dontgo					M 29	2	30	Th 29	6	15	S 29	6	30	Tu 29	7*	20
S 30	dontgo					Tu 30	6	0	F 30	6	40	Su 30	7*	0	● 30	8*	0
Su 31	6	0				W 31	6	20				● 31	7*	30			

☞ ● New Moon, ☽ First Quarter, ○ Full Moon, ☾ Last Quarter.

N. B. On the Days marked thus (*) the Bathing Packet will sail.—Stops one Hour and returns.

Figure 33   Passenger timetable of 1802 (front), for boats running between Chester and Ellesmere Port. One could bathe in the Mersey then

Excursion travelling by canal was also quite common. As early as 1776 the Chester Canal company was running special boats from Beeston to Chester Races. A handbill of the Edinburgh & Glasgow Union in 1834 offers ten miles for 6d (2½p) amidst most pleasant scenery and over highly interesting aqueducts, at one of which fruits, confectioneries and varieties of refreshments could be had.

Later, especially on rivers like the Thames and Severn, but also, for instance, on the Forth & Clyde Canal, excursion steamers were run. On this canal the famous 'Queens' worked from 1893 to 1939. Today, British Waterways, private firms and individuals, and many enthusiast bodies run excursion trips on the canals, and in doing so follow an old tradition.

It is interesting to note that the battle for passengers between water and rail was not known to be lost in 1835, when a prospectus was issued for a new canal in Scotland to connect Stirling with the Forth & Clyde Canal. This statement of the promoters says:

'In regard to the comparative amenity of the two modes of travelling, the noiseless smoothness of the Canal boats is unequalled. Nor must it be forgotten, that while a very large portion of the Liverpool Railway passengers are conveyed in uncovered waggons, exposed to wind and weather, all the Canal passengers have the privilege of well-lighted, comfortable, and elegant cabins.'[11]

Since the canal was never built, presumably the investing public thought better of the railway.

Though to our minds a boat drawn by horses on a canal does not seem a dangerous mode of travelling, accidents did occur. The following newspaper account in 1810 tells of one incident:

'Paisley. Nov. 11. Yesterday about half-past 12 the boat which tracks on the Ardrossan Canal, was about to set off for Johnstone: it was one of the days of our quarterly fair, and a great many boys and girls being off work—were attracted by its novelty (being the fifth day it had sailed); some had not got out from Johnstone, while others were crowding on board to go there; the boat was lying at the quay in the basin; the water about six feet deep, some were below, but most part on the top of the cabins or the deck. The boat was raised pretty high out of the water, and the weight getting too great above, she suddenly swayed on one side, and all on deck fell over. Some were able to leap upon the quay on the first motion: but upwards of 100 persons, men, women, boys and girls, and even children were precipitated into the basin. A few swam out, and others were got out before they sunk: but the greater number sunk to the bottom. Drags were got, and before one o'clock about 50 were got out. Every aid was given by the surgeons and inhabitants, and on Saturday night 18

July.			August.			September.			October.			November.			December.		
Days.	H.	M.	Days.	H.	M.	Days.	H.	M.	Days.	H.	M.	Days.	H.	M.	Days.	H.	M.
Th 1	8	*40	Su 1	9	*20	W 1	10*	0	F 1	10	10	M 1	11	20	W 1	12	10
F 2	9	*20	M 2	10*	0	Th 2	10*	30	S 2	10	50	Tu 2	12	20	D 2	1	10
S 3	9	50	Tu 3	10*	30	F 3	11*	0	Su 3	11	20	D 3	1	20	F 3	2	0
Su 4	10*	30	W 4	11*	0	S 4	11	40	D 4	12	20	Th 4	1	40	S 4	2	10
M 5	11*	0	Th 5	11	30	D 5	12	30	Tu 5	1	20	F 5	2	20	Su 5	dontgo	
Tu 6	11	40	D 6	12	10	M 6	1	30	W 6	2	20	S 6	5	40	M 6	6	0
W 7	12	20	S 7	1	0	Tu 7	2	30	Th 7	3	0	Su 7	6	0	Tu 7	6	20
D 8	1	0	Su 8	2	0	W 8	3	20	F 8	6	0	M 8	6	30	W 8	7	0
F 9	2	0	M 9	3	0	Th 9	5	40	S 9	6	15	O 9	7	20	O 9	7	40
S 10	3	0	Tu 10	5	40	F 10	6	20	Su 10	6	50	W 10	8	0	F 10	8	20
Su 11	3	30	W 11	6*	0	C 11	7	10	O 11	7	40	Th 11	8	40	S 11	9	0
M 12	5	40	Th 12	6*	30	Su 12	8*	0	Tu 12	8	20	F 12	9	20	Su 12	9	40
Tu 13	6*	0	O 13	7*	20	M 13	8*	40	W 13	9	0	S 13	10	0	M 13	10	20
W 14	6*40		S 14	8	10	Tu 14	9*	20	Th 14	9	40	Su 14	10	50	Tu 14	11	0
O 15	7*30		Su 15	8*50		W 15	10*	0	F 15	10	20	M 15	11	40	W 15	11	50
F 16	8*20		M 16	9*30		Th 16	10*	40	S 16	11	0	Tu 16	12	20	Th 16	12	30
S 17	9	0	Tu 17	10*20		F 17	11*	20	Su 17	12	0	C 17	1	0	C 17	1	0
Su 18	9*50		W 18	11	0	C 18	12	10	C 18	1	0	Th 18	1	30	S 18	2	0
M 19	10*30		Th 19	11*40		Su 19	1	10	Tu 19	2	0	F 19	2	0	Su 19	dontgo	
Tu 20	11*20		S 20	12	20	M 20	2	10	W 20	2	15	S 20	dontgo		M 20	dontgo	
C 21	12*15		S 21	1	20	Tu 21	3	10	Th 21	5	40	Su 21	6	0	Tu 21	6	0
Th 22	1	0	Su 22	2	20	W 22	5	40	F 22	6	0	M 22	6	15	W 22	6	15
F 23	2	0	M 23	3	20	Th 23	6	0	S 23	6	20	Tu 23	6	50	Th 23	6	30
S 24	3	0	Tu 24	5	40	F 24	6	40	Su 24	6	50	W 24	7	20	● 24	7	20
Su 25	3	30	W 25	6*15		S 25	7	20	M 25	7	20	● 25	7	50	S 25	8	0
M 26	6	0	Th 26	7*	0	● 26	8	0	● 26	8	0	F 26	8	30	Su 26	8	40
Tu 27	6*15		F 27	7*40		M 27	8	20	W 27	8	20	S 27	9	0	M 27	9	20
W 28	7*	0	● 28	8	10	Tu 28	8	40	Th 28	8	50	Su 28	9	40	Tu 28	10	10
● 29	7*50		Su 29	8*40		W 29	9	10	F 29	9	20	M 29	10	20	W 29	11	0
F 30	8*20		M 30	9*	0	Th 30	9	50	S 30	10	0	Tu 30	11	10	Th 30	11	40
S 31	9*	0	Tu 31	9*30					Su 31	10	40				D 31	12	30

Fare in the best Apartment, from Chester to Liverpool, 2s. 6d.; in the second Apartment, 1s. 6d.—Fare along the Canal and back, 2s. and 1s. 6d.

Parcels and Luggage are taken in at the Ellesmere Canal Tavern, Tower-wharf, where Information may be had respecting the Packet.

N. B. In the Passage from Chester to Liverpool, the Whole of the Fare is to be paid to the Captain of the Canal Packet, who will deliver a Ticket to each Passenger, which will free the Liverpool Packet; and in the Passage from Liverpool to Chester, the same must be done with the Captain of the Liverpool Packet, whose Ticket will free the Canal Packet.—The Proprietors will not be accountable for any Parcel above five Pounds Value, unless paid for as such; nor for any Parcel or Luggage, unless duly entered —An elegant Packet for Bathers, at 1s. 6d. and 1s. each Person, during the Season.—On the Day not appointed for bathing, the said Boat may be hired by Parties of Pleasure the whole Day, for 1l. 10s. exclusive of any other Expence whatever.

Chester, Fletcher print.

Figure 34   Passenger timetable of 1802 (back). At Ellesmere Port there were connections for Mersey packets to Liverpool

or 20 were recovered. The dragging continued all the afternoon. About 90 have been dragged out in all; but owing to the great number of families the sufferers belong to, it is not accurately known how many are dead. . . . Those in the cabin of the vessel were safe, the boat uprighting as soon as the crowd fell off.'[12]

The historian of Bury tells of another that happened on the Manchester, Bolton & Bury Canal:

'The catastrophe . . . was caused by the insensate folly of a party of passengers, drunken men, numbering near twenty, who overawed the quieter portion on board, and persisted, for amusement and to frighten the women, in swaying the boat, heavily laden and overcrowded, from side to side, until the window-sills of the cabin, below the deck, were almost on a level with the water of the canal. The brutal wretches, maddened with drunkenness and riot, paid no heed whatever to the remonstrances of the captain, the shrieks and piteous entreaties of the women, or the tears and cries of children who were on board; for the journey was a favourite Sunday trip, many families going that day to visit friends or relatives in Bolton. Opposition led only to more strenuous efforts, and they were blind to danger; and at length the dreaded apprehension was changed to reality. The heavily laden boat, urged by powerful impetus, gave one fatal dip below the water-line, turned upon its side, with its living freight, a hopeless multitude, and rose no more. . . .'[13]

The carrying of passengers, and the working of fly-boats, were affected by the experiments which were made in the years 1832 and 1833 on the Forth & Clyde, Oxford and Grand Junction Canals to increase the speed of boats. It was found with specially built light boats that if speed were increased beyond the normal three or four miles an hour, a wave was built up in front of the boat, but that a further increase of speed enabled the boat to pass the wave, rise in the water, and to travel at a speed of 11–12mph. Frequent changes of horses were of course necessary. It was as a result of these experiments that fast passenger services were operated successfully on the Glasgow & Ardrossan and other canals.

In 1839 the Forth & Clyde Canal experimented with locomotive haulage from the bank on a ½ mile stretch near Lock 16, but concluded it would be too expensive. Half a century later more trials were held, this time at railway initiative, when Francis W. Webb, the mechanical engineer of the London & North Western Railway, initiated trials on the Middlewich branch of the railway-controlled Shropshire Union, and showed that loaded boats could be towed at 8mph. Mechanical towage from the towpath using tractors was fleetingly used by the British Transport Commission, but on the

Continent both locomotive and tractor towage had a long life until self-propelled craft made it unnecessary.

Just as it is not easy nowadays to realise the canal activity of those times, when most of the heavy goods of the country, much of the lighter merchandise, and many passengers, were all moved by waterway, so it is difficult to generalise upon the prosperity of the canals without complete figures for every company. A few concerns were extremely prosperous, and they are often quoted as examples of the high profits made by navigation companies in the days before their monopoly was threatened. In 1833, for instance, these were the figures for seven of the leading companies:

Name	Dividend paid per cent	Market value of shares £
Loughborough Nav	108	1,240
Erewash	47	705
Mersey & Irwell	40	750
Trent & Mersey	75	640
Oxford	32	595
Coventry	32	600
Forth & Clyde	25	545

A number more were very satisfactory investments: such companies as the Staffordshire & Worcestershire, Cromford, Shropshire, Shrewsbury, Swansea or Grand Junction. Others were paying only small dividends, but had good prospects if locomotive railways were to prove only a flash in George Stephenson's pan: such were the Brecknock & Abergavenny, Peak Forest, Macclesfield, Ashby-de-la-Zouch, Kennet & Avon, Rochdale, Stratford-upon-Avon and the Regent's, none of which paid as much as 5 per cent in 1833.

Hundreds of thousands of pounds had, however, been spent on canals that were financially unsuccessful, and which never paid a dividend in their working existence, such as the Grand Western, Salisbury & Southampton or Leominster. The following sets of figures showing the dividends paid by three important companies are fairly representative. The Oxford was built before the war-time rise in prices, and its high dividends reflect its low construction cost of about £300,000. The Grand Junction and the Kennet & Avon were both built during the war, and each cost about a million pounds. One was financially very successful, the other less so. All three were of great commercial value.

Year	*Oxford (opened 1790) Dividend on £100 shares per cent*	*Grand Junction (opened 1805) Dividend on £100 shares per cent*	*Kennet & Avon (opened 1810) Dividend on £40 shares per cent*
1806	16	3	—
1807	19½	3	—
1808	22	4	—
1809	25	5	—
1810	25 plus 4%	6	—
1811	25 plus 6%	6	—
1812	25 plus 6%	7	—
1813	25 plus 6%	7	—
1814	25 plus 6%	7	1⅞
1815	25 plus 6%	8	1⅞
1816	25 plus 6%	2	—
1817	25 plus 6%	6	—
1818	25 plus 6%	8½	2½
1819	32	9	2¼
1820	32	9	2
1821	32	9	2
1822	32	10	2⅛
1823	32	10	2⅛
1824	32 plus 2%	10 plus 1%	2½
1825	32 plus 2%	10 plus 3%	2½
1826	32 plus 2%	10 plus 3%	2⅝
1827	32 plus 2%	10 plus 3%	3⅛
1828	32 plus 2%	13	3⅛
1829	32	13	3⅛
1830	32	13	3⅛
1831	32	13	3⅛
1832	32	12	3⅛
1833	32	12	3⅛
1834	32	12	2½
1835	32	12	2½
1836	30	12	2¾
1837	30	12	3⅛
1838	30	10	3⅜
1839	30	10	3⅜
1840	30	8	3¾
1841	30	7	3¾
1842	30	7	1⅞
1843	30	7	15/16

Year	Oxford	Grand Junction	Kennet & Avon
1844	30	7	$1\frac{5}{16}$
1845	28	7	$1\frac{5}{16}$
1846	25	6	$1\frac{5}{16}$
1847	20	5	$1\frac{5}{16}$
1848	20	5	$1\frac{5}{16}$
1849	20	5	$1\frac{5}{16}$

With the dividend figures should be compared those of toll receipts. These are comparable roughly, but not exactly, with one another.

Year	Oxford £	Grand Junction £	Kennet & Avon £	
1806	57,108	87,392		
1807	60,611	92,602		Canal
1808	72,051	107,295	4,204	not yet
1809	78,848	127,404	4,472	opened
1810	78,671	142,979	3,945	
1811	81,518	138,998	11,988	
1812	82,544	141,911	18,644	
1813	83,784	168,390	20,126	
1814	90,769	155,008	31,525	
1815	75,983	147,857	31,287	
1816	77,387	127,130	25,849	
1817	80,445	145,558	27,141	
1818	83,733	169,922	32,201	
1819	78,876	157,633	35,595	
1820	76,875	151,525	32,911	
1821	79,109	159,600 (est)	33,031	
1822	81,084	153,620	30,611	
1823	87,819	169,085	32,038	
1824	86,679	178,155	36,712	
1825	84,761	187,532	36,492	
1826	91,148	178,827	42,649	
1827	90,727	189,131	47,173	
1828	90,618	181,932	42,930	
1829	89,992	181,144	43,818	
1830	92,962	176,541	42,009	
1831	87,918	168,540	42,550	
1832	75,490	167,039	42,601	
1833	73,840	170,460	43,858	
1834	73,638	174,722	41,240	

Year	Oxford £	Grand Junction £	Kennet & Avon £
1835	72,465	180,125	39,939
1836	81,523	198,086	41,026
1837	86,176	155,718	42,219
1838	86,638	152,657	44,355
1839	85,570	138,263	44,328
1840	84,159	121,140	48,269
1841	86,217	121,753	46,704
1842	73,119	113,012	36,395
1843	74,483	116,685	32,045

(NB—The Kennet & Avon figures include tonnage receipts from the River Kennet Navigation from 1814.)

It is odd that waterway interests met the threat of railways bravely and progressively up to a point, and then resigned themselves to passive defence of their positions or to active efforts to get themselves bought out at favourable prices. The force of private enterprise in railways overbore that of the waterways, and the latter succumbed. In France, Germany and the Lowlands, on the other hand, State or local authority intervention early in the struggle led to partial nationalisation, co-ordination of water and rail transport, and the modernisation and standardisation of the waterways.

Here and there a canal company believed in itself, for a time at least. In 1841 the Birmingham Canal company wrote: 'The circumstance . . . of the Birmingham Canal being kept in a navigable state during the winter, whilst the neighbouring Canals were closed, affords strong proof of what can be done by energy and determination, and is well calculated to add to the impression, now rapidly gaining ground, that the low price of Canal stock and diversion of Traffic, is less to be ascribed to opposing railways, than to the inactivity, want of foresight, and absurd jealousies of the Canal Companies themselves.'[14] One is indeed struck by all three in many cases. Take the Staffs & Worcs, a neighbour of the Birmingham. Here was a very prosperous canal in a key position, run by a small group of apparently able men who could always spare a little money for the poor, or to help build a church or a school. Yet throughout its long career from its opening in 1772 it spent no substantial sum on the improvement of its winding narrow line and single locks, except to build reservoirs. It watched the Worcester & Birmingham take part of its Birmingham–Severn trade and then the Birmingham & Liverpool Junction take most of that from Liverpool to Birmingham with no action more effective than petitions against the Bills, and in the second case, provision for heavy compensation payments. A few concerns stood up, fought, and succeeded. It never seems to have occurred to the Aire & Calder that they might be defeated, though even they were willing to sell to a railway group at one time. They were broad-based and prosperous, well managed and well breeched, and showed what could be done. If more companies had been like them, more could have been saved. Across the Pennines, the Weaver's reactions were much the same. This navigation was publicly owned, by Cheshire, and is the sole British example of what happened so often on the Continent. The Weaver trustees also stood up and fought, and indeed were so formidable that railway companies treated them with respect. It is, I think, significant that both, many times modernised, are today among Britain's principal commercial waterways.

On the whole each waterway lived for itself. Very few working agreements were made to pass traffic, and those that were made often broke down. One is struck too by the fewness of canal amalgamations in pre-railway or early railway times. Only the Ellesmere with the Chester, and later with others to form the Shropshire Union, the Mersey & Irwell with the Bridgewater, the Birmingham with the Wyrley & Essington and the Dudley, and the North Wilts with the Wilts & Berks spring to mind, though it must be remembered that canals were interlocked in some cases by shareholders prominent in the affairs of more than one company. Even in the railway period amalgamations were few.

So ended the canal age, which had made the already navigable rivers a basis for an inland waterway system of some 4,000 miles in all, serving nearly all the important towns and industrial areas as well as many country districts. In the eighty years to 1840 it had provided the chief means of transporting goods in bulk, and by its means the Industrial Revolution had taken place. The country now stood on the threshold of a new era—the Victorian or railway age.

CHAPTER X

The Rivers during the Canal Age

+++++++++++++++++++++++++++++++++++++◆+++++++++++++++++++++++++++++++++++

As we have seen, over a thousand miles of river had been made navigable before the Duke of Bridgewater built his canal. Further miles were added throughout the canal age by work under a number of Acts for small rivers, and by efforts to improve the drainage of the Fens which resulted also in better navigation facilities.

River navigations were built in a variety of ways. In some very early cases individuals were appointed to do the work, like Thomas Skipwith in 1634 by letters patent to make the Soar navigable. Later, some river Acts named commissioners, local people with property near the river, who in turn appointed undertakers, sometimes called trustees, to do the actual work. Money was then borrowed, usually at a fixed interest. The Weaver was made navigable like this. In other cases, commissioners themselves undertook the work, as on the River Ure, Calder & Hebble, or, indeed, the Thames. Where drainage was part of the exercise, trustees might be given local rating powers, as under the River Axe Act of 1802 or the Adur in 1807.

Joint stock companies were also formed, as for building the Aire & Calder, the Don or the Mersey & Irwell. During the second half of the eighteenth century and afterwards, the joint stock type of company organisation became more usual, the Calder & Hebble and later Ure changing to this type.

The coming of canals caused great changes in the transport pattern of the country. Rivers usually benefited, for they became the trunks from which canals branched out. Some promoted linking canals, as the Aire & Calder the Barnsley, or the Don the Dearne & Dove and the Stainforth & Keadby. Others found their interests so closely linked with canals that amalgamation took place, as the Kennet or the (Bristol) Avon rivers with the Kennet & Avon Canal, or the river was leased to the canal, as the Upper (Warwickshire) Avon to the Stratford-upon-Avon Canal; some, on the other hand, found themselves in bitter competition with a canal, like the Tone with the Bridgewater & Taunton Canal, or the Upper Trent Navigation with the Trent & Mersey Canal, and a battle took place that often ended with the new canal buying the old river, as later in other circumstances the new railway bought the old canal. Lastly, there were the great rivers of Thames and Severn, throughout the canal age always to some degree navigable yet never fully so until after that age was over.

In 1778 the opening of the Aire & Calder company's new Selby Canal provided an artificial by-pass to the difficult natural navigation of the lower Aire. Forty years later the Selby Canal was itself by-passed, when the company obtained an Act in 1818 to build a new canal from Ferrybridge on the Aire to Goole on the Ouse. Engineered by George Leather jun, this new large-scale canal was opened in 1826. Immediately afterwards the Aire & Calder's routes upwards from Ferrybridge to Castleford and then to Leeds and Wakefield were rebuilt to the same standard, with 7ft depth and locks 18ft wide. It was during this rebuilding that the tied-arch aqueduct at Stanley Ferry (now by-passed by a new one) was constructed.

The port of Goole was the creation of the Aire & Calder. From 1826 it grew throughout the nineteenth century and into our own, new lock entrances being added as traffic, canal and later rail-borne also, increased. This company demonstrated how a river company that was connected to canals, and which used the science of canal building to shorten and make easier its own line, could attain and maintain prosperity. As we shall see later, the Aire & Calder was still a leading waterway concern when it was taken over by the British Transport Commission, and its routes are active today.

To the south, the Don company, controlling the river from Tinsley near Sheffield nearby to the Dutch River, was nearly as energetic. Authorised in 1726 and 1727, the line was finished to Tinsley in 1751, with 17 locks and a number of cuts by-passing river sections. During the canal mania they took the lead in getting the Dearne & Dove and Stainforth & Keadby canals built: the first connected them to the coalfields north of Barnsley, the second gave them an outlet to the Trent more efficient than the Dutch River passage to the Ouse. Later, too, in 1819, the Sheffield Canal was opened to their navigation at Tinsley. From 1821 onwards, the Don company rebuilt much of their line, so that when the railway age began, they were well placed to meet it.

As an example of a river that was closely connected with a canal, and later became incorporated with it, we may take the Kennet, the navigation of which ran from Newbury to within a mile and a half of the Thames at Reading, at which point it came under the jurisdiction of the Thames Commissioners. In that distance there is a fall of 126ft.

The first Bill to make the river navigable was introduced in 1708,

Page 202, Plate X (*above*) Sailing barges at Spalding gasworks on the Welland about 19
(*below*) loading sugar beet at Ludham bridge on the Ant, one of the Broads rivers, in 19

with the support of towns like Westbury and Hungerford, and with the opposition of Reading, which feared the loss of its transhipment trade, and of one Finch, a pensioner of the turnpike on Reading road, who presumably feared that if the navigation were successful the road would no longer be able to pay his pension.

The Act was passed in 1715, in favour of seven partners, holding between them the 32 shares in the navigation. In 1718 John Hore was taken on as engineer; he built 21 locks and made a number of artificial cuts joining sections of river, the whole being ready in 1723 except for the towpath, which took longer to finish. He became a surveyor of the river and wharfinger at Newbury, and a son or relation of his was later an engineer of the Kennet & Avon Canal. The proprietors were not successful, until:

'. . . about the year 1767 when, instead of being under the direction of a large body of men who were continually at variance with each other, the late Mr Page purchased the whole of the shares which were intitled to any profit . . . and giving up his time and attention to it he raised it from the ruinous state in which it was getting. . . .'[1]

The Pages, first the father Francis Page, then the sons Frederick and Francis Page, did their own carrying. By 1798 they had built up the trade to 20,000 tons a year and the tolls (apart from freight) to £2,140pa; three years later the effect of the still uncompleted Kennet & Avon Canal had raised them to £3,115. At that time there was a trade in malt, flour and timber to London, peat to Marlow and Henley, and coal, Baltic and West Indian goods from London to Bath, Bristol and Salisbury by land carriage from Newbury.

The building of the Kennet & Avon Canal greatly increased the profits of the Pages. When, therefore, the canal company soon afterwards in 1809 interested itself in a possible link from Newbury to Old Basing on the Basingstoke Canal, which would have by-passed the Kennet, Frederick Page opposed the proposal on behalf of himself and the Thames Navigation. For doing so he earned some criticism from 'A Friend of the People', who pointed out that as owner of the Kennet Navigation he charged for a load of timber 5s (25p) for 18½ miles, while the Basingstoke Canal charged 6s 2d (31p) for 27 miles, and 2½d per ton per mile for corn against the Basingstoke's 1¾d. Mr Page's opposition, combined, one suspects, with a little pressure behind the scenes, caused the canal company to buy him out for £100,000 in 1812. A few years earlier his property had been valued at a little over £23,000, so he drove a hard bargain, though it is fair to say that the increased prosperity brought by the canal had increased its value.

It is amusing to find that in 1824, when the Basingstoke link was

again being discussed, Frederick Page was this time representing the
Kennet & Avon Company, and was giving evidence in favour of the
link and against his former ally the Thames Navigation. Later he
became for a short time chairman of the canal company, until his death
in 1834.

Figure 35   Seal of the Norwich & Lowestoft Navigation
Company

There were a number of rivers which were physically independent
of the waterway system of the country. Some were great rivers, like
the Tyne or the Tees; others were small affairs, like the Adur and the
Eastern Rother, but all to their capacities performed a useful service
in opening up the country to trade. Of these a prosperous example
was the Weaver. This Cheshire river was first made navigable in
1732 under an Act of 1721, and by a further Act of 1760 was put under
the control of a body of county trustees, which continued to be
responsible for the waterway till the Transport Act of 1947.

The first locks were of wood, taking boats of about 40 tons while
the river itself could only be entered from the Mersey estuary at high-
water ordinary spring tides. From 1760 onwards, however, the locks
were rebuilt and the navigation improved at several points, a new
lock being built at Frodsham where it entered the Mersey so that it
was accessible at most states of the tide. It was at this time that the
trustees made great efforts to connect their river to the proposed
east–west canal that later became the Trent & Mersey. Failure, however, hardly affected the salt trade which was the staple of the Weaver,
and in 1807 a further improvement was made when the trustees were
authorised to cut a canal from the river to Weston Point on the

Mersey. This Weston Canal, opened in 1810, avoided the difficult navigation of the lower Weaver, and provided a basin where craft could wait for the tide, and a river lock. The basin is the ancestor of the British Waterways Board's present Weston Point docks.

By 1830 the waterway was receiving some £30,000pa from its trade, and was handing considerable sums to the county authorities in relief of rates. Traffic was mainly salt (432,000 tons) and coal (124,000 tons). From 1832 onwards, the trustees carried out major improvements, by increasing depth from 6ft (itself an increase on the original 4ft 6in) to 7ft 6in, and enlarging the locks to 88ft × 18ft, which could take vessels carrying 100 and more tons of cargo. Oddly, it was not until well into the railway age that this well-managed river was connected to the canal system, first by the building of the short Runcorn & Weston Canal in 1859, which linked it with the Bridgewater Canal docks at Runcorn, and later by the Anderton lift in 1875, which connected it with the Trent & Mersey Canal, and enabled narrow boats from the latter to pass down the river.

The most interesting of the failures amongst river navigations was the Norwich & Lowestoft. The ancient communication of Norwich with the sea had been by way of Yarmouth, but this line of waterway grew so shallow as to be of little use. In order to make Norwich once more a port, therefore, a plan was put forward for a ship canal to Lowestoft. After great opposition from Yarmouth, this was authorised in 1827. The River Yare was deepened from Norwich to Reedham. There a cut of 2½ miles was made to the River Waveney, which took the line to Oulton Dyke, which was enlarged to Oulton Broad. Thence a short cut took the line of waterway into Lake Lothing, which was made into a tidal harbour by cutting through the bank separating it from the sea. The ship canal, which cost £150,000 to build, was opened in 1833, and was a financial failure, the expenses of maintaining the channel exceeding the revenue. Money borrowed from the Exchequer Loan Commissioners could not be repaid, and the canal was sold by the commissioners to a new company, which soon afterwards resold to a group of railway promoters.

The rivers that were either independent of the canal system, or fitted well into it, were a large group. There were some, however, which found themselves directly in competition with canals. Just as in the next chapter we shall see what effect the competition of railways had upon waterways, and shall note the price-cutting, and the buying up of waterways by railways, that resulted from the impact of a more upon a less efficient means of transport, so during the canal age we can trace the same development in the impact of the newer canals upon the older river navigations. This impact was very local, and occurred whenever a canal was projected, sometimes at the very end of the canal age.

The case of the River Tone is typical. This little river, running down from beyond Taunton in Somerset to its confluence with the River Parrett near Bridgwater, on the Bristol Channel, had been made navigable to Taunton under an Act of 1699, which set up conservators to keep the navigation open from Bridgwater. Under the General Proposals signed in 1697–8 by the thirty-four gentlemen who moved for an Act, Article Five said:

' 'Tis agreed that when the Moneys Subscribed shall be paid and the work wholly finished; That every Subscriber shall be reimburst both the Principal Money and Profit at the Rate of Seven pounds per Cent with all Cost and Charges they shall be at for the Carrying on and effecting the said work, and after such ample satisfaction made out of the Profitts, Touls, or Customs that shall be settled by Act of Parliament on Coals or other goods brought up the said River, That then the remainder shall be to the said Company and every one of them, their Heires and Assigns for ever, In Trust for the use of the Poor of Taunton and Taunton St. James to be given or laid out from time to time for the Relief and good of the said Poor, as the major part of the Subscribers or their Heirs or Assigns shall think fitt.'[2]

The navigation, completed in 1717 to Taunton with 1 lock and at least 2 half-locks, had been a small affair, but had slowly increased in prosperity through the eighteenth century, and more rapidly in the nineteenth, as the figures show:

Date	Tolls received £
1728	388
1789	668
1821	2,369

When the Bridgwater & Taunton Canal Bill was put forward the conservators bitterly but unsuccessfully opposed it. The canal was opened in 1827, and price-cutting followed. The tolls became absurdly low, and the canal company felt the strain to such an extent that, in spite of the strong opposition of the conservators, they applied to Parliament for leave compulsorily to buy out the River Tone navigation and so get the trade into their own hands. While the Bill was before the House the two parties came to agree. Various things were to be done and payments made by the canal company, including a sum of £2,000 in discharge of the charitable trust for the poor, and the only powers left to the conservators were those of inspection, to see that the communication between Bridgwater and Taunton was kept free and available. These powers of the conservators to complain at Quarter Sessions were used at times up to nationalisation.

In some cases the river navigation succumbed to the competition, and ceased to be used. The River Salwarpe gave way to the Droitwich Canal, as did the River Idle from Bawtry to the Trent when faced with the Chesterfield Canal. In other cases amalgamation took place. For instance, in 1783 the Leeds & Liverpool Canal bought the River Douglas Navigation; the Derby Canal bought the River Derwent Navigation when the canal was authorised in 1795, and closed it; and the Bridgewater Canal bought the Mersey & Irwell Navigation in 1844. The competition between these last companies had been long-standing. The navigation company had failed to oppose successfully the building of the Duke of Bridgewater's Canal from Manchester to Runcorn. Thereafter followed a competition for Manchester traffic that lasted till 1844. During this time the river company was active in shortening its line by artificial cuts, and by overcoming shortages of water. In the last years of its life it took such a progressive line that it was worth while for the Bridgewater trustees to buy it up. On the one hand the river company started a plan to deepen the rivers to allow vessels of 300 tons to reach Victoria Bridge, Manchester, while on the other they successfully promoted the Manchester & Salford Junction Canal (buying it in 1840) which joined their navigation to the Rochdale, already linked to the Bridgewater.

Another type of river navigation usually had a more fortunate history—that which formed an integral part of a through line of canal. The Kennet & Avon proprietors, for instance, found that if traffic was to be efficiently handled they must own the two rivers that were connected by their canal. On the one hand, therefore, as we have seen, they bought the Kennet Navigation from its owner, Mr Page, for a good price, and on the other they acquired a majority of Avon shares.

The outstanding example of a river that lived in plenty on the connection it made with canals was the Soar, usually known as the Loughborough Navigation. Originally built during canal times as an inexpensive project for making navigable the River Soar from the Trent to the town of Loughborough, this company with an authorised capital of only £10,000 had the good fortune to find itself connected in 1794 with Leicester, and thence in 1814 with the Grand Junction Canal by means of the Leicestershire & Northamptonshire Union and Grand Union Canals. As a result its earning capacity was greatly increased, the average dividend rising from an average of 1½ per cent in 1782–94 to 40 per cent in 1797–9, 108 per cent in 1812–14, and 154 per cent in 1827–9, before falling to 107 per cent in 1839–41.

Two great rivers, the Thames and the Severn, remain to be dealt with. Both were vital to the canal network, for both carried great quantities of goods not only for the towns along their own banks, but to and from the many river and canal navigations that joined them. How important these two arteries were can be seen from the map of the waterways system, yet, for reasons to be examined, neither was improved to a good navigation standard during the canal period. Because of this failure, they not only prevented the canal system itself from functioning as efficiently as it might, but contributed to that system's inability to compete with the railways.

Severn, but not Thames, was a free navigation at the beginning of the canal age. The general responsibility of the City of London for the Thames before 1730 was only strictly exercised below Staines, whilst the only other authority was the Oxford-Burcot Commission set up in 1624 to build three pound-locks between Oxford and Abingdon and so improve the navigation of the part of the river between those towns. In 1695 a commission was set up for the river, and in 1751 a new Act included as commissioners all persons rated to the land-tax for an estate of £100 a year in the seven upper riverside counties, together with various official members from the towns along its banks. It was not until 1771 that the commissioners, now increased by including more representatives of local authorities and other interested bodies, as well as clergy and Members of Parliament, obtained powers to borrow and to regulate charges. Three years later the river downwards from Staines was formally transferred to the City of London. They were now able on the part above Staines to build pound-locks and make towpaths, to buy the old flash-locks and to arrange for regular flashes. It was, however, provided in the Act that the same tolls as before had to be paid to the owners of the old flash-locks, even through barges passed through new pound-locks on which tolls were also payable. A result of improvement was therefore to turn some old lock-owners from millowners into landowners or publicans, with a second and substantial source of income. Only very slowly over the following decades were the flash-lock owners bought out.

The navigation of the Thames at that time was entirely by flash-locks except for the three pound-locks built in the previous century by the Oxford-Burcot Commission.* So bad was it in the light of the

* The Oxford-Burcot Commission was absorbed by the Thames Commission in 1790.

improved waterway standards set by canals that in 1770 Brindley suggested to the city corporation that a long stretch of the river should be avoided by a canal (to be called the London Canal) from Monkey Island below Maidenhead to Isleworth. The project, and another for a Reading–Monkey Island canal, gave place to the Act of 1771 to improve the navigation of the river itself, under which the commissioners built eight timber pound-locks on the stretch of river between Reading and Maidenhead. Between 1777 and 1795 they built a new series from above Reading to Oxford. The river below Oxford, as far as Maidenhead, was now in fair condition, with locks able to take 150 ton barges, but on the one hand the dredging of the channel and the layout and construction of the older locks was not always good, while on the other many of the old weirs still remained, upon which tolls were payable. The improvements had not, however, been able to prevent the building of the Grand Junction Canal from the Oxford Canal at Braunston to London: this broad waterway diverted much midlands traffic from the older route via the narrow Oxford and the Thames.

Below Maidenhead, only one lock had been built before 1800, Romney near Windsor in 1797. Expecting that the newly built Kennet & Avon Canal (it was opened in 1810) would bring additional trade to the Thames between its junction with the river at Reading and London, the city built six locks below Staines between 1811 and 1815. The Thames Commissioners followed with others in the length between Staines and Windsor, and more to fill gaps, till Bray lock in 1845 completed the series below the junction with the Oxford Canal at Oxford.

To the proprietors of the Thames & Severn Canal, however, which entered the Thames at Lechlade not much lower than the extremity of the commissioners' jurisdiction, and which had been opened in 1789, it was the state of the Thames above Oxford that was especially important. In 1784 the newly formed canal company had indeed interested itself in a scheme for a canal from Lechlade to Abingdon, but the Bill failed. Jessop did survey the upper river, at that time without pound-locks, and with four bridges with small navigation arches. Osney lock was then built, and Radcot bridge enlarged. Five more locks followed, by which time the Thames Commissioners reckoned they had done well by the new and unproven canal. However, they called in the elderly, rather cantankerous, but expert Robert Mylne to make a survey. On behalf of the commissioners he wrote:

'I consider the Navigation, across the Island, from the Severn to the Thames, is totally barred and locked up; unless, it is opened by the means herein recommended; or some other way, that may appear proper.'[3]

Eventually the question was taken before a committee of the House of Commons in 1793. Among those giving evidence was Christopher Chambers, a Thames & Severn shareholder, who said:

'. . . the present State of the Navigation of the River Thames is injurious to the Thames and Severn Canal; that Applications have been made to the Commissioners to improve it, and he recollects the Improving of the River being objected to, until such Time as the Trade was brought thereon from the Canal, sufficient to satisfy the Expence; that if the Thames was put into as perfect a State as possible he thinks he should receive a fair Dividend for his Money, but now receives none; that the Canal was made in full Confidence that the Commissioners of the Thames Navigation would complete their Navigation by the Time it was opened, but the Proprietors have been disappointed.'[4]

The committee, after hearing the evidence of both sides, expressed itself firmly:

'. . . by a reference to the Journals of the House, it will appear that the Commissioners of the Five upper districts have opposed every Attempt at Improvement by Canals, though the Evidence given to your Committee affords abundant testimony of their Negligence in endeavouring to perfect the River.'[5]

This was unfair to the commissioners who, in 1811, were unrepentant, stating:

'In the district above Oxford, these [towing paths] are the only expences of any magnitude which your Committee think themselves justified in recommending, and it is with regret that they observe that the doubts expressed by a former Committee . . . have been too well founded, and the favourable expectations formerly entertained, of the accession of trade, to be expected from the Thames and Severn Canal, have not yet been realised. Of the four canals, namely, the Kington and Leominster, Hereford and Gloucester, Berkeley, and Worcester and Birmingham, which were stated by Mr Josiah Clowes, in his evidence in 1791 [sic], before the House of Commons, as then forming; and all the goods from which were expected to pass down the Thames and Severn Canal, not ONE has yet been finished.'[6]

This collection of tactlessly expressed home truths was too much for the Thames & Severn company, which in 1813 joined with the Wilts & Berks to promote the North Wilts Canal to join them together, and so allow narrow boats to avoid the upper Thames altogether. Thenceforward, a good deal of trade left the Thames, but whether the Thames lost profit by its diversion is doubtful. It was not until the 1890s, in the last days of the Thames & Severn Canal, that a number of new locks were built to bring the upper river to the standard of the lower, or until our own century that the last flash-lock disappeared from it.

By the time the Thames Conservancy was set up (in 1857 for the part below Staines till then controlled by the City of London, and in 1866 for the whole river), and modern administration established, the Thames & Severn, Wilts & Berks, Basingstoke and Wey & Arun tributary canals were moribund, the Kennet & Avon had passed into railway ownership, and the Londonwards traffic from the midlands once brought into the river by the Oxford Canal had long ago been diverted to the Grand Junction. So low had the commissioners fallen through railway competition that in their last year of existence the £100 stock units were valued at 2s (10p), and the annual income from tolls, which had once been £13,000, was only £3,000.

The story of the Severn shows less movement still. Throughout the canal period the river had no controlling authority at all, for the Severn Commission was not set up until 1842, and then only for the portion between Stourport and Gloucester. Before the coming of canals the river had been a great artery of trade in spite of its imperfections, and such it remained. For instance, in 1797 seventeen trows went weekly between Bristol and Bewdley, and twenty-eight between Bristol and Stourport. Yet only two serious efforts were made to do something about its condition, though in the rather abnormal year 1796 Telford tells us barges could only be navigated for two months with a paying load. These efforts were made at the instance of the Staffs & Worcs and of the Gloucester & Berkeley companies respectively.

The Staffs & Worcs Canal entered the river at Stourport, and when another canal from Birmingham to the Severn, the Worcester & Birmingham, was projected to join the river lower down, the former company obtained an Act in 1790 to deepen the river channel between Stourport and Worcester, not by using locks, but by building projecting jetties to increase the speed of the current and so its scouring effect upon the river bottom. The boatmen found them obstacles to navigation, however, and they were removed. Lower down, the Gloucester & Berkeley Canal (see pp 150–6) was promoted in 1793 to by-pass the worst stretch of the river, where shifting shoals and strong tides made navigation difficult.

One other improvement was carried out under various Acts between 1772 and 1811 to incorporate companies to build horse towing paths from Shrewsbury to Gloucester. On the Severn, as well as on the Thames and many smaller rivers, the towpath was an addition of the canal era. Before the building of the Gloucester & Berkeley Canal, which was opened in 1827, the trows went up to Gloucester under sail and with the tide, and thence to Worcester and Stourport partly under sail on the tide and partly by bow-hauling by gangs of men who better than horses could get past the obstructions of the river bank before the towpath was built. The heavy river barges needed gangs of men just as later they needed teams of horses—as many as twelve horses on one barge were usual on the Thames when working upwards. Before the opening of the Gloucester & Berkeley Canal goods going downstream were normally transhipped to trows at Worcester or Stourport, though a few narrow boats that worked from Stourport or Worcester to Maisemore for the Herefordshire & Gloucestershire Canal, or to Framilode for the Stroudwater and the Thames & Severn Canals, were given sails or bow-hauled. Later, bow-hauling died out, and many narrow boats worked down from Stourport or Worcester to Gloucester without transhipping their cargoes.

The only effort within our period for dealing with the channel of the river was by a company, the Severn Navigation Company, that was formed at Worcester in 1835. It proposed by a series of locks and weirs to give 12ft of water to Worcester, and 6ft thence to Stourport. This proposal affected a number of interests. In favour were the merchants of Worcester, who would have found themselves at the head of a ship canal made of the Gloucester & Berkeley and the newly deepened Severn from Gloucester to Worcester, and also the Staffordshire & Worcestershire Canal, which was always in trouble because of the lack of water below Stourport to carry its midlands' goods down to Worcester. Against the proposal were the Gloucester & Berkeley Canal and the merchants of Gloucester, who foresaw that the transhipment trade of Gloucester would be transferred to Worcester, and feared that the imposition of charges on the river would in any case injure traffic by waterway. This too was the fear of the Worcester & Birmingham proprietors, who also had an interest in diverting to their waterway midlands' trade that might otherwise go up the Staffs & Worcs. The opposition was the more powerful party, and the Bill was thrown out. While the Navigation Company now put forward a smaller scheme, for 6ft 6in to Worcester, an opposition company, the Severn Improvement Company, was sponsored by the Worcester & Birmingham Canal with support from the Gloucester & Berkeley, which sought to get 5ft to Worcester only by means of two movable weirs.

The Navigation Company's Bill was again defeated, and after a deputation had been sent from the Gloucester & Berkeley a compromise was arrived at by which the latter would support a Bill for the improvement of the river by public commissioners. Thereupon the Navigation Company dissolved itself after £20,000 had been spent in Parliamentary expenses. A Bill was introduced in 1841 for this purpose, but by this time the canal interests (except the Staffordshire & Worcestershire) had gone back on their support, fearing damage to the river. Only when it was agreed to put no lock lower than Diglis, near Worcester, but to dredge thence to Gloucester, did the Bill pass in 1842. A commission was then constituted, representative of the towns and navigation interests on the river, and at last the Severn had a controlling authority.

Compared with the Severn, the Shannon had much more attention paid to it, and money spent, prior to 1842. Afterwards, development was somewhat similar.

The Shannon, longest river in the British Isles, includes canal sections and also lakes or loughs, some of considerable size. As far as navigation is concerned, we can start with Lough Allen. Then follows a section by Battlebridge and Carrick-on-Shannon to Jamestown; then Lough Boderg, Roosky, Lough Forbes, and a section to Lough Ree (18 miles long). At the lough's far end is Athlone, whence the river runs past Shannon Harbour and Banagher to Portumna, whence it enters Lough Derg (24 miles). From Killaloe beyond the lake lies the final section to Limerick, below which the estuary begins.

This great river has several natural tributaries, which include the River Boyle, joining the Shannon above Carrick-on-Shannon, itself made navigable into and just beyond Lough Key. In course of time, also, three canals were to join it. The Ballinamore & Ballyconnell, entered by the Leitrim river just north of the Boyle, an ambitious effort opened in 1842 to connect the Shannon with the Upper Lough Erne, the Ulster Canal, Lough Neagh, Belfast and Newry, was a total failure. Seven miles above Lough Ree, the Royal Canal from Dublin, completed in 1817, the canal mania's contribution to Ireland, entered, and at Shannon Harbour the Grand Canal from Dublin came in. Opened in 1805, it was in 1828 continued across the river and completed to Ballinasloe.

There had been proposals to make the river navigable even before the general enabling Act of 1715, which included the Shannon's improvement from Limerick to Carrick-on-Shannon. Action, however, waited until 1755, when Thomas Omer, on behalf of the Corporation for Inland Navigation, began work on both the Limerick–Killaloe section and on the upper Shannon. The first, an example of optimistic estimates, insufficient technical supervision, and therefore

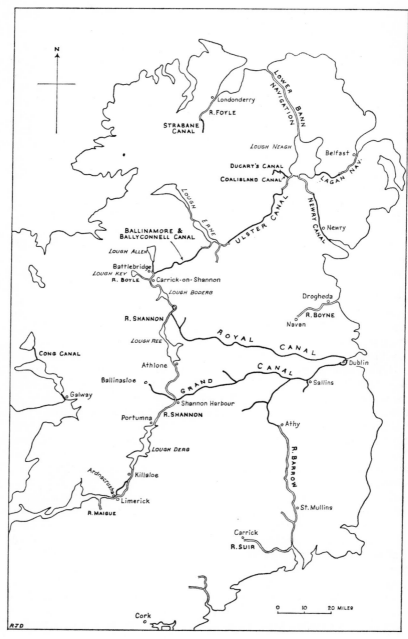

Map 17 The canals of Ireland

highly intermittent progress, was transferred to the Limerick Navigation Company in 1767, but not opened until 1799, and then only for small boats. To complete this system of three by-pass canals with two intervening river stretches, with 14 locks, a tidal lock and 12 others, six being in staircase pairs, together with a flood lock at Killaloe, the Directors General of Inland Navigation had to take the section over in 1803. They kept it, finished it, and handed it back to the company in 1829. It had cost £96,000, took craft 74ft × 14ft, but was still imperfect.

Higher up, the length from Battlebridge to Lough Allen was begun, but not completed until 1822, with two slightly smaller locks. Between Roosky and Killaloe, the river was reputed navigable in 1769, with locks and half-locks, and the remaining by-pass, the Jamestown Canal, a few years later. So, while the Jamestown–Killaloe section had early been canalised, though unsatisfactorily, the top and important lower sections had to wait for the 1820s to be perfected.

In the 1790s the directors of the Grand Canal, which was to join the Shannon in 1805, began to take an interest in the condition of the middle length between Portumna, at the top of Lough Derg, and Athlone, at the bottom of Lough Ree. If they could get a grant towards the cost, they were willing to take it over and improve it. William Jessop, called in, reported on the river up to Lough Allen, and made proposals, on the basis of which the company asked the Government for a £130,000 grant. This failed to go through, but a modified scheme for the middle Shannon (Portumna–Athlone) got a £54,634 grant in 1806, the year after the canal's opening, and was finished by 1810. However, even after the whole river was open, tonnage was negligible—in 1835, under 9,000 tons north of Athlone, under 20,000 on the middle Shannon, and in 1836, just over 36,000 tons on the Killaloe–Limerick section.

Thereafter, a concern for public works to relieve unemployment combined with drive from passenger steamboat interests produced reports from the engineer Thomas Rhodes in 1832 and 1833, proposing major improvements. As a result, Shannon Commissioners were appointed under an 1845 Act to take charge of the whole river: they included Rhodes and also William Cubitt. Their work was done in the middle section, from Killaloe northwards to Battlebridge: this they rebuilt, enlarging some lock cuts but eliminating others and using the dredged river channel instead to take steamers 102ft × 30ft. Below Killaloe, dimensions remained smaller and bridges lower, as also on the unimportant Lough Allen section above Battlebridge. The improvements increased traffic: in 1845, 16,113 passengers were carried on the river and 105,084 tons conveyed, 31,537 of which was interchange traffic with the canals, mainly the Grand. To get these increases, nearly £600,000 had been spent.

CHAPTER XI

War with the Railways

♦♦♦

THOUGH the early railways had mostly been built as feeders to canals, and the early locomotives had been used on such lines—Trevithick's on a canal feeder in South Wales, Stephenson's on a coal line to the Tyne—yet even before the days of steam, railways and canals had competed. There was, for instance, the Surrey Iron Railway, which had struggled with the Croydon Canal for the carriage of goods from the Thames to Croydon. No existing navigation interest was affected by the building of the Stockton & Darlington Railway (though a canal had first been proposed), but during the two years 1824 and 1825 that saw the opening of that historic line, a number of railway Bills were promoted, and some Acts obtained, which foreboded the coming struggle.

For instance, a meeting was held in Gloucestershire on 24 September 1824 to promote a railway, for which locomotives were recommended, from Framilode on the Severn or from Frampton on the Gloucester & Berkeley Canal to Stroud, with a capital of £50,000, to be called the Stroud & Severn Rail Road.

It is not quite clear how serious the promoters were in their intentions to proceed with a railway, for they authorised their committee to enter at once into negotiation with the Stroudwater Navigation for a reduction in rates of tonnage. The canal company refused to do so, and the railway committee then decided to go ahead with the promotion of a Bill. This attitude of the railway promoters seriously frightened the canal company, who pointed out that they were not profiteers, over forty years their average profit having been only $5\frac{7}{8}$ per cent, but agreed to reduce their tonnage rate for the whole length of their navigation from 3s 6d (17½p) to 2s 9½d (14p) per ton, and agreed also to reduce it by another 6d (2½p) if the railway project were abandoned. The railway promoters insisted, however, on presenting their Bill in the Session of 1825, saying:

'. . . that . . . they did not consider the suggested reduction of Tonnage to be a sufficient inducement to them to enter into any negociation for the abandoning the Railway.'[1]

The Bill was opposed by the landowners, the Stroudwater and the Thames & Severn Canal companies, and was defeated.

The lesson that competition would reduce canal tolls was not lost on businessmen. There was no other way, so long as the companies did not exceed the maxima laid down in their Acts. The very high profits of many canal companies, and the refusal of reductions when railway competition threatened—for not all companies were as accommodating as the Stroudwater—led to railways being regarded by the public as their saviours from canal monopoly. The story of the Erewash valley coal trade, told at the Canal Conference of 1888, illustrates the point.

'The Derbyshire and Nottingham colliery proprietors had exclusively supplied Leicester with coal,* until the opening of the Swannington line, in 1832, placed the trade in the hands of the West Leicestershire colliery people. A reduction of 3s. 6d. per ton on coal delivered at Leicester, from the Erewash valley, was needed to enable the Derbyshire and Nottinghamshire proprietors to retain the trade. As this traffic amounted to 160,000 tons a year, it was a great question, both for canals and colliery proprietors. The question was whether coal-owners or canal proprietors should make the sacrifice. The Erewash Canal received, for toll and wharfage, 2s. per ton for 12 miles; Loughborough, 3s. per ton for 8 miles; Leicester, 1s. 8d. for 14 miles —total, 6s. 8d. per ton (exclusive of boating and haulage charges) for 34 miles, or 2½d. per ton per mile. Conferences were held with the canal committees, who decided each to allow a drawback of 6d. per ton "on such coal only as shall be delivered at Leicester at 10s. per ton". The coal-owners, who held that the canals should allow 1s., "promptly rejected" these proposals, and the meeting broke up, with the colliery proprietors determined to free themselves from the monopoly of these canals by making a railway. . . . The result was, the railway secured the traffic to the detriment of the canals, who are now, in 1888, glad to pass coal at 2d. per ton each, or 6d. per ton for the whole 34 miles.'[2]

The use of locomotives upon a railway that competed directly with navigations began in 1830, when the Liverpool & Manchester Railway was opened. With it a new situation was created, for steam traction brought to railways two advantages, speed and the ability to haul heavy loads. The waterways bitterly opposed the early railway Acts, and made their obtainment an expensive matter for the railway shareholders. Indeed, inducements had to be offered them to withdraw their opposition. A curious situation then developed. Early railways were thought of much as if they were land canals; proprietors said they only wished to be toll-takers, and Parliament in

* In the 1790s there had been an attempt to link the Leicestershire collieries to Leicester by means of tramroads and a canal through Charnwood Forest. This had failed.

Page 219, Plate XI Waterways of Scotland: (*above*) the pleasure steamer *Fairy Queen* on the Forth & Clyde Canal; (*below*) Slateford, one of the magnificent aqueducts of the Edinburgh & Glasgow Union Canal

Page 220, Plate XII Waterways of Ireland: (*above*) sods of turf at Rahan near Tullamore on the Grand Canal await transport in 1894. The 'kish' or basket on the crane was used as a turf measure; (*below*) Athlumney mill near Navan on the Boyne Navigation in 1894. Craft with square transom were unusual in Ireland

Page 221, *Plate XIII* Waterways of Ireland: (*above*) Grange mills above 12th lock, Grand Canal, with a bye-trader's boat, in 1884; (*below*) the *Countess of Mayo* at the pierhead, Killaloe, River Shannon, about 1910

some cases empowered any carrier to run trains who wished, land-owners to make branch lines to connect with the railways, and lords of the manor to use free of charge those parts of the lines that passed through their property. The Upper Medway Navigation Co in 1845 indeed bought their own locomotive to haul coal trains on the South Eastern Railway, but quickly found that Parliamentary powers were little use against the railway's determination not to allow their loco-motive to run. On the London & Birmingham all carrying was done by private carrier for a time, the company only providing waggons and engines, while on the Great Western and the Grand Junction Railways carriers competed with the railway company.

We are nowadays so used to thinking of all matters of trade in national terms that it is difficult for us to realise that both the canals in their day and the railways in theirs began as essentially local affairs. The canals had indeed grown into a national system by the fact of joining up with one another, but they had never got over the stage of being small, independent and jealous units, often competing with each other as well as with rival methods of transport such as roads, coastal ships and horse tramroads; they were constructed of all sizes and shapes, and traffic passed from one to another with difficulty.

The railways began in the same way, as local affairs—the Stockton & Darlington, the Liverpool & Manchester, the Canterbury & Whitstable, built to improve communication between two towns, or along one route. Even the bigger projects, such as the London & Birmingham, were still local in the sense that they were not, and were not thought for practical purposes to be, part of a national scheme.

Competition began, therefore, as local competition between a waterway and a railway for the same passenger and goods traffic between two points, as happened between Manchester and Liver-pool. In the 1830s the annual reports of almost every canal company carried some statement to the effect that a railway in competition with that undertaking was projected. An extraordinary general meet-ing of the Basingstoke proprietors, for instance, was called for 22 September 1831:

'. . . to adopt such measures as may be necessary for the Interests of this Company, in regard to the proposed Railway, from London to Southampton.'[3]

Just as the river navigations had bitterly opposed in the Parlia-mentary committees the making of canals, so now the latter set them-selves to oppose the railway Bills in a way that, till the railway mania of 1845–7, did not differ much from a standard pattern. First, pam-pheteering, meetings, and a little misrepresentation; then petitions and the organising of Parliamentary opposition; then, if the canal was important enough, compensation or possibly purchase. The Kennet & Avon committee reported in 1835:

'The necessity of watching and opposing the Great Western Railway Bill, during the last two years, has materially added to the law expenses of the company; but the committee beg to inform the proprietors, that such arrangements have been made as rendered unnecessary a continuance of opposition to the Bill, and as cannot, in the opinion of the committee, fail (if the bill should pass) to be satisfactory to the proprietors.'[4]

These arrangements consisted of a payment of £10,000 by the railway company, less the value of lands carrying a rent-charge of £100 per annum that were transferred to the railway. Since the gross annual receipts of the canal company for the previous five years had averaged £45,213, the compensation payment was not large, and reflected the bad bargaining position of the canal.

The railway Bills obtained, the canal companies then gained a few years of extra prosperity by carrying the materials to build their rivals. For instance, the receipts of the Kennet & Avon rose from the average given above to a peak of £48,269 in 1840. Then the railway was opened, and competition began, fly-boat services being affected first. Takings on the Kennet & Avon in three years dropped to £32,045, caused not by loss of tonnage but by the drastic cut in tolls necessary to keep it.

Price-cutting was the commonest competitive weapon, and it was sometimes taken to the point at which a weak canal company charged no toll at all, only freight charges being taken by the carriers. At the same time, steps were taken to improve the service, as when on 27 March 1844 the Gloucester & Berkeley company agreed to a proposal of Pickfords, the carriers, that trows be permitted to move at all hours of the night to expedite carriage and so enable water carriers to compete more successfully with railways.

This lengthening of the permitted hours during which boats could move through locks and tunnels, in some cases to the extent of 24 hour working, combined with the religious revival of the time to cause pressure to be brought on the canal companies against Sunday canal work. In 1839, for instance, 140 boatmen at Shardlow petitioned the Trent & Mersey company to close the canal on Sunday, and in the next year that company in turn petitioned Parliament 'for the general prevention of Traffic on all Canals and Railways on Sundays'.[5] The Lancaster and the Worcester & Birmingham companies took the same view. Protests against Sunday working also came in from canalside towns, such as that from Stourport in 1839.

Companies varied in their attitudes: on the Manchester–Wakefield line, the Calder & Hebble closed its line on Sundays from 1836, but the Rochdale did not agree, and, in one instance defended a boatman accused by the Calder & Hebble of contravening their bye-law.

Most of the money of the early railways was made from passenger carrying—rather against their own expectations—the heavier goods remaining for the time being upon the canals, though at a lower rate of toll. In 1843 the railways received from the carriage of passengers £3,110,257, and from goods £1,424,932. Five years later, in 1848, the receipts from passengers had risen to £5,720,382, but those from goods to £4,213,169. Canal dividends had also as yet suffered little from the railway competition that so far existed: the Oxford paid 25 per cent in 1846, as against 32 per cent in 1833, the Coventry 25 per cent as against 32 per cent; the Trent & Mersey 30 per cent at against 37½ per cent.

There is a close parallel between the development of canals—first, the building of isolated lines of waterway; then the evident success of the new type of transport, and then the canal mania—and that of railways. From 1830, the date of the opening of the first really successful railway operated by locomotives, to 1844 was a time of construction. Towards the end of the period, the local view that had so far been taken of railways gave way to the national in the minds of those most concerned with the companies. The importance of through routes, the necessity for spheres of influence, seized upon such enterprising railway directors as George Hudson. The railway mania began. It consisted of a mad scramble to promote companies and to buy up competitors. Twenty-three railway Acts were passed in 1843, 48 in 1844, and 108 in 1845. These competitors might be either other railways or canals, and anyone who reads the annals of that time realises that there was little difference in the minds of railway directors between the two types of competitor; both represented a threat to the golden dreams raised up by the dividends of the Stockton & Darlington or the Liverpool & Manchester.

The Government at first was doubtful of the wisdom of allowing an unrestricted amalgamation policy, whether of railways with railways, or of railways with canals, and it was laid down that all amalgamation Bills must be examined by the Board of Trade, who would determine whether they were in the public interest. The tide was, however, coming in too strongly; soon afterwards the decision was reversed, and no further attempt to control the leasing or sale of one line of transport by another was made until after the railway mania was over. The control policy had, however, reversed the leasing in 1843 of the Calder & Hebble to the Manchester & Leeds Railway.

After protest by the Aire & Calder to the Board of Trade, it was ruled that the lease must either be cancelled or a legalising Act sought. It was cancelled.

In 1846, a committee of the House of Commons, in its second report, recommended a number of precautions to be taken before railway and canal amalgamations were allowed, such as the inclusion in authorising Acts of low maximum canal tolls, and provisions to ensure that railway-owned canals were kept in repair and supplied with water. It led to an Act of the same year which set up a policing Railway Commission. *Laissez-faire* ideas, however, caused its abolition in 1851, its duties going to the Board of Trade.

Parliament now chose to put railways and waterways upon competitive equality. Canal companies' Acts had bound them to charge the same tolls for any one mile of their line as for any other, and not to discriminate between customers, though this rigidity was a little lessened by drawbacks on tolls for cargoes carried a minimum distance and discounts for those passing a minimum annual tonnage over the canal. In 1844, however, a railway Bill sought power to vary tolls, whereupon, led by the Aire & Calder, representatives of canal companies met in London, calling themselves the United Body of Canal Proprietors.

Canal companies' Acts, again, unlike railway Acts, did not specifically authorise the companies to operate carrying craft. Neither had they forbidden the practice. Some companies had carried extensively in the past, others occasionally, others had operated through nominally independent firms. In their carrying role they could quote ad hoc rates which, as toll-takers, they were prevented from doing, and the resulting anomaly must have looked unsafe to the United Body. They therefore drafted, and in 1845 got through Parliament, the Canal Tolls Act, which empowered canal companies to charge different rates per ton-mile on different parts of their line, though the varied rates had to be applied equally to all, and the Canal Carriers' (or Clauses) Act, which enabled companies to carry and provide towage services on their own or other waterways, though not to discriminate between customers in doing so. This second Act also empowered companies to make traffic agreements with railway or other canal companies and to lease themselves to any other canal or navigation company, in a section whose implications were not then seen. In 1847 a third Act enabled companies to borrow money to set up carrying departments.

Very few canal companies seem to have had any feeling that there was a general waterway interest opposed to a general railway interest, or that the one kind of transport was locked in battle with the other.

One of the few was the Staffs & Worcs, which proposed to send a circular letter to other canal companies (I do not think it was ever sent) which said:

'An experience of seventy years has established the utility and importance of Inland Water Communication. It has become intimately interwoven with the great manufacturing, trading, and agricultural industry of this country, and has been mainly instrumental to the development of its resources and the growth of its power and importance. But although your Committee are quite ready to admit the advantage and necessity of Railways as a great step in advance of the old modes of conveyance for passengers and many articles of commerce, they conceive that a stoppage of any part of the great chain of inland water communication, would cripple the whole system and produce irremediable mischief to the interests of the Canals and Navigable Rivers and to those of the Community at large. At present their ramifications extend into every part of the manufacturing portions of the Kingdom which have thus a mutual dependence on each other, and a common interest in maintaining unbroken the existing water communication, and they afford to the public the only salutary check to and control over those charges and regulations which the Railway Companies may at pleasure impose if left uncontrolled by such check.'[6]

On the other hand, a month later, when it seemed likely that the Regent's, Warwick & Birmingham and Warwick & Napton would all be bought for conversion to railways, such a powerful company as the Grand Junction could write mildly to the Board of Trade saying that: 'altho' this Committee is not aware that any reasonable objection can be urged to the whole, or even the greater portion, of any thorofare line of Canals being converted into Railways, it is to be hoped that with a view to protect the inland navigation of the Country Her Majesty's Government will be disposed to oppose in Parliament, the principle of partial conversion.'[7]

The first incident of the war with the railways was a case of desertion to the enemy, for in 1831 the Manchester, Bolton & Bury Canal proprietors obtained an Act authorising them to make a railway at or near the line of canal, and altering their name to the Company of Proprietors of the Manchester, Bolton & Bury Canal Navigation & Railway. A successful take-over bid by a group of railway promoters now brought about a change of control. It was decided not to turn the canal into a railway, as had been the intention, but to build a railway alongside the waterway. It was opened in 1838. In 1846 the company amalgamated with the Manchester & Leeds Railway, which the following year changed its name to the Lancashire & Yorkshire.

Other canal companies later followed the example of the Manchester, Bolton & Bury, and turned themselves into railways, among them the Ellesmere & Chester, Liskeard & Looe Union, Thames & Medway, Monmouthshire, and the Carlisle. The important Don company followed its own path in order to dominate south Yorkshire traffic, on the one hand absorbing three other waterways, the Stainforth & Keadby, Dearne & Dove and Sheffield Canals, on the other encouraging the formation of what became the South Yorkshire, Doncaster & Goole Railway. With this line the Don company amalgamated in 1850 to form the South Yorkshire Railway & River Don Company, which operated as a combined rail-waterway transport concern until it was leased in 1864 by the Manchester, Sheffield & Lincolnshire Railway, whereupon the waterway side became much less important.

Before the mania began, only one or two other waterways had been sold or leased to a railway company: for instance, the Kensington, vested in the West London Railway in 1839, following an agreement made in 1836, and the Croydon, bought by the London & Croydon Railway also in 1836. By 1845, however, there was a double interest at work; the railways wishing to eliminate a competitor and using their shareholders' money to do so; and canal proprietors who had experienced a year or two of what railway competition meant, and who were in many cases anxious to sell out while the golden shower continued. In 1845 five navigations, beginning with the Norwich & Lowestoft, of a total length of 78¼ miles, came under railway control; in 1846, seventeen navigations with a total length of 774½ miles, and in 1847, six navigations with a total length of 96¼* miles. In these three years about four-fifths of the mileage of all railway-controlled canals was acquired, being one-fifth of all the navigable waterways in Great Britain. They included the 160 miles of the Birmingham Canal Navigations, and the 204 miles of the Shropshire Union system, on which railway control did not become effective for some time.

There was one curious case of the reverse process; of a canal company that leased a railway. The Lancaster Canal, which had increased the tonnage carried upon it from 459,000 tons in 1825 to 617,000 tons in 1840, was seriously hit by the opening in 1840 of the Lancaster & Preston railway—as after 1846 by the Lancaster & Carlisle. The canal company therefore obtained a lease of the Lancaster & Preston in 1842 for 21 years, for an annual rent of £13,300. In 1848, however, the Lancaster & Preston, wishing to sell itself to the Lancaster & Carlisle, offered the canal proprietors £4,875 a year for the remainder

* These figures include the canals that turned themselves into railways.

of their lease, as well as the cessation of the annual rent. This offer was accepted. In 1859 these lines were leased (later sold) to the London & North Western Railway, in 1864 the canal itself was leased to the same railway, and in 1885 bought outright. Part of the separate southern portion of the canal, from Johnson's Hillock to Wigan, was in 1864 leased to the Leeds & Liverpool Canal Company, since it formed part of their line.

Whereas railway competition greatly affected Irish waterways, most of which were economically less secure than those in Britain, only one waterway was bought by a railway, and another leased for a time. The Royal Canal, less prosperous than the Grand, received an offer to purchase from the Midland Great Western at some £300,000, 40 per cent of its written-down capital and rather over one-fifth of original cost. The railway wanted its land to build their line; the canal company were agreeable, and the purchase was authorised in 1845. Thereafter it remained open, but in steadily deteriorating condition.

The same railway then tried to buy the Grand Canal. The latter company had been working a haphazardly observed rates agreement with the rival Great Southern & Western Railway since 1847, and in 1848, bankrupt, had had to write down its capital. In 1850 the GS & WR ended the agreement, and in 1852 offered to buy the Grand Canal. The MGWR made a higher offer, which was accepted. The authorising Bill was, however, defeated by the GSWR, and the MGWR then leased the Grand for seven years from 1853 at £19,564pa. During the lease the two railway companies agreed to buy the canal jointly, but the MGWR had been losing money on it, and when in 1860 the proposed canal rates seemed too low, the Bill was dropped and the canal returned to its own company, who then negotiated rates agreements with both railways.

Railways bought canals for three reasons; because they could not get their Bills without coming to an arrangement with their principal opponents; because they were actual or potential competitors; or because they wanted to use the line of the canal for a railway.

Those canals, the purchase of which was authorised as part of the Bill giving powers to a railway company to construct its line, included the Stratford-upon-Avon, the Stourbridge Extension, the Ashby-de-la-Zouch, and the Cromford. They were in a position to make a good bargain, and in addition, to make sure that the acquisition of the waterway by a railway company did the least possible harm to other waterway interests. For instance, in the Act for the sale of the Ashby Canal, in 1846, it was laid down that the maximum tolls charged should not exceed the railway charges, and that:

'. . . if, owing to railway competition, coal from the Moira collieries is diverted from the Oxford canal (which is a continuation of the Coventry Canal, and is in communication of course with the Ashby Canal), and in order to meet such diversion the Oxford Canal lower their tolls for this traffic, then the Midland Railway must lower the tolls on the Ashby Canal proportionately, provided that the tolls shall not be reduced below ¼d. per ton per mile. . . . There is a further clause to this effect, that if any one or more of the canals forming the route to London, combine to reduce their rates, the Midland Company are bound to reduce the tolls on the Ashby Canal correspondingly.'[8]

Junction with the Trent and Mersey Canal.

ETRURIA WHARF.																
0½	0½	Chatterley's Bridge and Caldon Place.														
1½	1½	1	Heath's Shed.													
2	1¾	1¼	0½	Close's Wharf.												
2¼	2	1½	0¾	0½	Ivyhouse.											
2½	2½	2	1	0¾	0½	Keeling's Lane.										
3½	3¼	2¾	2-	1½	1¼	1	Prime's Wharf.									
4¾	4½	4	3¼	3	2½	2¼	1½	Milton.								
5½	5½	5	4	3¾	3½	3	2¼	1	Cockshead.							
6	5¾	5¼	4½	4	3¾	3½	2½	1¼	0½	Heakley.						
7	6¾	6¼	5½	5	4¾	4½	3½	2¼	1½	1	Stockton Brook.					
7½	7¼	6¾	6	5½	5¼	5	4	2¾	2	1½	0½	Stanley.				
8	7¾	7¼	6½	6	5¾	5½	4½	3¾	2½	2	1	0½	Post Lane Bridge an			
8½	8½	8	7	6¾	6½	6	5¼	4	3	2¾	1¾	1¼	0¾	Parklane.—(E		
10	9¾	9¼	8½	8	7¾	7½	6½	5¼	4½	4	3	2½	2	1½	Junct	
10	10	9½	8½	8¼	8	7½	6¾	5½	4½	4¼	3¼	2¾	2¼	1½	0¼	H.
10½	10¼	9¾	9	8½	8¼	8	7	5¾	5	4½	3½	3	2½	2	0½	
11½	11½	11	10	9¾	9½	9	8¼	7	6	5¾	4¾	4¼	3¾	3	1¾	
1 0¼	1 0	11½	10¾	10½	10	9¾	9	7½	6¾	6½	5½	5	4½	3¾	2½	
1 1½	1 1½	1 1	1 0	11¾	11½	11	10¼	9	8	7¾	6¾	6¼	5¾	5	3¾	
1 3	1 2¾	1 2¼	1 1½	1 1	1 0¾	1 0½	11½	10¼	9½	9	8	7½	7	6½	5	
1 3¼	1 3	1 2½	1 1¾	1 1½	1 1	1 0¾	1 0	10½	9¾	9½	8½	8	7½	6¾	5½	
1 5	1 5	1 4½	1 3½	1 3¼	1 3	1 2½	1 1¾	1 0½	11½	11¼	10¼	9¾	9¼	8½	7¼	
1 5¼	1 5	1 4½	1 3¾	1 3½	1 3	1 2¾	1 2	1 0½	11¾	11½	10½	10	9½	8¾	7½	
1 6¼	1 6	1 5½	1 4¾	1 4½	1 4	1 3¾	1 3	1 1½	1 0¾	1 0½	11½	11	10½	9¾	8½	
1 6½	1 6½	1 6	1 5	1 4¾	1 4½	1 4	1 3¼	1 2	1 1	1 0¾	11¾	11¼	10¾	10	8¾	
1 8	1 8	1 7½	1 6½	1 6¼	1 6	1 5½	1 4¾	1 3½	1 2½	1 2¼	1 1¼	1 0¾	1 0¼	11½	10¼	
1 10	1 10	1 9½	1 8½	1 8¼	1 8	1 7½	1 6¾	1 5½	1 4½	1 4¼	1 3¼	1 2¾	1 2¼	1 1½	1 0¼	1
2 0½	2 0½	2 0	1 11	1 10¾	1 10½	1 10	1 9¼	1 8	1 7	1 6¾	1 5¾	1 5¼	1 4¾	1 4	1 2¾	1
2 1½	2 1½	2 1	2 0	1 11¾	1 11½	1 11	1 10¼	1 9	1 8	1 7¾	1 6¾	1 6¼	1 5¾	1 5	1 3¾	1
2 2	2 2	2 1½	2 0½	2 0¼	2 0	1 11½	1 10¾	1 9½	1 8½	1 8¼	1 7¼	1 6¾	1 6¼	1 5½	1 4¼	1
2 2½	2 2½	2 2	2 1	2 0¾	2 0½	2 0	1 11¼	1 10	1 9	1 8¾	1 7¼	1 7¼	1 6¾	1 6	1 4¾	1
2 4½	2 4½	2 4	2 3	2 2¾	2 2½	2 2	2 1¼	2 0	1 11	1 10¾	1 9¾	1 9¼	1 8¾	1 8	1 6¾	1
2 6¼	2 6	2 5½	2 4¾	2 4½	2 4	2 3¾	2 3	2 1½	2 0¾	2 0½	1 11½	1 11	1 10½	1 9¾	1 8½	1

J. PIGOT AND SC

Figure 36 Tolls on the Trent

The situation envisaged in this Act later came about.

Many canal companies, whose opposition to railway Bills had not brought forth an acceptable offer, or who at first were prepared to ride the whirlwind, later became uncertain of their ability to compete, and tried to bring the railway companies to the point of making a proposal. One way of doing this was to promote a Bill for a rival railway. In 1845, for instance, the committee of the Kennet & Avon Canal reported:

'The Committee have had under their consideration the expediency of converting the Canal into a Railway, and they intend taking immediate steps to obtain every information and order an actual survey

RATES OF TONNAGE

ON THE

Caldon, Leek, & Uttoxeter Canals,

AT ONE PENNY PER TON PER MILE.

———ooo———

Commencing 19th November, 1832.

———ooo———

)

ek Canal (to Leek 2¾*d.*)

ford Turn Bridge.

Bridge.

akmeadow Ford Lock.

1½	Crowgutter.													
1¾	0½	Consall Flint Mill.												
3½	2¼	2	FROGHALL Junction with the Uttoxeter Canal.											
3¾	2½	2	0¼	Froghall Mill.										
4¾	3½	3	1¼	1	Ross Bridge.									
5	3¾	3½	1½	1½	0½	Jackson's Wood Lock and East Wall.								
6½	5¼	5	3	3	2	1½	Oak-a-moor.							
8½	7¼	7	5	5	4	3½	2	Alton or Alveton (Lord Shrewsbury's.)						
11	9¾	9½	7½	7½	6½	6	4½	2½	Quickshill.					
0	10¾	10½	8½	8½	7½	7	5½	3½	1	ROCESTER.				
0½	11¼	11	9	9	8	7½	6	4	1½	0½	Cambridge.			
1	11¾	11½	9½	9½	8½	8	6½	4½	2	1	0½	Hooklane.		
3	1 1¾	1 1½	11½	11½	10½	10	8½	6½	4	3	2½	2	Spath.	
4¾	1 3½	1 3	1 1¼	1 1	1 0	11¾	10¼	8¼	5¾	4¾	4¼	3¾	1¾	UTTOXETER.

. MANCHESTER.

, Leek and Uttoxeter branches

to be made, that they may be prepared (if it be found practicable) to lay before the Proprietors the best mode of proceeding.'[9]

The canal owners were on a good wicket. It was with crocodile tears that the committee reported in the following year:

'The Committee regret to report the loss of the Bill which was applied for in the present Session of Parliament . . . for making the London, Newbury and Bath Direct Railway, in conjunction with the Kennet and Avon Canal, but they trust that as a General Meeting will be shortly held, the explanations which will there be given, of the arrangement come to with the Great Western Railway Company and the Wilts, Somerset and Weymouth Railway Company, will be satisfactory.'[10]

It was in 1852 that the Great Western Railway finally agreed to take over the canal for a payment capitalised at £210,415. The capital cost of the waterway had been just over £1 million, but the highest dividend paid had been 3¾ per cent, and since the railway had been opened the usual distribution had been under 1 per cent.

Again, railways were sometimes forced to acquire canals by the extent of the competition that developed, and the losses on carriage by rail which showed themselves. The opening of the Bristol & Exeter Railway by way of Taunton in 1844, and especially of its Tiverton branch in 1848, brought it into direct competition with the Grand Western Canal from Tiverton to Taunton.

From 1845 the canal company had been unable to pay its mortgage interest, and had had to maintain itself with further loans. It was indeed a matter of life or death to defeat the railway, even though a forlorn hope. The canal and the railway proceeded to cut rates against each other, the former about 1851 charging coals from Taunton to Tiverton at tolls of ¼d per ton per mile to enable the canal traders to sell at Tiverton at the same price as the railway company delivered, and later they carried coal free of any toll. At the same time the railway was losing money, but was able to recoup itself elsewhere. The situation was only appreciated by the consumers at Tiverton.

The extent of the price cutting can be seen by comparing the figures for tolls and tonnage in the years 1849 and 1853. In each year the canal carried 37,000 tons, but whereas it received £2,351 in tolls in 1849, this had fallen to £734 in 1853. The canal company had, however, succeeded in raising the tonnage carried on the through haul from Taunton to Tiverton from 1,961 in 1850 to 4,373 in 1852.

It was estimated that the railway was losing £6,000 a year by the competition, and so both parties were anxious to come to terms, and did so after the railway had opened negotiations with the Bridgwater & Taunton Canal, so threatening the source of the Grand Western's coal supplies.

The railway refused to buy the canal, but agreed to lease it for £2,000 a year, and in 1853 the tolls upon it and upon the Bridgwater & Taunton were raised to the full Parliamentary levels, while the railway charges rose also. Traffic left the canal almost entirely. Then, ten years later when it was clear that the canal company was unable to revive its business, the railway made an offer for purchase of £30,000, which was accepted. The Taunton to Holcombe Rogus portion was dismantled, but the part that carried the stone traffic from Holcombe Rogus was preserved.

Lastly, in a few cases canals were bought or leased in order that they could be converted into railways, the rails being laid along their banks, such as the Aberdeenshire, Glastonbury, Oakham, Andover, or part of the Leominster.

Financially, the waterways that sold out made no bad bargain for their shareholders, who fared far better than did most of those who remained owners of independent canals. For instance, the Stratford-upon-Avon, owing to a cost of construction far above the estimate, had never been a great success. Authorised in 1793, it was not completed until 1816. In 1824 it paid its first dividend of $3\frac{1}{3}$ per cent, which rose to a maximum of $6\frac{2}{3}$ per cent for seven years. It had cost altogether some £300,000, and the owners of bonds and shares received between them £160,434 for their property from the Oxford, Worcester & Wolverhampton Railway company. The little Stourbridge Extension Canal was sold to the same company for more than its capital value. The proprietors of the Cromford Canal, which had cost about £79,000 to build before the war-time rise of prices had become severe, judiciously agreed during the railway mania to sell to the Manchester, Buxton, Matlock & Midlands Junction Railway before the most seriously competitive line, the Erewash Valley Railway, was opened in 1847. Since by 1850 the canal tolls had fallen from £14,198 in 1840 to £7,588, though the traffic only from 346,208 tons to 284,889, they were perhaps lucky to get £103,500 for their property. The Fossdyke Navigation was leased for 894 years to the Great Northern Railway for a yearly rent of £9,570, and the Witham to the same company for 999 years at £10,545 a year and the interest on mortgages amounting to £24,692. These rents were calculated on the basis of the previous three years' profits, plus 5 per cent.

The canals that the railways acquired while they were consolidating their position became in most cases an embarrassment to them. The companies were by statute bound to maintain them in good order, and therefore many waterways were fortunately kept in more or less navigable condition up to the date of nationalisation, which would have decayed if they had been in private hands.

On the other hand, the railway companies naturally wished to carry traffic by rail and not by water, since otherwise they would have been maintaining a competition with themselves. Partly by intention,

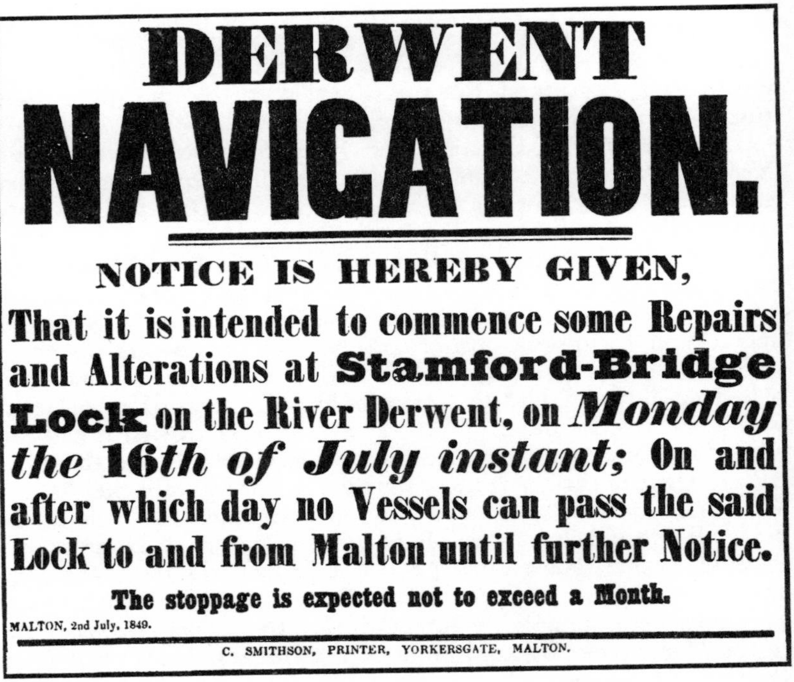

DERWENT NAVICATION.

NOTICE IS HEREBY GIVEN,

That it is intended to commence some Repairs and Alterations at **Stamford-Bridge Lock** on the River Derwent, on *Monday the 16th of July instant;* On and after which day no Vessels can pass the said Lock to and from Malton until further Notice.

The stoppage is expected not to exceed a Month.

MALTON, 2nd July, 1849.

C. SMITHSON, PRINTER, YORKERSGATE, MALTON.

Figure 37   A gift to railway competition

partly by neglect, the general effect of high tolls, lack of dredging, closings for leisurely repairs, decaying warehouses and wharves, failure to provide or maintain cranes, and no effort to get business, was to divert trade from the water to the land.

There were exceptions, either because the canals were indispensable for certain purposes, or because they served an area or attracted traffic not otherwise available to the railway company. The two most important were the Birmingham Canal Navigations and the Shropshire Union system.

The Birmingham Canal Navigations came under railway control by deferred action. The canal company was a powerful one, with a near-monopoly position in the Birmingham area, which had been strengthened by its amalgamation in 1840 with the Wyrley & Essington, and the making almost immediately afterwards of two additional links between the Walsall lines of the former and the Wednesbury canals of the latter. Yet the beginnings of railway competition caused strain, and when the London & Birmingham Railway company proposed a joint venture for a railway taking in Birmingham, Wolverhampton and Dudley, the canal company agreed. Because the Dudley Canal company would obviously be affected, an amalgamation was arranged in 1846 between the two waterway concerns, a second railway, the Shrewsbury & Birmingham, being taken into the partnership. In 1846 the canal company subscribed to the new railway, the Birmingham, Wolverhampton & Stour Valley, and at the same time came to an arrangement with the London & Birmingham Railway, by which the latter would guarantee the dividends of the canal company at 4 per cent, and nominate half the canal committee. So long, however, as the canal company did not need the guarantee, the canal directors should have the casting vote; but in any year in which the guarantee was needed, the railway directors should have the casting vote. With the exception of 1868, however, the dividends of the canal company did not need support from the guarantee until 1874. Thereafter the canal company's income never reached the sum required to pay 4 per cent on its stock in any year, and the company came under continuous railway control. However, in the original agreement a clause stated the canal company should not vary its tolls without the consent of the railway, which thus gained much immediate advantage in the competition for business.

In 1878 the clerk to the company, Mr Thomas, retired after more than fifty years' service, and the then chairman of the company made some revealing remarks at the half-yearly meeting, at which he looked back to Mr Thomas's early days, and went on to say: 'The company would concur in thinking that the directors had done wisely in placing themselves under the tutelage of the L. & N.W.R. instead of leaving themselves to contend against the continually increasing encroachments of the railways, which were now more than ever going on in the district. They might rest under the shadow of the £4 per share which the L. & N.W.R. Company guaranteed to them.'[11]

The case of the Birmingham Canal Navigations illustrates how precarious was any unity of waterway interests in face of the problems with which each company's self-interest confronted it. In December 1844 the Staffs & Worcs, one of the few canals which maintained an anti-railway policy throughout the mad year of 1845, proposed a meeting with the Birmingham 'to confer on the propriety of arranging a Coalition of the Canals in this District, in opposition to the projected Lines of Railway'.[12] The meeting took place, and a joint fund was set up, and agreement reached to oppose railway Bills at any rate to second reading. Alas, only a fortnight later the Birmingham had had second thoughts in the light of the moves by the London & Birmingham Railway, and wrote to say that 'under all the Circumstances . . . [it is] no longer expedient to carry on any united opposition to the various projected Railways'.[13]

The Birmingham Canal Navigations remained busy from the time they came under railway control to the present century. Indeed, the important Cannock Extension and Wyrley Bank branches were constructed, and the Netherton tunnel was built with a double towing path after the agreement with the London & Birmingham Railway. The high figures of trade done upon these canals mask, however, the change that in fact took place. Birmingham and its neighbourhood were intersected with this elaborate network of some 160 miles of canal, along the banks of which had grown up hundreds of works (there were some 550 private basins), which depended for their coal and raw material supplies, and in many cases for the removal of their finished products, upon the waterway. It would have been impossible to divert all this traffic from canal to rail without causing intense dislocation, since in many cases the construction of rail sidings was impossible in such a crowded area. Instead, the railway policy was to use the canal like the road, for a collection and delivery service. Instead of goods being sent from the canalside works for long hauls by waterway to London, Hull or Liverpool, they were sent by water to a railway basin, where they were transferred to rail for the remainder of their voyage. Figures put before the Royal Commission of 1906 show that between 53 per cent and 63 per cent of the goods transhipped could not have completed their journey by waterway; taken the reverse way, the figures show what a large tonnage could in fact have remained upon the water for long hauls.

Railway basins were built upon the Birmingham system by three railways, the London & North Western, Midland, and Great Western. Only for short hauls within the Birmingham system did goods remain upon the water. In 1905, out of 7,546,453 tons of goods conveyed on the Birmingham Canal Navigations, only 1,376,165 tons moved outside them.

Within these limits the Birmingham Canal Navigations were well maintained and improved. Widening and deepening of channels, widening under bridges, new pumping machinery and extensive

BRECON AND ABERGAVENNY
CANAL NAVIGATION.

REDUCTION
of
TONNAGES.

From and after the First day of February, 1863, the Rates, Tolls, & Tonnages, payable to the Company, in respect of their Canal and Railways, will be as follow :

		heretofore				will be		
Coal & Coke		2d. per Ton per Mile,				¾d. per Ton per Mile.		
Lime & Limestone	„	1d.	„	„	„	½d.	„	„
Pitwood, Cordwood, & Sleepers	„	1½d.	„	„	„	1d.	„	„
Round Timber, Deals, Fine, Lath, Helves, &c.	„	1½d.	„	„	„	1½d.	„	„
Iron, Iron Mine, Iron Ore, Cinders, Slates, Stone, Clay, & Bricks	„	1d.	„	„	„	½d.	„	„
Hay, Straw, & Compost.	„	1d.	„	„	„	1d.	„	„
Goods and other Merchandize not above described.	„	2¼d.	„	„	„	1½d.	„	„

Canal Office,
Llanelly, Nr. Abergavenny,
January, 29th, 1863.

By Order,
GEORGE L. HILEY,
Clerk to the Company of Proprietors

PRINTED BY J. HILEY MORGAN, HIGH STREET, ABERGAVENNY.

Figure 38   An example of heavy price-cutting

walling of banks were all carried out under railway control, which showed a gross profit on canal working as well as an indirect gain to the railway system. For instance, in 1905, gross receipts were £190,873 and the working expenses £99,207, but the balance was not enough to pay the guaranteed 4 per cent dividend to the shareholders, and £39,861 was paid to the canal company by the railway company.

The Shropshire Union system, which afterwards controlled over 200 miles of waterway, was authorised in 1846 to include the Ellesmere & Chester (already united with the Birmingham & Liverpool Junction), the Shrewsbury and the two parts of the Montgomeryshire Canal. The object of the company, in which two railways were given powers to hold stock, was to convert part of the canal lines to railways, and to build certain new lines of railway. One of these lines, from Wellington to Stafford, was in fact built; then in 1847* the whole system was leased to the London & North Western Railway, and later part of the Shropshire Canal was added. Since this system covered an area not fully served by the leasing railway, it was encouraged to receive trade. Later, when the Manchester Ship Canal was built. Ellesmere Port upon the Mersey which was the outlet for the canal system became a port on the ship canal. This fact was important enough to persuade the railway to operate the canal as fully as possible, as supplementary to their own system, and to avoid a loss upon the heavy maintenance cost of the waterways. They spent over £250,000 upon new quays, warehouses and a barge dock at Ellesmere Port, and became carriers on the canal. In 1905 the tonnage carried was 469,950, having increased from 371,978 in 1898. After deducting the cost of maintenance and of the carrying business, the company was still making a profit of £6,765, but without any contribution towards interest on capital.

When the railway mania ended in 1847, the greater part of those canals that were destined to pass into railway ownership had already done so. Only fifteen more, with a mileage of 300, were subsequently transferred, though others came for a time under railway direction.

Of the remainder of the canal network, which continued an independent existence in competition with the railways, it was the canal with plenty of factories on its banks that survived, often making its money from only a small portion of its waterway, while long hauls

---

* The lease was authorised in 1847, but not signed till 1857. It guaranteed the shareholders half the rate of dividend of London & North Western Railway ordinary shares, and also the surplus profits of their undertaking up to 6 per cent, and half profits above that amount. The debentures were to be taken over by the railway. Management was by an equal number of directors from the Shropshire Union and the London & North Western Railway.

Page 239, Plate XV   Early days of pleasure cruising: (*above*) a horse boat on the Llangollen Canal; (*below*) on the Ripon Canal in the early 1900s

Page 240, Plate XVI Hope and disaster: (*above*) children and teachers at the Boatmen's Institute, Brentford, in 1912; (*below*) after the Regent's Park explosion of 1874. Sir Laurence Alma-Tadema's house was one of those damaged

fell away. It benefited by the long time lag that intervenes before a user changes from one method of transport to another. All along the banks of canals in Manchester or London stood works that had been built during a time of water transport that might go back for eighty years. It was often impossible to build sidings, and James Wheeler the historian of Manchester wrote quite truly in 1836:

'Railroads have one disadvantage in the carriage of coal for manufactories, which appears likely to give the canals a permanent superiority over them in this branch of traffic. The banks of the latter being generally studded with manufactories (to which such a supply of water as canals afford is indisputable); coals conveyed in boats is lodged without any second expense, at their very doors. The railroads are otherwise circumstanced. The coal is necessarily deposited by them regularly at the "stations", whence it must be carted to its destination. . .'[14]

The advantage was with the canal, though usually only if it cut both tolls and freights from their accustomed levels. It was clear to most manufacturers, however, that the railways were more efficient and offered a wider distribution system. Therefore new factories tended to be situated alongside the rails rather than the waterway, and branches built where a change in the type of transport used was practicable. Indeed, it was often the case with an industrial canal that it was not the original line of competing railway that did the serious damage: it was the subsequent building of branches and sidings into works after works which had formerly sent its goods by canal.

While the industrial canals kept their tonnage at the expense of their receipts, the independent waterways that ran through agricultural districts, and had no wealth of works upon their banks (like the Wilts & Berks) or the heavily locked long-haul canals such as those over the Pennines (like the Rochdale) mostly succumbed sooner or later to the competition of the railway. During the railway mania and afterwards, the railway companies had brought under their control over one-fifth of the navigable waterways of Britain. In the century between the mania and nationalisation another quarter was driven out of active existence by the competition of newer forms of transport, first railways, then motor lorries. It was the relentlessness of this pressure, quite as much as the actual purchase of waterways by railways, that broke the waterway system of the country up into units, and forced it back to the local trade from which it had sprung.

HEREFORDSHIRE and GLOUCESTERSHIRE CANAL.

In the Matter of The Newent Railway Act, 1873, and

In the Matter of The Ross and Ledbury Railway Act, 1873.

TAKE NOTICE, that in pursuance of the powers in that behalf contained in the Newent Railway Act, 1873, and the Ross and Ledbury Railway Act, 1873, it is intended on and after the 30th day of June, 1881,

TO STOP UP AND CLOSE

so much and such part of the CANAL known as the Herefordshire and Gloucestershire Canal as is situate BETWEEN the Worcester and Hereford Railway at LEDBURY in the County of Hereford and the River Severn in the City of GLOUCESTER, and that all rights of way or navigation and other rights and privileges if any along, upon, or over such part of the said Canal with the Banks and Towing Path will as from the said 30th day of June cease and determine accordingly.

AND FURTHER TAKE NOTICE, that all persons who will be affected by the closing of the said portion of the Canal are required, on or before the said 30th day of June, to remove their Barges, Boats, and other Craft accordingly.

Dated this 2nd day of June, 1881.

BY ORDER,

Waterlow and Sons Limited, Printers, London Wall, London.

Figure 39 A canal is closed so that a railway can be built on its track

CHAPTER XII

The Years of Decline

THE completion of the Birmingham & Liverpool Junction Canal in 1835 marked the end of major canal development. It was Telford's great effort to show that an improved canal, straight and comparatively level even though narrow, could compete with a railway, and it cost so much more than the estimate that at one time there was doubt whether it could be opened. A few waterways were built later: the Tame Valley and Netherton tunnel lines of the Birmingham Canal Navigations, and its link to the Warwick & Birmingham Canal that was known as the Birmingham & Warwick Junction; the Chard Canal from that town to the Bridgwater & Taunton, which it joined at Creech St Michael; the continuation of the Herefordshire & Gloucestershire from Ledbury to Hereford; the Manchester & Salford Junction to link the Rochdale Canal with the Mersey & Irwell Navigation; the Runcorn & Weston, to join the Bridgewater Canal to the Weaver; and the Droitwich Junction to join Droitwich to the Worcester & Birmingham, and in the twentieth century one further important link, the New Junction Canal* in Yorkshire. In addition, some new branches were built to existing lines, notably the Bentley, Rushall and Cannock Extension canals on the Birmingham system, and the Slough branch of the Grand Junction.

In the previous chapter we saw what happened to those canals which, in their war with the railways, were taken prisoner or disarmed. What of the remainder, the independent waterways that continued to compete, either from choice or because they could not find a rich enough captor?

The Oxford Canal was built in the days before the Napoleonic Wars inflated construction costs. It had been prosperous from the time that its line from Longford, where it joined the Coventry Canal, to Oxford had been completed in the first days of January 1790. It was additionally benefited when, by the building of the Grand Junction to Braunston, a portion of its line became incorporated in the through route from London to Birmingham, because of the substantial compensation payment to which it became entitled. If we take the year 1870 as marking the date by which the affairs of the water-

* See p 270.

ways had attained some sort of stability in their relation to the railways, we can see at once that the Oxford had in fact lost no traffic, measured in terms of tonnage carried upon it. The figures are these:

1828	450,000 tons	1858	400,000 tons
1838	520,000 ,,	1868	482,000 ,,
1848	420,000 ,,		

They show that tonnage rose from 1828 to 1838, partly by natural increase of trade, partly because the canal was carrying railway constructional material; then the effect of railway competition drove down the tonnages for twenty years, after which the effect both of improvements on the waterway itself, and of generally expanding trade, brought an increase.

Financially, however, the position of the Oxford Canal greatly deteriorated, for its tonnages were maintained at the expense of a steady decrease in tolls and compensation receipts, and so in dividends. Only the fact that its position had been so good at the beginning of the period enabled it to reach the end still in a reasonably strong position. These are the figures, taken every five years:

Year	Toll receipts £	Rate of dividend per cent
1825	84,761	34
1830	92,962	32
1835	72,465	32
1840	84,159	30
1845	76,211	28
1850	46,198	20
1855	23,464	9
1860	25,898	$8\frac{1}{4}$
1865	27,314	$8\frac{3}{4}$
1870	23,632	$8\frac{1}{2}$

Thus the receipts at the end of the period had fallen to about one-quarter, while the tonnage carried remained constant. No exact comparison can be made, however, because of variations in the tolls on the kind of goods carried and in the length of the hauls. We can see, however, that a great change took place in the balance of the trade, and that the traffic had become much more local.

The three great interchange points of Hawkesbury (to the Coventry Canal), Braunston (to the Grand Junction Canal) and Napton Junction (for Birmingham), had accounted in 1830 for 67 per cent of the total receipts. By 1869 the long hauls had so far fallen away that the proportion of total receipts taken at these three points had dropped to 47 per cent, Hawkesbury having suffered least and Napton Junction most. Oxford had not had much interchange traffic with the Thames within the period of comparison, and must be counted as a local centre. Trade to it, to Enslow, to Aynho, to Cropredy, and to Hillmorton (for Rugby) had fallen away heavily owing to railway competition, but where that competition fell less heavily, takings could be maintained, as at Banbury, or indeed increased, as at Stretton.

The Oxford was a major canal which formed part of important through lines of waterway; the Stour was a minor river not joined to any other navigation. Yet this small concern, through whose minute and account books run the names of Gainsboroughs, Constables and Lotts, met the railway threat bravely, made the most of a good competitive position, and survived into the twentieth century as a going concern.

The Stour Navigation from Manningtree to Sudbury had been authorised by an Act of 1705 and by 1835 was paying a dividend of 14 per cent upon its nominal capital of £4,800. On 10 February of that year the minute book recorded the appointment of a surveyor to investigate and report upon the state of the river, and stated:

'That it be a particular instruction to the surveyor that his attention be drawn to the possibility of there being shortly established two lines of Rail Roads through Colchester and Bury Saint Edmunds to Yarmouth and Norwich, and how they are likely to affect the interests of all parties concerned.'

The proprietors at once got back the lease of the tolls from a lessee who had held them for many years, and proceeded to manage the river themselves. They decided to abolish all staunches and to build a number of new locks, dredge and clean the river, improve the towing paths, cut tolls and revise schedules of rates. The improvements were paid for partly by issuing twelve new £100 shares at £400, so raising £4,800, and partly by taking considerable amounts from revenue during two and a half years when no dividends were paid. The result of these measures of reconstruction was to increase the rate of dividend upon the larger capital to 20 per cent in 1840 and 30 per cent in 1846.

In 1845 a railway company offered to buy the shares, and the proprietors with spirit offered them at £1,000 each, the market price having reached £850. They seem to have been sure that the railway would accept the offer, but it was refused, and the proprietors began a long and losing battle. They had the advantage of connection with the sea, and so of the opportunity to handle sea-borne imports, mainly of foreign corn for the mills along the river, and coal for Sudbury and other towns. Exports, chiefly flour, and also bricks from Sudbury for the building of the suburbs of South London, also went by sea for many years. They reduced tolls when they had to, got every possible competitive advantage from quoting special rates, kept the river in good repair, and even experimented with a steam barge. Though the gross income from tolls, which had reached £3,415 in 1847, was less than £2,000 in 1849, it did not finally fall below £1,000 till 1869. A dividend of 15 per cent was still being paid in 1863 and of 6 per cent in 1871; the last, of 1½ per cent, was declared for 1890.

The canal boom of 1888 brought a moment of hope to the weary proprietors, when a vague proposal was made to join the Stour with the Ouse and the Cam. Thereafter mills began to close, the new county councils set up in 1888 began to insist on more expensive standards of maintenance for bridges, and money to keep the navigation alive and in repair was only found from sales of land and property. At last, in 1913, the shareholders resolved to wind up the company. It was revived, unsuccessfully, as a public trust in 1918, and again collapsed in 1935. Navigation may yet be revived once more.

Such was the decline of prosperous companies. Those other concerns which had not at the beginning of the competitive period the small capital and high earning power of such waterways as the Oxford Canal or the Stour Navigation found that by being forced to cut their tolls they eventually brought their receipts below their maintenance costs. These maintenance costs were indeed an important factor, for they slowly rose throughout the century, and formed one jaw of the pincers, the other being falling revenue per ton carried. On the Basingstoke Canal, for instance, an estimate of tonnage and receipts made by the company in 1787 was 30,700 tons and £7,783, or 5·07s per ton carried; in 1801–2 the actual tonnage carried was 18,737 and the tolls 4·08s. In 1814–15, at the end of the Napoleonic War, the position was similar (21,695 tons and 4·17s), and in the boom year of 1825–6 15,258 tons and 4·06s. By 1838–9 the tonnage had risen to 33,717 because of materials being carried for railway building, but tolls were 3.2s. The next year the figures were down to 26,965 and 2·79s; by 1865–6 they had fallen to 20,598 and 1·03s a ton.* At this point the company went into liquidation, though it was later revived more than once under various names before passing into decrepitude or dereliction, except for the small portion between the

---

* For the same reasons as were given earlier, these figures are only roughly comparable. The general trend is clear enough.

Wey and Woking. In 1949 it was bought by a new company, which obtained revenue from the sale of water. The canal was in 1972-3 bought by the Surrey and Hampshire County Councils, and much of it is now being restored.

All canals suffered from the tendency: for instance, the revenue of the very prosperous Somersetshire Coal Canal fell from 2.61s per ton carried in 1828 (113,442 tons and £14,809), to 0.84s per ton in 1868 (140,112 tons and £6,120), and that of the Leeds & Liverpool from 1.59s per ton (1,436,160 tons and £114,518) in 1828 to 1.13s per ton (1,884,140 tons and £94,207) in 1868. It will be noticed that the tonnage carried increased in both these cases, as it did in many others.

Some of the smaller concerns went into voluntary liquidation, retiring with dignity from a contest to which they were not equal. Such a one was the Wey & Arun Junction, which from 1830 to 1865 paid a dividend in all but three years. In 1864 it went into liquidation while there were still assets to divide. Many followed, especially in the seventies, including the Tavistock, Baybridge, Coombe Hill, Ivel, Melton Mowbray and Sleaford Navigation. A few, like the Wilts & Berks, just faded away. The receipts became less and less, till meetings ceased to be held and offices were shut for lack of means to pay wages. The long pounds became slowly un-navigable and stagnant, a nuisance to towns and villages. Then some public authority would take steps to end the life of the canal and stop the nuisance.

In the Fens, where the waterways had been built or enlarged primarily for drainage reasons, a great water-borne trade had grown up before and during the canal age. The coming of the railways saw this trade up and down the rivers and drains of fenland slowly die away, except here and there when the railways did not quite serve local purposes. In this case, however, the waterways themselves continued to be maintained for their primary purpose of drainage.

By the early 1850s a considerable mileage of canals was railway-controlled. Parliament in 1854 passed the Railway & Canal Traffic Act to ensure that these railway canals provided 'reasonable facilities' for traffic, and did not hinder through freights to or from independent waterways. Complaints were to go to the courts. The Act was well-intentioned, but had no teeth, and not until the appointment of commissioners under the Regulation of Railways Act 1873 did policing become effective, or the quotation of through rates compulsory.

Some canals were bought by railways long after the railway mania. This was not illegal, but in order to do so, railways needed authorisation Acts, and as the 1850s moved on, Parliament became less and less inclined to see canal companies absorbed. Railways therefore looked round for expedients whereby they could control canals without having to go before Parliament. One way was to use the leasing clause of the 1845 Canal Carriers' Act in an unintended way. If a railway already owned a canal company, that company could legally lease others. Thus a consortium of three canal owning railways in 1850 jointly leased the Leeds & Liverpool Canal for twenty-one years, and in 1855 another of four companies leased the Rochdale Canal for what became thirty-six years, thus killing the trans-Pennine canal trade in finished textiles. As the Huddersfield was already owned by the LNWR, all three Pennine canals were for a time railway-controlled.

The Rochdale case, taken to the Board of Trade by the vigilant and powerful Aire & Calder, and an effort by the Oxford, Worcester & Wolverhampton Railway also to use the Canal Carriers' Act to lease the Worcester & Birmingham Canal, taken also to the Board of Trade, in this case by the Gloucester & Berkeley company, led to the Government inserting into the Cheap Trains Bill then before Parliament a clause to prevent the practice except after a special Act.

Another way was never prevented. In 1855, three officials of the North Eastern Railway in their own names bought the Yorkshire Derwent Navigation from Earl Fitzwilliam, then leased it to their own company. The same technique was used in 1859 when the Upper Avon was sold to an individual who resold it to the Oxford, Worcester & Wolverhampton Railway, and, more importantly but differently in 1871, when the Bridgewater trustees sold their waterways to the chairmen of the Midland and the Manchester, Sheffield & Lincolnshire railways: these then formed the Bridgewater Navigation Company to take over their purchase.

From the 1840s to the 1870s one gets the impression that the waterways were becoming more and more old-fashioned and unable to cope with the changing world of the mid-nineteenth century. The independent canals seemed mostly to lose heart from the beginning of railway competition. They had been created as local lines of communication, and local they largely remained. Of the race to amalgamate, to form national lines of communication, that gave its driving force to the railway mania, there was little sign. From time to time, however, the bigger of them met together to try to evolve a common policy. For instance, a conference was held in May 1841 of all the companies on the Liverpool and Manchester to London route, the main purpose of which was to complain of the excessive tolls demanded at that time of acute competition by the Oxford company. The Regent's, Grand Junction, Coventry, Trent & Mersey,

Macclesfield, Peak Forest and Ashton-under-Lyne companies were represented: the Oxford was not. These were the figures produced at the meeting of the respective companies' share of the through toll from Manchester via Preston Brook, Fradley and Braunston to Paddington.

Canal	Miles	Toll	
		s	d
Bridgewater	25	1	0
Trent & Mersey	67	2	9½
Coventry (Fradley section)	5½		2¾
Birmingham (Fazeley section)	5½		5½
Coventry	21¼		11
Oxford	23⅝	2	11
Grand Junction	101	4	2½
	248⅞	12	6¼ (62½p)

These figures are tolls only: at the time the freight charge for the distance made by the carriers was £2 2s 5½d (£2.12½), making £2 15s (£2.75) in all, which was a quite inadequate differential in favour of the canals against the railway charge of £2 17s 6d (£2.87½) for the same distance, which had recently been reduced from £3 5s (£3.25).

The meeting passed a resolution that 'the course which the Oxford canal is pursuing is destructive of the thoroughfare trade'.[1] The Oxford did nothing, and the situation got worse. In July 1845 there was another meeting, this time with the Oxford present. They took the offensive, its representatives complaining that the Grand Junction was giving preference for coal traffic to the Leicestershire line over their own. The Grand Junction replied that the Oxford charged 1¾d per ton for coal to London, and 3d for other goods, against their own rates of ¼d and ½d respectively, 'by which exactions the Oxford Canal Company had been and were still enabled to Share a Dividend of 30 per Cent, while the Grand Junction Canal Company were sharing one of only seven per Cent'.[2] Still the Oxford company refused to lower its tolls, or to go to arbitration. The Grand Junction then approached the two Warwick canals and others for 'a general amalgamation of their common interests'.[3] This proposal does not seem to have been seriously meant but to have been intended to force the Oxford's hand by isolating that company. It worked, and the Oxford agreed to arbitration and a lowering of tolls. No more was heard of amalgamation for many years.

We can see in this episode the difficulties with which a number of long-established and independent canal companies were faced in competing against railways. For a time the tonnage carried was to be unaffected, but the heavy fall of revenue that resulted from price cutting might have been to some extent counteracted, and the conservatism of management and engineering policy mitigated, by amalgamation into bigger units, or at the least by following a common policy.

There was one water line where such a policy was pursued with a good deal of success: that from Birmingham or Liverpool by way of the Staffs and Worcs Canal to the Severn and the Gloucester & Berkeley. The initiative came from the Staffs & Worcs, whose energetic management combined much foresight in respect of other waterways with an inability to improve its own canal. From the beginning in about 1835 of serious proposals to improve the navigation of the Severn, the Staffs & Worcs had supported them with money and Parliamentary influence. When the Severn Commission was at last set up in 1842, the canal company agreed to guarantee the commission's bonds up to £180,000, which enabled locks to be built between Stourport and Diglis, and the river to be dredged lower down.

When the railway mania began, two or three railway companies interested themselves in the Severn, offering to guarantee its revenue in exchange for a clear run with their Bills. Of them, the offer of the Oxford, Worcester & Wolverhampton Railway was accepted, so that the Severn bond-holders were doubly protected: the OW & W guaranteed the revenue of the waterway, and the Staffs & Worcs the capital and interest of the bonds.

Through many years and manoeuvres it then became the object of the Staffs & Worcs, who had meanwhile entered into guarantees for additional capital for improvements to the river, to get rid of the influence first of the OW & W, and then of the Great Western Railway behind it. It took the canal company until 1890 to do so, and at a heavy cost. When it was done, there was once more an independent waterway route to Gloucester. It was ironical, however, that the S & W's old rival for the Birmingham trade, the Worcester & Birmingham, was now owned by the Gloucester & Berkeley, and therefore had an automatic preference, while all three main feeders into the Staffs & Worcs which should have contributed most to this water line, the Shropshire Union, the Trent & Mersey, and the Birmingham Canal Navigations (including the Dudley line) were railway controlled. Only the little and extraordinarily supine Stourbridge Canal was independent, though its feeder the Stourbridge Extension was not.

Again, a waterway company could stay in business if it could encourage traffic originating on its line to remain, was largely self-contained, well managed, and had reasonable access to funds. This was the case with the Aire & Calder.

The company was well-placed to meet competition, for between 1820 and 1826, it had built the broad and deep Ferrybridge & Goole Canal as a more modern alternative to its older line to the Yorkshire Ouse by the Selby Canal, and had then developed Goole as a port. It had also enlarged and straightened its main lines from Castleford to Leeds and Wakefield between 1828 and 1839, so that it entered the railway age with a recently modernised waterway.

Basic traffics were coal, much of it from collieries beside its own waterway, with East Anglian corn as back carriage upwards. To enlarge the area from which coal could be drawn, the company leased the largely coal-carrying Barnsley Canal in 1854 (later it was bought and the locks enlarged), and the Calder & Hebble for twenty-one years in 1865. To keep traffic on the water, they followed a vigorous carrying policy. Steam tugs had been used since 1831, and by 1855 they were steam hauling two-thirds of their own carrying mileage, after which they put on public tugs to haul bye-traders' craft.

It is difficult to say that railway ownership of or influence over important canals prevented a movement to bring the waterways closer together, because there were so few signs of such a movement even along routes that remained independent. But it was undoubtedly one of the factors working against an energetic canal policy. The difficulty in getting a quotation for a through toll from a railway-controlled canal such as the Trent & Mersey, for instance, was a discouragement in itself. By the time the law compelled railways to quote through tolls,* the possibilities of keeping long-haul traffic on the canals had largely gone.

Part of the drag that kept canals back was due, of course, to their many sizes and shapes. Part, especially in agricultural areas, came from the repeal of the Corn Laws and the transfer of mills to the ports; part also to changing industrial techniques, such as the substitution of a few large steelworks served by railways for many small ironworks alongside canals.

In sum, the canals fell behind because the public no longer believed in inland water transport. Railways were to the general mind more efficient, more speedy, more flexible, more widely spread, and more

---

* The Railway & Canal Traffic Act, 1888; though the Railway & Canal Traffic Act, 1854, laid it down that railway-owned canals should afford reasonable facilities for traffic from other canals or railways.

suited to the adventurous Victorian times. This being so, the canal proprietors and officials lost heart; doing so, they found capital for improvements almost impossible to obtain.

Throughout the period, the canals that were successful in retaining trade upon themselves did so by keeping the short hauls, which stayed with them because old-established industry was placed on the canal banks. The long-distance trade decreased a good deal, not only because of the difficulty of passing goods from one company to another with different tolls and classifications, a different size of lock and depth of waterway, but also because portions of many through routes were in railway hands. The tendency towards the short haul can be seen also on the system of a single waterway. Upon the 145 miles of the Leeds & Liverpool, for instance, in 1905 the average haul for a ton of goods was 19.6 miles; upon the 189 miles of the extended Grand Junction 23.2 miles; upon the 144 miles of the Thames Navigation 16.7 miles.

Canal companies were hampered by several factors in any effort they made to extend their hauls. The first was the old distinction between toll-taking and carrying.

A number of navigation and canal concerns had always had their own carrying fleets, like the Aire & Calder, the Mersey & Irwell or the Bridgewater; others had organised the business of carrying by accepting goods freight-paid, and then themselves employing independent craft to carry them, like the Don or the Calder & Hebble; others again had agreed with carriers that they would run regular services—the so-called contract vessels of, for instance, the Rochdale Canal. But the majority of companies had only intermittently or never been concerned with carrying, but had confined themselves to taking tolls from anyone who wished to put a boat upon the waterway and use it for the carriage of goods. We have seen that this system was abandoned in the early days of railways, and its maintenance upon many canals meant that the necessary business organisation for successful competition, of offices, regular services, warehouses, cranes, and so on was not available to the businessman.

The carrier might be the owner of a single boat, or might be a manufacturer, or a carrying company like Fellows, Morton & Clayton, who carried goods over many canals. The fact that, unlike the railway, the canal did not usually do its own carrying meant that it had not the same vital interest in the state of its line. If a carrier's boat went aground the company did not feel the same urgent sense that a railway company did when a train was derailed. Again, manufacturers who wanted goods moved by water had to go to more trouble; they had to find a carrier, and then to entrust him with the necessary money to pay tolls and charges on his way, and sometimes the money was otherwise spent, especially by the small men, or there was pilfering from the cargo, compensation for which was difficult to recover.

A number of companies continued to carry; others adopted the powers of the Canal Carriers' Act: others made no attempt to go beyond their toll-taking functions. Of the companies that did carry, let us look at the experiences of a well-managed concern.

The Grand Junction set up a direct carrying business in 1848, soon after the authorising Act, with a capital of some £100,000. While only toll-takers, they had only been indirectly concerned with rate-cutting against the railways through pressure from the independent carriers for reduced tolls. Now that they were themselves in the carrying business, however, they were directly involved, and as early as 1851 came to an agreement with the LNWR by which both companies undertook not to cut rates against each other. In this agreement the Grand Junction bound themselves not only to peg their own freight charges, but also those of the independent carriers. This, not surprisingly, they found themselves unable to do, and in 1854 had to tell the railway so. The railway thereupon began to cut rates again, causing further reductions in both tolls and rates on the canal, until in October 1857 a meeting of canal companies and carriers was held. The chairman of the Grand Junction reported to it that he had been to see the managers of the LNWR and the GWR, who had complained that 'they could not retain their fair proportion of the heavy Trade in consequence of the Carriers on the Canal being enabled to carry at such low rates'.[4]

The meeting must have decided not to fight further, for in December a rates agreement was concluded with both railways which gave small fixed differentials to the canal carriers, which the Grand Junction accepted for itself and undertook to enforce on the independents. This was perhaps made easier by some rises in rates on both railway and canal as a result of the agreement, a tendency about which the (old) Grand Union company warned that 'any decided combination between the Railways and Canals may materially affect the interest of the Canals with the Board of Trade',[5] and refused to join the understanding on tolls that the Grand Junction, in the light of its agreement with the railways, had now reached with the Oxford and other canals.

Price-cutting by the independent carriers caused further trouble, however, and for a moment the company thought of following the example of the Bridgewater trustees, controlling the Duke of Bridgewater's Canal, who had had the same difficulty, and who had converted the independent carriers on their canal into their agents, to whom certain working expenses and a commission were paid in exchange for agreements to charge uniform rates.

All seems thereafter to have gone well until the Regent's Park explosion of 1874 (see p 77), which, although on the Regent's Canal, involved Grand Junction Canal carrying craft. The damage brought 632 claims totalling £74,418, and the final cost of the settled claims, together with legal costs and those of reinstating Macclesfield bridge, proved so daunting that in 1876 the company for many years closed its carrying business.

It was not until the 1880s that serious efforts were made to negotiate through tolls, even on lengths of waterway which were not interrupted by railway ownership. At no time did the canal companies set up an equivalent to the Railway Clearing House for the settlement amongst themselves of mutual debts (an institution that saved railway companies and railway users an immensity of time and trouble) though they were expressly authorised to do so by the Railway & Canal Traffic Act, 1888. There was not even an Association to promote the interests of the waterways during the critical early period of their history. In the canal age there had from time to time been *ad hoc* meetings, or groups of meetings, between representatives of canal companies, such as the group of proprietors of inland navigations who called a meeting in 1797 to protest against a proposed tax on goods carried by canal. Common action had to wait until 1844. Then, on the initiative of the Aire & Calder company, meetings of canal representatives in London drafted and helped to push through the Canal Tolls and Canal Carriers' Acts of 1845. This United Body of Canal Proprietors continued in loose form to watch current Bills and consider what the future of the canal interest required. In 1855 it became the Canal Association, with an Aire & Calder chairman and secretary. Neither was there a journal devoted to canal affairs until the short-lived *Canal Journal* of the 1890s, though several periodicals covered railway interests.

Meanwhile a steady deterioration of the condition of many canals took place. As receipts fell, maintenance was cut in order that dividends might still be paid; money for capital expenditure was hard to find in face of dropping revenues with which to pay interest on borrowings. Canals began to look less prosperous, and that did not attract new customers. Mud accumulated, boats could not carry full loads, delays increased, and even old customers began to look for alternative transport.

The decline of the canals introduced a new figure to the scene, the tourist, who always arrives when the ordinary is becoming exceptional. In 1867 a party took a boat through the Wey & Arun Junction

and down to the sea at Littlehampton shortly before that canal was
closed, and published the results of their adventures as *The Thames to
the Solent by Canal and Sea* (by J. B. Dashwood) in 1868. The following
year a similar book, *The Waterway to London*, appeared anonymously,
and described a canoe trip by three men from Manchester to London
by way of the Mersey, Shropshire Union, Severn, Thames & Severn
Canal and Thames. In both cases the accounts are written as if their
authors were pioneers of this type of amusement, and it is interesting

Figure 40   Pleasure cruising on the Arun in 1867

to notice that in neither case do they regard the canals themselves,
or the people upon them, as picturesque. The boats are taken for
granted—as would be natural in an age when the waterways were
still a familiar means of transport—and the people also.

Earlier, of course, there are occasional references to short pleasure
trips on canals, such as the 'Barge with a party of Ladies and Gentlemen'[6] for whom tolls on the Swansea Canal were remitted in 1809.
The Rev. John Skinner, rector of Camerton in Somerset, describes in
his diary such an occasion in 1823 on the Somersetshire Coal Canal:

'Having engaged one of the coal barges, I had it fitted up for the ladies with an awning and matting against the sides, and tables and chairs from the public-house, in which we proceeded to Combe Hay. . . . As the day was delightful, the whole party much enjoyed the excursion.'[7]

Plate XVII Two aspects of maintenance: (*above*) a Grand Junction Canal steam
ab dredger at work in 1898; (*below*) a cloudburst in 1973 causes a breach in the Peak Forest
Canal at Disley

Page 258, Plate XVIII   The Manchester Ship Canal: (above) under construction; (below) a Barton in 1973. The Bridgewater Canal can be seen on each side of the ship canal, with Leade Williams's aqueduct swung to allow the ship to pass. Below is Barton road swingbridg

CHAPTER XIII

Time of Hope

++◆++

UNTIL the 1870s the development of the railway system so astonished and benefited the country that the people were on the one hand content to think the waterways obsolete, and on the other to overlook the dangers of railway monopoly. A letter written to the Secretary of the Royal Society of Arts at the time of the Canal Conference of 1888, says:

'Sixteen years ago anyone advocating water transport was promptly accused of galvanizing a corpse. . . .'[1]

A change of heart was brought about by a number of factors all operating over the same period.

The dangers of railway monopoly began to be understood when for the first time since the Industrial Revolution foreign manufactured goods began seriously to compete with our own in the home market, open to them because of the universally held doctrine of free trade. It began to be said that cheap transport was vital, and that on the Continent both railways and waterways were cheaper than British railways, the latter by a good deal. There were complaints that railway rates on imported goods were less than those the home manufacturer had to pay, and statements that manufacturing firms were moving from the interior of the country to the seaboard to avoid the high railway rates. Critics of the railways pointed to their high capital charges, and suggested that new capital was being raised to carry unprofitably heavy traffic which could better go by water. It was in 1873 that the Regulation of Railways Act was passed, the first to provide machinery adequate to control railway influence over canals. It compelled railway and canal companies to quote through tolls or rates and to publish them, forbade railways to acquire a controlling interest in a canal unless approved by commissioners appointed under the Act, and stated that railways controlling canals already must maintain them:

'. . . so that the whole of such canal or part may be at all times kept open and navigable for the use of all persons desirous to use and navigate the same without any unnecessary hindrance, interruption or delay.'

The Act set up Railway Commissioners to whom matters of dispute were to be referred, who were to see that through rates were fair, and who were to be the guardians of the public interest.

From the 1870s to the Royal Commission of 1906 an argument raged between the two groups of interests. Those who supported the waterways argued that the water had an important part to play, but in order that it could do so, amalgamation of the existing companies was needed, probably with help from the State or local authorities, followed by modernisation. This would take the form of uniformity of gauge on the great through waterway routes, an enlarged sectional area in order to increase speed, the substitution of lifts for flights of locks, the protection of canal banks by walls, and the use of steam haulage. On the other side railway supporters pointed out that canals had a network not nearly as comprehensive as that of the railways, that storage in railway waggons was an essential convenience to coal and other merchants, that speed of conveyance was becoming more and more important as traders held smaller stocks and traded on less capital, and that the enormous expenditure involved in any major reorganisation of the waterways system would be out of all proportion to the possible benefits.

By the 1880s so active had interest become in the revival of the waterways that in 1888 the Royal Society of Arts held a two-day conference on the subject, at which the leading waterway engineers and managers read papers and entered into discussion. It emerged from the conference that the raising of the necessary capital by private enterprise was unlikely, and that in any case a strong hand was needed to make sure that railway influence was not still exercised over waterways. Several speakers supported nationalisation, such as General Rundall, who put forward a proposal for a Water Commission very similar to the later recommendation of the Royal Commission of 1906, or the formation of public trusts under local authorities. Nationalisation had not then the political significance it has since gained, and proposals for acquisition by the State were judged on their merits as likely or unlikely to lead to the end desired. A speaker at the conference summed up this point of view when he said:

'The traditional independence of Englishmen is opposed to Government interference, and yet the descendants of Englishmen in Canada and the United States are now enjoying the benefits of artificial waterways provided by their Governments.'[2]

In the end the following resolution was carried:

'That the Legislature should seriously consider the necessity of encouraging and assisting the improvement and extension of the canal system, by State acquisition or otherwise; and that meanwhile the Conference urges the Council of the Society of Arts to petition the House of Commons for the amendment of the Railway & Canal Traffic Bill by authorising local authorities to constitute Public Trusts, for the development of the existing system of canals.'

Such an authorisation was in fact included in the Act, and, as we shall see, was used. Thenceforward to the end of the century the controversy continued, but with very little action. At last, in 1906, a Royal Commission was appointed to study the whole matter and make recommendations.

This revival of interest in the waterways that began in the 1870s led to developments along several lines. The beginning in 1876 of the discussion at meetings and in newspapers of the proposal that became the Manchester Ship Canal is dealt with in the next chapter, but it must be remembered that all thought about waterways was from that time coloured by the slowly maturing ship canal. It drew public attention to the possibilities of waterway development, and led to interest in other ship canal projects, notably one from Birmingham to the sea. Again, the passing in 1877 of the Canal Boats Act was the culmination of many years of work by George Smith in drawing attention to the working conditions of boat people. Again, the purchase in 1874 of the Worcester & Birmingham Canal and two associated waterways by the Gloucester & Berkeley and the negotiations by the Staffs & Worcs that led in 1890 to the freeing of the Severn from railway influence, were forward moves of importance by waterway concerns, which in the case of the Worcester & Birmingham Canal also marked the defeat of a long effort by a railway company to acquire the canal.

In Ireland, unlike most of Britain, there was a continuing conflict between the interests of navigation and drainage. Navigation tended to be put first by a Royal Commission of 1880, chaired by Lord Monck, which considered the future of the very unsatisfactory north–south waterway that nominally existed from Belfast or Newry to Lough Neagh and then by way of the Ulster and the Ballinamore & Ballyconnell canals to the Shannon and so to Limerick. Subsequent commissions, the Allport of 1887 on Irish Public Works, and that of 1905 on Arterial Drainage, thought navigation, drainage and other water interests should be the responsibility of a single government department.

Proposals for a ship canal from Birmingham to the sea arose out of complaints at the high railway rates from that town during the trade depression of 1885. On 5 April 1887 the Birmingham Town Council passed this resolution:

'That this Council deems it to be of the utmost importance to the trade and commerce of Birmingham and the surrounding district that improved canal communication should be opened up, which should connect this great centre of industry with the sea. . . .' and a committee was set up to make investigations. There were two principal candidates: a Birmingham & Liverpool ship canal project, for a line 64¼ miles long from the Weaver at Winsford by way of the Potteries to Stafford, Wolverhampton and Birmingham, and the Birmingham & Bristol Channel Improved Navigation, to include a Worcester & Birmingham Canal enlarged to 200–250 ton capacity. A third improved line, to London, had less support.

The committee reported in March 1888, pointing out that though the Severn was the greatest channel for Birmingham's imports, her exports went to London and Liverpool, and it was these routes that needed most attention. The committee recommended that action should be taken by public trusts to rebuild the main lines of canal— those joining Trent, Mersey, Severn and Thames—to a uniform depth of 8–10ft, and width of 70–100ft, to take steamers of 600 tons. Lifts should be substituted for locks wherever possible. It was thought that the cost of acquiring the waterways concerned would be £8–12 million, and of converting them the same figure. This proposal was indeed an adumbration of the Royal Commission's recommendations of twenty years later (see Chapter XV). Little was done. In 1891 the North Staffordshire Railway got an Act to enlarge the Trent & Mersey to Stoke-on-Trent, but did not implement it; in the 1930s the Grand Union between Birmingham and London was enlarged, and in 1943 an enlarged canal was surveyed from the Weaver to Birmingham via the upper Weaver to Audlem and the Shropshire Union.

Meanwhile, during the long time of decline, what of the human side of the canals? Earnings had fallen in terms of real wages as the prosperity of the industry declined, and this tended to bring more families on to the boats, in place of the crews of men and boys who seem usually to have manned the craft during the canal age. The canal people, the men and women and children who lived on the boats, brought up children, aged and died, were ignored by legis- lators, reformers, novelists and clerks of canal companies alike. Be- cause they moved about, they did not fall within the jurisdiction of any local government authority; their boats paid no rates, and they no taxes. Factory Acts did not apply to them, and Acts pro- hibiting the employment of women and young children, or Sunday work, had no application to the canals. No Engels studied them as he studied the condition of the labouring classes in Manchester in 1844; no Royal Commission investigated hours or conditions; no

Charles Kingsley took canal people for his theme. Like the colliers, they were feared as a rough, ignorant and drunken race; but unlike colliers, they moved about, and carried on their mysterious pursuits unknown to society. The Church alone, as so often, amateurishly in the eyes of the critics, sometimes patronisingly in the eyes of the boat people, but yet working in love, did do something when none else cared. In 1841 a Boatmen's Pastoral Instruction Society was founded; little schools were run, Boatmen's Institutes were started, boaters' services were held, and the vicar of Paddington married boat couples,

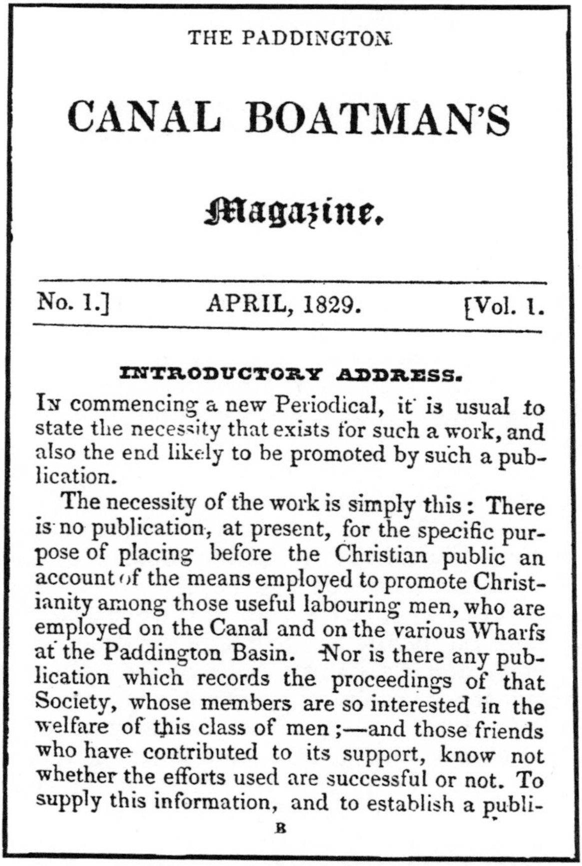

THE PADDINGTON

CANAL BOATMAN'S

Magazine.

No. 1.]   APRIL, 1829.   [Vol. 1.

INTRODUCTORY ADDRESS.

In commencing a new Periodical, it is usual to state the necessity that exists for such a work, and also the end likely to be promoted by such a publication.

The necessity of the work is simply this : There is no publication, at present, for the specific purpose of placing before the Christian public an account of the means employed to promote Christianity among those useful labouring men, who are employed on the Canal and on the various Wharfs at the Paddington Basin. Nor is there any publication which records the proceedings of that Society, whose members are so interested in the welfare of this class of men ;—and those friends who have contributed to its support, know not whether the efforts used are successful or not. To supply this information, and to establish a publi-

B

Figure 41   The Church cares for boatmen's souls. The magazine ran until December 1832

many of whom had dispensed with the ceremony until late in life, free of charge.

Now and then a glimpse appears: of the part played by canals in spreading cholera, for instance, when in 1835 the Grand Junction company paid £50 to the Braunston Board of Health towards its expenses, 'it appearing that the disease first attacked a woman who had been employed in washing the bedding of a boatman who had died of it . . .';[3] of poachers when a Cromford Canal bye-law prohibited any boat from stopping at night in Crich Chase, or in any wood or coppice; of drunken boatmen, when the lock-keepers on the Staffs & Worcs were told to report them to the committee, especially if they had wines or spirits on board; of sober boatmen, in the Penkridge parish magazine for February 1891: 'At our last Temperance Meeting, addressed by Mr Mundin, the Lincolnshire Navvy . . . our own people were supplemented by several of the frozen up Canal Boat people, some of whom took the pledge. . . . Many of our own people might well learn a lesson from their reverence and attention in the House of God. . . .'

It was a deeply religious man, a Nonconformist, George Smith, 'of Coalville', though he was born near Tunstall and died at Crick, who first took an interest in the boat people. He had earlier in his life taken up the cause of the children who worked in brickyards, having himself begun work in a brickyard when he was nine years old, and by persistence and publicity had obtained an Act to regulate their employment, losing his well-paid job as manager of a large brickyard in doing so, and thenceforward being boycotted by employers all his life.

Since he lived near a canal, the state of the canal people, and especially of the children, also affected him. In his two books, *Our Canal Population* (1875) and *Canal Adventures by Moonlight* (1881) can be read accounts of the state of the floating population, at a time when canals were much more crowded than they are now. It is not a pleasant picture to a lover of what he imagines as the good old days.

George Smith put before the people of England, by means of a Press campaign, the facts about the life of the boat people. Their numbers he put at 100,000 (as it turned out, an over-estimate for the time when he worked: the figure was probably about 30,000. He reckoned that 98 per cent of them were illiterate, and 50 per cent unmarried. He pointed out that there was no statutory limit to the number of people who could occupy a boat cabin, nor were powers given to any public body to inspect boats for health reasons. Especially he pointed to the state of the children, worked hard for seven days a week, irreligious and illiterate.

His campaign roused a good deal of interest, and almost entirely as a result of his efforts the Canal Boats Act was passed in 1877. This measure was very much less comprehensive than Smith wanted; for in his opinion children should not live upon the boats at all, and he was strongly in favour of both women and children leaving them to the men. The Act provided that all boats should be registered, and that the registration certificate should give permission for the boat to carry so many adults and so many children, according to the cubic capacity of the living accommodation. It provided also that the boat should be registered as belonging to a local authority for purposes of licensing and of bringing the children within the interest of the educational system.

The Act left much undone. It suffered because it was permissive, and only a few local authorities made any serious attempt to use it, especially since no penalties for non-observance were provided. Smith himself tramped the towpaths and travelled the boats, watching; he found that his Act was of no practical help to the canal children he loved, so once again he began the struggle, helped by another Nonconformist, the Rev Guy Mark Pearse, who published a tract in 1878 called *Rob Rat: A Story of Barge Life*. In 1884 another Canal Boats Act was passed, appointing an inspector under the Local Government Board, requiring the local authorities to make annual reports to the Board upon the action they had taken, and instructing local authorities to make sure that the children attended school. The difficulties in enforcing school attendance on a moving population of children, many of whose parents had no interest in giving their children learning they themselves had done well without, were great. Some education authorities in areas where many canal boats were registered, like Birmingham and Runcorn, did all they could; others very little. But the problem was never really solved: instead it disappeared with the boat people themselves.

This second Act, now centrally supervised, did much to improve the sanitary condition of canal boats, and to reduce the overcrowding upon them. George Smith later turned his efforts more towards the gypsies, for whom he had worked at the same time as the boat people, but this time unsuccessfully. He died in 1895.

From 1884 to 1921 the law did not take further care of the increasingly unimportant canals. In the latter year a departmental committee of the Ministry of Health reported on the practice of living-in on canal boats. The committee were impressed by the theoretical objections to living-in, but they were unable to find practical fault with a system which produced canal boat-dwellers of whom it could be said:

'. . . the majority of the witnesses have agreed that, so far as health, cleanliness, morality, feeding and clothing are concerned, they are fully equal, if not superior, to town dwellers of a similar class.'

The committee did, however, recommend strongly that children of school-age should be prohibited from living-in on canal boats during term-time. They stated that there were not more than 1,000 such children on canal boats, of whom 85 per cent were almost un-educated.

In the same year of 1921 an Education Act was passed, which pro-vided that canal children were subject to the bye-laws of the education authority in whose area a canal boat was registered, unless the parents could certify that the children were being efficiently educated else-where. The recommendation of the departmental committee was not, however, included, the Act did not succeed in ensuring regular education for canal children, and much illiteracy persisted. This prob-lem was again tackled in the Education Act of 1944, which made it unlawful for a child not to attend school for at least 200 days a year, after which one local authority established a boarding school for boat children, who returned to the boats in the holidays.

The original regulations made under the Canal Boats Acts of 1877 and 1884 were amended in 1925, and the Acts themselves were re-placed by Part X of the Public Health Act of 1936, which codified all existing public health legislation. The amended regulations are still in force and are chiefly concerned with the living cabins, and their

Figure 42   A canal child

most important provisions are that an after-cabin must contain at least 180cu ft of free air space, and a fore cabin 80cu ft. The amount of space allowed for a person over twelve years old is 60cu ft, of under twelve, 40cu ft. A cabin occupied as a sleeping place by a husband and wife must not be occupied also as a sleeping place by a girl above twelve years old, or a boy above fourteen.

Thus far did George Smith succeed in concerns that had greatly moved him. What he could not foresee was the gradual decline of family boat carrying. Very few narrow boats are still working. Bigger carrying craft on the larger waterways are crewed with day men. Nowadays a boat family cruises for pleasure, not livelihood, or lives on board, as an alternative to a house or a caravan.

As previously mentioned it was grasped in the 1870s that there was a danger to the country in railway monopoly, and that one way of lessening it was to revive the waterways. The Joint Select Committee on Railway Amalgamation of 1872, the Select Committee on Railway Rates and Fares of 1882, the Select Committee on Canals of 1883, and the final Report of the Royal Commission on the Depression of Trade of 1886, all recommended that waterways should be developed and freed from the railways. The 1883 report also recommended that the Irish canals should be taken over by public trusts or local authorities. Several Acts from 1858 to 1888 protected canals against railways, encouraged canal amalgamations, gave canal companies and carriers powers such as those of compulsory reduction in certain conditions of the tolls of railway-owned canals, and empowered local authorities to take over canals which their owners wished to abandon. But to legislate was easier than to obtain action.

Apart from the acquisition of the Worcester & Birmingham, Droitwich, and Droitwich Junction canals by the Gloucester & Berkeley, already described in Chapter VIII, two important amalgamations took place towards the end of the century. The Grand Junction Canal, one of the most powerful in the country, in 1894 bought the Leicestershire & Northamptonshire Union and the old Grand Union. This purchase was followed by an agreement upon through tolls with the Loughborough, Leicester and Erewash companies, under which the Grand Junction offered a guarantee of minimum receipts, and was given options to purchase. The object of the purchase and the agreements was to get the coal trade of the Erewash Valley, but it was partly frustrated by the bad condition of the railway-owned Cromford Canal and the abandonment of the privately owned Nutbrook, partly by competition from other coalfields in the Grand Junction market. As a result, the Grand Junction had to pay out on its guarantees of receipts, and also to relinquish its options to purchase.

The company also proposed an amalgamation in 1895 with the Warwick canals on the Birmingham route, but this seems to have been defeated by opposition from local authorities on rating grounds.

The Butterley tunnel of the Cromford Canal had been seriously affected by mining subsidence in 1889, and closed. It was reopened in 1893 after £8,000 had been spent on it, but when R. H. de Salis went through he found it very low and for bad condition 'unsurpassed by any other I have ever seen'. In July 1900 there was a worse subsidence which closed the tunnel completely. It was never reopened. The canal below the tunnel, which served most of the collieries and connected with the Erewash Navigation, was also reported by de Salis to be 'in very bad condition'.

The law would have allowed an appeal to the Board of Trade to compel the railway company to reinstate the canal. But things were not as they seemed, and the hard-headed Grand Junction told the Royal Commission of 1906:

'It has always been considered that there would be a very great deal of risk for one independent canal to endeavour to compel a railway company to reopen its canal or make it navigable.'[4]
Their opinion was not unique.

In the north of England local interests maintained that the navigations which linked Sheffield with the Aire & Calder system should be removed from railway control. We have seen that the River Don company encouraged the building of the Stainforth & Keadby and Dearne & Dove canals, and later had absorbed them, along with the Sheffield Canal. Then in 1850 it amalgamated with the South Yorkshire, Doncaster & Goole Railway to form the South Yorkshire Railway & River Don Navigation. Later, in 1864, the Manchester, Sheffield & Lincolnshire Railway (later the Great Central) had leased the whole undertaking of the South Yorkshire & River Don, and so had acquired all four navigations. The railway company then built a line from Mexborough past Rotherham to Sheffield which used part of the navigation's Rotherham cut, this being replaced by a more circuitous route via two new cuts and a section of the old river, which was opened in 1868.

In 1888, as a result of strong local initiative, a new company, the Sheffield & South Yorkshire, was formed to buy the former navigation from the railway, and to modernise and enlarge the main line. After years of negotiation, agreement was reached in 1894 on a price of £1,140,000, payable £600,000 in cash, the balance in ordinary shares to be held by the railway until bought from them at par by the S & SY. However, though the company raised enough in preference shares to pay the cash (some of it, however, subscribed by the railway company), the enthusiasm for waterways of the years between 1888 and the opening of the Manchester Ship Canal in 1894 had diminished, and they could raise no more. The railway therefore retained very strong influence upon the company, which in turn prevented the Aire & Calder from giving the Sheffield & South Yorkshire the financial support it might otherwise have been willing to provide.

The Aire & Calder was the most successful of the independent concerns. It depended for its prosperity largely on traffic generated on its own system, though that to and from the Barnsley, Calder & Hebble and Leeds & Liverpool added palatable icing to an already satisfactory cake. But it was fortunate in being managed from the late 1770s onwards by an energetic board and served by highly competent officials and engineers, men like William Martin, Joseph Priestley, the Maudes and the Bartholomews. In the 1820s and 1830s we saw the new and modern Ferrybridge & Goole Canal built, the port of Goole founded, and the Castleford–Leeds and Castleford–Wakefield lines realigned and rebuilt.

Steam tugging was introduced in 1831 and by the 1850s most of the company's own craft were steam-hauled. The resultant barge trains suggested much longer and wider locks. The first of these, Pollington, 206ft long and partially widened to 22ft, was opened in 1860, and followed by all others to Castleford by 1867, and throughout the navigation by 1873. Meanwhile in 1862 the company's engineer, William H. Bartholomew, got the board's approval to experimental construction of his newly patented invention of compartment boats. These, later to be called 'pans' or 'Tom Puddings' were rectangular iron boats which could be built up into trains. Each was then fitted with spring-loaded buffers and a protruding vertical iron bar in front of which fitted a corresponding slot at the back of the boat ahead. By putting a steam tug at the back, running cables through fairleads on each boat to a false bow at the head of the train, and working the cables by windlasses, it was possible to bend the train to pass round curves in the waterway. At Goole these coal-carrying compartment boats would then be separated, raised in a hydraulic hoist, and tipped into ships' holds.

Over the years, Bartholomew modified his invention: he dropped push-towing from behind, and his elaborate steering system, in favour of a tug in front pulling a long train of boats which adjusted themselves to curves. The boats' design was also simplified. The system was a tremendous success. By 1897 half a million tons a year were being carried in 400 boats, 1½ million tons in 1913 in some thousand boats which operated, of course, alongside conventional barges and steam tugs. From the 1880s onwards, locks began to be further enlarged, and in 1896 the company began to build the New Junction Canal, 5½ miles long with one lock, to join the Sheffield & South Yorkshire to the Aire & Calder, mainly so that compartment boat trains working to the Goole hoists could now be introduced to the Don line. Finally, from 1884 onwards the company took over control of the River Ouse from Goole downwards to its junction with the Trent at Trent Falls, and enlarged it so that bigger ships could reach Goole, the port facilities of which had been greatly enlarged and extended in the previous half century.

The effect upon revenue of operating a large modern waterway with big barges or long barge trains, compared with narrow-boat canals, whether highly industrialised and short-haul, like the BCN, or long-haul on a good sized waterway like the Grand Junction, can be seen from the following figures of revenue earned and tonnage carried in 1905:

Company	Tonnage	Revenue
Birmingham	7,546,453	£190,873
Grand Junction	1,794,233	£101,926
Aire & Calder	2,810,988	£317,468

In the last thirty years of the century, therefore, there were prosperous concerns such as the Aire & Calder and the Weaver, viable but less secure companies like the Grand Junction, and one or two efficient railway-owned canals like the Trent & Mersey or the Shropshire Union main line. There were also many canals in difficulties. Some became entangled with railway companies; others just died. Perhaps the story of the later years of the Thames & Severn will epitomise the first process, that of its neighbour the Wilts & Berks the second.

As long ago as 1836 the Thames & Severn Canal had put forward a Bill to turn itself into a railway. The occasion for this move was the promotion of the Cheltenham & Great Western Union Railway to run from Swindon to Stroud, Gloucester and Cheltenham, with a branch to Cirencester, along a route parallel with the canal from Cirencester to Stroud. The line along which the canal had been built, and the possession of a ready-cut tunnel, were advantages that led the canal company not only to oppose the railway Bill, but to promote their own. The battle, however, became complicated, for in opposition to the broad-gauge proposal of the Cheltenham & Great Western Union there was promoted a standard-gauge railway, the Cheltenham, Oxford & London & Birmingham Union Railway, to build a line from the London & Birmingham Railway at Tring through Aylesbury, Thame, Oxford, Witney and then over the Cotswolds by way of Burford and Northleach to Cheltenham, a more direct but hillier route from London. The canal company opposed the Swindon and supported the Tring line, since the latter would not have affected their traffic. However, the Swindon line was authorised and the other two Bills were lost. It was not until 1845 that this line was completed, and by that time the company that had built it had been absorbed in the Great Western. The Swindon line had a serious effect upon the revenues of the canal.

By the early 1860s the canal company was in a bad way; its last dividend was paid in 1864. There were at the time a number of railway proposals for new lines, and among them three that were of interest to the company, and to the bankers, Stevenson, Salt & Sons, who from the early days of the waterway had been large shareholders. These lines were the Stonehouse & Nailsworth, from the Midland at Stonehouse, with a branch to Stroud, the East Gloucestershire, from Cheltenham to Fairford and Witney to join an existing branch from Oxford, and the Severn Junction to bridge the Severn. All these proposals were for standard-gauge lines, and if they could be linked together they would serve to invade the broad-gauge territory across the Severn and draw traffic thence towards London. The canal company therefore proposed the Severn & Thames Railway, to join the Stroud branch of the Stonehouse & Nailsworth at Stroud, and to run through the canal tunnel (on a single line) and along the waterway to a point beyond South Cerney, where it would leave the canal and swing away to Fairford to join the Witney branch from Oxford. The part of the canal between Stroud and Brimscombe was to be maintained, and water for the Stroudwater and the Gloucester & Berkeley canals was to be brought through pipes from Thames Head. It was this latter proposal that lost the Bill in 1866, for there was opposition to the transfer of Thames water to the Severn Valley, though other factors in railway politics also had their influence.

Richard Potter had been a director of the Great Western Railway for several years, and chairman from 1863 to 1865. He was a man with many other interests, and he resigned in 1865 in order to give more time to them. It was in 1876 that he began to buy the shares of the Thames & Severn Canal, as far as one can see with the intention of turning it into a railway to compete with his old company. He acquired large blocks of shares, and eventually controlled over 2,000 out of the 2,450 issued. A railway already existed from Swindon to Andover to link with another line to Southampton. In 1881 an extension was authorised from Swindon to Cheltenham. In 1882, therefore,

Potter and the canal company promoted a Bill for a railway to join this line at Siddington, near Cirencester, and to run to Stroud, where it would connect with the Stroud branch of the Midland. The Severn Bridge had been opened in 1879, and therefore Welsh trade would have a direct link with the places served by the new line and its connections. This time the whole of the canal was to be closed.

It was on the initiative of a section of the Board of the Gloucester & Berkeley Canal that a number of navigations opposed the Bill, and interviewed the President of the Board of Trade. Potter did what he could to persuade the navigations that the Thames & Severn and its connection the Wilts & Berks could never compete successfully with the railway. He failed, and the Bill was withdrawn. The fact that Potter, a man of wealth, position, and influence, was behind the Bill caused the Great Western to be nervous lest the rival railway might re-emerge later. Therefore it seemed best to that company to make sure the Thames & Severn remained a canal, by buying the control from Potter at a comfortable profit to him, and adding shares held by others. The company acquired 2,205 of the shares through nominees, in order not to contravene the Regulation of Railways Act, 1873.

The railway had not bought the canal to work it, but to make sure that it was not converted into a rival railway, but remained a canal until it could safely be abandoned. The associated navigations, who who had been discussing rather vague proposals for leasing the canal, now firmly offered to do so for 21 years, but the railway asked a prohibitive price, and instead allowed the canal to deteriorate. On local initiative a Board of Trade inspection of the waterway took place in 1886 and a report stated:

'. . . I must express my opinion that it is eminently desirable that the management of the Canal should vest in persons more nearly interested than the present proprietors in keeping the Canal and all Reservoirs, Works and Conveniences thereto belonging in thorough repair and dredged and in good working condition . . . the harmonious working and development of the Canal system . . . cannot be effectually carried out if this duty is neglected and the interests of the public will suffer as long as it is neglected.'[5]

Nothing happened until a memorial was presented to the local Members of Parliament in 1893, signed by 152 traders, boat-owners and others, which brought from the Great Western notice to close 26 miles of the canal, leaving only 4 miles open. Thereupon the local authorities took action. The Gloucester County Council and the Cirencester and the Stroud Boards of Health joined a deputation of members of Chambers of Commerce, navigation concerns and others to Mr Mundella, President of the Board of Trade, which reiterated the willingness of the associated navigations to take over the canal. The Board of Trade put pressure on the railway, and in 1895 the Act was passed that set up a Trust for the canal, giving the associated navigations and local authorities powers to improve and manage it, but not to turn it into a railway. It was estimated that some £10,000 was needed to put the canal into repair, and there were also debentures to be paid off. The Act therefore gave power for £15,000 to be raised. Losses were to be borne as to the first £600 a year by the navigations, and after that half by them and half by various local authorities. The £15,000 was spent, together with a further £4,000 (as well as £20,000 by the Thames Conservancy on the improvement of the river between Lechlade and Oxford), but it was not enough to restore the canal. In 1900 it was transferred to the Gloucestershire County Council, though limited liabilities of the associated navigations and public bodies continued. Of the five years during which the canal had been in the hands of the Trust it had only been open throughout its length for three months.

The chief hindrance was the leakage on the summit or topmost level that had troubled the canal ever since it was built, and the county council therefore spent some £20,000 in completely clearing out and repuddling about 2½ miles. The waterway was reopened in 1904, but traffic never recovered, and it was finally closed in 1927, except for 6¼ miles between Stroud and Chalford, which were put under the management of the Stroudwater company, and later closed also.

The Wilts & Berks was an independent canal. As we saw in Chapter IV, its earlier years were not without excitement, and until the Great Western came along the Vale of White Horse it brought coal and took away produce from the area between its junction with the Thames at Abingdon and with the Kennet & Avon at Semington, to the benefit of the inhabitants. The coming of the railway ruined the concern, which struggled on until 1876, by which time the tolls had fallen from some £15,000 a year to £1,158. After the Great Western Railway had considered buying the canal, and had decided not to do so, the original company sold out to a new group, the capital being reduced from £321,613 to £30,000. The new company in its turn leased the waterway in 1882 to a group of Bristol merchants for 21 years. The merchants thought that they could make the canal pay, but after six years they parted with £1,000 to break the lease, having lost some £16,000. The company of 1876 then worked the canal until 1891, by which time the tolls were down to £617. Then again a fresh company was formed, which spent about £7,000 in dredging and other improvements, and put on a fleet of twelve fly-boats that ran regularly to Bristol. Once again no money could be made out of the canal, and in 1897 the company applied for a warrant of abandonment. The closure was opposed on the one hand by the neighbouring waterways, and on the other by the landowners, who found its water convenient for their farms. The abandonment application broke down on a legal point, and the company survived. Traffic did not, however, and had entirely ceased by 1906. The corporation of Swindon, through whose town the canal ran, eventually found it so much of a nuisance that they applied for and obtained in 1914 an Act of closure, taking over Coate Water, the canal reservoir, for local purposes.

It is very noticeable during this period that the best progress was made by the river navigations, though more could have been done if the non-tidal portion of each river had been under the control of a single authority. Some rivers, like the Severn, for long had none; others had several: in the case of the Witham, at one time seventeen. Increases in capacity could be obtained more easily and at less cost on rivers, even if partly canalised, than on pure canals. The smaller river navigations still suffered, however, from the old trouble of the rights of millers to draw off or withhold water and to charge tolls, but the improvement of large rivers was general: the Severn and the Weaver will serve as examples.

The Severn Commission, representative of the county and municipal authorities interested, and of the neighbouring navigations, was set up in 1842 to improve the waterway from Gloucester to Stourport, the rest of the river being left without a controlling authority. Its work was, however, hampered by the existence of two parties upon it, one representing the interests of Gloucester and the other of Worcester. The former wanted no other improvement than dredging to be carried out below Worcester, in order to keep tolls low; the latter, supported as we have seen by the Staffs & Worcs company, wanted locks to be built in order to increase traffic above Worcester both on the river and the canals. Work proceeded under the enabling Act, the bonds of the commission up to £180,000 having been guaranteed by the canal company. Four locks were built between Diglis (near Worcester) and Stourport, while below Diglis the river was dredged to a depth of 6ft, thereby meeting Gloucester's wish that the channel should not be obstructed. It was found impossible to maintain the dredged depth, and, after much opposition, a proposal for a lock and weir at Tewkesbury was sanctioned, and completed in 1858.

British canals post-war: (*above*) barges on the Gloucester & Sharpness Canal; (*below*) cruising and angling on the Shropshire Union

Page 276, Plate XX A canal boatwoman in her cabin during World War II

When the Severn Commission's engineer, Leader Williams, wrote in 1864 a pamphlet on the state of the river, he advocated large improvements that would bring a foreign as well as a coasting trade to Worcester, and Gloucester interests so far withdrew their opposition as to support a plan for obtaining a firm 6ft to Worcester by a lock on each branch of the river at Gloucester. Clegram, the engineer to the Gloucester & Berkeley, pointed out that the shallow state of the river prevented the full use of steam tugs, and caused expense through the lightening of deep-draughted vessels, remarking that it:

'. . . greatly interrupts that regularity of traffic which is essential to keep the water communication between Gloucester and the interior of the country in fair competition with the railway system'.[6]

The waterway interests had seen where the danger lay. When in 1868 the commission announced its intention to apply for an Act, the Gloucester & Berkeley agreed to guarantee £750 a year to the commission, and the Staffs & Worcs helped also. The Act provided for complete canalisation by the construction of two locks and weirs at Gloucester.

When the Oxford, Worcester & Wolverhampton Railway obtained its Act in 1845 for a railway that largely paralleled the river and the Staffs & Worcs Canal from Worcester to Wolverhampton, the Severn Commission represented that £180,000 had been spent on the river, and the estimated yield from tolls was £14,000 a year. The railway therefore undertook to make up the tolls to this amount, should they fall short of it. Further bond issues for improvements to the river with the encouragement of the Staffs & Worcs, however, put the railway guarantee into abeyance. It was renewed in 1868 by an agreement between the Staffs & Worcs and the GWR which had absorbed the OW & WR, and was, as we have seen, eventually commuted in 1890 for cash payments and mortgage cancellations totalling £129,000, much of which was used to repay part of the debt owed by the commission to the Staffs & Worcs company.

In 1888 the river had a minimum depth of 6ft with 9ft in most parts. Tugs towing 10 or 12 boats navigated it, and in that year carried 323,000 tons. Though in 1890 further improvements were made in the river, including the enlargement of the lock at Gloucester which connected the river with the ship canal basin, and thenceforward the condition of the navigation remained adequate, the tonnage carried declined from that time to 120,000 tons in 1927, in spite of great efforts by the Severn Commission and the Severn & Canal Carrying Company to get traffic. Then oil traffic boomed, but by 1967 most had been lost again, and tonnage was down to 109,365. Planned enlargement to Worcester now offers new hope.

The River Weaver depended for its traffic upon an export trade in salt, and an import trade in coal, raw materials and china clay to be transhipped at Anderton for the Potteries. From the late 1840s to 1870s the 11 locks were reduced to 9; most were also doubled, new 100ft × 22ft × 10ft locks being built alongside the old 88ft × 18ft × 7ft 6in ones. An additional dock and Mersey entrance lock were also built at Weston Point, and opened in 1856. The result was to increase both tonnage and revenue by 50 per cent between the 1840s and the 1870s.

Then Edward Leader Williams, son of Leader Williams of the Severn Commission, was appointed engineer. Further dock extension was begun, a steam tugging service for Weaver traffic inaugurated on the Mersey, and the Anderton vertical boat lift opened in 1875, thus providing a direct connection between Weston Point docks, the Weaver, and the Trent & Mersey Canal leading to the Potteries. This structure, prototype of many lifts on the Continent and the only one now working in Britain, raises boats 50ft 4in, each caisson being 75ft × 15ft 6in × 5ft, able to take two narrow boats or one barge. In 1903 electric had replaced steam power at the lift, and in 1908, when it was found that the hydraulic rams and cylinders were worn out, the lift was provided with a new framework that enabled each caisson to be separately worked, using counterbalance weights.

In the early 1870s, following recommendations Leader Williams had made in 1865, the Weaver trustees began to build new locks, 220ft × 42ft 6in × 15ft, able to take craft carrying 1,000 tons and, except for the Manchester Ship Canal, the biggest inland waterway locks so far built in Britain. Four of these were built in tandem with the larger of the earlier pairs, to replace all existing locks down to the old entrance at Frodsham, and the new one at Sutton. There a new lock was also built alongside the existing smaller one. The gates of these new locks were power-operated by two Pelton wheels to each gate. The programme was completed by 1885, the year a further dock was also opened at Weston Point. By the 1880s the income of the Weaver Navigation had reached £60,000 a year, and £10,000 or more was being handed over to the relief of the Cheshire rates by the 105 trustees. The principal traffic was salt, which had grown from 14,524 tons in 1732 to 1,250,543 tons in 1880–1, apart from another 500,000 tons sent by rail. Thereafter the salt traffic tended to move to pipeline and rail. Coal carrying fell also, but thanks to modernisation, the losses were replaced by a rapid growth of traffic to the chemical works that had been built near the Weaver.

The last half of the century saw a number of major engineering improvements on waterways. In 1850 the Blackhill inclined plane had been completed on the Monkland Canal. With a rise of 96ft, its twin caissons carried 70ft × 13ft 4in barges longitudinally down its 1 in 10 slope. Steam engines provided the power. Blackhill plane did not replace the flight of four staircase pairs of locks beside it, but supplemented it, loaded boats coming down the locks, empties passing up the plane.

Then came three major improvements, the removal of Fenny Compton tunnel on the Oxford Canal in 1868 at a cost of £15,000, and its replacement by a cutting, the Anderton lift in 1875, and in 1893 a new swinging aqueduct to carry the Bridgewater Canal over the Ship Canal, then being built. The Barton swing aqueduct, replacing Brindley's old Barton aqueduct over the Irwell, was, and is, unique in the world. Designed by Edward Leader Williams, then engineer of the Ship Canal, its hydraulic-powered swinging span is 235ft long and weighs 1,450 tons.

Finally came Foxton inclined plane on the Leicester line of the Grand Junction after that company had taken over the two canals between Norton Junction and Leicester. The Foxton incline replaced the ten locks of the Foxton flight. Opened in 1900, steam-powered, it had a rise of 75ft, each of its two caissons taking two narrow boats or one barge. Unlike Blackhill, which had closed about 1887, Foxton's caissons carried boats sideways down the slope. The hoped for trade did not materialise, however, and the incline was abandoned in 1910 in favour of the old locks. Some waterways themselves were also improved. For instance, the Bridgewater Canal was walled, and a depth of 7ft obtained on the towing side, road bridges were rebuilt to give greater canal width, and additional water supplies were found; traffic was now normally worked by a tug towing four boats with a total cargo of 200–240 tons.

Though steam-driven craft had been used experimentally on canals from early days, and soon came into use as tugs in tunnels and on the bigger waterways, they did not seriously threaten the horse-drawn boats as cargo-carriers on the narrow canals until about the 1870s. These 'steamers' were similar in design to the present diesel-engined craft, with an engine-room separate from the living accommodation and an overhanging counter to protect the propeller. The earlier craft were adapted from horse-drawn boats by adding a separate counter: later, they were specially built.

Coke-fired boilers were designed to take up the least space: they were 6ft long by 4ft in diameter, and worked at a pressure of 140lb to the square inch. The boats had tall brass funnels, hinged so that they could be lowered under bridges if necessary, and a brass steam whistle. The engines usually had one high-pressure and one low-pressure cylinder in tandem vertically, operating on a single crank, and were fitted with Stephenson link motion for reversing.

Two main reasons for the decline of 'steamers' before semi-diesel-engined craft were the greater space needed for the engine, boiler and coke supplies, and the heavy crew. There were usually two men on the 'steamer' and two on the butty, or, if the boats were working 'fly' round the clock, four on the steamer and three on the butty, of whom three were off duty at any one time. The whole crew was employed by the captain. Later, a family sometimes took over the butty, but not the steamer.

About 1910 the biggest canal carriers, Fellows, Morton & Clayton, began to fit single-cylinder, two-stroke semi-diesel units to their boats, and other carriers followed. The last 'steamer' left the Grand Junction in 1932, but on the northern canals occasional steam-driven craft, usually maintenance boats, lasted much longer. From the early 1930s two-cylinder, four-cycle diesels began to be fitted, which did not need the pre-heating of the older type.

On the operational side, a great reform carried through in this period was the reclassification of the freights carried on canals, and the fixing of new tolls for each waterway. In his opening address to the Canal Conference of 1888, Sir Douglas Galton had said:

'. . . there are many anomalies of classification in the tolls authorised by Parliament to be charged on different canals forming part of a through route; and without uniformity of classification the difficulties of arranging through rates on contiguous canals are much enhanced.'

An inquiry on rates was held during 1887 and 1888, and the result was embodied in the Railway & Canal Traffic Act, 1888, which laid down that each waterway company must submit a revised classification of traffic and schedule of rates to the Railway & Canal Commission also set up under the Act to supersede the Railway Commission of 1873. The commissioners were to discuss these with the company in the interests of uniformity, and when agreement had been reached, they were to become law. A procedure for use in case of disagreement was also laid down. A great deal of work was done by the commission as a result of the Act in this respect, and in 1894 a series of Acts was passed to give the new classifications and charges (which latter were on balance lower than before), the force of law. This Act was damaging to some of the small canals, since it reduced their already small revenue, collected perhaps from a single article in the carriage of which they had a local monopoly.

The Act also enabled waterways to be taken over by local authorities or public trusts, a recommendation of the 1883 Select Committee which had been reiterated during the Canal Conference of early 1888.

Towards the end of the century Henry Rodolph de Salis, a member of a family who had for long been connected with the Grand Junction Canal, a director of Fellows, Morton & Clayton, the canal carriers, and a seeker after greater efficiency, began an examination of the waterway system of England and Wales. In the course of eleven years he travelled 14,000 miles, and prepared a systematic survey that was first published in 1904 as *Bradshaw's* Canals and Navigable Rivers of England and Wales*, a handbook intended to inform commercial users of the possibilities of water transport. The third and last edition appeared in 1928.

* 'Bradshaw' because published by the proprietors of the then well-known Bradshaw's railway guides, Henry Blacklock & Co Ltd.

CHAPTER XIV

The Manchester Ship Canal

In transport history Manchester and Liverpool have been Tweedledum and Tweedledee; sometimes they have been friends, and sometimes they have had a battle.

We have already noticed the formation of the Mersey & Irwell Navigation, and the reasons that led the Duke of Bridgewater to build his Worsley–Manchester canal and later to extend it to Runcorn on the Mersey.

The river company, carriers as well as toll-takers, had not been prosperous even before the Duke had opened his Runcorn extension in 1776, and in 1779 they had sold out to a new group for £10,000. These worked to build up the fleet and improve the navigation, notably by a canal extension from Warrington to Runcorn, and to put on a passenger service. They benefited a good deal from their connection with the Manchester, Bolton & Bury Canal, much less from the Manchester & Salford Junction to link the river to the Rochdale Canal, to which the Bridgewater was already joined. Keen competition developed between the two concerns, both of which shared in the prosperity that good water transport and the rise of the cotton industry brought to the district. In 1844, when Egerton of the Bridgewater bought the river navigation and so united the two waterways, the Mersey & Irwell Navigation £100 shares (£70 paid up), were still valued at £800 each, in spite of railway competition.

The Liverpool & Manchester Railway was opened in 1830. It had been promoted partly because the rapid growth of traffic offering had been greater than the waterways' ability to carry it efficiently, in spite of improvements they made; partly because it seemed to the railway promoters that there were lucrative pickings to be got. In fact, the railway company found their principal source of revenue was not, as they had thought, goods, but passengers. Ten years after the railway had opened, the railway was still only carrying one-third of the total goods traffic.

Meanwhile, in 1824, a proposal had been made for a small ship canal to carry 400 ton vessels to Manchester, not however from the Mersey, but from the Dee, by a line 45 miles long, and at a cost of £1 million. The scheme reached Parliament in 1825, but was thrown

out on standing orders. That it would have been strongly opposed
by the port interests of Liverpool can be seen from the tenor of these
verses, which appeared in the *Liverpool Mercury* on 18 February 1825.

'Oh, ye Lords of the loom,
Pray avert our sad doom,
We humbly beseech on our knees;
We do not complain
That you drink your champagne,
But leave us our port, if you please.

Sweet squires of the shuttle,
As ye guzzle and guttle,
Have some bowels for poor Liverpool!
Your great Ship Canal
Will produce a cabal,
Then stick to the jenny and mule.

Your sea scheme abandon
For rail-roads the land on:
And to save us from utter perdition,
Cut your throats if you like
But don't cut the dyke,
And this is our humble petition.'[1]

The Manchester & Dee scheme dropped, but the idea of a ship
canal remained in the minds of Manchester men, and references to it
occur at intervals during the next fifty years. As the century wore on,
there was increasing criticism, on the one hand of the exactions of
the Liverpool port authorities, and on the other of the railway transport monopoly that was growing up between Liverpool and Manchester, and which was solidified when in 1872 a new railway-
influenced company, the Bridgewater Navigation Company, bought
the canal, carrying interests and waterway property of the Bridgewater
trustees for £1,115,000.

The beginning of the process that led to the building of the ship
canal was probably a walk beside the river taken by Mr George Hicks
in 1876. He saw barges stuck on the mud, and wrote a letter to the
Manchester Guardian pointing out that a good waterway was neglected.
This letter was noticed by a London engineer, Hamilton Fulton, who
wrote to Mr Hicks and expressed his interest in helping any scheme
to improve the navigation of the Mersey. The two men met, and a
preliminary report was made by the engineer and put before a meeting

of the Chamber of Commerce. A trading slump set in, however, and nothing was done until in 1881 Sir William Harcourt made a speech in which he praised the energy of the citizens of Glasgow in making the Clyde navigable for ocean-going steamships. Correspondence to the newspapers began, and interested a man who was to be prominent in ship canal affairs, Daniel Adamson. He consulted an engineer friend, James Abernethy, upon the project, and, getting a favourable reply, he took the lead in organising the demand for a canal.

The slump also played its part, for it was especially severe in Manchester, where it was attributed:

'. . . to the excessively keen competition to which Manchester was subjected by reason of the great cost of transit of goods from this district as compared with that to which other manufacturing centres were put.'[2]

The effort towards a ship canal really dates from 1882. In May of that year a pamphlet was issued by 'Mancuniensis', *Facts and Figures in Favour of a Tidal Navigation to Manchester*, which set the proposal within a frame of statistics. It went quickly through a number of editions and had a large sale. In June Adamson called at his house a meeting of 68 prominent businessmen and representatives of interested towns, to meet Hamilton Fulton and Edward Leader Williams, now engineer of the Bridgewater Navigation Company. Fulton's proposal was for a tidal canal without locks, to cost £4½ million. The meeting was enthusiastic, a provisional committee of the Manchester Tidal Navigation company was formed, and plans made to raise money for preliminary expenses. In the autumn it was decided that, following the advice of Leader Williams and James Abernethy, a canal with locks was more practicable than one open to the tides, and the plan was changed.

Meetings were held, newspaper correspondence sprang up, money was raised, and songs were written. A representative verse of one of these is:

'Monopoly has vexed me long,
   It's done the like by you;
Down with the monster in the mud
   And give fair play its due.
Then cotton, timber, corn, and beef,
   Will come to us right through;
And ham and eggs and well-filled kegs
   With savoury things for you.

Chorus
Then love your neighbour as yourself,
We'll sing whilst sailing through
The Ship Canal by Liverpool
On board our *Ocean Screw*.'[3]

The Manchester and Salford city councils supported the project, and before the end of the year the plans for the Parliamentary Bill had been deposited. From this time until 5 August 1885 there raged a Parliamentary war, during which two Ship Canal Bills were thrown out, the one by the Lords and the other by the Commons, and nearly £350,000 was spent. The opposition came from the railway companies, from the Bridgewater Navigation Company, and from Liverpool interests. Whilst the Parliamentary battle was being fought, a steady newspaper war also went on, the Manchester papers varying from indifference to keen support, and those of Liverpool from slight to ferocious opposition.

The third Bill was passed after various alterations had been made to placate Liverpool, especially by altering the route so that the canal, instead of passing down the estuary, left the river at Eastham and ran beside it. Liverpool opinion greatly feared that the works would in the former case have damaged the estuary farther down. The estimated cost of the works was £6,311,137, but in addition certain commitments were entered into, notably to buy the Bridgewater Navigation Company for £1,710,000, nearly £600,000 more than the railway interests had paid for the waterway a few years before. The Act provided for a capital of £8 million in shares, with power to raise a further sum by loan, of which £5 million as well as the purchase price of the Bridgewater concern, was to be raised before 6 August 1887.

The Act did not give power to pay interest on capital during construction. Daniel Adamson was optimistic that the money needed would be raised without difficulty in spite of that handicap, and a prospectus was issued. It was a shock to the promoters when only £750,000 came in, and a Bill was quickly prepared to authorise the company to pay interest whilst the ship canal was being built. The Act was passed, only to be followed by an issue of shares that failed, partly because the promoters had tried to economise on Stock Exchange commissions, chiefly because the public were not sufficiently impressed either by the strength of the Board of Directors or by the soundness of the estimates.

It was therefore a wise move of the board to set up a consultative committee, upon which there were men like C. P. Scott, the editor of the *Manchester Guardian*, who had not strongly supported the scheme. This committee was asked to study the practicability of the ship canal, and after a careful inquiry it reported that it was perfectly satisfied with the estimates, and that the project was a thoroughly sound commercial undertaking. They did, however, suggest that the board should be strengthened.

The board were not agreed as to the next step, but eventually Daniel Adamson resigned as chairman in favour of Lord Egerton, a kinsman of the Duke of Bridgewater whose canal had first connected Liverpool and Manchester by an artificial waterway. Now began a rush to get the money. Meetings were held all over the Midlands; a Bill was hurried through Parliament to allow the creation of preference shares, which were then underwritten by two London financial houses, and before 6 August 1887 it was proudly announced that two-thirds of the share capital authorised had been issued and accepted in accordance with the Act of 1885. An agreement was signed with T. A. Walker, the contractor, builder of the Severn Tunnel, and on 11 November 1887, the first sod was cut by Lord Egerton upon the site of Eastham lock, where the canal was to enter the Mersey. Work upon the great project had begun.

It led off with energy, and within a year, 11,000 men were at work, and cutting was up to time. Then Walker died, and with his death there came both natural disasters, in the shape of floods that delayed the work and added to the expense, and also arguments with the executors of the contractor. These led the company at the end of 1890 to take the work into its own hands, unfortunately at a time when bad weather was to cause further difficulties, and when the price of labour and materials was to rise beyond the estimates.

It soon became clear that the money in the hands of the ship canal company would not be sufficient to finish the canal. The chairman therefore approached Manchester Corporation, which so well understood the seriousness of allowing the works to stop, that it agreed to promote a Bill in Parliament allowing it to lend £3 million to the company upon debentures, and to have five directors upon the Board. So loyal were the shareholders to the company that they in turn raised almost no objections to the placing of such a large sum in front of their own interest.

The influence of the corporation upon the scheme led to a tightening up of the canal administration, and work was pushed on. It became clear in 1892, however, that still more money would be needed to finish the canal. The corporations of Salford and Oldham, feeling that their interest in the canal had not been given practical form, promoted Bills to allow them to lend, the former £1 million, the latter £250,000; but the corporation of Manchester had offered to lend a further £2 million, and this was accepted by the ship canal company in debentures to rank *pari passu* with those existing. It was agreed that until half the total of £5 million owing to the Manchester Corporation had been paid off, the corporation should appoint a majority of the directors. This majority still exists today. In 1904 the interest on the loan was reduced, and it became irredeemable and non-transferable.

Among the last works on the canal to be completed was the Barton swing aqueduct, which carries the Bridgewater Canal over the ship canal. At the same time Brindley's old aqueduct was pulled down, the oldest large piece of engineering on an English canal making way for the newest.

So, on 1 January 1894 the canal was opened for business, by a procession of boats headed by the *Norseman* carrying the directors, and followed by a trail of merchant ships, seventy-one of which entered the docks. On 21 May the formal opening took place by the Queen in front of packed crowds of jubilant Mancunians. The ship canal was open, at a cost of £14,347,891, against the £8,408,936 estimated in the prospectus of July 1886. Given the vicissitudes through which all great works pass, it was not excessive, but the greatly increased cost did mean, as so often when the earlier canals were being built, that those who had taken the initiative and the risk, the Ordinary shareholders, were the greatest sufferers. In this case some £5 million of debentures and £4 million of Preference capital had been put in front of their shares. It was many years before they saw a dividend.

The early years of the canal were filled with difficulties; among them a lack of co-operation from the railways which caused the slow handling of goods, and the habit of shipping companies in conferences of binding shippers by means of rebates to use certain channels that were not easy to change. It was indeed thought possible for the first year or two that the canal would have to close. Then slowly its fortunes changed. Cheaper costs attracted imports to Manchester, and the total tonnage handled rose from 1,826,237 in 1896 to 2,595,585 in 1898. With it rose the prosperity of Manchester. A paper read in 1912 before the Manchester Statistical Society by J. S. McConechy, *The Economic Value of the Ship Canal to Manchester and District*, shows the great economic effect it had, exemplified in the increase in the rateable value of the township of Manchester (a part only of the city) as follows:

| 1884 | £1,481,182 | 1904 | £1,886,913 |
| 1894 | £1,504,607 | 1912 | £2,043,854 |

The indirect benefit in lowered freight rates to Manchester was great, both on canal-borne and railway goods, since the railways had lowered their Liverpool–Manchester rates when the canal was opened.

Dr D. A. Farnie has excellently written the canal's history in *The Manchester Ship Canal and the rise of the Port of Manchester*. Here I can only sketch outlines.

First steps were its close association with Trafford Park Estates in 1896, which were developed for new industry likely to use the canal, and in 1898, with Christopher Furness of the shipping line, the formation of Manchester Liners Ltd, intended to increase carryings of Canadian produce to industrial England, and which soon added services also to the USA.

Then came the provision of facilities especially for the import trade, mainly in timber, grain, cotton, oil, cattle, and later, wood-pulp. Outside interests being reluctant to provide such necessaries as warehouses for raw cotton, grain elevators, cattle lairages, cold stores and oil tanks, the ship-canal company had to act, directly or indirectly, to provide them. Manchester remained a mainly importing port: imports as a percentage of total traffic were 60 in 1900, 70 in 1920, 71·5 in 1950 and 75 in 1970. Actual import tonnages in those years were, 1,678,379, 2,877,733, 6,968,519 and 11,380,000. The greatest battle of all was with Liverpool for raw cotton, especially American, and Manchester never succeeded in winning more than a large share of the trade.

Exports were mainly coal, salt, manufactured goods and machinery, the mechanised Partington coal basin of 1894 on the canal being the forerunner of a continuous development of mechanised handling of varied cargoes.

By now the canal had 179 acres of water space in its docks at Manchester and Salford alone, and 5⅝ miles of quays. The largest entrance lock to the canal at Eastham was 600ft × 80ft, the upper locks being 600ft × 65ft.

In its first half century cotton dominated the ship canal's trade, but oil imports, which succeeded it, date back to 1897, first from Russia, then the world's largest oil producer, later from the United States. Oil arrived in casks, but as tankers took over, so special oil docks began to be opened, two on the canal at Stanlow (5 m from Eastham) in 1922 and 1933, and Britain's then largest oil dock, the Queen Elizabeth II at Eastham, taking ships of over 30,000 dwt, in 1954.

Figure 43   Irlam locks on the Manchester Ship Canal at the time of its opening

The building of the first Stanlow dock, to which the canal had been deepened, marked a basic change, as activity began to move from Manchester docks lower down the canal to the Eastham–Runcorn section. Moreover, when the Tranmere Oil Terminal was opened in 1960 at Birkenhead, in much deeper water, all the canal's oil docks were seriously affected. The old barge canal-served ports of Runcorn and Ellesmere Port were now increasing in importance until the export trade of the latter, after it had gained a container terminal in 1972, exceeded that of Manchester itself.

A historic link was broken in the seventies when the Bridgewater Canal, by that time a cruising waterway, was transferred to a separate Bridgewater Canal Trust.

For 1981 the chairman reported to shareholders: 'No longer is there any demand for deepsea general cargo vessels in the heart of the greater Manchester area—the purpose for which the Ship Canal was originally constructed'. The company was doing a good trade lower down the canal at Runcorn and Ellesmere Port, but the port of Manchester was sharing the experience of others on the west coast; business was moving to the south and east. It had one special disadvantage: its approaches, and even more the canal itself, taking vessels up to 15,000 dwt to Stanlow and 12,500 dwt to the terminal docks, could not accommodate big modern containerships and bulk carriers.

Historic moments came in 1981 when Clan Line withdrew their Indian service, operative since 1896, and in 1983 when Manchester Liners themselves moved their Mediterranean service from the terminal docks to Ellesmere Port. Soon afterwards, Manchester ceased to have any regular liner service. The docks were left with only eighteen dockworkers, and the upper part of the canal with only an occasional ship, serving a land drainage purpose more important than that of commerce.

CHAPTER XV

From Royal Commission to 1948

THE last years of the century saw increasing interest in waterways, partly the result of the opening of the Manchester Ship Canal, partly of a general wish to reduce railway rates, especially upon the raw materials upon which British industry increasingly relied, partly of a greater knowledge of what overseas waterways were achieving. Papers on these had been read at the Royal Society of Arts' Conference of 1888, and had been followed by two notable books, J. S. Jeans' *Waterways and Water Transport in Different Countries*, 1890, and the second rewritten edition of L. F. Vernon-Harcourt's two-volume engineering work, *Rivers and Canals*, 1896.

In the year 1900 this interest clarified itself in a resolution passed unanimously by the Associated Chambers of Commerce, which asked the government to appoint a Royal Commission to consider the whole question of the waterways. In the following year, on the initiative of the same body, a Bill was introduced into Parliament which favoured the setting up of public canal trusts, but was not proceeded with. The Associated Chambers of Commerce continued to press their views, somewhat altering them as they did so, and Bills were introduced in 1904, 1905 and 1906. The memorandum attached to the Bill of 1906 shows its object to be:

'To constitute a strong Central Canals Board for the purpose of obtaining provisional orders authorising the board to take over, improve and manage, in the first instance, certain canals which form a chain of navigation between the principal ports in England. Powers are also taken for subsequently acquiring by provisional orders other canals (with the exception of the Manchester Ship Canal) and for their improvement and management. The object of the Bill is, by such a consolidation of interests and management, to improve the facilities for water carriage and to establish a complete system of intercommunication.'[1]

This pressure, kept up for a number of years, led to the appointment of the Royal Commission of 1906, which presented its Report in twelve volumes in 1911. This Report is the most comprehensive study of the waterway system of the British Isles (it included Ireland) that has ever been made. In addition, the commissioners studied the Continental waterways with some care, and tried to balance fairly the undoubted progress they had made when compared with British waterways against the different commercial and economic conditions of this country.

They summed up the situation of their time as they saw it in these words:

'On a few waterways or sections of waterways, favoured by special conditions, combined in two or three cases with enterprising management, traffic has been maintained and even increased. On other waterways it has declined, on some it has virtually disappeared. Everywhere the proportion of long-distance traffic to local traffic by water has become small. Considered as a whole, the waterways have had no share in the enormous increase of internal transport business which has taken place between the middle of the nineteenth century and the present time. Their position, so far as regards their total traffic, has been at best one of a stationary character, since the development of steam traction on railroads and on the sea, while the whole transport business of the country, including that taken by railways and that taken by coasting vessels, has multiplied itself several times over.'[2]

The commission recommended the widening and deepening of the trunk waterway routes called the Cross, which connected Thames, Severn, Humber and Mersey, with a centre at Birmingham. If these lines were reconstructed to take larger barges, and to eliminate many of the locks, they thought a large saving in time and so in labour costs would result.

Their final proposals were to enlarge these routes, partly to a 100 ton barge standard, and partly (chiefly where there were river navigations) to a 300 ton barge standard.

The routes were as follows:

A. Birmingham and Leicester to London, both at Brentford and Paddington.
    To be improved to 100 ton barge standard. The Regent's Canal was left out, since it was already capable of taking 100 ton barges

B. Leicester, Burton and Nottingham to the Humber.
    To be a 300 ton route from Fradley Junction on the Trent & Mersey Canal, and from Leicester on the Soar, to Nottingham, and a 750 ton barge route thence to the Humber.

C. Wolverhampton and Birmingham to the Mersey.

   To be a 100 ton route, though a portion of it, the River Weaver, was already capable of taking much larger craft.

D. Wolverhampton and Birmingham to the Severn.

   To be of 100 ton standard from Wolverhampton to Stourport, and from Birmingham to the Severn via Droitwich. To be of 600 ton standard from Stourport to Worcester and of 750 ton standard from Worcester to Gloucester, whence the Gloucester & Berkeley Canal could take 1,200 ton vessels to the Severn at Sharpness.

It was considered to be impossible to widen the Birmingham canals themselves, and this system was therefore thought of as a collecting ground for the enlarged waterways. No immediate recommendations were made for the other canals in the country, but it was suggested that after the Cross had been dealt with, one of the trans-Pennine canals should also be enlarged.

The commission's proposals for enlargement would have meant the complete reconstruction of the trunk waterways to bring them up to date, and to enable them to handle a great deal more traffic in an efficient way. For instance, the proposals of the consulting engineers for the treatment of the route from Birmingham to Sharpness suggested that 7 inclines and 6 locks should replace 62 existing locks.

The cost of improving 533¾ miles of main waterway was estimated at £15,238,909, with an extra £2,295,001 for 514 miles of branch canals that would be in close communication with the Cross, and would need some improvement. This figure did not include the cost of acquisition, or a number of subsidiary charges such as the cost of new warehouses. The commission estimated that the annual charge for the improvements, including interest and sinking fund, management and maintenance, would be £1,098,025, against which the revenue of the existing owners of the waterways affected was £567,971. In other words, the takings would have to be doubled if the improvements were to be paid for.

The commissioners were doubtful whether they would in fact be paid for, and were in no doubt at all that their proposals were not such as to interest private enterprise. They therefore recommended nationalisation of the trunk waterways and their branches under a Waterways Board of three or five, which should not however have power to act as carriers. The board would issue stock or raise loans guaranteed by the State, first to acquire the waterways and then to improve them. It was also recommended that the two existing State canals, the Caledonian and the Crinan, should be transferred to the board.

As regards Ireland, the commission's report was not radical: it recommended some expansion to meet certain anticipated increases of traffic and also state control of both navigation and drainage by a single water authority.

Though it was clear that if the waterways were improved on the lines recommended, a great saving in transport costs to the user was to be expected (for instance, a reduction in the cost of carrying coal from Leicestershire to London from 6s 8d (33½p) to 3s 10d (19p) a ton was envisaged), the report of the commission was still-born, partly because it carried no very great conviction, partly because of two well-written books by a railway supporter, E. A. Pratt, *British Canals* published when the commission began its sittings, and *Canals and Traders* after it had finished. Against it were the powerful and reasonable arguments that only some of the canals were to be dealt with, that their improvement would virtually subsidise certain traders at the expense of all others on railways or unimproved waterways who were not so fortunately placed, and that a state system of waterways would be put in competition with a privately owned system of railways. On the Continent the usual practice was for both the railways and the waterways to be state-owned or state-assisted, and for the transport system to be planned as a whole.

It sounds curiously in our ears that Pratt should go far towards accusing the Liberal Party of engineering the whole business as a means of helping them to nationalise transport. He says in *Canals and Traders* (1910):

'It certainly is the case that the proposal for a reorganisation of the waterway system, in the assumed interest of British traders, was brought forward by the late Sir Henry Campbell-Bannerman in a speech which he delivered in the Albert Hall on the eve of the general election of four years ago. It is, also, the case that the report of the Royal Commission, appointed, apparently, as the outcome of the declaration in question, was published, at the end of December 1909, on the eve of another general election. No less true is it that a depreciation of values would, in fact, facilitate the acquisition of the railways by the State; while the Report itself says: "The whole tendency of the civilized world, both on the Continent and in most of the British dominions, is towards the vesting of all important means of inland communication, whether by waterways, railways or roads, in public authorities. We are unable to make a recommendation which would be out of harmony with the policy which practical experience has led so many nations to adopt." [3]

In the minds of the public the proposals of the commission looked too much like an expensive gamble. In any case, Irish Home Rule and the long struggle of the Liberal Government with the House of Lords diverted public opinion to other more exciting topics until the outbreak of World War I. Meanwhile an Act of 1908 had transferred responsibility for the Thames below Teddington to the new Port of London Authority, and a beginning was made with a scheme to improve the Trent.

On the outbreak of war the railway-owned canals were immediately put under the control of the State through the Railway Executive Committee, together with the railways themselves. Nothing was done to control the independent waterways, however, and their tonnage fell as their men left to join the Forces. It was not until 1 March 1917 that most of them were brought under a Canal Control Committee of the Board of Trade, which worked through three committees for the northern, midland and southern areas in Britain, and a fourth for Ireland. This committee tried to restore some of the lost traffic to the canals, but much had gone for good. In 1913 31,585,909 tons were carried on British canals, and in 1918 21,599,850.

On 31 August 1920 the canals reverted to private control, £3 million having been paid out to controlled companies and carriers since 1 March 1917, though the Ministry of Transport agreed to continue nominal government control of certain waterways for a time after 1920 as a means of raising tolls to an economic level pending new legislation. The rise in the prices of labour and materials made it unlikely that the recommendations of the Royal Commission would be carried out, but in order that the post-war position could be reviewed the government appointed a committee under the chairmanship of Neville Chamberlain, of which Ernest Bevin was a member. A first interim report in February 1921 suggested immediate action for the improvement of the Trent, and a second, in May, recommended against nationalisation (Mr Bevin dissenting) on the grounds that it would involve liabilities greater than the nation was prepared to face, since the waterways had further deteriorated since the report of the Royal Commission, and prices and wages had risen.

This was the time when the railways were being formed into four great groups, and the committee therefore suggested the formation of seven regional groups of waterways, which were to include railway-owned canals, each under a public trust made up of representatives of local users, public bodies, the Ministry of Transport and the stockholders, and financed by the State and the local authorities concerned. These trusts should have carrying powers, though not to the exclusion of bye-traders, and the railways should be debarred from uneconomic competition with them. The groups proposed were:

1. The River Trent and its connections.
2. The Yorkshire canals.
3. The Lancashire canals.
4. The canals joining Liverpool with the Midlands.
5. The River Severn with its connections.
6. The River Thames and its connections with the Midlands and Bristol.
7. The Birmingham canals and their connection in the Midlands.

The committee recommended that the groups should not all be brought into being at once, but that an experimental start should be made with the Trent group, since Nottingham was already committed to an improvement scheme on that river.

The committee never produced a final report, and nothing was done officially to follow up its recommendations, or the similar ones of the Royal Commission on Transport which reported in 1930, and which suggested that failing voluntary amalgamation schemes, the Ministry of Transport should set up public trusts to take over the waterways of the Cross.

In the Irish Free State, independent from 1922, a Canals and Waterways Commission was appointed. Its recommendation that a Waterways Board should be established was not, however, implemented. In the south, the Grand Canal Company from 1927 onwards built up extensive road services, though canal carrying on all waterways fell, except during the artificial years of World War II. In the north, canals began to be disused for commercial traffic: the Ulster in 1929, the Strabane in 1932, the Newry, oldest of all, in 1938–9. Once disused, they soon decayed.

The time between the wars saw on the one hand a few developments, but on the other the rise of a new competitor, the motor lorry, which took much of the short-haul traffic left to canals, the further working out of coal seams and quarries on canal routes, and the replacement of coal by electricity from the grid as a source of power. There was therefore a deterioration in the condition and use of most waterways, and the extinction of some.

Of the developments, two are of especial interest.

The River Trent has always been of great importance as a navigation, and the building of the Trent & Mersey Canal made it a link in a through route from the Humber to the Mersey. The original Trent Navigation company, formed in 1783, was concerned with the state of the river, especially that part of it below the canal entrance at Wilden Ferry, while the Newark Navigation Commissioners controlled the cut of 4 miles at Newark. Later the Humber Conservancy Board was formed to control the portion of river from Trent Falls, where the river joins the Humber, to Gainsborough, where the control of the Trent Navigation company began.

The navigation was good from Trent Falls to Newark, but between there and Nottingham lay a shallow and fast-running part of the river, with a fall up to 19in to the mile. It was therefore necessary for goods to be transhipped at Newark to smaller craft, which added to the transport costs of those carried up to Nottingham. The corporation of that town had been interested in improving the navigation for many years, and it welcomed an Act obtained by the Trent Navigation company in 1906 to dredge the river to a minimum depth of 5ft and width of 60ft, and to build six new locks and cuts. The Act provided that the works were to be done within ten years, but shortage of money resulted in only one new lock and cut, at Cromwell, 188ft × 30ft being built, and the river being dredged below Newark so that 120 ton vessels could come up to that town, before the outbreak of war in 1914.

The city council then took a hand, and appointed a committee to discuss with the navigation company what part they could play so that the works could be completed before parliamentary powers expired. It was finally agreed that the corporation, helped by development commissioners whose task it was to provide work for the unemployed, should finance the remainder of the works, and an Act was passed in 1915 for this purpose, after opposition from the railway companies. By this time, however, the war had caused money to be tight and labour scarce, and nothing was done. It was not until after the war was over that the river was dredged and new locks the same size as Cromwell built to take three Trent boats and a cargo-carrying tug at once, each 82ft 6in × 14ft 6in and carrying between them up to 600 tons. The single-boat lock at Nether Newark was replaced by a four-boat lock, and a new channel later provided at Holme lock so that the biggest craft using the river could work through to Trent Bridge, Nottingham. From Nottingham up to Shardlow and Leicester, however, the waterway still only took Upper Trent boats 71ft 6in × 14ft 6in. Nottingham was now less than twenty-four hours away by river from Hull, where the craft could be loaded direct from seagoing ships. The work authorised under the 1906 Act was completed in 1927: Nottingham corporation had spent about £450,000 on the navigation.

A second important development was the formation of the Grand Union Canal company and the modernisation of its route. In 1894 the Grand Junction company had absorbed the Leicestershire & Northamptonshire Union and the (old) Grand Union, and so had carried its waterway to Leicester. Now, in 1929, it joined with the Regent's Canal in London and the three canals on the Birmingham route—the Warwick & Birmingham, the Warwick & Napton, and the Birmingham & Warwick Junction—to form a new company, the Grand Union, the name of the old company that had been absorbed in 1894 being used to symbolise a greater purpose. A through route from Regent's Canal dock at Wapping to Birmingham was now under one ownership with the exception of a short length of the Oxford Canal which formed part of the waterway, and over which the Grand Union company had running powers.

The amalgamated company three years later absorbed three more concerns, the Leicester Navigation, the Loughborough Navigation, and the Erewash Canal. These took its line past Leicester to Trent Junction, and across the river to Langley Mill. The length of the new combined waterway was over 300 miles. With the help of a government guarantee of interest for a number of years, about a million pounds was then spent on the London–Birmingham route. As it stood, it had been built as a barge canal to Braunston, while the remainder was narrow. Fifty-one new broad locks on the Birmingham–Braunston section were built to take two narrow boats at once. In order to work 14ft beam barges through the canal it would, however, have been necessary to rebuild so many bridges that it was decided for the time being to maintain the 14ft standard from London to Berkhamsted, and a 12ft 6in standard thence to Sampson Road, 1 mile from Birmingham, and the nearest practicable point to which the improvements could be carried. The Grand Union company intended to build boats of 12ft 6in beam, and prototypes were constructed, but there were so many lengths of canal where two 12ft 6in boats could not pass that the canal beyond Berkhamsted continued to be worked by narrow boats in pairs.

Much dredging was done, and over many stretches of the canal the cross-sectional area was increased by walling and piling the sides, so enabling the boats to travel faster. At the same time banks were protected. Most of this programme was completed by 1934.

Meanwhile the canal company had begun carrying by buying the small firm of Associated Canal Carriers Ltd, and in 1934 changing the name to the Grand Union Canal Carrying Co Ltd, and greatly expanding its fleet. It had, however, over-expanded, and had to be considerably cut down and reorganised before heavy losses could be ended. These had their repercussions on the canal company itself, which paid no dividend on its ordinary shares between 1933 and 1945.

In Ireland, there was one major new work. In 1925 the building of hydroelectric works at Ardnacrusha on the Shannon above Limerick was authorised. They were completed in 1930. The old locks and cuts on the Killaloe–Limerick section were now eliminated, the navigation channel remaining in the river to Parteen, where a new navigation cut led to the power station and a staircase pair of locks, one 60ft, one 40ft deep. These were built 105ft × 19ft 6in, narrower, curiously, than the nineteenth-century ones built above Killaloe by the Shannon Commissioners.

The time between the wars was one of steady contraction. The main railway-owned canal-carrying concern, the Shropshire Union, ceased to carry in 1921, it being reported that the loss was too great, due to the eight-hour day, higher wages and higher costs of material. Before the war this concern had operated 670 craft of various kinds. It was followed by other canal companies with carrying departments, like the Rochdale. The influence of the country lorry, again, ended the last loads on many semi-derelict waterways. The Grantham Canal, which in 1905 had carried 18,802 tons, in 1924 carried 1,583, and was closed in 1929. Another railway-owned canal, the Grand Western, had carried its last loads of stone some years earlier. Independent canals also suffered. The Thames & Severn, owned by the Gloucestershire County Council, was closed in 1927, except for 6 miles from Chalford closed in 1933. The Droitwich and Droitwich Junction, owned by the Sharpness New Docks and Gloucester & Birmingham Navigation company, were abandoned in 1939. There were many others, including the Louth, Wisbech, Aberdare and Bradford canals, and the Rother (Sussex) Navigation, and a number of canal branches. That quietude—in whatever sense—had fallen upon old rivalries is shown by the agreement reached in 1933 between the four railways and the Canal Association for joint traffic conferences and the elimination of price-cutting and the quotation of uneconomic rates.

In an earlier chapter I mentioned tourists on the canal system in the 1860s of the last century, who of course had predecessors even before the famous journey of fiction described in *Crotchet Castle*. It was probably George Westall who first made cruising by canal at all popular when he published *Inland Cruising on the Rivers and Canals of England and Wales* in 1908. The book gave an account of a tour through 870 miles of waterway by motor boat in twenty-five days under way, which Westall had carried out the previous year. He later became the President of the National Inland Navigation League which existed for a time after World War I.

Several other books followed, among them C. J. Aubertin's *A Caravan Afloat*, which was partly an account of life on a canal house-boat and partly a plea for the canals; E. Temple Thurston's *The 'Flower of Gloster'*, an account of a tour by canal boat through the Oxford, Stratford-upon-Avon and Thames & Severn Canals, a book which has happily been reprinted; and, published during World War I, P. Bonthron's popular *My Holidays on Inland Waterways*, staccato descriptions of explorations of many canals, some of which are no longer navigable.

In Scotland, passenger steamers had run for many years on the Crinan and Caledonian Canals, and on the Forth & Clyde the 'Queens' plied from 1893 to 1939.

Between the wars the literature of canal cruising partly transferred itself to the motor boating and yachting magazines. William Bliss's writings were popular, but the only book on the subject which interested the general public was the very popular *Narrow Boat* by L. T. C. Rolt, which was published in 1944, but which went back to the last year of peace. The hiring of motor cruisers on canals had begun in 1935, when G. F. Wain and others started the Inland Cruising Association at Christleton near Chester, and in 1938 what was probably the first canal boat club, the West London Motor Cruising Club, was formed on the Paddington Arm.

On the outbreak of war in 1939 the railway-owned canals came at once under the control of the Ministry of Transport as part of the railway undertakings. The independent canals remained for the time being on their own, the government deciding against immediate control on the main grounds that the cost would be too great, and that so much traffic would in any case find its way to them that they would not need assistance. The coming of the war caused a great shift in the channels of trade. There was much less use of the east coast ports facing Europe, and much more of those on the west coast facing America. Traffic also changed its character and its usual destination. All this had its effect on canal trade, because the limited mileage of the waterways made the water transport system far less flexible than that of the railways or the roads. The canal companies began to lose revenue, and therefore in June 1940 a subsidy of 50 per cent of the tolls was given to the carriers on traffic moved by canal. Tolls were pegged at one-third above pre-war, and freight rates could only be moved upwards with the consent of the Ministry of

Transport. It was considered that with this subsidy, which lasted until nationalisation, and which was paid to registered carriers, prices competitive with other forms of transport could be quoted. The canal companies found, however, that the pegged tolls they were receiving were insufficient to enable them to maintain their waterways, which deteriorated in consequence.

The government, however, soon came to feel that the greatest use was not being made of canals in the war, and in 1941 Frank Pick was appointed to investigate and report upon the best steps to take. He recommended that the government should assume responsibility for them. The first steps were to strengthen the advisory central and regional canal committees that had been set up at the beginning of the war, by including on them not only the two sides of the canal industry, but representatives of the government departments controlling the traffic and of the trade unions. The Parliamentary Secretary to the Ministry of War Transport became chairman of the Central Committee. These committees were not really executive, but found themselves carrying out certain executive functions because they were the most convenient bodies to do so. At the ministry Brig-Gen Sir Osborne Mance was appointed Director of Canals.

By now, pressure on the nation's transport was such that it was clearly necessary to maintain in reasonable order those waterways which could contribute to the war effort. Therefore by three Orders dated between July and October 1942, eighteen undertakings and a number of carriers were taken under control. Financial agreements provided that all income should go to the ministry, which would pay fixed annual sums equivalent to average revenue in the last three pre-war years, plus outgoings considered necessary for war purposes. The subsidy was continued to those carriers who were not controlled, and these were also represented on the canal committees. The cost to the end of the war to the government was £2,600,000.

Efforts were made to put as much traffic as possible on to the waterways, but a number of factors made this difficult. Apart from the diversion of trade caused by the war, the canals suffered from the poor standard of maintenance some of them had had previously, and from the drain of skilled men and women, not only from the boats themselves, but from such ancillary industries as the boat-building and repairing yards. Owing to the different gauges of the canals, it was almost impossible to transfer craft from those parts of the system not fully used to those other parts, such as the Mersey and Severn areas, where more traffic could have been carried by water if the boats had been available. The chief transfer carried out was that of petroleum tank barges from the Humber to the Severn; these helped to build up what later became a substantial trade in petroleum by water from Avonmouth to Gloucester, Worcester and Stourport.

The six regions into which the waterways were divided were:

> *North-East*, based on the Aire & Calder system, with head-quarters at Leeds.
> *North-West*, based on the Leeds & Liverpool and Bridgewater Canals and the River Weaver, with headquarters at Manchester.
> *East Midland*, based on the Trent, with its headquarters at Nottingham.
> *West Midland*, based on the Birmingham Navigations, with its headquarters at Birmingham.
> *South-Western*, based on the Severn, with its headquarters at Gloucester.
> *London*, based on the Grand Union and the Lea, with its head-quarters in London.

These regions were also used for the joint industrial negotiating machinery which was set up in 1942, with a National Council and Regional Councils.

Women had for long partnered men on some canal boats, but as the result of the enterprise of two, later three, women who ran a boat in 1941 on the Worcester & Birmingham Canal, a scheme was started for training women to work pairs on the Grand Union. The numbers included in the scheme at any one time were small, and a maximum of eleven pairs of boats were worked by women at the same time, but it was not the less valuable for that. The scheme was later taken over by the Ministry of War Transport, and was wound up at the end of 1945, when the last woman volunteer left the cut. Three books, *Maiden's Trip* by Emma Smith, *Idle Women* by Susan Woolfitt, and *The Amateur Boatwomen*, by Eily Gayford, describe what happened to the cut when the women invaded it.

We saw that at the end of World War I the tonnage carried on canals had dropped to 21½ million tons. Through the inter-war years it fell steadily to about 17 million tons in 1924 and 13 million in 1938. The dislocation of trade routes in the early years of the war caused a further fall to about 11 million tons, of which about half was coal, which by the year 1946 had fallen still further to 10 million. The war years also saw the passing of abandonment Acts covering some 200 miles of waterway, including most of the Huddersfield, Glamorganshire, and Manchester, Bolton & Bury canals, and much of the Shropshire Union system; in one case, however, the Shropshire Union line from Hurleston to Llangollen, the canal remained open for pleasure traffic and has now been re-authorised as a cruise-way.

In 1946 a few people gathered in Robert Aickman's flat founded the Inland Waterways Association, choosing Aickman as chairman, L. T. C. Rolt, author of *Narrow Boat*, as secretary, Charles Hadfield, part-author with Frank Eyre, of *English Rivers and Canals* (1945), as vice-chairman, and Frank Eyre as treasurer.

The passing of the Transport Act of 1947 ended the era of private ownership for the great majority of waterways. The battle on the Bill was chiefly fought upon the nationalisation of road transport, and there were few mentions of canals in the debates. The nationalisation of the waterways, which had been seriously debated since 1888, came about almost without controversy.

In the Republic of Ireland, as the Irish Free State had become, nationalisation came with the Transport Act of 1944. It was followed by the setting up of the road-rail amalgamation Coras Iompair Eireann (the Transport Company of Ireland) in 1945. CIE took over the railway-owned Royal Canal, which it closed in 1961, and in 1950 acquired the Grand and the Barrow.

CHAPTER XVI

Transformation Scene

++◆++

ON 1 January 1948 the British Transport Commission took over most of the waterways owned by independent companies, and the Caledonian and Crinan canals from the Ministry of Transport, with the result that the annual loss on these two waterways would now appear in the commission's accounts. The former railway-owned canals were transferred during the following two or three years. Important exceptions to nationalisation were: the Manchester Ship Canal and its appendage the Bridgewater Canal, because, curiously, it ranked as a dock enterprise; the Exeter Canal; the Wey; and several small semi-derelict canals, such as the remaining part of the Bude, Basingstoke, Rochdale, Derby, Glamorganshire, Neath and Tennant. Also omitted was the Thames, which under its conservancy was presumably considered a pleasure rather than a commercial waterway, and an important group on or near the east and south coasts, which had not been included in the wartime canal control scheme upon which the nationalisation schedules had been based. This included the Yorkshire Ouse, Foss, and Linton Lock Navigations, the navigations of the Hull River, the Market Weighton and Ancholme, the Nene, Great Ouse, Yare, Broads and Chelmer & Blackwater. The mileage taken over was 2,172. The nationalised canals were at first grouped into five areas, soon reduced to four, with headquarters at Leeds, Northwich (later Liverpool), Gloucester and London (later Watford).

Under the commission, the Docks & Inland Waterways Executive were given responsibility for the canals. This body consisted of a chairman, Sir Reginald Hill, formerly of the Ministry of Transport, and three full- and three part-time members appointed by the ministry. Among the original members were Robert Davidson, former general manager of the Leeds & Liverpool Canal, and George Cadbury, former chairman of the Severn & Canal Carrying Co.

The commission had the duty to promote efficient modern transport, and powers, *inter alia*, to carry, provide traffic facilities, warehouse and consign goods, build, repair and maintain equipment for their own use, lend money to carrying concerns, acquire transport businesses, license carriers, and build barges. The abandonment procedure by warrant authorised in the Railway & Canal Traffic Act 1888 was retained, the authority now to be the Ministry of Transport instead of the Board of Trade.

Nationalisation of British waterways had been talked of at any rate since the Canal Conference of 1888, and had been recommended for the principal routes by the Royal Commission in 1909. Now it had happened, with the canals forty years older. Government intended that transport should be planned and administered as a whole, and had therefore made the executive for each kind of transport subservient to the central Transport Commission, itself finally responsible to the Ministry of Transport. It was a situation that offered waterways the best chance of catching up the years that the locust had eaten, because they could now be accepted as part of the transport whole.

The executive had inherited a miscellany of obsolete and run-down facilities among which showed a few gleams of modernity. Their first priority was to overtake war-time arrears of maintenance, and then, as resources became available, to develop the waterways, track, warehousing and handling plant, traction methods, carrying and road distribution alike; and to build up a marketing organisation. For the time being, problems like the long-term viability of the narrow boat had to wait.

Track improvements in the commission's early days were mainly on the Severn and the Trent. On the former, dredging and the easing of bends enabled 400 ton craft to reach Worcester, where a new quay wall was built at Diglis to accommodate petroleum tankers, now increasing in number. On the Trent a larger Newark Town lock was opened in 1952, and another old one at Holme was eliminated as part of the River Board flood prevention scheme. As a result, craft up to 300 tons, 120ft × 17ft 6in, could now reach Nottingham. Elsewhere, dredging, bank protection work, and much needed improvement of terminal facilities went on, and in 1950 a small research department was set up at Bulls Bridge depot.

The executive took over the carrying fleets that had been directly owned by the former companies, like the compartment boats, barges and tugs of the Aire & Calder, and also a miscellany of subsidiaries. Among their acquisitions were the carrying, shipping, warehousing and other dependent companies of the Grand Union; Canal Transport Ltd on the Leeds & Liverpool, where the former partners were bought out; the Calder Carrying Co of the Calder & Hebble (soon sold), and the Trent Navigation Company's fleet. Simultaneously with nationalisation, Fellows, Morton & Clayton went into voluntary liquidation, and the executive bought their fleet of 172 craft. Fringe subsidiaries were either sold or transferred to other executives, and the carrying fleets organised divisionally under superintendents, but all as 'British Waterways'. For the time being, however, day boats formerly owned by the Great Western and London, Midland & Scottish railways on the BCN and the Staffs & Worcs Canal continued to be operated by the Railway Executive. In 1950 the commission's fleet represented some 20 per cent of capacity available and of ton-miles worked. In 1952, under their licensing powers, the executive licensed the Willow Wren narrow boat carrying concern.

On the carrying side, the executive built a number of big Aire & Calder self-propelled barges and motorised others; built two each also for the Trent and the Severn, and some of high-tensile steel for the Leeds & Liverpool, an experiment that reduced weight by 5½ tons and increased capacity 10 per cent. At Accrington (Church), Wolverhampton, Liverpool and elsewhere, warehousing capacity was increased, and at Mexborough on the Sheffield & South Yorkshire, loading staithes were built for coal to Doncaster power station. A three-wheeled petrol tractor was introduced on the Forth & Clyde Canal in 1953 for towing oil barges, and in the same year narrow tractors appeared on the Regent's and later the Lea and the old Grand Junction, at first petrol-driven, later diesel.

By 1951, their organisation beginning to settle down, the executive turned from the present to the future. In the commission's report they wrote:

'There is at present virtually no surplus of craft or crews. . . . To a large extent, therefore, short-term policy has necessarily been directed to ensuring improved use of available resources by a speeding up of repairs, reduction of empty mileage and an improvement in turn-round of craft at terminal points. Over a longer term, an increase in carrying capacity depends upon the construction of additional craft, the recruitment and training of additional crews, the improvement of handling facilities at terminals, combined with measures to improve operational efficiency by redesign of craft, extension of the compartment or floating container system, tractor towage, and so on.'

They went on to say that they considered water transport especially suitable for traffic to and from ports, especially if handled overside to and from ship; for traffic that could be carried from point to point in full barge loads; for that to or from waterside premises; for petroleum and liquids in bulk; that requiring bulk movement and storage in canalside warehouses; and for trunk hauls to river and canal waterheads with subsequent delivery by road. In addition, they saw waterways exchanging traffic with coastal shipping, and small ships penetrating inland where possible.

In 1948 there was, of course, hardly any pleasure boating on the waterways, and such as there was, the executive considered an oddity in a basically transport situation. A yacht and cruiser on the Crinan Canal were shown on the cover of the executive's magazine *Lock and Quay* in 1949 and indeed in 1950 an executive motor boat began running pleasure trips on the Crinan; a pleasure boat would not be depicted again, among the barges, working narrow boats and lock views, until 1957, when much had changed. Nevertheless, the first issue of *Lock and Quay*, in September 1949, carried a significant paragraph:

'A good deal of interest had been shown in pleasure cruising on the canals. Though primarily concerned with the commercial use of the waterways, we are anxious to encourage this interest, particularly if it helps to swell the revenue. . . . Some waterways are already in use for pleasure boating, and some, though apparently quite suitable, do not seem to appeal. Others that might be suitable require attention to make them serviceable, and we are seeing what can be done without undue expense to improve these.'

For the rest, the issue recorded, among other topics, the launch of new barges for the executive's carrying fleet, the working of compartment boats, and an effort to distribute toys, games and books to children on narrow canal boats.

Incidentally, in its first 1948 report, the executive mentioned discussions with government ministries on the old problem of canal boat children's education, and in 1952 Birmingham local Education Authority opened Wood End Hall, Erdington, as a boarding school for 16 canal children who would return to their parents' boats in the holidays.

Then came a new development. The Lower Warwickshire Avon, from Evesham to the Severn at Tewkesbury, had decayed until it was almost unnavigable, the navigation company not having money to repair it. Local people joined the Midlands Inland Waterways Association members under C. D. Barwell's leadership, and early in 1950 they bought the navigation for £1,500. The Lower Avon Navigation Trust was formed. Twelve years later, after £35,000 had been raised, the navigation was re-opened. Barwell had shown what volunteers, efficiently managed, and supported by professionals when necessary, could accomplish. What he taught for waterways, L. T. C. Rolt and the Talyllyn Railway Preservation Society were teaching for railways. The lesson was well learned and has been fruitful.

In 1949, L. T. C. Rolt had published *Green and Silver*, an account of cruising on Irish canals, and in the following year *The Inland Waterways of England*, a book as outstanding as *Narrow Boat*. Together with Robert Aickman's popular booklet, *Know your Waterways*, Eric de Maré's superbly illustrated *The Canals of England*, and Charles Hadfield's *Introducing Canals*, they constituted the beginnings of a post-war canals literature and an encouragement to venture upon cruising.

Simultaneously, canal history was beginning to be studied and written about. In 1950 Charles Hadfield published the first edition of this book. Four years later the Railway & Canal Historical Society was founded, in 1955 Hadfield's *The Canals of Southern England** appeared, the first of the 'Canals of the British Isles' series of regional histories, the last volume of which was published in 1977. Since those days so much has been written and published on canal history that it is difficult to realise how little was then accurately known. Nationalisation greatly helped the historical student, for it brought together the scattered archives of canal and railway companies in a single collection, British Transport Historical Records, in the care of an archivist, and made available to the student (see p. 344).

In their 1950 report, the executive recorded the standardisation of charges for pleasure boats, and the issue of 1,500 licences. They also mentioned that the Inland Waterways Association's rally at Market Harborough had been attended by some hundred craft, including some belonging to the commission. In 1951, however, a serious upset occurred in the association: some original members were expelled and independent local canal societies founded. The association itself chose a protest role as a pressure group which had some success in preventing possible abandonments, but for a time kept it out of a constructive part in decision-making or co-operation with the commission.

The forward-looking 1951 commission report had ended by roughly classifying the waterways into three groups: those that offer 'scope for commercial development': the Aire & Calder, Sheffield & South Yorkshire, Trent, Weaver, Severn and Gloucester & Berkeley Canal, the Lea to Enfield, and the Grand Union from Regent's Canal Dock and Brentford to Berkhampsted; those that should probably be retained in an inland waterway system: the Calder & Hebble, Leeds & Liverpool, Shropshire Union main line, Trent & Mersey, Birmingham and certain connecting canals, Coventry, northern section of the Oxford, and Grand Union above Berkhamsted; and the rest. Of these last, some 800 miles with little or no commercial traffic,

---

* Now replaced by two volumes, *The Canals of South and South East England* and *The Canals of South West England*.

600 miles seemed no longer required for transport, though they might be useful for pleasure boating, industrial water supply, or drainage. It seemed best to negotiate with local authorities, river boards and other bodies to take over what they needed, and to abandon others. Lengths of the Nottingham, Shrewsbury, Dudley and other canals were indeed transferred to local authorities; others were abandoned, among them the Swansea, part of the Monmouthshire, the old course of the Aire, the Monkland and the Barnsley (this had been initiated in Aire & Calder days) in the years to 1955.

A change of government in 1951 led to the Transport Act of 1953. Aimed at returning most road transport to private enterprise and at encouraging competition between modes of transport, it was a move away from a unified transport policy. Under it, the Docks & Inland Waterways Executive was replaced in October 1953 by a Board of Management under a weakened commission. Sir Reginald Hill continued as chairman. In its 1953 report, the commission noted it possessed a carrying fleet of 97 barges, 372 narrow boats and 647 compartment boats. Of its canal network, 1,250 miles were carrying 98 per cent of the traffic and yielding a net revenue of £160,000. The rest turned that into a deficit of £83,000 on the whole system. 'It becomes increasingly clear', they wrote, 'that the solution of this major problem requires more effective powers under new general legislation, specifically designed to deal with this highly complicated question.'

To help themselves towards a decision, in 1954 the commission appointed a Board of Survey under the chairmanship of one of its members, Lord Rusholme, to investigate and make recommendations. Their report, published in 1955, proposed that the waterways should be separated from the docks under their own general manager, that Scottish canals should be transferred to the Secretary of State for Scotland, and that the remainder should be divided into three groups.

Group I waterways, totalling 336 miles, 'should be improved by the elimination, where necessary, of accumulated arrears of maintenance, by dredging, bank protection and other improvements, and by the provision of suitable handling and terminal facilities'. These were the same waterways as the former executive had listed in 1951. Group II waterways, 994 miles, included all those from the 1951 list, and a few others: the used part of the Ashby, the Fossdyke, Avon (Bristol–Bath), Kensington Canal, Lea (above Enfield) and Stort, St Helens Canal, Staffs & Worcs, Stourbridge and Stourbridge Extension, Worcester & Birmingham, and Ure. However, the retention of either the Staffs & Worcs south of Aldersley or the Worcester &

Birmingham, was recommended, but not both. These 'appear, under existing conditions, to be worth retaining for transport purposes. ... They should be maintained for the present to an adequate standard of efficiency. Every encouragement should be given to the development of traffic.' The board recommended that if these expectations of traffic turned out not to be justified on any waterway, it should be transferred to the next class.

Group III waterways, 771 miles, were 'either disused, or carry insufficient traffic to justify their retention as commercial navigations'. These should be transferred to other bodies more appropriate than the Transport Commission. Some of them had already been abandoned for navigation, like the Huddersfield, though still retained for water supply; but they included a number popular for pleasure cruising, and some that were thought still to have commercial value. Among the more controversial were the Llangollen line of the Shropshire Union (legally abandoned but open), the Kennet & Avon, the southern section of the Oxford, the Forth & Clyde, Ashton-under-Lyne, Peak Forest, Macclesfield and Lancaster canals.

The commission's 1954 report illustrated the board's recommendations by showing the toll receipts per mile:

	Miles	£
Group I	336	3,600
II	994	438
III	771	19
IV*	69	217

The commission at once accepted the board's classification into groups, and the objects to be sought in the case of each, though they reserved their position in the case of the Scottish canals. In 1955 the docks and inland waterways undertakings were separated, Goole now being split off from the Aire & Calder, though Weston Point, Sharpness and Regent's Canal dock remained with waterways. British Transport Waterways, as they were now called, were to be run by a sub-commission under a general manager, this post being given to the energetic and forward-looking Sir Reginald Kerr.

Following the board's recommendations, early in 1956 Kerr persuaded the commission to announce that it hoped to spend £5½ million in the following five years on the development of Group I waterways. At this time the tonnage carried on all BTC waterways was just under 10 million tons, to which must be added some mil-

* Caledonian and Crinan canals.

lions for the independent canals and rivers other than the Manchester Ship Canal.

About £1 million was spent on the Aire & Calder, including channel straightening, bank protection, the mechanisation of several locks, new workshops at Goole, dredging equipment, 50 new compartment boats, and the building of a new depot at Knostrop near Leeds, opened in 1958. In 1962 preliminary work began on a plan to provide Ferrybridge 'C' power station with waterborne coal. On the Sheffield & South Yorkshire the main work was the new mechanised lock at Long Sandall, 215ft long, 22ft wide, with 9½ft over the sills, to replace the old 70ft lock. Opened in July 1959, it enabled compartment boat trains to reach Doncaster without the multiple pennings needed at the old lock. In 1960 the building of new warehouses began at Rotherham—a development continued by the later British Waterways Board, who turned it into a major depot. In 1961, the Dearne & Dove Canal, no longer connected to the derelict Barnsley Canal, and suffering from serious subsidence, was abandoned except for a short section at Swinton.

Where the Grand Union joined the Thames, the accommodation at Brentford depot was more than doubled between 1957 and 1960, and, like Knostrop and Rotherham, given modern handling equipment. The warehousing at Meadow Lane and Trent Lane, Nottingham, was similarly expanded and modernised. In 1959 a container service was introduced using small 4 ton fibreglass containers, from Knostrop and Hull, Nottingham, and Regent's Canal dock to the Continent. It was not, however, very successful, probably because the containers were too small. Today, Leeds depot can handle standard containers up to 40ft for water carriage.

On the Trent a start was made in 1957 on rebuilding Cromwell lock by absorbing the old extension lock of 1935 into the main chamber to provide one able to take eight Trent barges at once. It was reopened in 1960. Meanwhile, locks were mechanised, and dredging and bank protection work increased. On the Trent & Mersey, still carrying Potteries' traffic, a new cut at Marston and an anti-subsidence lock at Thurlwood were built to replace a damaged section. On the Lea, new enlarged locks were built at Ponders End, Stonebridge and Tottenham. This, with bank protection and dredging work, was intended to open 13½ miles of the navigation to Enfield to the largest barges, and halve the time taken. At Brentford Thames lock was enlarged and mechanised.

Among other craft built, four new 250 ton barges were provided for the Severn and Bristol Channel runs, and, scattered over the Group I system, money was made available for piling, cranes, dredgers and storage sheds. The whole added up to a considerable programme.

From the late 1950s more money began also to be put into the commission's docks, especially Weston Point and Sharpness, as their potentialities for development were realised. The Manchester Ship Canal Company were doing the same at Runcorn docks, but these, unlike Weston Point, were no longer to be canal served. Considerable extensions to depots began about the same time as their profit potential was realised, even though they could not always serve waterborne traffic.

Kerr saw clearly that pleasure cruising should be encouraged on canals. In 1956 he started a small fleet of hire cruisers based at Chester —the ancestors of the British Waterways Board's present two groups of hire craft at Nantwich and Hillmorton—and welcomed private firms starting up, as some had already done. In the same year he initiated the very popular Inland Cruising guides with no 1, *The Llangollen Canal*. That the sub-commission's thinking was still commercial, however, is shown by the introduction, 'Our Waterways', to this booklet, which describes the commercial system and ends: 'Ways are constantly being sought of attracting traffic to the waterways, and the co-operation of the public (including, of course, the readers of this booklet) is earnestly requested in the aim of saving as many of our heritage of canals as possible by seeing that they are provided with traffic to carry.' Another way of seeking the public's support was to signpost the canals at road bridges and railway sites, so that people would know which canal they were passing and might consider water transport.

Kerr also went into passenger carrying, in 1957 starting a 'Heart of England' day boat, passengers spending the night in hotels on the Oxford Canal, and in 1959 a Nottingham–Torksey–Boston and return run (later Nottingham–Lincoln), passengers sleeping on board *Water Wanderer*. Both ventures were maintained for a number of years, the latter until the boat's useful life ended. Other experiments were to participate from 1957 in the annual boat shows, and initiate the Boat Afloat Show at Little Venice, London, in 1962.

In 1961, 10,500 cruising licences had been issued, against the 1,500 of 1950, and in 1962, an old canalside building at Stoke Bruerne having been adapted, the Waterways Museum was opened with Charles Hadlow as curator. Later enlarged, it has been most successful in its own right and as an introduction to pleasure cruising and discovery of the world of the canals.

Almost as soon as the Rusholme Board of Survey had reported, and the new sub-commission and general manager been appointed, a considerable controversy broke out, to some extent centred on the Kennet & Avon but also on the future of the Group II and even more the Group III waterways, and in February 1956 a committee independent of the commission was appointed by the Government to 'consider and report on the future of the country's system of inland waterways. . . .' The chairman was Mr Leslie Bowes.

Reporting in July 1958, the Bowes Committee grouped waterways to be retained into two classes: Class A and Class B, which were very much the same as the Board of Survey's Group I and Group II and totalled 1,315 miles against the 1,330 miles in the board's report. However, they put more into Class A (380 miles against 336), and less into Class B (935 miles against 994). The committee recommended that waterways in these classes should be put into good working order and maintained to prescribed standards for not less than 25 years, the whole being made an integrated and efficient system of inland navigation.

Profits on Class A waterways should be spent on their improvement, financial relief being given to cover the cost of reinstatement of those in Class B, and of their operating deficit. The committee proposed that tolls should not be payable by commercial craft on Class B waterways: instead, craft carrying up to 60 tons should be licensed annually on the basis of £1 per ton of capacity per annum. For the remaining canals of the country, independent as well as nationalised, the committee proposed a Waterways Redevelopment Board which should prepare, or secure the preparation of, schemes to redevelop them for purposes not primarily concerned with navigation, or to eliminate them. The committee was divided upon whether the British Transport Commission should continue to administer the Class 'A' and 'B' waterways, a minority suggesting an autonomous Inland Waterways Corporation, a proposal supported by the Inland Waterways Association.

Following upon the report of the Bowes Committee, the government in April 1959 appointed an Inland Waterways Redevelopment Committee under the chairmanship of Admiral Sir Frederick Parham, to consider and recommend plans for the redevelopment of waterways which could not economically be maintained for commercial transport. This committee, whose members included L. T. C. Rolt and Lionel Munk, made a number of useful recommendations over the following three years, many of which were acted upon by the Ministry of Transport. The last three years of the commission saw a number of abandonments as the policy of freeing itself from Group III canals not considered useful was speeded up: among others the Forth & Clyde, Manchester, Bolton & Bury, much of the

Monmouthshire, the Grand Union's Buckingham arm, and parts of the Erewash, Cromford, Chesterfield and Lancaster canals.

The following figures from alternate years summarise the commission's period in control of the waterways:

Year	Toll recs	Operating loss	Carrying* loss	Tonnage carried 000s	Net ton-miles 000s
	£	£	£		
1948	811,333	226,277	66,457	11,231	190,265
1950	805,866	154,129	93,795	11,802	194,404
1952	962,185	122,584	59,452	12,442	205,896
1954	1,012,323	119,442	80,301	12,306	199,707
1956	1,240,181	299,783	169,418	10,456	183,832
1958	1,166,250	641,566	195,632	9,298	166,127
1960	1,153,119	469,679	185,306	9,621	168,773
1962	1,139,249	914,014	177,945	9,263	152,253

In the early years the figures rise:

	Coal, etc	Ton-miles Liquids in bulk	General merchandise
1948	79,801,000	37,832,000	72,632,000
1954	90,274,000	50,823,000	58,610,000

There is at this time a national need for coal, at home and for export; the end of petrol rationing and the expansion of industry increase oil carrying; but merchandise moves to road. In the next eight years the picture changes:

	Coal, etc	Ton-miles Liquids in bulk	General merchandise
1956	71,752,000	55,386,000	56,694,000
1962	49,720,000	55,737,000	46,796,000

Coal exports have fallen away, and have drastically affected waterway fortunes. At home, the gas grid is reducing gasworks demand: new oil-fired generating stations are being built, and both railways and

* Tolls paid by the carrying fleet exceeded the loss in earlier years, but not in later.

roads are seeking big shares of their business. General merchandise is still dropping, the figures somewhat affected by falling long-haul narrow-boat traffic and a general tendency towards shorter hauls. The modernisation programme has held the oil traffic, is helping to maintain general merchandise, but can do little to arrest the decline in coal. Overall, there has been a sharp increase in competition between rail, road and waterway, especially since the centralised Transport Commission was broken up in 1953. The fall in traffic has, of course, increased the ratio of overheads to traffic carried, including the servicing of the improvements carried out and the cost of the higher standard of maintenance. The burden of the less useful canals is increasing. Nevertheless, in its last year, 1962, the commission had net receipts of £69,000 on the Group I waterways. However, in this last year also they reduced their narrow-boat fleet in the South-east, and pruned their carrying concerns in the North-east.

Meanwhile, in the Irish Republic, Coras Iompair Eireann had ceased carrying on the Grand, Barrow and Shannon in 1959–60. In Northern Ireland the Inland Navigation Act (NI) of 1954 added the Upper Bann, Coalisland Canal and Lagan Navigation from Lough Neagh to Belfast to the Lower Bann, which had been government-owned since 1929. Commercial traffic had already ceased on the first two, and they were at once closed, as was part of the Lagan. Traffic ended on the Lagan in the early 1950s and it also was closed in 1958. Only the Lower Bann (a proposal to close it in 1962 was defeated) and the Newry Ship Canal remained open as commercial navigations. The Inland Waterways Association of Ireland was founded in 1954 with much the same objects as its earlier British counterpart. Since then it has done much to prevent closures, and to encourage cruising. In Northern Ireland the River Bann Association watched over the interests of the river. The Newry Ship Canal closed in 1974.

The Lower Avon was well on the way to restoration by its trust in 1958, when the Warwickshire County Council, wishing to lower a bridge at Wilmcote, announced its intention of applying for a warrant of abandonment of the southern section of the Stratford-upon-Avon Canal. Having become unnavigable while in Great Western Railway ownership, it had been inherited by the commission, who had left it alone. In 1956 the Stratford-upon-Avon Canal Society had been formed (succeeding an earlier canal club) to press for restoration. When the county council acted, the society linked itself with the Inland Waterways Association and the National Trust to restore the canal, whereupon the county council retreated. David Hutchings was appointed manager, some £20,000 was provided by the government, £7,500 and free water supplies by the commission (and later the British Waterways Board as its successor), £10,000 by the Pilgrim Trust, and the balance by the Inland Waterways Association and public subscription. In 1960 the commission leased the canal to the trust, work began in 1961 at Kingswood, and the canal was reopened to Stratford in 1964. Meanwhile, in 1963, the National Trust had also taken over the Wey navigation to Guildford from its former owner, Harry Stevens, and in 1969 its extention to Godalming. The reopening of the Lower Avon in 1962, and of the lower Stratford-upon-Avon Canal in 1964, led to the formasion of an Upper Avon Navigation Trust to rebuild the long disused connecting link between them. David Hutchings took charge of this operation, the through line being reopened, after many difficulties, in 1974.

As a result of a political decision to break up the British Transport Commission completely, denationalise much road haulage, and set up the rest under independent boards, the British Waterways Board was appointed towards the end of 1962, and took office on 1 January 1963. The chairman was F. D. Arney, the vice-chairman Sir John Hawton, a former senior civil servant of wide experience; among its members were Sir Frederick Parham,* who had been chairman of the Inland Waterways Redevelopment Committee, and Charles Hadfield.† Six months later, Mr Arney left the board upon appointment to the National Ports Council, whereupon Sir John Hawton became chairman and Admiral Parham vice-chairman. In 1968 Sir Frank Price took over the chairmanship, Sir John Hawton continuing as vice-chairman until 1974.

The board inherited from the commission a collection of waterways of all sizes and shapes, and in every sort of condition, about whose future there had been arguments going back to the nineteenth century, but no decisions. They were still grouped in three classes, and still thought of as separate, under their old company names. The board had also inherited the commission's policy of closing canals unlikely to be useful, and as they took over, some abandonments, like the St Helens Canal, were going through Parliament. Within a few months general lines of policy began to emerge, and decisions of principle to be taken for which the waterways had been waiting so long.

A list of waterways with current and potential commercial value was drawn up and published in January 1964, in an interim report, *The Future of the Waterways*: these were: the Aire & Calder, Sheffield

* 1963–7.   † 1963–6.

& S. Yorkshire, Calder & Hebble (part), Trent, Fossdyke, Weaver, Gloucester & Sharpness Canal, Severn, Lea (below Enfield), Grand Union (below Uxbridge), Caledonian and Crinan. As it was clear to the board that the future lay with big modern craft on big modern waterways, they regretfully decided that there was no real commercial future for narrow boats, and not much more for small barges. In 1963 the Board therefore ended most of their own carrying on the midlands canals and the Grand Union, and on the Leeds & Liverpool: many of their boats were rented cheaply to the Willow Wren Carrying Co and other private concerns, who endeavoured to maintain services. But these, too, ended in a few years, leaving only a few small independent firms, mostly operating with a large proportion of volunteer effort.

Canals other than those clearly commercial had now to find new reasons for existence if they were to be retained, among them higher revenues from water sales and estate work. Many were, however, being regularly and increasingly used by pleasure cruisers. But, just because their future had for so long been uncertain, investment in hiring and boatbuilding businesses was being held back. The board therefore planned in terms of creating a single cruising network which could be given statutory authority, and so long-term stability. When that was done, then, in their view, private capital could be attracted, and their future would be unquestioned. In the meantime, the public had to be persuaded that there was a future for canal cruising, for which licences would continue to be required to raise revenue, in competition with sea cruising, which was free; thereafter the government had to be convinced that the demand was there, and that progress towards financial viability could be made if they were willing to subsidise a cruising network. In planning such a network, many canals were certainties for inclusion: for others, evidence was needed both upon the engineering costs of maintaining them, and upon the degree of enthusiast and other support they would gain.

The network the board planned in its first year, explained (with the qualifications noted in the previous paragraph) in *The Future of the Waterways* (1964), backed with detailed figures in *The Facts about the Waterways* (1965), did indeed convince both public and government. In this the board were greatly helped by the wide-spreading support and publicity efforts of voluntary bodies, and such activities as the Inland Waterways Association's organisation of local authority conferences. The board's general line was accepted in principle in the White Paper on Transport Policy of July 1966: this, however, had certain objectionable aspects, among them a proposal for five-yearly reviews of canal viability that would have stultified enterprise. Widespread protests were headed by the Inland Waterways Association under Lionel Munk, and in 1967 a much more acceptable White Paper, 'British Waterways: Recreation and Amenity', was issued, a prelude to the 1968 Transport Act which established a cruiseway system little different from the board's earlier planned network.

Supplementing these major moves towards new commercial and cruising policies, the board early in its life made other decisions. One was to close no more canals. After the abandonment of those before Parliament when the board took over, only the Edinburgh & Glasgow Union (unopposed) and short lengths of no foreseeable value were closed: the days of abandonment were over. Another was to end the antagonism that had developed between the former British Transport Commission and enthusiasts in the Inland Waterways Association and canal societies, and to create instead a feeling of partnership.

When the board took over, the restoration of the lower Stratford-upon-Avon Canal was being carried out. It was completed in 1964, the National Trust then deciding to exercise·its option to take over the freehold of the canal rather than to hand it back to the board. Its restoration suggested that fruitful results might come from close co-operation between the board and the societies in restorations which, if successful, could then be added to the cruising network and maintained by the board. The pilot scheme was that for the restoration of the Wordsley 16 locks on the Stourbridge Canal, to link the Staffs & Worcs Canal to the Dudley no 1 line of the BCN via Stourton. A restoration plan was drawn up in consultation with the businesslike representatives of the Staffordshire & Worcestershire Canal Society, on the broad basis that the board would provide necessary new lock gates, other essential materials, and technical supervision, while volunteers would do the rest of the work. Union agreement was obtained, restoration began, and in 1967 the locks were reopened. Meanwhile talks had been held with the Retford and Worksop (Chesterfield Canal) Boat Club on helping to maintain their canal, with representatives of the Kennet & Avon Canal Trust on stage-by-stage restoration of that waterway, which began in 1965, and with what was then the Caldon Canal Committee. Discussions with other societies leading to action followed. Under Captain L. Munk's chairmanship, too, the Inland Waterways Association moved from the fringes of power towards co-operation and its centre, a policy continued by its three subsequent chairmen, John Humphries, John Heap and Ken Goodwin. As a result, the Association's views were, and are, sought and attended to by board and government alike. Simultaneously, the Association has grown in membership while the number of canal societies has multiplied.

It was soon clear, however, that for some prospective restorations, including the Kennet & Avon, more money would be needed than the government, through the board, was likely to be willing to supply, or than the canal societies could raise. Local authorities, however, would have a direct interest in the amenity value of a restored local canal; their support was therefore sought by many canal societies anxious to restore local lengths, and also by the board, eg for help in maintaining towpaths in exchange for making them rights of way. Local authorities indeed became involved, notably in the movement to restore the lower Peak Forest and Ashton-under-Lyne canals to reopen the 'Cheshire Ring', which had long been the aim of enthusiast bodies, and by s 114 of the Transport Act, 1968, they were empowered to assist in maintaining waterways for amenity purposes. Since then, they have become a third party with the board and the societies in restoration schemes.

The board had another urgent task: to end the historical but impossible financial position it had inherited, via the British Transport Commission, from the Transport Act, 1947. The board began with a capital debt of £19,252,928, upon which it was supposed to pay £725,835 pa interest to the Ministry of Transport. As the board had no present or future prospect of earning this profit, it had to borrow further sums from the ministry to pay the interest, so increasing the debt. The situation was cleared up in the 1968 Transport Act. This reduced the board's commencing capital debt to £3,750,000 plus borrowings since 1 January 1963. At the end of 1968 the total was £6,050,000. By then it was clear that whereas the commercial side should be able to pay its way, the amenity side would require a subsidy for the foreseeable future; this support grant was authorised under section 43 (2) of the Act.

The 1968 Transport Act listed the commercial waterways, 'to be principally available for the commercial carriage of freight': these were the Aire & Calder, Calder & Hebble from the tail of Greenwood lock to Wakefield, Caledonian and Crinan canals, Sheffield & South Yorkshire from the tail of Tinsley bottom lock to Keadby, New Junction, Trent from Nottingham, Weaver, Severn and Gloucester & Sharpness Canal, and Lea. It also listed the cruising waterways, or cruiseways, 'to be principally available for cruising, fishing and other recreational purposes'. These were therefore given security at last.

Thirdly, there were what the Act called 'the remainder'. Section 107 laid down as the duty of the board that each of these remainder waterways should be 'dealt with in the most economical manner possible (consistent, in the case of a waterway which is retained, with the requirements of public health and the preservation of amenity and safety), whether by retaining and managing the waterway, by developing or eliminating it, or by disposing of it.' An Inland Waterways Amenity Advisory Council was established to advise the board and the minister on developments for amenity purposes, and on any changes in the cruising waterways. Finally the old 'right of navigation' that all old canal Acts had conferred, was abolished.

The Act greatly increased the size and power of the impetus towards cruising growth and canal restoration. Now that the cruising canals had a secure future, new hire firms opened businesses and old ones expanded; boat-building yards multiplied; marinas were built; canalside pubs and other facilities were extended or created, and sections of towpath began to be opened as public rights of way. The movement to restore derelict waterways now moved to the remainder waterways. The board's interest was naturally that these should be restored, but without using money needed for its existing system. With the help of canal societies and local authorities, a drive began to bring sections of them back into use, such as parts of the BCN system, beginning with Parkhead locks to connect Dudley tunnel to the old Dudley no 1 line. These were reopened in 1973. It also began to take in canals which had already been abandoned, such as the old Ellesmere and Montgomeryshire line from Frankton by Carreghofa to Welshpool and beyond, the Wey & Arun, Stroudwater and others, some not owned by the British Waterways Board.

In most cases, however, restoration continues to be carried out very much along the lines found practicable for Wordsley locks: co-operation between the board and a local society, often now with local authority participation also. The volunteer labour available was greatly increased when the London Working Party Group, founded in 1965 as part of the Inland Waterways Association, began to organise groups of volunteers from further afield than could local societies, through the magazine *Navvies' Notebook*, later *Navvies*. Reorganisation in 1970 resulted in the Waterway Recovery Group being formed: this now organises nationwide assistance to local societies. A central means of fund raising for restoration purposes was then instituted: the National Waterways Restoration and Development Fund of the Inland Waterways Association, which makes grants to local societies.

As a result, the restoration for pleasure use of formerly navigable waterways has gained an impetus undreamed of a few years ago.

Go Trad This Easter

Tunnel Reopening at Dudley

Easter Saturday, Sunday and Monday, April 21, 22 and 23 at Parkhead, Peartree Lane, Dudley (off Dudley-Halesowen Road).

The Proprietors of the Dudley Canal Trust wish to Announce the Grand Reopening of the famous Dudley Tunnel and the re-built Parkhead locks on the Dudley Canal. The worthy Chairman of the British Waterways Board, Alderman Sir Frank Price has kindly consented to open the proceedings at 3 o'clock Easter Saturday, together with His Worship The Mayor of Dudley. A large Number of Canal Craft will be on Hand and Boat Trips will be available to the Public, both along the Dudley No. 2 line and also through the Dudley Tunnel, man-made Wonder of the Black Country.

A Pavilion of exhibitions will be erected and delicious Refreshments are being provided.

On the Saturday evening a Grand Barbecue will be commenced.

Maroons, rockets, bands and militia will be much in evidence.

The Proprietors will make no Charge for Admission; your attendance at this unique function will amply Reward their Efforts.

Figure 44   Parkhead locks on the Dudley Canal are reopened in 1973 with a flourish after restoration

In May 1974 the 'Cheshire Ring' was completed by the reopening of the lower Peak Forest and Ashton Canals to Manchester. It was followed in June by the Upper Avon from Evesham to Stratford-upon-Avon. Third in a remarkable year, the Caldon Canal was reopened in September, this and the 'Cheshire Ring' restorations being joint enterprises of the BWB, volunteers and concerned local authorities. So in one year some 53 additional miles of waterway were made available for cruising. In 1978 the Great Ouse was reopened to Bedford.

For some years from 1974, two opposite tendencies showed themselves on the amenity waterways: restorations continued, yet the cruising network, with not enough money to overtake maintenance arrears, continued to deteriorate. Straddling the two was the isolated remainder waterway, the Brecknock & Abergavenny (Mon & Brec), where in 1975 a breach at Llanfoist caused its central section to be closed pending study. This revealed the need for more expenditure by BWB than a remainder waterway was likely to get in the short term. In 1977, therefore, the Manpower Services Commission (MSC), which as a job-training body has since become important in the canal restoration world, approved a £170,000 grant for essential work, the Welsh Development Agency adding £231,000 and the board £82,000. Further grants followed, and the canal was reopened in 1981.

Similar outside help has been shown in the restoration of the Kennet & Avon. Because the canal's owners, BWB, are only empowered to maintain much of the line as it was in 1968 (this maintenance has included the replacement of Avoncliff aqueduct's old iron trough by a new concrete one), real restoration work must be financed from elsewhere. The canal trust itself has raised large sums, to which have been added considerable local authority, MSC and other grants. As I write (late 1983) the canal is in a fair way to reopening throughout: 44 locks have been restored, Crofton and Claverton pumping stations reactivated, and much bridge and channel relining work done.

A good start has also been made upon another major restoration of a BWB remainder canal, the Montgomery, the Carreghofa branch of the Ellesmere Canal from Frankton (where it joins the Llangollen Canal) to Llanymynech, and its continuation the Montgomeryshire Canal to Welshpool and on to Newtown. Work began upon a section of some 5 miles between Welshpool and Arddleen and a stretch through Welshpool, and continued at Frankton locks and between Welshpool and Newtown. A turning point was reached in 1983 when consultants employed by a consortium led by the Welsh Development Agency and including the BWB reported that greatest economic benefit would result if the whole 33-mile line from Newtown to Frankton, together with the Guilsfield branch, were to be restored.

MSC money, sums now being granted by local authorities and such bodies as the Countryside Commission and the English Tourist Board, and a more relaxed attitude towards cruisers by river and drainage authorities, have enabled existing restorations to be speeded up, and new ones begun, all over the country.

Most restorations on BWB waterways, those of river authorities, or those helped by strong local authorities, have good prospects. Among those making good progress are the Basingstoke and Droit-wich Canals, and the Sleaford Navigation. Bigger schemes are the Wey & Arun, Stroudwater–Thames & Severn and Rochdale and, virtually new navigations rather than restorations, the upper Thames (Lechlade to Cricklade) and upper Severn (Stourport past Bewdley and Bridgnorth initially to Ironbridge and later to Shrewsbury). A start has indeed been made on the Rochdale, a beautiful cruising line over the Pennines which, though heavily locked, has no summit tunnel. Thanks to the MSC, local authorities and other bodies, work was in late 1983 almost finished upon four miles from Todmorden to Hebden Bridge, with good hopes of continuing towards Sowerby Bridge.

Sensibly, those interested in the Wilts & Berks Canal, having decided that the canal is impossible to restore, are working along lines already applied in America. There structures are as far as possible maintained in good shape, as much towpath as possible made available to the public, maybe a stretch of locked canal reopened for horse-boat trips, and an interpretation centre provided. A canal thus looked after becomes a focus for instructional and yet enjoyable visits. BWB and local authorities seem to be following similar lines on the Forth & Clyde Canal.

One canal is in serious trouble, the southern Stratford. The National Trust, having restored it, made a serious mistake in not allowing its five-year lease to revert to BWB. Having decided to keep the canal, twenty years later it found the burden too great, and was in late 1983 trying to shed it. Interestingly, in 1983 also, the BWB obtained powers, subject to the Secretary of State's approval, to accept transfers of other inland navigations.

The Government's agreement in 1983, after years of pressure, to the first upgradings of some remainder waterways to cruising water-ways cannot but encourage restoration work on eg the Kennet & Avon and the Montgomery, and reassure doubting local authorities. Those upgraded were the Ashton, Erewash, Caldon, Lower Peak

Forest and Mon & Brec, along with the Leek and Slough arms. While restoration was accelerating, the amenity waterways were in the late '70s deteriorating, insufficient money having been granted to the board over many years to keep them in a proper state to carry their traffic, let alone to overtake maintenance arrears.

This quickly became more serious as structures, few less than a hundred years old and many nearer two hundred, became life-expired. Between 1973 and 1978, Harecastle, Blisworth, Netherton and Braunston tunnels, Pontcysyllte and Alvechurch aqueducts and Anderton lift had to be closed for long periods. That so many buildings and structures were either scheduled under Ancient Monuments Acts or listed under Town & Country Planning Acts as being of special architectural or historical interest increased the difficulty of maintaining working waterways.

Another problem faced the board: water shortages. These were causing restrictions on boat movements, or even the closure of canal lengths during summer months. They were partly due to maintenance arrears, especially in the care of reservoirs and locks. But they also resulted from the increasing use of canals for pleasure. Some locks, for instance on the Oxford and Llangollen Canals, are probably now passing more boats and using more water than ever they did in commercial days. Moreover, shortage of supervisory staff meant that more water was likely to be wasted. The need here was for better maintenance and supervision, for new equipment at many lock flights to pump water back to the top as well as for reservoirs to be repaired so that their full capacities could be utilised.

After pressure from the board and the IWA for additional funding, the government announced in 1974 that Peter Fraenkel & Partners had been appointed consulting engineers to make a survey of maintenance arrears on Britain's inland waterways. Their report, not published until November 1977, identified a backlog on both commercial and cruising waterways of some £60m at 1977 prices. This, they proposed, should be provided over fifteen years. The government thereupon granted £5m and a year later a similar sum.

The year 1978 marked a turning point, for the government confirmed, in the words of the BWB's 1979 report, that in future 'the Board's Undertaking should be managed as an entity charged with fulfilling the statutory duties and responsibilities placed upon them by Parliament'. It followed that the board would be granted money to eliminate the maintenance backlog within a reasonable time. Though unexpected new crises still occurred, as was inevitable on an old system, nevertheless the network was in 1983 in better shape than five years before.

On non-BWB waterways, one major new work is the rebuilt and enlarged Romney lock on the Thames, opened in 1980. By using conduits running lengthwise to enable water to enter at various points—a technique usually found on big commercial locks—turbulence when filling is minimised.

By 1979 the enthusiast market was large enough to support two independent magazines, *Waterways World* (founded 1972) and *Canal and Riverboat Monthly* (now *Canal and Riverboat*), in addition to BWB's *Waterways News*, IWA's *Waterways*, the inland-waterway sections of many yachting and boating periodicals, and the journals or newsletters of IWA's regions or of canal societies, among which *The Butty* of the Kennet & Avon Canal Trust is outstanding.

There has been parallel growth in the number of canal and boat societies and clubs, and in the membership and number of branches of the IWA. One notes, too, widenings in the interest people take in canals: fishing, short- and long-distance walking along towpaths that now needs no permit, photography, nature study, history, industrial archaeology, and their role in education among them.

The 1,500 cruising licences on the nationalised waterways in 1950 had by 1978 risen (excluding Scotland) to 22,698 for private craft (4,898 unpowered), together with 1,708 hire-boats, these last immensely important because they introduce so many newcomers to inland waterways. Then recession began to take effect, causing a near-standstill to expansion. Signs of the times were the formation in 1982 of UK Waterway Holidays Ltd by BWB and the Association of Pleasure Craft Operators (APCO), to approach overseas visitors, and in 1980 of a trade association for the cruising waterways, the Canals & Navigations Alliance.

Side effects of waterway revival have been the refurbishing of canalside pubs, the opening of interpretation centres as at Welshpool and Devizes, and new museums. Among these, the Boat Museum at Ellesmere Port is outstanding, as is the Blist's Hill site at Ironbridge, with its restored Hay inclined plane and sections of the former Shropshire Canal, but others are well worthwhile, like that in the Clock Warehouse at Shardlow. Meanwhile, BWB's museum at Stoke Bruerne has improved every time one revisits it. In a different category are the redevelopments, not yet fully agreed, at Limehouse basin and Gloucester docks, both too cramped for modern commercial use.

In Northern Ireland there is cruising on Lough Neagh, the Bann and Lough Erne, part of which borders the Republic. There the main cruising ground has become the Shannon and to a lesser extent the Grand Canal and the Barrow. After considerable expenditure on these waterways by the Board of Works, Coras Iompair Eireann (the national transport authority), local authorities and the Irish Tourist Board, the Irish themselves have begun to take to cruising; previously most hirers were Continentals. Some restoration work has been undertaken by the Inland Waterways Association of Ireland on Grand Canal branches previously closed to navigation, and a good start has been made upon restoring the beautiful Royal Canal. In Northern Ireland, interest centres on the possible restoration of the Newry Canal, with Northern Ireland Tourist Board support and help from Enterprise Ulster.

On the commercial side of waterways, the years between 1963 and the 1968 Transport Act presaged basic changes. The break-up of the Commission produced strong competition with railways, now operating merry-go-round trains and similar services. Combined with a rapidly expanding motorway system, rail and road attracted some traffics from water, eg, coal to power stations. Coal carryings to gasworks also died away as North Sea gas was introduced, while changes in oil refinery and distribution patterns caused pipelines and rail to take more traffic.

The years after 1963 saw the establishment of Freight Services Division of BWB to operate the board's carrying, warehousing and docks enterprises on a commercial basis. New warehouses were built, old ones modernised, money well spent at Sharpness and Weston Point docks. With traffics falling, the board's carrying fleets had to be further contracted, and their Bristol Channel carrying ended in 1969. Independent carriers also tended to reduce their fleets, and some working the narrow canals, notably Willow Wren and Blue Line, ended operations.

Improvements were made. On the Caledonian Canal the sea-lock at Corpach was lengthened and lock mechanisation, begun by the Commission, continued; Monk Meadow wharf on the Gloucester & Sharpness was built, the Aire & Calder adapted to take 500-tonne craft, and the Weaver improved to Anderton depot. The Limehouse Cut was linked to Regent's Canal Dock in 1968, thus eliminating its old Limehouse entrance. A new coal-carrying service to Ferrybridge 'C' power station on the Aire & Calder, worked by Cawoods-Hargreaves with push-tugs each handling three 160-tonne barges, was initiated in 1966. A scheme to enlarge the Sheffield & South Yorkshire Navigation from Doncaster to Rotherham, submitted to the government in 1966, was turned down in 1967, apparently on the grounds that the traffic should go by rail, an argument that did nothing to hinder the construction of the later motorway.

The 1968 Transport Act had given BWB's commercial waterways

a security similar to that of the amenity side. It was now necessary to relate waterways and their craft to a transport pattern moving towards through-carrying and away from transhipment. The Board started to build push-tugs and standard 140-tonne compartment boats; the first was delivered in 1970. In 1967 they also commissioned an engineering study of 'a craft which could both navigate the North Sea and also (either as a unit or compartmentalised) use the larger waterways of the north-east'.[1] Contact was then made with an interested Danish group. The result was the BACAT (Barge Aboard Catamaran) ship, the construction of which began in 1974. She carried 10 140-tonne compartment boats and three LASH (Lighter Aboard Ship) lighters between the Humber and the Continent. However, an unofficial group of dockers at Hull, notwithstanding an agreement with them, soon afterwards blacked not only the BACAT ship herself, but all BWB craft and inland terminals in the north-east. At the end of 1975 the BACAT ship was driven from England without the men's union, the Docks Board* or the government taking effective action.

Another major change in water transport patterns was now taking place. In former times Britain's established big ports had handled deep-sea as well as short-sea trade, ocean ships either transhipping cargoes for Continental destinations or sailing on to European ports to complete discharge or loading. But, thanks to labour intransigence bolstered by the National Dock Labour Scheme and weak, inefficient management overbalanced by Continental enterprise, most deep-sea (except container) and some short-sea traffic left the big ports. There was one major exception, Felixstowe, a non-Scheme port. Large ships have gone to the Continent, lesser ones to a host of increasingly busy small ports round our coasts and up our navigable rivers. Among many of these latter providing new inland-waterway traffics are Rochester, Colchester, Mistley, Ipswich, Norwich, Wisbech, newly reopened Fosdyke on the Welland, Gunness, Gainsborough, Howdendyke, Selby, those like Runcorn and Ellesmere Port on the lower Manchester Ship Canal, Weston Point, Anderton and Sharpness. Indeed, special types of ship have been designed to serve such as these, or their bigger equivalents on Continental rivers and canals; ports such as Paris, Liège, Duisburg and Basle. Usually called low-profile coasters and mainly developed by Britain and West Germany, they combine features of coasters and seagoing barges, and run from about 250 to over 2,000 dwt. Operated by companies such as Crescent Shipping, Union Transport (London) or Freight

* The former British Transport Docks Board has been privatised as Associated British Ports.

Express–Seacon, they are proving a major influence in British inland-waterway development.

Such vessels have to be long, with comparatively narrow beam and low draught to pass through Continental locks, yet with an air draught, particularly when unladen, that will get them under bridges. They must have high cargo capacity and, so that they need carry only a small crew, be highly efficient to work and also conform to measurement rules that produce ships with high capacities per registered ton. Hence a design such as Crescent Shipping's *Vibrence* in the 1,800–2,000 dwt range. She has a simple box-shaped hold for maximum capacity, with mechanically operated folding steel hatch covers. Water ballast tanks under the side decks help to trim the ship when cargo is being worked, and can be filled to reduce air draught when the ship is unladen. A wheelhouse mounted on a hydraulic column lowers into a well when necessary, mast and radar being also lowerable. Thus the tops of the hatch covers can become the ship's highest points.

This development of the maritime link between inland waterways and the sea has been paralleled by a decline in carrying between one inland-waterway point and another, and the ending of some traditional traffics: for instance, coal from Park Hill colliery near Wakefield to Ferrybridge in 1983. Other movements have, however, been given more efficient craft: in autumn 1981 Blue Circle Industries replaced tug and lighter carrying on the Thames cement run from Northfleet to Hurlingham by two new 850-tonne self-propelled craft.

Organisationally, we see increased concentration. John H. Whitaker of Hull earlier took over Harker's barge operations on Merseyside and Tyneside, and more recently absorbed those on Humberside also. Whitaker's, now with a large barge fleet, are adding to it.

The heavy decline in the number of deep-sea ships visiting British ports, and a lesser one in short-sea traders, reduced the work available for pilots. The Pilotage Act 1983 confirms many of the provisions of the Merchant Shipping Act 1979, which established the Pilotage Commission, and allows (but does not compel) pilotage authorities to propose changes to the bye-laws governing pilotage in UK coastal waters, ports and estuaries. Any change would require prior approval from the Secretary of State for Transport (formerly Trade), who would seek the advice of the Pilotage Commission before making any decision.

Many pilotage authorities used the Act to propose changes to their bye-laws, a common feature being the extension of compulsory pilotage to include many smaller vessels whose size or trading patterns had previously rendered them exempt. These authorities wish to exempt only vessels below 50 grt, whereas the current limit is generally about 1,500 grt. Shipping companies and many others lodged objections with the Minister, pointing out that the changes were not only unnecessary to maintain safety of navigation, but would also add significantly to the costs of operation of estuarial barges, coasters and short-sea traders.

To date (late 1983) the Minister has not endorsed Pilotage Commission advice that any such new bye-laws be introduced. Currently, certain trading interests are indeed suggesting that the Act be used to allow a relaxation of some pilotage rules, notably an end to compulsory pilotage on the lower Trent.

These and other developments have been straws in the wind of change. The BWB, chaired by Sir Frank Price, and having O. H. Grafton as Director, Freight Services, was active, but it was time for a well-informed pressure group to work closely with Freight Services Division taking a national view of the future of commercial waterways, given that most tonnages moved on non-BWB routes. So, in June 1971 the Inland Shipping Group was set up within the IWA initially under Charles Hadfield's chairmanship. Later, it was to have in turn as chairmen three outstanding men, Fred Doerflinger, Mark Baldwin and David Hilling. As something of a think-tank as well as an unobtrusive means of persuasion, the ISG has had considerable success, and two of its publications were influential: *Barges or Juggernauts?* (1974) and *British Freight Waterways To-day and To-morrow* (1980). Soon after 1971, lightermen and others in the waterway business formed another mainly London group, TOW (Transport on Water).

In 1972 the board had submitted a revised Sheffield & South Yorkshire scheme, to have it again turned down in 1973, though the government did agree to the introduction of an enabling Bill, which was passed in 1974. Perhaps the S&SY's rejection and BACAT's withdrawal helped to create a new mood of aggressive belief in the future of commercial waterways to modern Britain. One manifestation was BWB's organisation of the first international waterways conference to be held in Britain, 'Freightwaves '75'. There a new trade body was formed, the National Waterways Transport Association, planned to include waterway authorities, carriers, and all firms and organisations concerned with British commercial waterways. Suggested originally by the ISG, the idea was supported by the board, and by many organisations whose representatives formed a steering committee to do the preparatory work. Since its formation NWTA has

played a steadily increasing role as spokesman for the whole waterway industry.

Not since 1888 had an international conference on waterways (see
p. 260) been held, or since the Royal Commission a serious study
made of Continental waterways. But 'Freightwaves '75' was attended
by Continentals and Americans, and after it more of those involved
with British freight waterways began also to concern themselves, as
the ISG was already doing, with what was happening abroad. There
was much to learn, about engineering techniques, craft and administration, and leaders of waterway opinion began to learn it, to the
benefit of the future. Representatives of BWB began to travel overseas, NWTA to include overseas news in its documentation, the IWA
to organise frequent visits to overseas freight waterways, and the ISG
to publish *Report on Continental Waterways* (1975). In 1982 NWTA
organised another smaller international conference, 'Waterfreight
80s'.

Freight waterway track improvements in the 1968–78 period included the removal of obstructions, notably the notorious Torksey
shoal, to give 7ft depth on the Trent. Specially built 1,000-tonne
tankers could now use the Gloucester & Sharpness Canal, and lock
rebuilding and channel improvement had upgraded the Aire &
Calder's line to Leeds to 700 tonnes. That to Wakefield had to wait
for a decision upon the future of the fine iron aqueduct at Stanley
Ferry, then in poor condition.

On the side of craft, the idea of using waterways to by-pass built-
up areas and provide interior transhipment points to road was also
taken up, most successfully with the board's barge groupage services
from Brentford, Enfield, and elsewhere to docks. Craft developments
included Humphery & Grey's four push-towed 800-tonne Thames
lighters, and Whitaker's 570-tonne tankers *Humber Jubilee* and
Humber Pride. Continental barges were also bought to use on British
waterways, for instance the two 800-tonne Dutch-built self-trimming
craft bought by Mercantile Lighterage.

The matter of waterway statistics is an odd one in an age when
there is a statistic for almost everything. National waterway freight
traffic figures had been compiled only three times, in 1888, 1898 and
1905. When in 1947 most canal and navigation concerns were
nationalised, it became accepted that the figures published by the
BTC and later by the BWB were equivalent to national statistics. But
this was far from being so, for many navigations or parts of them,
eg the Mersey, Thames, Humber, Trent below Gainsborough, as
well as all estuaries and the Manchester Ship Canal, are not BWB-
controlled. Therefore no national figures existed as a basis for

government decisions upon the relative performance of roads, railways and waterways.

A member of the ISG, Dr Mark Baldwin, compiled figures for 1974, which listed a total of 1,569km of commercial waterway, only 545km BWB's, with a tonne-km total of 3,217 millions, some 30 times the BWB figure published in the *Annual Abstract of Statistics*.

Meanwhile, the government had announced in 1971 that the BWB would be ended in 1974, and that its functions would be absorbed into the proposed regional water authorities. The board were strongly defended, and in 1973 left in possession of their waterways. Those controlled by river authorities, however, such as the Thames, were transferred by the Water Act, 1973, to the new bodies; the rest, whether the board's or independent, remained with their existing owners. The Act laid upon the new authorities a duty to make the best use of the water they controlled for recreation and amenity, and set up a Water Space Amenity Commission with John Humphries as chairman to advise the government and regional water authorities upon the exercise of these functions.

In 1976 the government published a Green Paper which now proposed that the board should be merged with a new National Water Authority heading the whole water industry, then become the nucleus of a national inland navigation authority. Eventually in July 1977, a White Paper appeared which reiterated the proposals and added that 'the water industry will be required to assume the major financial responsibility in view of the substantial benefits they derive from the waterways'. Simultaneously, Devolution Bills were being discussed that included proposals to transfer powers over canals in Scotland and Wales.

Meanwhile BWB in 1977 had doggedly submitted another revised plan for the Sheffield & South Yorkshire, supported by the South Yorkshire County Council, and with good hope of financial help from the EEC once government approval was forthcoming.

It was against this background of turmoil that in mid-1977 Sub-Committee 'A' of the House of Commons Select Committee on Nationalised Industries began an examination of the board and their affairs. After studying a wide range of evidence, early in 1978 it made recommendations so remarkable for their practical commonsense—in that they agreed so closely with what the board, NWTA, the IWA and others had been saying for years—that I shall quote them in full.

1. (a) The Government should announce immediate acceptance of the findings of the Fraenkel Report;
   (b) the Government should publicly undertake to finance from

the Exchequer the maintenance backlog identified in the Fraenkel Report over the next twelve to fifteen years on the scale indicated in the Report;

(c) the British Waterways Board should plan their maintenance programme on this basis; and

(d) any further expenditure on maintenance of the waterways in accordance with the Transport Act 1968 which cannot be met by the British Waterways Board from their own resources should continue to be paid for by grants from the Exchequer.

2. The Government should devise a standard technique and standard criteria for the appraisal of all forms of transport investment including waterways.

3. The Government should henceforth compile statistics relating to inland waterways on the basis of the submission made by the Inland Waterways Association.

4. The Government should announce immediate approval of the Sheffield & South Yorkshire Navigation improvement scheme, and should apply forthwith to the EEC for a grant from the Regional Development Fund.

5. The Government should immediately announce its intention to abandon its proposals to merge the British Waterways Board into a National Water Authority.

6. The Government should table amendments to remove the British Waterways Board from the provisions of the Scotland and Wales Bills.

7. Ministerial responsibility for the British Waterways Board should be transferred from the Department of the Environment to the Department of Transport.

The official reception given to these recommendations was un-enthusiastic. In June 1978 the government promised to review waterway statistics and use cost-benefit analysis for waterways; otherwise they rejected them. Nevertheless, in August the government accepted a House of Lords amendment to the Transport Bill then going through, which laid a duty on the Secretary of State 'to promote a national policy for the use of inland waterways for commercial transport', and in September the Secretary of State for the Environment at last approved the Sheffield & South Yorkshire improvement scheme. The minister, while referring to the 'obvious under-use of our waterways', stated that the money was to be borrowed from the National Loans Fund, and that: 'The Board will be required to charge an economic price for traffic on the canal and the traffic and pricing will be regularly monitored', provisions which certainly do not apply to single short stretches of road.

Since then No 3, as we shall see, has been carried out, and by other means recommendations 5 and 6 have also come about. We await action upon No 2, upon the duty laid upon the Secretary of State 'to promote a national policy for the use of inland waterways for commercial transport', and also on No 7, upon which, however, the amenity and commercial sides of the inland-waterway business have not themselves been able to agree. As for No 1, the Government accepted the basis of the Fraenkel report, that enough money should be made available over a period of years to overtake the maintenance backlog. This being so, the board could get on with repairing and reopening major structures, and also with the multifarious tasks of maintaining a waterway system: bank protection, channel relining, culvert rebuilding, swing-bridge and lock-gate renewals, bridge strengthening or replacement, and routine tunnel and aqueduct repairs.

Nevertheless, time-expired structures still continued to fail. One after another tunnels had to be closed for short or long-term repair: Braunston, Wast Hill, King's Norton, Foulridge, Preston Brook, Saddington, Crick, not to speak of aqueduct closures and one at Anderton lift. But by 1980 reopenings had begun. The board now felt sufficiently confident to start looking for future trouble before it occurred instead of rushing from one patching job to another.

Fifteen years after it had been first proposed to the board in 1964, work began on 24 April 1979 upon the Sheffield & South Yorkshire Canal, the rebuilding of the old 90-ton barge route between Doncaster and Rotherham to take a single 700-tonne barge or push-tow units totalling 420 tonnes. The new line, opened on 1 June 1983, included seven new locks, the enlargement of another, and much new channel cutting and bridge reconstruction. The cost was some £16 millions, of which about one-third came from the EEC and South Yorkshire County Council. Below Doncaster, and mostly considered part of normal BWB expenditure, Long Sandall lock on the S&SY and Sykehouse on the New Junction Canal were lengthened, and aqueducts on the latter enlarged. Taken with the Aire & Calder improvements and good use of the Yorkshire Ouse (non-BWB) to Selby, the north-east now possesses the nucleus of a modern waterway system. Meanwhile a new concrete-trough Stanley Ferry aqueduct had been opened in November 1981, Stoke Bardolph lock on the Trent had been rebuilt after wall failure, and the nineteenth-century water-hydraulic paddle-gear on the Weaver's locks had been replaced by electro-hydraulic.

That the much-publicised Sheffield & South Yorkshire Canal was

indeed being built caused a favourable change in the political,
industrial and press atmosphere. Influential, too, was the publication
in August 1982 of the statistical study* that the government had
commissioned. It used as definition of an inland waterway all waters
inland of a point on any estuary or river where the surface width of
water does not exceed 3km at low water or 5km at high water, and
for statistical purposes excluded waterways unable to take 50-ton
barges. The result for 1980 showed 2,351km of track mostly radiating
from the Humber, Mersey, Severn and Thames estuaries, of which
285km carried no freight in that year.

The traffic in 1980[2] was:

	Millions of Tonnes carried	Millions of Tonne-km performed on:			
		Sheltered water	Maritime waterways	Non-maritime waterways	Total
Internal	11·28	36·8	295·5	101·1	433·4
Coastwise	14·48	—	384·1	8·3	392·4
Special (to/from) sea bed)	13·96	—	594·4	9·2	603·6
Foreign	22·99	—	865·5	29·4	895·2
	62·71	36·8	2139·8	148·0	2324·6

It therefore confirmed Mark Baldwin's findings that inland-waterway
traffics were some 30 times greater than the BWB figures previously
used, the figure of 62·71 million tonnes lifted, at 4 per cent of the
national total, comparing well with the 154 million tonnes and 9 per
cent of railways. Because waterway transport tends to be regionalised,
local percentages are higher.

Principal inland-waterway traffics were shown to be petroleum
products (24 per cent of tonne-km), sewage sludge (17 per cent),
crude minerals (16 per cent), cereals (5 per cent) and solid fuel (5 per
cent). A survey of vessels showed powered craft averaging 305 tonnes
(maximum 1,500 tonnes), dumb craft 231 tonnes (maximum 800
tonnes), and tugs ranging up to 1,000 bhp. The Marine Transport
Centre of Liverpool University which had compiled the figures, also
produced the first directory of UK inland-waterway facilities to be
published for many years, while about the same time NWTA brought
out Britain's first freight waterways map.

* Curiously, the study still does not provide national figures, as Ulster is not included.

These publications did succeed in fixing in the minds of the influential that Britain's freight waterways were more important than had been realised. One early result was that the government extended the system of grants given since 1973 for new rail freight facilities to waterways by Section 36 of the 1981 Transport Act, the first such, of £369,000 to a firm at Gainsborough on the Trent, being made in mid-1983. Commenting, the Secretary of State for Transport said: 'I want freight to go by waterways or by rail wherever it makes sense ... Grant funds are available and I hope industry will take advantage of them to put more of its business on our waterways'.

The Marine Transport Centre's analysis shows the great change that has come about. Of total inland-waterway tonnage, 87 per cent moves in ships, not barges; 81 per cent passes direct to or from the open sea; 39 per cent moves directly to a foreign country, this last group, incidentally, revealing a much greater mix of commodities carried than the average. Inland-waterway carrying has come a very long way from the days of narrow boats and Westcountry barges. Thanks to the spread of low-profile coasters able to reach ports far inland, Britain is becoming part of the European waterway system. The future of ocean-going barge-carrying ships is still uncertain, but it is indeed interesting that the latest development, the Severn Corridor scheme, is based upon the latest design of low-profile coasters, barge-carriers, including the largest ship-borne barges built, and a third development steadily spreading on the Continent against strong rail and road competition, container-carrying by barge.

The Severn Corridor scheme, made public in March 1983 after considerable discussion by the BWB with other concerned bodies, is to enlarge the Gloucester & Sharpness Canal to Monk Meadow, Gloucester for 2,500 dwt vessels, and via a new lock at Gloucester, the Severn thence to Worcester for craft of 1,500 dwt. Currently, capacities on the canal are 1,000 dwt for specially built tankers and 750 dwt for other vessels, and on the river up to 350 dwt.

Prospects for developing inland-waterway traffic look good, with one exception, the lower Thames, that 69-mile stretch of river between Teddington lock and a line across the estuary some 50 miles below London bridge which is controlled by the Port of London Authority and burdened by the National Dock Labour Scheme. As one travels Europe, one finds ports on navigable rivers busy with inland waterway and seagoing traffic. Rouen, Bremen, Hamburg, all lie well up tidal rivers. Yet London, once the world's greatest port, is now only a shadow, most of her docks becoming housing, office or leisure sites, less than two dozen once-busy river wharves still used for craft-handling. With decay, and with the dockers' ruling that transport by water within the Port area is dockers' work, whereas transport by road is not, has gone the erosion of the lighterage trade from over 13m tons twenty years ago to less than 1m today. Gone are such great names as Mercantile Lighterage, Thames & General and Humphery & Grey, though BWB with Darling Brothers in 1982 did form Lee & Brentford Lighterage to preserve its groupage services. Only a substantial container-ship trade remains at Tilbury and some business at riverside wharves; for the rest, big ships and coasters have gone outside the Port limits.

When in 1950 the first edition of this book was reviewed in a well-known weekly, the reviewer suggested that I should have given my views on the future of the waterways. But *British Canals* is a history. Interestingly, indeed, an age-old pattern is showing through. Before and during the Middle Ages, people and light goods moved by road, most heavy goods, if they could, by water. In those days the maritime link was strong, sailing vessels navigating rivers and the sea alike. Our turnpike mania widened and improved road facilities, and the subsequent canal mania did the same for waterways. The two, along with maritime-linked rivers and canals, made the first industrial revolution. Then came railways, to sweep away much road and water transport alike. But now railways are of minor importance for most freight and passenger carrying except specialised traffics, and we find ourselves back with roads and waterways, fulfilling their old functions, but upon improved roads and improving waterways, and with very different vehicles and craft. There are two changes: rail and to a smaller extent road have lost passengers, though little freight, to a new means of transport, the air, and road, though rail only marginally, has gained a maritime link by means of RoRo ferries.

In the mid-80s, we find ourselves in an inland-waterway world which, on the side of pleasure cruising, has since the war grown from almost nothing to a major amenity, and in doing so has recreated an obsolete small-canal network. On the freight side, we find ourselves not supporting a losing and old-fashioned transport mode, but running fast to keep up with technological, traffic, vessel and political changes. My readers have only to compare the closing pages of this edition of *British Canals* with its predecessor of 1979 to see that.

The history of British canals continues.

AUTHOR'S NOTES AND ACKNOWLEDGEMENTS

FIGURES 1, 2, 3, 4, 17, 18, 24, 25 and 28 are taken from Samuel Smiles, *Lives of the Engineers*, 1862; 5 and 6 from Rees' *Cyclopaedia*, 1819; 8 from Tomlinson's *Cyclopaedia of Useful Arts*, 1866; 10, 12 and 42 from the Rev Mark Guy Pearse's *Rob Rat*, ND; 13 from George Smith's *Our Canal Population*, 1878 ed; 15 from John Phillips *A Treatise on Inland Navigation*, 1785; 27 and 29 from the cover of a prospectus for the proposed Stirling Canal, 1835; 35 from William Cole, *A Poetical Sketch of the Norwich & Lowestoft Navigation Works*, 1833; 40 from J. B. Dashwood, *The Thames to the Solent by Canal and Sea*, 1868; and 43 from the *Illustrated London News* for 30 December 1893. The picture on p 148 (above) is from the *Transactions of the Royal Scottish Society of Arts*, IV, 82, and that on p 166 (below) from A. F. Tait, *Views on the Manchester and Leeds Railway*, 1845.

I am indebted to Mrs Ruth Heard (formerly Mrs Delany) for making Figures 14, 19 and 32 available to me; Westminster (Marylebone) Public Libraries for 20 and 21; Dr Jean Lindsay for 30; Shrewsbury Public Libraries and Museum for 33 and 34; the Waterways Museum for 26 and 31; the British Museum for 41; Mr Ian Langford and the Dudley Canal Trust for 44; and Mr Peter Davis for 45.

My thanks are due to the following for allowing me to use photographs: Collection of Hugh McKnight Photography, p 129 (above); Mr Peter Le Neve-Foster, ARPS, 129 (below); British Railways Board, pp 130, 147 (above) and 239 (above); Waterways Museum, 147 (below), 148 (below), 165 (above), 183, 184 (below), 210 (below), 219 (above), 240 (above), 257 (above), 258 (above); Mitchell Library, Glasgow, 148 (above); Michael W. Wheeler, 165 (below); Bodleian Library, 166 (above); Manchester Central Library, 166 (below); E. Paget Tomlinson, 185 (above); Westminster (Marylebone) Public Libraries, 201 (above), 240 (below); Mr L. A. Edwards, 202; Dr Jean Lindsay, 218 (below); Richard Shackleton, 220, 221 (above); National Library of Ireland, 221 (below); Dr W. A. McCutcheon, 222; A. D. Boddy and D. T. Atkinson, 238 (below); R. Keaveney, 256 (below); Manchester Ship Canal Co, 258 (below); British Waterways Board, 247; Central Office of Information, 275.

Miss Sheila Doeg of the British Waterways Board, Mrs Ruth Heard, Dr Jean Lindsay, Mr L. A. Edwards, Mr R. J. Hutchings of the Waterways Museum, Dr Michael Lewis and Dr W. A. McCutcheon have all helped me greatly in my search for pictures.

Maps 2 and 3 are from *River Navigation in England, 1600–1750*, by permission of Professor T. S. Willan and the Clarendon Press.

SOURCES OF QUOTATIONS

British Canals is the introductory volume to the 'Canals of the British Isles' series, published by David & Charles. I have therefore not burdened it with references. Those who would like to follow up the history of a canal or navigation will find it in one of the series volumes, accompanied by full notes on sources. An index to these volumes by waterway will be found on pp 344–50. The bibliography on pp 339–43 will, I hope, also help readers who would like to follow up any aspect of waterway history that may appeal to them.

Notes to Chapter I

1. *A Report of the Committee of the Commissioners of the Navigation of the Thames and Isis, appointed to survey the rivers from Lechlade to Whitchurch* . . . 1791 (Institution of Civil Engineers).
2. H. C. Darby, *The Mediaeval Fenland*, 1940.
3. Quoted in H. C. Darby, *The Draining of the Fens*, 1940.
4. Quoted from the Journals of the House of Lords in T. S. Willan, *River Navigation in England, 1600–1750*, 1936.
5. F. G. Blacklock, *The Suppressed Benedictine Minister and other Ancient and Modern Institutions of the Borough of Leominster*, 1898.
6. Mersey & Irwell Act, 7 Geo I c 15.
7. 2 Geo I c 12 (Ireland).
8. *Dublin News-Letter*, 30 March 1742.
9. Obituary notice of Henry Berry, *Liverpool Mercury*, 7 August 1812.
10. *Annual Register*, 1760, p 160.
11. E. Meteyard, *Life of Josiah Wedgwood*, 1866.
12. C. Humbert, *The History and Description of the County of Shropshire*, 1837, p 94n.

Notes to Chapter II

1. Thomas Telford, *A Survey and Report of the proposed extension of the Union Canal from Gumley Wharf, in Leicestershire, to the Grand Junction Canal, near Buckby-Wharf, in Northamptonshire*, 1804.
2. H. F. Killick, *Notes on the early history of the Leeds and Liverpool Canal. The Bradford Antiquary*, July 1897.
3. J. A. Langford, *A Century of Birmingham Life*, 1868, quoting a local newspaper.
4. J. Farey, *General View of the Agriculture of Derbyshire*, 1817.
5. W. Cobbett, *Rural Rides*, 1912 (Everyman edition).
6. *Thames Navigation. Observations upon the evidence adduced before the Committee of the House of Commons upon the* . . . *Hants and Berks Canal*, 1825.

7. *Felix Farley's Bristol Journal*, 22 March 1794.
8. E. Meteyard, *Life of Josiah Wedgwood*, 1866.
9. *Felix Farley's Bristol Journal*, 5 October 1793.
10. J. S. Padley, *Fens and Floods of Mid-Lincolnshire*, 1882.
11. Gloucester & Berkeley Canal Minute Book, 23 December 1794 (BTHR).
12. Thames & Severn Canal records (Glos CRO).
13. Op cit at 3 above.
14. Ashby-de-la-Zouch Canal Minute Book, 1 July 1794 (BTHR).
15. Birmingham Canal Minute Book, 14 July 1769 (BTHR).
16. Op cit at 8 above.
17. Op cit at 2 above.
18. *Gentleman's Magazine*, September 1788.
19. Kennet & Avon Canal Minute Book, 10 April 1797 (BTHR).
20. Shropshire Canal Minute Book, 12 February 1816 (BTHR).
21. Quoted from D. R. Phillips, *The History of the Vale of Neath*, 1925.
22. Unidentified newspaper cutting (author's collection).

Notes to Chapter III

1. C. Nicholson, *The Annals of Kendal*, 2nd ed, 1861.
2. Swansea Canal Minute Book, 9 June 1803 (BTHR).
3. J. A. Langford, *A Century of Birmingham Life*, 1868.
4. Anon, *An Authentic Description of the Kennet and Avon Canal . . .*, 1811 (Institution of Civil Engineers).
5. J. Plymley, *A General View of the Agriculture of Shropshire*, 1813. Article by Telford on 'Canals' dated 1797.
6. Grand Junction Canal Minute Book, 9 July 1811 (BTHR).
7. Charles Dickens, 'On the Canal', *Household Words*, 11 September 1858.
8. Grand Junction Canal Minute Book, 10 November 1825 (BTHR).
9. W. Hutton, *A History of Birmingham*, 2nd ed, 1783.
10. Grand Junction Canal Minute Book, 13 September 1808 (BTHR).
11. Driffield Navigation Minute Book, 6 July 1841.
12. Op cit at 5 above.
13. L. F. Vernon-Harcourt, *Rivers and Canals*, 2nd ed, 1896.
14. Birmingham Canal Act, 23 Geo III, c 92.
15. A. Rees, *Cyclopaedia*, 1819. Article on 'Canals' written 1805.
16. Illustrated in *Country Life*, 22 December 1955, article 'History in Ceramics', by Stanley W. Fisher.
17. Staffs & Worcs Canal Minute Book, 14 September 1832 (BTHR).
18. Basingstoke Canal Report, 20 May 1802 (Hants CRO).
19. *Illustrated London News*, 10 October 1874.
20. Swansea Canal Minute Book, 3 March 1818 (BTHR).
21. Peak Forest Canal Minute Book, 16 May 1806 (BTHR).
22. Staffordshire & Worcestershire Canal Minute Book, 23 August 1823 (BTHR).

23. Quoted in F. S. Thacker, *The Thames Highway: A History of the Locks and Weirs*, 1920.
24. Regent's Canal Minute Book, 1 December 1830 (BTHR).

Note to Chapter IV

1. J. Phillips, *A General History of Inland Navigation*, 4th ed, 1803.

Notes to Chapter V

1. *Case of the Birmingham Canal Committee, in opposition to the Dudley Canal Extension Bill*, ND.
2. Rev S. Shaw, *A Journey to the West of England in 1788*, 1789.
3. C. Vancouver, *A General View of the Agriculture of the County of Devon*, 1808.

Notes to Chapter VI

1. *Exeter Flying Post*, 2 January 1794.
2. J. Latimer, *The Annals of Bristol in the Eighteenth Century*, 1893.
3. Salisbury & Southampton Canal records (Southampton PL).
4. Peak Forest Canal Minute Book, 7 July 1794 (BTHR).
5. J. Plymley, *A General View of the Agriculture of Shropshire*, 1813. Article by Telford on 'Canals' dated 1797.
6. Kennet & Avon Canal Report, 14 June 1797 (BTHR).
7. Kennet & Avon Canal Report, 26 June 1798 (BTHR).
8. Letter to shareholders, 29 January 1798. Kennet & Avon Canal records (BTHR).
9. Grand Junction Canal Minute Book 5 July 1797 (BTHR).
10. Basingstoke Canal Report, 26 October 1803 (Hants CRO).
11. *Records of the Borough of Nottingham, 1760–1800*, vol VII, 1947.
12. Grand Junction Canal Minute Book, 5 May 1801 (BTHR).
13. Tavistock Canal Report, 16 March 1803 (Devon CRO).
14. Tavistock Canal Report, 27 September 1816 (Devon CRO).
15. Ibid.

Notes to Chapter VII

1. J. Knox, *A View of the British Empire, more especially Scotland, with some proposals for the improvement of that country, the extension of its fisheries and the relief of the people*, 1784.
2. J. Phillips, *A General History of Inland Navigation*, 4th ed, 1803.
3. Quoted in E. A. Pratt, *Scottish Canals and Waterways*, 1922.
4. *Prospectus of the advantages to be derived from the Crinan Canal*, 1792.
5. Daniel Defoe, *A Tour thro' the whole Island of Great Britain*, 1724–6.
6. H. W. Dickinson, *James Watt*, 1936.

7. English & Bristol Channels Ship Canal Report, 23 June 1828.
8. *Canals and Waterways Journal*, January 1922.

Notes to Chapter VIII

1. J. Phillips, *A General History of Inland Navigation*, 2nd ed, 1795.
2. Gloucester & Berkeley Canal Minute Book, 28 October 1794 (BTHR).
3. Ibid, 11 August 1795.
4. Ibid, 2 June 1797.
5. Ibid, 14 July 1818.
6. Ibid, 19 April 1827.
7. Gloucester & Berkeley Canal Report, 6 October 1871 (BTHR).

Notes to Chapter IX

1. Basingstoke Canal Report, 21 October 1816 (Hants CRO).
2. Ibid, 11 October 1822.
3. Kennet & Avon Canal. Minutes of a meeting of the Western sub-committee, 10 November 1840.
4. E. Meteyard, *Life of Josiah Wedgwood*, 1866.
5. H. F. Killick, *Notes on the early history of the Leeds & Liverpool Canal. The Bradford Antiquary*, July 1897.
6. E. A. Pratt, *Scottish Canals and Waterways*, 1922.
7. T. Grahame, *Essays and Letters on . . . Inland Communications*, 1835.
8. Quoted in *LMS Railway Magazine*, November 1928. Article on 'The Lancaster Canal and its Connection with Railways'.
9. J. Farey, *A General View of the Agriculture of Derbyshire*, 1817.
10. Charles Lever, *Jack Hinton: the Guardsman*, ch XX, 1843.
11. Prospectus of the Stirling Canal, 1813 (author's collection).
12. *Exeter Flying Post*, 22 November 1810.
13. B. T. Barton, *History of the Borough of Bury*, 1874.
14. Birmingham Canal Proprietors' Minute Book, 14 May 1841 (BTHR).

Notes to Chapter X

1. MS History of the Kennet Navigation, ND (*c* 1810) (Institution of Civil Engineers).
2. Bridgwater & Taunton Canal records (BTHR).
3. *A Report of the Committee of the Commissioners of the Navigation of the Thames and Isis, appointed to survey the rivers from Lechlade to Whitchurch. . . .*, 1791 (Institution of Civil Engineers).
4. *Report from the Committee of the Hon the House of Commons appointed to enquire into the progress made towards the amendment and improvement of the navigation of the Thames and Isis*, 1793 (Institution of Civil Engineers).
5. Ibid.

6. *Report of a Survey of the River Thames from Lechlade to the City Stone. . . .*,
1811 (Institution of Civil Engineers).

Notes to Chapter XI

1. Thames & Severn Canal Report, 25 January 1825 (Gloucester PL).
2. Report of Canal Conference of 1888. Royal Society of Arts. Paper on
the *History, Rise and Progress of Canal and River Navigation in Great
Britain and Ireland*, by M. B. Cotsworth.
3. Basingstoke Canal, Notice of Meeting, 12 September 1831 (Hants
CRO).
4. Kennet & Avon Canal Report, 21 July 1835 (BTHR).
5. Staffs & Worcs Canal Minute Book, 7 May 1840 (BTHR).
6. Ibid, 4 September 1845.
7. Grand Junction Canal Minute Book, 23 October 1845 (BTHR).
8. *Report of the Royal Commission on the Canals and Inland Navigations of
the United Kingdom.* Answers to questions 23965 and 23970.
9. Kennet & Avon Canal Report, 15 July 1845 (BTHR).
10. Kennet & Avon Canal Report, 21 July 1846 (BTHR).
11. Birmingham Canal Navigations Minute Book, 22 February 1878
(BTHR).
12. Staffs & Worcs Canal Minute Book, 12 December 1844 (BTHR).
13. Ibid, 30 December 1844.
14. James Wheeler, *Manchester: Its Political, Social and Commercial History,
Ancient and Modern*, 1836.

Notes to Chapter XII

1. Grand Junction Canal Minute Book, 28 May 1841 (BTHR).
2. Ibid, 16 July 1845.
3. Ibid, 21 May 1846.
4. Ibid, 2 October 1857.
5. Ibid, 7 January 1859.
6. Swansea Canal Minute Book, 5 September 1809 (BTHR).
7. *Journal of a Somerset Rector*, 1930.

Notes to Chapter XIII

1. *Report of Canal Conference of 1888* (Royal Society of Arts). Letter from
W. M. T. Campbell.
2. Ibid, paper on *The Relative Cost of Transport by Railway and Canal*, by
W. Shelford.
3. Grand Junction Canal Minute Book, 6 March 1835 (BTHR).
4. *Report of the Royal Commission on the Canals and Inland Navigations of
the United Kingdom*, 1907–9. Answer to question 19,214.

5. *Report to the Board of Trade on the Thames and Severn Canal*, 1888 (Glos CRO).
6. Gloucester & Berkeley Canal Report, 1 April 1864 (BTHR).

Notes to Chapter XIV

1. Quoted in Sir Bosdin Leech, *History of the Manchester Ship Canal*, 1907.
2. A. Woodroofe Fletcher, *The Economic Results of the Ship Canal on Manchester and the Surrounding Districts*, 1899.
3. Op cit at 1 above.

Notes to Chapter XV

1. *Report of the Royal Commission on the Canals and Inland Navigations of the United Kingdom*, 1907–9. Vol VII. Final Report, para 28.
2. Ibid, para 20.
3. E. A. Pratt, *Canals and Traders*, 1910.

Note to Chapter XVI

1. British Waterways Board, Annual Report and Accounts, 1967.
2. S. Burn, M. Garratt and D. M. Hayter, *Inland Waterway Freight Statistics*, Marine Transport Centre, University of Liverpool, 1982.

BIBLIOGRAPHY

THE following is a selection of useful books on canals and river navigations in the British Isles. The dates given are those of the first editions unless otherwise stated.

Of further sources of information, the most important are the original records of the canal companies themselves. Most of these are in the British Transport Historical Records Collection, now held at the Public Record Office, Ruskin Avenue, Kew, Surrey, but some are in county record offices or public or institution libraries. Other essential information is contained in Acts of Parliament, files of local newspapers, and various government and parliamentary publications to be found in the House of Lords Record Office or the Official Publications Library (at the British Museum). Useful periodicals include *Economic History Review*, *Industrial Archaeology*, *The Journal of the Railway and Canal Historical Society*, *The Journal of Transport History*, *Minutes of Proceedings of the Institution of Civil Engineers* (and its *Journal*, and *Proceedings*), *Transactions of the Newcomen Society*, and *Transport History*, and the periodicals published by numerous local history and canal societies. There is a good bibliography (for material published before 1916) in Jackman's *The Development of Transportation in Modern England*.

History, general and regional

ALBERT, WILLIAM. *The Turnpike Road System in England, 1663–1840*. 1972.
ANON. *The History of Inland Navigation*. 1766.
BAGWELL, PHILIP S. *The Transport Revolution from 1770*. 1974.
BAXTER, BERTRAM. *Stone Blocks and Iron Rails*. 1966.
BOYES, JOHN and RUSSELL, RONALD. *The Canals of Eastern England*. 1977.
DE SALIS, H. R. *A Chronology of Inland Navigation in Great Britain*. 1897.
DELANY, V. T. H. and D. R. *The Canals of the South of Ireland*. 1966.
FORBES, U. A. and ASHFORD, W. H. R. *Our Waterways: a history of inland navigation considered as a branch of water conservancy*. 1906.
GLADWIN, D. E. *The Canals of Britain*. 1973.
HADFIELD, CHARLES. *The Canal Age*. 2nd edn 1981.
——. *The Canals of the East Midlands*. 2nd edn 1970.
——. *The Canals of North West England* (with Biddle, Gordon). 1970.
——. *The Canals of South and South East England*. 1969.
——. *The Canals of South Wales and the Border*. 2nd edn 1967.
——. *The Canals of South West England*. 1967.
——. *The Canals of the West Midlands*. 2nd edn 1969.
——. *The Canals of Yorkshire and North East England*. 1972–3.

JACKMAN, W. T. *The Development of Transportation in Modern England*. 1916. Reprinted.

LEWIS, M. J. T. *Early Wooden Railways*. 1970.

LEWIS, M. J. T., SLATCHER, W. N. and JARVIS, P. N. 'Flashlocks on English Waterways', *Industrial Archaeology*, vol 6, no 3 and vol 7 no 2.

LINDSAY, JEAN. *The Canals of Scotland*. 1968.

McCUTCHEON, W. A. *The Canals of the North of Ireland*. 1965.

PAGET-TOMLINSON, EDWARD W. *The Complete Book of Canal & River Navigations*. 1978.

PHILLIPS, J. *A General History of Inland Navigation*. 1792. 5th edn. Reprinted.

PRATT, E. A. *Scottish Canals and Waterways*. 1922.

PRIESTLEY, J. *Historical Account of the Navigable Rivers, Canals and Railways, throughout Great Britain*. 1831. Reprinted.

REES, A. *Cyclopaedia*. 1819. Article, 'Canal'.

ROLT, L. T. C. *Navigable Waterways*. 1969.

RUSSELL, RONALD. *Lost Canals and Waterways of Britain*. 1982.

WILLAN, T. S. *River Navigation in England 1600–1750*. 1936. Reprinted.

WRIGHT, IAN L. *Canals in Wales*. 1977.

Single waterways or localities

BROADBRIDGE, S. R. *The Birmingham Canal Navigations*, vol I (1768–1846). 1974.

CAMERON, A. D. *The Caledonian Canal*. 1972.

CLARK, E. A. G. *The Ports of the Exe Estuary 1660–1860*. 1960.

CLEW, KENNETH R. *The Kennet & Avon Canal*. 2nd edn 1973.

——. *The Somersetshire Coal Canal and Railways*. 1970.

COMPTON, HUGH J. *The Oxford Canal*. 1976.

DALBY, L. J. *The Wilts & Berks Canal*. 1971.

DELANY, RUTH. *The Grand Canal of Ireland*. 1973.

DENNEY, MARTYN. *London's Waterways*. 1977.

DUCKHAM, BARON F. *The Yorkshire Ouse*. 1967.

FARNIE, D. A. *The Manchester Ship Canal and the Rise of the Port of Manchester 1894–1975*. 1980.

FAULKNER, ALAN H. *The Grand Junction Canal*. 1972.

HADFIELD, CHARLES and NORRIS, JOHN. *Waterways to Stratford*. 2nd edn. 1968.

HARRIS, HELEN. *The Grand Western Canal*. 1973.

HARRIS, HELEN and ELLIS, MONICA. *The Bude Canal*. 1972.

HASSELL, J. *Tour of the Grand Junction*. 1819. Reprinted.

HOUSEHOLD, HUMPHREY. *The Thames & Severn Canal*. 2nd edn 1983.

JOHNSON, GUY. *Save the Stratford Canal!*. 1983.

LEECH, BOSDIN. *History of the Manchester Ship Canal*. 1907.

LINDSAY, JEAN. *The Trent & Mersey Canal*. 1979.

MATHER, F. C. *After the Canal Duke*. 1970.

OGDEN, JOHN. *Yorkshire's River Aire*. 1976.

——. *Yorkshire's River of Industry: the story of the River Calder*. 1972.

STEVENS, PHILIP. *The Leicester Line.* 1972.

STEVENSON, PETER. *The Nutbrook Canal: Derbyshire.* 1970.

SUMMERS, DOROTHY. *The Great Ouse.* 1973.

TEW, DAVID. *The Oakham Canal.* 1968.

THACKER, F. S. *The Thames Highway: General History.* 1914. Reprinted.

——. *The Thames Highway: Locks and Weirs.* 1920. Reprinted.

VINE, P. A. L. *London's Lost Route to Basingstoke.* 1968.

——. *London's Lost Route to the Sea.* 3rd edn 1973.

——. *The Royal Military Canal.* 1972.

WILLAN, T. S. *The Navigation of the River Weaver in the Eighteenth Century.* 1951.

——. *The Early History of the Don Navigation.* 1965.

People

BOUCHER, C. T. G. *James Brindley, Engineer, 1716–1772.* 1968.

BURTON, ANTHONY. *The Canal Builders.* 2nd edn 1981.

DICKINSON, H. W. *Robert Fulton, Engineer and Artist.* 1913. Reprinted.

HADFIELD, CHARLES and SKEMPTON, A. W. *William Jessop, Engineer.* 1979.

HODDER, E. *George Smith (of Coalville).* 1896.

MALET, HUGH. *Bridgewater, The Canal Duke, 1736–1803.* 1977.

ROLT, L. T. C. *Thomas Telford: a biography.* 1958.

SMILES, SAMUEL. *Lives of the Engineers.* 1861–2. Reprinted.

General works—1939 and earlier

CADBURY, G. and DOBBS, S. P. *Canals and Inland Waterways.* 1929.

Canals and Inland Waterways Commission (Eire). *Report.* 1923.

DE SALIS, H. R. *Bradshaw's Canals and Navigable Rivers of England and Wales.* 1904, 1918, 1928. 1904 edn reprinted.

FAIRBAIRN, W. *Remarks on Canal Navigation, illustrative of the advantages of the use of steam, as a moving power on canals.* 1831.

FULTON, R. *A Treatise on the Improvement of Canal Navigation.* 1796.

NETTLEFOLD, J. S. *Garden Cities and Canals.* 1914.

PALMER, J. E. *British Canals: problems and possibilities.* 1910.

PRATT, E. A. *British Canals: is their resuscitation practicable?* 1906.

——. *Canals and Traders.* 1910.

Royal Commission on Canals and Waterways. *Reports.* 1906–11. 12 vols.

VERNON-HARCOURT, L. F. *Rivers and Canals.* 2nd edn 1896.

General works—since 1939

British Transport Commission. *Annual Reports.* 1948–1962.

——. *Canals and Inland Waterways: report of the Board of Survey.* [The 'Rusholme Report']. 1955.

British Waterways Board. *Annual Reports.* 1963–date.

——. *The Facts about the Waterways.* 1965.

——. *The Future of the Waterways: interim report of the Board.* 1964.

BURTON, ANTHONY and PRATT, DEREK. *Canal.* 1976.

DE MARÉ, ERIC. *The Canals of England*. 1950.

EDWARDS, L. A. *Inland Waterways of Great Britain*. 5th edn 1972.

HARRIS, ROBERT. *Canals and their Architecture*. 2nd edn 1980.

Inland Waterways Association. *British Freight Waterways Today & Tomorrow*. 1980.

McKNIGHT, HUGH. *The Shell Book of Inland Waterways*. 2nd edn 1981.

——. *Waterways Postcards 1900–1930*. 1983.

RANSOM, P. J. G. *Waterways Restored*. 1974.

Report of the Committee of Enquiry into Inland Waterways [The 'Bowes Report']. 1958.

ROLT, L. T. C. *The Inland Waterways of England*. 1950.

——. *Landscape with Canals*. 1977.

SQUIRES, ROGER W. *Canals Revived: the story of the waterway restoration movement*. 1979.

WARE, MICHAEL E. *A Canalside Camera, 1845–1930*. 1975.

——. *Historic Waterway Scenes: Britain's Lost Waterways: Vol 1: Inland Navigations*. 1979.

——. *Historic Waterway Scenes: Britain's Lost Waterways: Vol 2: Navigations to the Sea*. 1979.

——. *Narrow Boats at Work*. 1980.

Boats and boatpeople

CARR, FRANK. *Sailing Barges*. Revd edn. 1971.

CHAPLIN, TOM. *The Narrow Boat Book*. 1978.

CLARK, ROY. *Black-Sailed Traders: the keels and wherries of Norfolk and Suffolk*. 1961.

D'ARCY, G. *Portrait of the Grand Canal*. 1969.

GAYFORD, EILY. *The Amateur Boatwomen: canal boating, 1941–1945*. 1973.

HANSON, HARRY. *The Canal Boatmen, 1760–1914*. 1975.

——. *Canal People*. 1978.

LEWERY, A. J. *Narrow Boat Painting*. 1974.

MALSTER, ROBERT. *Wherries and Waterways*. 1971.

SMITH, D. J. *The Horse on the Cut: the story of the canal horses of Britain*. 1982.

SMITH, EMMA. *Maidens' Trip*. 1948.

SMITH, GEORGE. *Canal Adventures by Moonlight*. 1881.

——. *Our Canal Population*. 1875. Reprinted.

WILKINSON, TIM. *Hold on a Minute*. 1965.

WILSON, ROBERT J. (series of booklets published by).

WOOLFITT, SUSAN. *Idle Women*. 1947.

Canals for pleasure—1939 and earlier

ANON. *The Waterway to London*. 1869.

AUBERTIN, C. J. *A Caravan Afloat*. ND. [1916]. Reprinted.

BLISS, W. *The Heart of England by Waterway*. 1933.

BONTHRON, P.* *My Holidays on Inland Waterways*. ND [1916].

DASHWOOD, J. B. *The Thames to the Solent by Canal and Sea*. 1868. Reprinted.

NEAL, AUSTIN E. *Canals, Cruises and Contentment.* ND. [1921].
THURSTON, E. TEMPLE. *The 'Flower of Gloster'.* 1911. Reprinted.
WESTALL, G. *Inland Cruising on the Rivers and Canals of England and Wales.* 1908.

Canals for pleasure—since 1939

Broads Book, The (annually).
BURTON, ANTHONY. *Back Door Britain.* 1977.
Canals Book, The (annually).
DOERFLINGER, FREDERIC. *Slow Boat through England.* 1970.
——. *Slow Boat through Pennine Waters.* 1971.
EDWARDS, L. A. *Holiday Cruising on the Broads and Fens.* 1972.
GAGG, JOHN. *5,000 Miles, 3,000 Locks.* 1973.
HADFIELD, CHARLES. *Inland Waterways.* 1978.
——. *Introducing Canals.* 1955.
——. *Waterways Sights to See.* 1976.
HADFIELD, CHARLES and STREAT, MICHAEL. *Holiday Cruising on Inland Waterways.* 1968.
LILEY, JOHN. *Journeys of the Swan.* 2nd edn 1983.
MALET, HUGH. *Voyage in a Bowler Hat.* 1960.
OWEN, DAVID E. *Water Byways.* 1973.
——. *Water Highways.* 1967.
——. *Water Rallies.* 1969.
PILKINGTON, ROGER. *Thames Waters.* 1956.
RANSOM, P. J. G. *Holiday Cruising in Ireland.* 1971.
ROLT, L. T. C. *Narrow Boat.* 1944.
——. *Green and Silver.* 1949.
SEYMOUR, JOHN. *Sailing through England.* 1956.
——. *Voyage into England.* 1966.
Thames Book, The (annually).

SERIES INDEX

to the volumes of the 'Canals of the British Isles' series

THIS index notes the volume in the series that contains the principal historical account of each important canal, river navigation, branch or project in the British Isles. Subsidiary but useful references also, of course, occur in other volumes covering neighbouring regions, eg the principal account of the Rochdale Canal is in *The Canals of North West England,* but there is much subsidiary information in *The Canals of Yorkshire and North East England.* All volumes have been published.

Abbreviations	B	= Branch	pr = project
	C	= Canal	R = River
	Nav	= Navigation	

Key		
	BC	*British Canals*
	CEE	*The Canals of Eastern England*
	CEM	*The Canals of the East Midlands*
	CNI	*The Canals of the North of Ireland*
	CNWE	*The Canals of North West England*
	CS	*The Canals of Scotland*
	CSI	*The Canals of the South of Ireland*
	CSSEE	*The Canals of South and South East England*
	CSWB	*The Canals of South Wales and the Border*
	CSWE	*The Canals of South West England*
	CWM	*The Canals of the West Midlands*
	CYNEE	*The Canals of Yorkshire and North East England*
	WS	*Waterways to Stratford*

Aberdare C	CSWB	Anson B	CWM
Aberdeenshire C	CS	Ant R	CEE
Abingdon–Lechlade C pr	CSSEE	Arram Beck	CYNEE
Adelphi C	CEM	Arun R	CSSEE
Adur R	CSSEE	Ashburnham's, Earl of, C	CSWB
Aike Beck	CYNEE	Ashburton C pr	CSWE
Aire & Calder Nav	CYNEE	Ashby-de-la-Zouch C	CEM
Aire & Dun C pr	CYNEE	Ashton-under-Lyne C	CNWE
Alford C pr	CEE	Avon (Bristol) R	CSSEE
Allen, Lough, C	CSI	Avon (Hants) R	CSSEE
Ancholme R	CEE	Avon, Lower (Warws) R	WS, CWM
Andover C	CSSEE	Avon, Upper (Warws) R	WS, CWM
Anglesey B	CWM	Axe R	CSWE

Aylesbury & Abingdon C pr	CSSEE	Bude C	CSWE
Aylesbury B	CEM	Bumblehole B	CWM
		Bure R	CEE
		Burnturk C	CS
Bakewell C pr	CNWE	Burry R	CSWB
Ballinamore & Ballyconnell C	CSI	Burwell Lode	CEE
Ballinasloe B	CSI	Bury & Sladen C pr	CNWE
Bann, Lower R	CNI	Bute Ship C pr	CSWB
Bann, Upper R	CNI	Caistor C	CEE
Barking & Ilford Nav	CEE	Calder & Hebble Nav	CYNEE
Barnsley C	CYNEE	Caldon C	CWM
Barnsley–Don C pr	CYNEE	Caledonian C	CS
Barrow R	CSI	Cam R	CEE
Basingstoke C	CSSEE	Campbeltown C	CS
Bath & Bristol C pr	CSSEE	Campsie C	CS
Baybridge C	CSSEE	Cann Quarry C	CSWE
Beat Bank B	CNWE	Cannock Extension C	CWM
Bedale Beck	CYNEE	Canterbury Nav & Sandwich Harbour pr	CSSEE
Bedford–Grand Junction C pr	CEM	Carlingwark C	CS
Bedford Level	CEE	Carlisle C	CNWE
Beeston Cut	CEM	Central Junction C pr	CSSEE
Bentley C	CWM	Central Union C pr	CEM
Beverley Beck	CYNEE	Chard C	CSWE
Birmingham C Navs	CWM	Charnwood Forest B	CEM
Birmingham & Liverpool Junc C	CWM	Chelmer & Blackwater Nav	CEE
Birmingham & Warwick Junc C	CEE CS	Chester C	CWM
Blyth Nav	CEE	Chesterfield C	CEM
Bo'ness C	CS	Chet R	CEE
Bottisham Lode	CSSEE	Chichester C	CSSEE
Bourne Eau	CEE	Churchbridge B	CWM
Boyne R	CSI	Cinderford C	CSWB
Bradford C	CNWE	Circular Line	CSI
Bradley B	CWM	Clifton & Kearsley Coal Co's C	CNWE
Brandon R	CEE	Clywd, Vale of; C pr	CWM
Braunton C pr	CSWE	Coalisland C	CNI
Brecknock & Abergavenny C	CSWB	Cod Beck	CYNEE
Brede R	CSSEE	Colne R	CEE
Breydon Water	CEE	Commercial C pr	CEM
Bride R	CSI	Compstall Nav	CNWE
Bridgewater C	CNWE	Coombe Hill C	CWM
Bridgwater & Taunton C	CSWE	Corrib, Lough	CSI
Brighton C pr	CSSEE	Cosham Cut pr	CSSEE
Bristol Avon R	CSSEE	Cottingham & Hull C pr	CYNEE
Bristol–Cirencester C pr	CSSEE	Coventry C	CEM
Bristol Junction C pr	CSSEE	Crier Cut	CYNEE
Bristol–Salisbury C pr	CSSEE	Crinan C	CS
Bristol & Severn C pr	CSSEE	Cromford C	CEM
Bristol & Taunton C pr	CSWE	Croydon C	CSSEE
Bristol–Thames Head C pr	CSSEE	Crymlyn & Red Jacket C	CSWB
Bristol & Western C pr	CSWE	Cuckmere R	CSSEE
Briton C	CSWB	Cumberland Arm	CEM
Brown's C	CSWE	Cumberland C pr	CNWE
Brue R	CSWE	Cyfarthfa C	CSWB
Buckingham B	CEM	Dane Nav pr	CNWE

Danks B	CWM	Fossdyke	CEE
Dartford & Crayford Nav	CSSEE	Foston Beck	CYNEE
Dartmouth B	CWM	Foxhole C	CSWB
Daw End B	CWM	Foxley C	CWM
Deal Junction C pr	CSSEE	Frodingham Beck	CYNEE
Dearne & Dove C	CYNEE		
Dee R	CWM	Galton's C	CSWE
Derby C	CEM	Garforth C pr	CYNEE
Derbyshire Derwent R	CEM	General Warde's Cs	CSWB
Derwent (Derbyshire) R	CEM	Giant's Grave & Briton	
Derwent (Yorks) Nav	CYNEE	Ferry C	CSWB
Dewsbury Cut	CYNEE	Gipping R	CEE
Dick Brook	CWM	Glamorganshire C	CSWB
Digbeth B	CWM	Glan-y-wern C	CSWB
Dixon B	CWM	Glasgow, Paisley & Ard-	
Doctor's C	CSWB	rossan (Johnstone) C	CS
Don (Dun) Nav	CYNEE	Glasson B	CNWE
Donnington Wood C	CWM	Glastonbury C	CSWE
Dorset & Somerset C	CSWE	Glen R	CEE
Douglas Nav	CNWE	Glenkens C pr	CS
Driffield Nav	CYNEE	Gloucester C pr	CSSEE
Droitwich (& Junc) Cs	CWM	Gloucester & Berkeley	
Ducart's C	CNI	(Sharpness) C	CSSEE
Duckett's C	CEM	Glynne's, Sir John, C	CWM
Dudley C	CWM	Godalming Nav	CSSEE
Duke's Cut	CEM	Goole C	CYNEE
Dunkirk B	CWM	Gowdall Cut pr	CYNEE
Durham C pr	CYNEE	Grand C	CSI
Dutch R	CYNEE	Grand Commercial C pr	CNWE
		Grand Imperial Ship C pr	CSSEE
Eardington Forge C	CWM	Grand Junction C	CEM
Eastwood Cut	CYNEE	Grand Southern C pr	CSSEE
Eden R	CNWE	Grand Surrey C	CSSEE
Edenderry B	CSI	Grand Towy C pr	CSWB
Edinburgh & Glasgow		Grand Union C (new)	CEM
Union C	CS	Grand Union C (old)	CEM
Ellesmere C	CWM	Grand Western C	CSWE
Ellesmere & Chester C	CWM	Grantham C	CEM
Elsecar B	CYNEE	Grantham–Sleaford C pr	CEM
Emmet's C	CYNEE	Gravesend & Rochester C	CSSEE
English & Bristol		Greasbrough C	CYNEE
Channels Ship C pr	CSWE	Great Ouse R	CEE
Erewash C	CEM	Greenland B	CYNEE
Erne, Lough	CSI	Gresley's, Sir Nigel, C	CWM
Exeter C	CSWE	Griff C	CEM
Exeter & Crediton Nav	CSWE	Grosvenor C	CEM
Exeter–Uphill C pr	CSWE		
		Hackney C	CSWE
Fairbottom B	CNWE	Haddiscoe Cut	CEE
Fairburn C	CYNEE	Halifax B	CYNEE
Fall Ing Cut	CYNEE	Hampton Gay C pr	CEM
Fearnley's C	CYNEE	Hants & Berks Junc C pr	CSSEE
Fergus R	CSI	Haslingden C pr	CNWE
Fleet C	CEM	Hawarden C	CWM
Fletcher's C	CNWE	Hayle–Camborne C pr	CSWE
Flint Coal C	CWM	Heathcote's C	CWM
Forth & Cart C	CS	Hedon Haven	CYNEE
Forth & Clyde C	CS	Helston C pr	CSWE
Foss Nav	CYNEE		

Herefordshire & Gloucestershire C	CSWB
Hertford Union C	CEM
Heywood B	CNWE
High Peak Junc C pr	CNWE
Hollinwood B	CNWE
Holne C	CYNEE
Hopkin's C	CSWB
Horbury Cut	CYNEE
Horncastle C	CEE
Howden C pr	CYNEE
Huddersfield Broad C	CYNEE
Huddersfield C	CYNEE
Hull R	CYNEE
Humber Arm	CWM
Humber R	CYNEE
Ickham Nav	CSSEE
Ickles Cut	CYNEE
Idle R	CEM
Inverarnan C	CS
Ipswich & Stowmarket Nav	CEE
Isle of Dogs C	CEM
Itchen R	CSSEE
Ivel R	CEE
Ivelchester & Langport Nav	CSWE
Jersey C	CSWB
Kempsford–Abingdon C pr	CSSEE
Kennet R	CSSEE
Kennet & Avon C	CSSEE
Kensington C	CEM
Kent & Sussex Junc C pr	CSSEE
Ketley C	CWM
Keyingham Navigable Drains pr	CYNEE
Kidwelly & Llanelly C	CSWB
Kilbagie C	CS
Kilbeggan B	CSI
Kilgetty C	CSWB
Kilkenny C	CSI
Knaresborough C pr	CYNEE
Knostrop Cut	CYNEE
Knottingley & Goole C	CYNEE
Kyle Nav pr	CYNEE
Kyme Eau	CEE
Kymer's C	CSWB
Lagan C	CNI
Lake Lock–Bottom Boat C	CYNEE
Lancaster C	CNWE
Langstone Docks & Ship C pr	CSSEE
Lark R	CEE
Lea (Lee) R	CEE
Lea Wood B	CEM
Lechlade–Abingdon C pr	CSSEE
Leeds & Armley Nav pr	CYNEE
Leeds & Liverpool C	CNWE
Leeds & Selby C pr	CYNEE
Leicester Nav	CEM
Leicestershire & Northamptonshire Union C	CEM
Leigh B	CNWE
Leominster C	CSWB
Leven C	CYNEE
Limehouse Cut	CEE
Limerick–Killaloe C	CSI
Linton Lock Nav	CYNEE
Liskeard & Looe Union C	CSWE
Lismore C	CSI
Little Ouse R	CEE
Little Stour R	CSSEE
Liverpool C pr	CNWE
Llandeilo & Llandovery C pr	CSWB
Llangollen C	CWM
Llansamlet C	CSWB
Llechryd Cut	CSWB
Lockington Nav	CYNEE
Long Sandall Cut	CYNEE
London C pr	CSSEE
London & Birmingham C pr	CEM
London & Cambridge Junc pr	CEE
London & Hampshire C	CSSEE
London & Portsmouth C prs	CSSEE
London (Regent's) C pr	CEM
London & Southampton Ports Junc C pr	CSSEE
London & South Western C	CSSEE
London & Western C pr	CEM
Lord Hays B	CWM
Lothing, Lake	CEE
Lough Allen C	CSI
Lough Corrib	CSI
Lough Erne	CSI
Lough Neagh	CNI
Loughborough Nav	CEM
Loughor R	CSWB
Louth C	CEE
Lower Avon (Warws) Nav	CWM, WS
Lower Bann R	CNI
Lower Douglas Nav	CNWE
Lower Medway R	CSSEE
Lugg R	CSWB
Lydney C	CSWB
Macclesfield C	CWM

Mackworth's C	CSWB
MacMurray's C	CSSEE
Maidenhead–Isleworth C pr	CSSEE
Maigue R	CSI
Mallow–Lombardstown C	CSI
Manchester & Birmingham C pr	CWM
Manchester, Bolton & Bury C	CNWE
Manchester & Dee Ship C pr	CNWE
Manchester & Salford Junc C	CNWE
Manchester Ship C	BC, CNWE
Mardyke C	CEE
Market Weighton C	CYNEE
Medway (Lower) R	CSSEE
Medway (Upper) R	CSSEE
Medway & Thames C pr	CSSEE
Melton Mowbray Nav	CEM
Merionethshire C pr	CWM
Mersey & Irwell Nav	CNWE
Mersey R	CNWE
Methley Cut	CYNEE
Mexborough Cut	CYNEE
Middle Level Nav	CEE
Middlesborough–Redcar Ship C pr	CYNEE
Middlewich B	CWM
Millwall C	CEM
Monkey Island–Isleworth C pr	CSSEE
Monkey Island–Reading C pr	CSSEE
Monkland C	CS
Monmouthshire C	CSWB
Montgomeryshire C	CWM
Moorfields C pr	CEM
Morris's C	CSWB
Mountmellick B	CSI
Muirkirk C	CS
Mundon C	CEE
Naas B	CSI
Nar R	CEE
Neagh, Lough	CNI
Neath C	CSWB
Neath & Swansea Junc C	CSWB
Nene R	CEE
Nent Force Level	CNWE
New Bedford R	CEE
New Chapel C	CSWB
New Junction C	CYNEE
Newark Nav	CEM
Newbiggin B	CYNEE
Newcastle–Hexham–Haydon Br–Carlisle–Maryport C prs	CYNEE
Newcastle-under-Lyme C	CWM
Newcastle-under-Lyme Junc C	CWM
Newdigate Cs	CEM
Newport B	CWM
Newport Pagnell C	CEM
Newry C	CNI
Newry Ship C	CNI
Newton Abbot C pr	CSWE
Nore R	CSI
Norfolk Broads	CEE
North Eastern Junc C pr	CNWE
North Riding C pr	CYNEE
North Walsham & Dilham C	CEE
North Wilts C	CSSEE
Northampton B	CEM
Nottingham C	CEM
Nutbrook C	CEM
Oakham C	CEM
Ocker Hill B	CWM
Old Bedford R	CEE
Old Union C	CWM
Old West R	CEE
Oldbury Loop	CWM
Oulton Broad	CEE
Ouse, Great, R	CEE
Ouse, Little, R	CEE
Ouse (Sussex) R	CSSEE
Ouse (Yorks) R	CYNEE
Oxford C	CEM
Oystermouth C pr	CSWB
Paddington B	CEM
Par C	CSWE
Park Gate C	CYNEE
Parnall's C	CSWE
Parrett R	CSWE
Parrott's C	CEM
Peak Forest C	CNWE
Pembrey C	CSWB
Pen-clawdd C	CSWB
Penrhiwtyn C	CSWB
Penshurst C pr	CSSEE
Pensnett C	CWM
Pen-y-fan C	CSWB
Petworth C pr	CSSEE
Pidcock's C	CSWB
Pinxton B	CEM
Pitfour C	CS
Plas Kynaston C	CWM
Pocklington C	CYNEE
Polbrock C pr	CSWE
Poole C	CSWE
Portsea C	CSSEE
Portsmouth & Arundel C	CSSEE
Portsmouth Ship C pr	CSSEE

Prees B	CWM	Shropshire C	CWM
Preston Ship C pr	CNWE	Shropshire Union C	CWM
Public Devonshire C pr	CSWE	Slaney R	CSI
		Sleaford Nav	CEE
Ramsden's, Sir John, C	CYNEE	Slough B	CEM
Ravenhead C	CNWE	Smith's C	CSWB
Reach Lode	CEE	Soar R	CEM
Reading–Monkey		Soham Lode	CEE
Island C pr	CSSEE	Somersetshire Coal C	CSSEE
Reading–Windsor–		South Forty Foot Drain	CEE
Isleworth C pr	CSSEE	Southam C pr	CEM
Red Jacket C	CSWB	Southampton C pr	CSSEE
Red Moss C pr	CNWE	Southampton &	
Regent's C	CEM	Salisbury C	CSSEE
Retyn C pr	CSWE	Springs B	CNWE
Rievaulx Abbey Cs	CYNEE	Stamford C prs	CEM
Ripon C	CYNEE	Staffs & Worcs C	CWM
Rochdale C	CNWE	Stainforth & Keadby C	CYNEE
Roding R	CEE	Staniland's C	CYNEE
Rolle C	CSWE	Stanley Dock B	CNWE
Romford C	CEE	Stella–Hexham C pr	CYNEE
Rother (Eastern) R	CSSEE	Stevenston C	CS
Rother (Western) R	CSSEE	Stirling C pr	CS
Royal C	CSI	Stockport B	CNWE
Royal Clarence Ship C pr	CSSEE	Stockton & Auckland	
Royal Military C	CSSEE	C pr	CYNEE
Rufford B	CNWE	Stockton & Darlington	
Runcorn & Latchford C	CNWE	C pr	CYNEE
Runcorn & Weston C	CNWE	Stort R	CEE
Rushall C	CWM	Stour (Kent) R	CSSEE
		Stour, Little (Kent) R	CSSEE
St Columb C	CSWE	Stour (Suffolk) R	CEE
St Helens C	CNWE	Stour (Worcs) R	CWM
St Nicholas Bay Harbour		Stourbridge C	CWM
& Canterbury C pr	CSSEE	Stourbridge Extension C	CWM
Salisbury &		Stover C	CSWE
Southampton C	CSSEE	Strabane C	CNI
Saltney C	CWM	Stratford-upon-Avon C	CEM, WS
Salwarpe R	CWM	Stroudwater Nav	CSSEE
Sankey Brook Nav	CNWE	Suir R	CSI
Scarborough C prs	CYNEE	Suffolk Broads	CEE
Scarsdale & High Peak		Surrey & Hampshire C	CSSEE
C pr	CNWE	Surrey & Kent C	CSSEE
Seaton Nav	CSSEE	Sussex Ouse	CSSEE
Selby C	CYNEE	Sutherland's, Duke of, C	CWM
Settle C pr	CNWE	Swaffham Lode	CEE
Severn Junc C pr	CSSEE	Swale R	CYNEE
Severn R	CWM	Swansea C	CSWB
Severn & Wye Rly & C	CSWB		
Shannon R	CSI	Tamar C pr	CSWE
Sharpness New Docks &		Tamar Manure Nav	CSWE
Gloucester & Birming-		Tame Valley C	CWM
ham Nav	CWM	Taunton–Uphill C pr	CSWE
Sheffield C	CYNEE	Tavistock C	CSWE
Sheffield & Chesterfield		Tees C prs	CYNEE
Junc C pr	CYNEE	Tees R	CYNEE
Sheffield & South		Teign R	CSWE
Yorkshire Nav	CYNEE	Teme R	CWM
Shrewsbury C	CWM	Tennant C	CSWB

Thames & Medway C	CSSEE	Welland R	CEE
Thames Nav	CSSEE	Wendover B	CEM
Thames & Severn C	CSSEE	Went C pr	CYNEE
Thanet's, Lord, C	CNWE	Went & Wakefield C pr	CYNEE
Thatto Heath C	CNWE	Wern C	CSWB
Thorne & Hatfield Moors		Werneth Co's C	CNWE
Peat Cs	CYNEE	West Croft C	CEM
Thornhill Cut	CYNEE	Western C	CSSEE
Thurne R	CEE	Western Junc C pr	CSSEE, CEM
Tinsley Cut	CYNEE	Western Union C pr	CSSEE
Titford B	CWM	Weston B	CWM
Toll End B	CWM	Weston C	CNWE
Tone R	CSWE	Westport C	CSWE
Torridge C pr	CSWE	Wey & Arun Junc C	CSSEE
Torrington C	CSWE	Wey Nav	CSSEE
Trent & Balby C pr	CYNEE	Wey (Godalming) Nav	CSSEE
Trent C pr	CEM	Weybridge, Woking &	
Trent & Mersey C	CWM	Aldershot C	CSSEE
Trent (Newark) Nav	CEM	Whaley Bridge B	CNWE
Trent R	CEM	Wharfe R	CYNEE
Trewyddfa C	CSWB	Whitby C prs	CYNEE
Tyne R	CYNEE	Whitchurch B	CWM
Tyne–Wear C prs	CYNEE	Wilkinson's C	CNWE
Tyrone C, Nav	CNI	Willenhall B	CWM
		Wilts & Berks C	CSSEE
Ulster C	CNI	Wimbledon &	
Ulverston C	CNWE	Wandsworth C pr	CSSEE
Upper Avon (Warws) Nav	CWM, WS	Wirral Line	CWM
Upper Bann R	CNI	Wisbech C	CEE
Upper Douglas Nav	CNWE	Wissey R	CEE
Upper Medway R	CSSEE	Witham Nav Drains	CEE
Ure Nav & Ripon C	CYNEE	Witham R	CEE
Uttoxeter B	CWM	Woking, Aldershot &	
		Basingstoke C	CSSEE
Vauxhall C	CSWB	Wombridge C	CWM
Vavasour's, Sir Edward, C	CYNEE	Womersley B pr	CYNEE
		Wood's, Sir Andrew, C	CS
Wakefield & Ferrybridge		Woodeaves C	CEM
C pr	CYNEE	Woodlesford Cut	CYNEE
Wakefield & Went C pr	CYNEE	Woolston Cut	CNWE
Walsall C pr	CWM	Worcester & Birming-	
Walton B	CNWE	ham C	CWM
Ward's, Lord, B	CWM	Worcester & Gloucester	
Warde's, General, Cs	CSWB	Union C pr	CWM
Wardle B	CWM	Wormald's Cut	CYNEE
Warwick & Birmingham C	CEM	Worsbrough B	CYNEE
Warwick & Napton C	CEM	Worsley Brook Nav pr	CNWE
Waveney R	CEE	Worsley Underground Cs	CNWE
Weald of Kent C pr	CSSEE	Wye R	CSWB
Wear R	CYNEE	Wyrley Bank B	CWM
Wear–Tyne C prs	CYNEE	Wyrley & Essington C	CWM
Weaver Nav	CNWE		
Wednesbury B	CWM	Yare R	CEE
Weedon Arm	CEM	Yeo R	CSWE
Welford Arm	CEM	Yorkshire Derwent R	CYNEE
Well Creek	CEE	Yorkshire Ouse R	CYNEE

INDEX

Aberdare Canal, 34, 164, 299
Aberdeenshire Canal, 233
Abernethy, James, engineer, 284
Abingdon, 23, 91-2, 171, 208-9, 273
Accrington (Church), 89, 306
Adamson, Daniel, promoter, 284-6
Adur River, 199, 204
Aickman, Robert, 303, 308
Aire & Calder Navigation, 26, 43, 46, 57, 59, 72, 86, 88-9, 107, 113, 139, 144, 160, 163, 171-2, 185, 198-200, 226, 248, 251-2, 254, 268-70, 302, 305-6, 308-11, 316, 319, 326, 330, 333
Aldersley, 96n, 309
Ancholme Navigation, 304
Anderton, 68, 165, 205, 278-9, 324, 326-7, 333
Andover Canal, 95, 233
Aqueducts, canal, 46, 82, 191, 333; Alvechurch, 324; Avoncliff, 322; Barton, 32, 82, 279, 287; Barton Swing, 258, 279, 287; Chirk, 103, 105; Holmes, 102; Kelvin, 138; Longdon-on-Tern, 102; Lune, 159; Marple, 160, 162; Pontcysyllte, 102, 104-6, 134, 324; Slateford, 219; Spencer's Bridge, 93; Stanley Ferry, 200, 330, 333
Ardnacrusha, 299
Arney, F. D., 316
Arun River, 174, 255
Ashby-de-la-Zouch Canal, 44, 46, 57, 70-1, 112, 115, 194, 229-30, 309
Ashton, John, promoter, 30
Ashton-under-Lyne Canal, 43, 112, 160, 249, 310, 319, 322-3
Associated Canal Carriers, 298
Athlone, 189, 213, 215
Athy, 94
Aubertin, C. J., author, 300
Autherley, 85, 96, 106, 178
Avon (Bristol) River, 20, 27, 81, 86, 90-2, 142, 144, 199, 207, 309
Avon (Hants) River, 26
Avon (Warws) River, 23, 178, 199, 248, 307, 316, 322. See also Lower Avon, Upper Avon
Axe (Somerset) River, 199
Aylesbury, 126, 271

BACAT ship, 327, 329
Baldwin, Dr Mark, 329, 331, 334
Ballinamore & Ballyconnell Canal, 178-9, 213, 261
Ballinasloe, 187, 213
Banagher, 93, 213
Banbury, 85, 245
Banks, and canal companies, 34, 38, 48-9, 55, 101, 271
Banks, Sir Edward, contractor, 43
Bann, River, 222, 315, 325
Barge-carrying ships, 327, 329, 335
Barge groupage services, 330, 336
Barges or Juggernauts?, 329
Barnes, James, engineer, 120-1, 124
Barnsley Canal, 33, 43, 46, 65, 112–13, 163, 199, 251, 269, 309, 311
Barrow River, 29, 94, 171, 187, 303, 315, 325
Bartholomew, W. H., engineer, 269
Barton, 82, 258, 279, 287
Barwell, C. D., 307
Basingstoke Canal, 37-8, 43-4, 76, 95, 100-2, 119-20, 159, 172, 203, 211, 223, 246, 304, 323
Bath, 90, 142, 163, 179, 203
Battlebridge, 213, 215
Bawtry, 207
Baybridge Canal, 247
Bedford, 322
Bedford, Dukes of, 24, 123-4
Belfast, 29, 92, 171, 178, 213, 261, 315
Berkhamsted, 298, 308
Berry, Henry, engineer, 30
Beverley Beck, 35, 163
Bewdley, 21, 60, 211, 323
Bilston, 59, 98
Birmingham, 34, 36, 59, 64, 85, 92, 95, 98, 100, 106, 108, 126, 156, 159, 178, 197, 211, 235-6, 243-4, 250, 261-2, 265, 268, 292-3, 298, 302, 307
Birmingham Canal (and Navs), 33, 36, 43, 45-6, 56, 60-2, 65-6, 69, 85, 95-6, 98-100, 108-9, 126, 147, 154, 178, 185, 197-8, 228, 234-6, 238, 243, 249-50, 270, 293, 296, 302, 306, 308, 318, 320
Birmingham & Liverpool Junc Canal, 46, 66, 96n, 106, 169, 177-8, 197, 238, 243

Birmingham Ship Canal projects, 261-2
Birmingham & Warwick Junc Canal, 243, 298
Bishop's Stortford, 128
Blackburn, 89, 159
Blackhill incline, 148, 278-9
Blackwater River, 29, 171, 178
Bliss, William, author, 300
Blisworth, 43, 61, 117, 120, 124, 324
Blue Line, carriers, 326
Board of Trade, 225-7, 248, 253, 268, 272-3, 295, 305, 328
Board of Works (Ireland), 179, 326
Boatmen's Institutes, 240, 263
Boatpeople, 55, 72-80, 120, 201, 225, 255, 261-7, 276, 307
Bolton, 193
Bonthron, P., author, 300
Boston, 21, 163, 312
Boulton & Watt, 151
Bow-hauling, 18, 59-60, 212
Bowes Committee, 313
Boyle River, 213
Boyne River, 29, 94, 220
Bradford, 36, 86, 88
Bradford Canal, 88, 94, 299
Bradshaw, Robert H., canal official, 32
Braunston, 57, 124, 126, 178, 209, 243-4, 249, 264, 298, 324, 333
Brecknock & Abergavenny Canal, 34, 37, 72, 109, 115, 117, 164, 194, 237, 322, 324
Brecon, 34, 111, 164
Brentford, 124, 126, 240, 292, 308, 311, 330
Bridges, canal, 40, 61-3, 65, 236, 246, 254, 279, 288
Bridgewater, Duke of, 30-3, 82, 102, 169, 176, 180, 199, 282
Bridgewater Canal, 30-3, 45-6, 57, 81-2, 89, 94, 102-3, 107-8, 159-61, 164, 182, 185, 198, 205, 207, 243, 248-9, 252-3, 258, 279, 282-3, 287-8, 290, 302, 304
Bridgwater, 140, 142, 206-7
Bridgwater & Taunton Canal, 141, 199, 206, 232-3, 243
Brimscombe, 71, 271
Brindley, James, engineer, 30-2, 39, 44-5, 58, 65, 81-2, 85-6, 140, 177, 209, 279
Bristol, 20-1, 38, 57-8, 91-2, 100, 108, 111-12, 140, 142, 144, 150-1, 171, 179, 203, 211, 273-4, 296
Bristol & Taunton Canal project, 57
British Transport Commission, 136-7, 193, 200, 304-16, 318-19, 326, 330
British Transport Docks Board, 327
British Transport Historical Records, 308
British Transport Waterways, 310
British Waterways Board, 72, 136-7, 191, 205, 288, 311-12, 316-27, 329-36
Broads, The, 202, 304

Brownrigg, John, engineer, 46
Buckingham, 126, 171, 314
Bude Canal, 59, 66-7, 101, 141, 174-5, 304
Bulls Bridge, 126, 305
Burnley, 89, 159
Burry Port, 164
Burscough, 88
Burslem, 39
Burton (Upper Trent) Navigation, 81-2, 199
Burton-on-Trent, 81, 292
Bury, 193
Bury St Edmunds, 245
Butterley, 268

Cadbury, George, 304
Calder Carrying Co, 305
Calder & Hebble Navigation, 27, 46, 55, 73, 89, 160, 199, 225, 251-2, 269, 305, 308, 317, 319
Caldon branch, 45, 230-1, 318, 322-3
Caledonian Canal, 46, 57, 119, 124, 133-7, 143, 154, 294, 300, 304, 317, 319, 326
Calne, 91
Cam River, 18, 128, 131, 246
Camberwell, 127, 157
Cambridge, 21, 23, 128
Canal Association, 254, 299
Canal Boats Act (1877), 261, 265-6
Canal Boats Act (1884), 265-6
Canal Carriers' Act (1845), 72, 266, 248, 253-4
Canal Carriers' Act (1847), 226
Canal, etc, companies, formation, organisation of, 35-8
Canal Conference (1888), 218, 259-61, 280-1, 291, 305
Canal Control Committee (1917), 295
Canal cutting machines, 39n, 150
Canal mania, 34-5, 91, 95, 107ff, 139-40, 150-2, 200, 213, 225
Canal restoration, 307, 315-16, 318-24, 326
Canal and Riverboat, 325
Canal Tolls Act (1845), 70, 226, 254
Canal Transport Ltd, 305
Canals, construction, dimensions of, surveying for, 38-51, 91, 107, 112, 151, 177-8, 258
Canals & Navigations Alliance, 325
Canals, Select Committee on (1883), 267, 280-1
Canals & Waterways Commission (IFS), 296
Cannock Extension Canal, 236, 243
Capital of canals, 34-5, 48-51, 82, 91, 94, 101, 107-9, 118-19, 141, 152-4, 172, 245-6, 250
Cardiff, 71, 142, 156, 164, 167
Carlisle Canal, 35, 139, 182, 228

Carne, John, engineer, 39, 150
Carrick-on-Shannon, 178, 213
Carrying, by canal, etc, companies, 55, 72, 203, 226, 238, 251-4, 267, 282, 293, 298-9, 304ff; by others, 59, 63, 69, 71-5, 78, 120, 222, 224, 249, 251-4, 267, 281, 301, 304-6, 317, 326-30
Castle, Richard, engineer, 29, 46
Castleford, 163, 184, 200, 251, 269
Cawoods-Hargreaves, carriers, 326
Cement, carried on canals, etc., 328
Central Union Canal project, 178
Chalford, 273, 299
Chamberlain Committee, 295
Chapman, William, engineer, 46, 93-4
Chard Canal, 66, 243
Charlotte Dundas, 139
Charnwood Forest, 218
Cheap Trains & Canal Carriers' Act (1858), 248
Chelmer & Blackwater Navigation, 304
Cheltenham, 171, 270-1
Chepstow, 27, 109
'Cheshire Ring', 319, 322
Chester, 35, 94, 103-4, 106, 190-2, 300, 312
Chester Canal, 33, 35, 57, 94-5, 102-4, 106, 151, 178, 185, 191, 198
Chesterfield Canal, 57, 70, 94, 118, 163, 207, 314, 318
Chichester, 174
Chippenham, 91
Chirk, 103, 105
Church, *see* Accrington
Cirencester, 90, 270, 272
City Road basin, 128
Clachnaharry, 135
Clark, Edwin, engineer, 68
Claverton, pumping station, 322
Clegrams, engineers, 151, 277
Cloondara, 113
Clowes, Josiah, engineer, 90, 210
Clyde River, 21, 57, 132, 284
Coal, carried by coasting trade, 20, 30, 37, 119, 171; by road transport, 20, 30, 95, 119, 141, 171; on canals, etc, *passim*; on railways, 218, 223, 232, 241, 260; on tramroad, 113, 175; sold by canal, etc, companies, 72
Coalbrookdale, 59-60, 98, 108, 115, 169
Coalisland, and Canal, 29, 171, 315
Coalport, 169
Coasters, *see* Sea-going barges
Coasting trade, 20-1, 27, 37, 63, 69, 74, 86, 102, 119, 121, 137, 139, 144, 146, 155, 159, 167, 170, 172, 222-3, 277, 292, 307, 334, 336
Colchester, 245, 327
Colne, 159
Combe Hay, 256

Commercial Canal project, 57
Commissioners, appointed under canal Acts, 47-8, 70
Compartment boats, 184, 269-70, 305, 307, 308, 311, 327
Congreve, Sir William, engineer, 68
Constables Act (1840), 75
Containers, carried on barges, 89, 311, 335
Contractors, for canals, etc, 43-4, 47, 74, 153
Coombe Hill Canal, 247
Coras Iompair Eireann, 303, 315, 326
Corpach, 135-6, 326
Coventry, 54, 82, 85, 308
Coventry Canal, 33, 45, 57, 70-1, 82, 85, 109, 115, 126, 178, 194, 225, 230, 243-4, 248-9
Crediton, 146, 149
Crescent Shipping, 327-8
Crinan Canal, 34, 51, 133, 136-7, 294, 300, 304, 307, 317, 319
Crofton pumping station, 322
Cromford Canal, 46, 64, 95, 108, 160, 167, 194, 229, 233, 264, 267-8, 314
Cromford & High Peak Rly, 160, 175
Cromwell lock, 297, 311
Crosleys, William, engineers, 46
'Cross, The', 292-3, 296
Croydon Canal, 43, 127, 157-8, 217, 228
Cruiseways, *see* Pleasure boating
Crumlin, 109, 164
Cubitt, William, engineer, 178, 215
Cyfarthfa, 108

Dadford, James, engineer, 151-2
Dadford, Thomas, sen, engineer, 44, 46
Darby family, 108, 169
Dashwood, J. B., author, 255
Davidson, Matthew, engineer, 134
Davidson, Robert, 304
Dearne & Dove Canal, 33, 65, 112-13, 163, 199-200, 228, 268, 311
Dee River, 94, 102-3, 105, 109, 175, 282
Denver sluice, 26, 60
Derby, 23, 70, 167, 185
Derby Canal, 36, 70, 102, 115, 167, 185, 207, 304
Derwent (Derbyshire) River, 23, 27, 207
Derwent (Yorkshire) River, 26, 234, 248
De Maré, Eric, author, 268, 281
De Salis, R. H., author, 268, 281
Devizes, 91-2, 111, 147, 325
Diesel-engined boats, 59-60, 280
Diglis, 213, 250, 274, 305
Dividends, on canal shares, 36, 38, 49, 51, 55, 91, 95, 99-100, 102, 112-13, 156, 175, 194-6, 207-8, 210, 225, 232-3, 235, 238, 244-7, 249, 254, 271, 287, 290, 299
Docks & Inland Waterways Executive, 304-9

Dodd, Ralph, engineer, 157
Don Navigation, 73, 90, 113, 117, 163, 171, 182, 199-200, 228, 252, 268, 270. *See also* Sheffield & South Yorkshire Navigation
Doncaster, 60, 163, 183, 306, 311, 326, 333
Donnington Wood Canal, 35, 66, 169
Dorset & Somerset Canal, 51, 68, 112, 141-2
Douglas River, 27, 30, 86, 88, 171, 207
Drainage works, etc, 22, 29, 37, 39, 128, 178, 199, 247, 261, 290, 294, 309, 323
Drawbacks, 70, 218, 226
Dredging, 22, 63-4, 156, 209, 234, 257, 272, 274, 298, 305, 309, 311
Driffield Navigation, 43, 65, 163
Droitwich, 21, 85, 243, 293
Droitwich Canal, 36, 45, 57, 85, 108, 156, 207, 267, 299, 323
Droitwich Junction Canal, 156, 243, 267, 299
Dublin, 29, 79, 93, 113, 120, 171, 187-9, 213
Ducart, Davis, engineer, 46, 66, 171
Ducart's Canal, *see* Tyrone Canal
Dudley Canal, 96, 98, 198, 235, 250, 309, 318, 320-1
Dukinfield, 160
Dun River, *see* Don Navigation
Dundas, Charles, Lord Amesbury, 91
Dutch River, 163, 200

Eastham, 285-6, 288, 290
Edinburgh, 137, 172, 182, 187
Edinburgh & Glasgow Union Canal, 138, 165, 172, 181, 191, 219, 318
Edson, Dennis, engineer, 151
Egerton family, 282, 286
Electricity works, and canals, 124, 311, 326
Ellesmere Canal, 34, 46, 67, 102-6, 109, 112, 185, 190, 198, 239, 310, 312, 320, 322, 324
Ellesmere & Chester Canal, 72, 106, 228, 238
Ellesmere Port, 103, 144, 178, 190, 192, 238, 288, 290, 325, 327
Elsecar, 163
Enfield, 308, 311, 317, 330
Engineers, canal, 44-7, 55, 151, 153, 203, *and see under names*
English & Bristol Channels canal projects, 119, 139-43, 175
Environment, Dept, of the, 332
Erewash Canal, 43, 57, 95, 167, 194, 218, 267-8, 298, 314, 323
European Economic Community, 331-3
Evans, Richard, engineer, 46
Evesham, 307, 322

Exchequer Bill Loan Commissioners, 51, 153-4, 178, 205
Exe River, 140, 146
Exeter, 35, 57-8, 91, 141, 146, 149-50
Exeter Canal, 23, 28, 35, 57, 141, 146, 149-50, 304
Exeter Maritime Museum, 150, 175
Explosives, carried on canals, etc, 77
Eyre, Frank, author, 303

Facts about the Waterways, The (1965), 317
Falkirk, 165, 172, 182
Farmer's Bridge, 85
Farnie, Dr D. A. (author), 288
Fazeley, 85, 96, 108, 126, 249
Fellows, Morton & Clayton, carriers, 252, 280-1, 305
Fenland waterways, 21, 23-6, 58, 128, 144, 168, 199, 247
Ferrybridge, 163, 172, 200, 251, 269, 328; 'C' power station, 311, 326
Fishing and fisheries, 17, 20, 22, 28, 132-4, 136-7, 319, 325
Flash-locks, 18-20, 22-3, 27, 129, 208, 211, 245
Flats, 28, 58
Fleet River, 20
Floods and flood protection, 22-3, 26, 63, 92, 286, 305
Fly-boats, 73, 75, 77, 92, 172, 179-80, 193, 224, 274, 280
Fort Augustus, 134
Fort William, 132, 134
Forth & Clyde Canal, 46, 51, 57, 86, 93, 109, 117, 133, 136-9, 172, 180-2, 186-7, 191, 193-4, 219, 300, 306, 310, 313, 323
Forth River, 57, 132, 138
Fosdyke, 327
Foss River, 112, 304
Fossdyke, 28, 163, 233, 309, 317
Foulridge, 89, 333
Foxton, 127, 279
Fradley, 82, 249, 292
Fraenkel report, 324, 331-3
Framilode, 212, 217
Frankton, 103-4, 320, 322-3
Freight Services Division, BWB, 326, 329
'Freightwaves' conference, 329-30
Frindsbury, 52, 127
Frodsham, 204, 278
Fulton, Hamilton, engineer, 283-4
Future of the Waterways, The (1964), 316-17

Gainsborough, 167, 297, 327, 330, 335
Gasworks, canalside, 202, 314, 326
Gauging, 71-2, 78
Gayford, Eily, author, 302

Gilbert, John, agent, 30-2, 82, 169
Gilbert, Thomas, agent, 31, 169
Glamorganshire Canal, 33-4, 55, 71, 108, 164, 167, 302, 304
Glan-y-wern Canal, 164
Glasgow, 136-9, 163, 172, 182, 185, 187, 284
Glasgow, Paisley & Ardrossan Canal, 182, 191, 193
Glastonbury Canal, 130, 233
Glen River, 25
Gloucester, 21-2, 60, 109, 111-12, 146, 150, 152, 155-6, 171, 211-13, 250, 270, 274, 277, 293, 302, 304, 325, 335
Gloucester & Berkeley (Sharpness) Canal, 43, 47, 51, 57, 109, 146, 150-6, 185, 210-13, 217, 224, 248, 250, 261, 267, 271-2, 275, 277, 293, 308, 317, 319, 326, 330, 335. *See also* Sharpness New Docks
Gloucestershire County Council, 156, 272-3, 299
Godalming, 316
Goole, 59, 63, 144, 163, 172, 200, 251, 269-70, 310-11
Goole Canal, 43, 46, 172, 251, 269
Gower, Earl, promoter, 31-2, 38-9, 169
Goyt River, 159-60, 162
Grand Canal, 29, 79, 93-4, 171, 182, 187, 189, 213, 215-16, 220-1, 229, 296, 303, 315, 325-6
Grand Junction Canal, 43, 46, 48, 54-7, 61, 63, 66, 71, 92-3, 109-10, 112, 117, 119-21, 124, 126-8, 166, 171, 185, 193-7, 207, 209, 211, 227, 243-4, 248-9, 252-4, 257, 264, 267-8, 270, 279-81, 298, 306
Grand Surrey Canal, 127, 151, 157-8
Grand Union Canal (old), 126-7, 207, 253, 267, 298
Grand Union Canal (new), 64-5, 262, 298, 302, 305, 308, 311, 314, 317
Grand Union Canal Carrying Co, 298-9
Grand Western Canal, 43, 57-8, 66-8, 91, 102, 112, 140-2, 194, 232-3, 299
Grangemouth, 138, 172
Grantham Canal, 109, 299
Gravesend, 52, 127
Great Haywood, 75, 82
Great Western Rly, 91, 156, 175, 223-4, 232, 236, 250, 253, 271-2, 274, 277, 306, 315
Green, James, engineer, 67, 141-2, 149, 164
Gresley, Sir Nigel, industrialist, 57
Grosvenor Canal, 55
Guildford, 180, 316

Haddlesey, 88
Hadfield, Charles, 303, 308, 316, 329
Hadlow, Charles, 312

Half-locks, *see* Flash-locks
Halifax, 55
Hampton Gay Canal, *see* London & Western
Hanley, 57
Hants & Berks Junct Canal project, 37-8, 102, 203-4
Harecastle, 46, 61, 82, 84, 163, 177, 324
Hatherton branch, 35
Hawkesbury, 126, 244-5
Hawton, Sir John, 316
Hay Railway, 34, 117
Heap, John, 318
Hebden Bridge, 166, 323
Hedon, 144
Henshall, Hugh, engineer, 44
Henshall, Hugh, & Co, carriers, 72
Hereford, 108-9, 111-12, 115, 243
Herefordshire & Gloucestershire Canal, 39, 109, 112, 150-1, 210, 212, 242-3
Heywood, 159
Hill, Sir Reginald, 304, 309
Hills of Blaenavon, 117
Hillmorton, 245, 312
Hinckley, 118
Hobbacott Down incline, 67, 174-5
Hodgkinson, John, engineer, 114
Hollin Ferry, 30, 32
Holme, 297, 305
Hore, John, engineer, 203
Horncastle, 41
Hotels, canal, 187
Houston, William, shareholder, 182
Howdendyke, 327
Huddersfield Broad Canal, *see* Ramsden's
Huddersfield Canal, 43, 89, 112, 119, 160-1, 248, 302, 310
Hull, 57, 81, 163, 236, 297, 311, 327-8
Hull River, 163, 304
Humber River, 27, 86, 139, 144, 163, 171, 292, 297, 301, 327-8, 330, 334
Humphery & Grey, carriers, 330, 336
Humphries, John, 318, 331
Hungerford, 91, 203
Hurleston, 104, 106, 303
Hutchings, David, 315-16

Ice, on canals, 63, 264
Idle River, 207
Inclined planes, 46, 58-9, 66-8, 160, 293; Blackhill, 66, 148, 278-9; Bude Canal, 59, 66-7, 141, 174-5; Chard Canal, 66; Donnington Wood Canal, 66, 169; Foxton, 66, 279; Ketley, 66-7, 102; Kidwelly & Llanelly Canal, 58, 66; Morwellham, 123; Shropshire Canal, 66, 169, 325; Somersetshire Coal Canal, 68; Trench, 66, 148, 169; Tyrone Canal, 172; Wellisford, 66, 141

Inglesham, 90
Inland Cruising Association, 300
Inland Navigation, Corporation for, 93-4, 213
Inland Navigation, Directors General of, 113, 124, 179, 215
Inland Navigation (NI) Act (1954), 315
Inland Shipping Group, 329-31
Inland Waterways Amenity Advisory Council, 320
Inland Waterways Association, 303, 307-8, 313, 315-20, 324-5, 329-32
Inland Waterways Association of Ireland, 315, 326
Inland Waterways Redevelopment Committee, 313, 316
Interpretation Centres, 323, 325
Inverness, 132-3, 135
Ipswich, 327
Irlam, 28, 289
Iron, carried by pack-horse, 167; by road transport, 167; on canals, etc, 59, 69, 98, 113, 163-4, 167; sold by canal, etc, companies 72
Iron barges, boats, 59, 63
Iron ore, carried on canals, etc, 69, 157
Irwell River, 23, 28, 32, 279. See also Mersey & Irwell Navigation
Isle of Dogs Canal, 127
Isleworth, 209
Islington, 59, 61
Itchen River, 26, 119
Ivel (Beds) River, 247

Jamestown, 213, 215
Jeans, J. S., author, 291
Jessop, William, engineer, 44, 46, 57, 93, 102, 124, 133, 140, 144, 161, 209, 215
Johnson's Hillock, 89, 229
Johnstone, 182, 191
Joliffe & Banks, contractors, 43

Keadby, 163, 319
Keels, 21, 27, 58, 65, 73, 75, 158, 183
Kemmett, John, projector, 90
Kendal, 54, 159, 185
Kennet & Avon Canal, 37-8, 43, 46, 49, 55, 57-8, 91-2, 100, 102, 118-19, 142, 147, 163, 171, 179, 182, 194-7, 199, 203-4, 207, 209, 211, 224, 231-2, 273, 310, 313, 318-19, 322-3, 325
Kennet River, 23, 28, 58, 90-1, 100, 197, 199-200, 203, 207
Kensington Canal, 228, 309
Kerr, Sir Reginald, 310, 312
Ketley Canal, 66-7, 102, 169
Kidwelly & Llanelly Canal, 43, 58, 66, 141, 164
Killaloe, 213, 215, 221, 299
Killaly, John, engineer, 46, 93, 178

King's Lynn, 20-1, 24, 60, 144
Kingswood, 98, 316
Knostrop depot, 311
Knottingley, 27
Knox, John, author, 132, 136, 138

Lagan Navigation, 29, 92-3, 171, 178, 315
Lake Lothing, 205
Lancaster Canal, 43, 46, 54, 89, 109, 112, 117, 159-60, 182, 185, 224, 228, 310, 314
Land purchase and ownership, 47-8, 54
Land carriage, see Road transport
Langley Mill, 298
Langport, 140
Lappal, 98
Lark River, 26
LASH barges, ships, 327
Latton, 92
Lea River, 22-3, 128, 302, 306, 308-9, 311, 317, 319
Leather, George, engineer, 46, 200
Lechlade, 90, 92, 209, 273, 323
Ledbury, 171, 243
Lee Navigation, see Lea
Lee & Brentford Lighterage, 336
Leeds, 23, 27, 59, 86, 88-9, 163, 200, 251, 269, 302, 304, 311, 330
Leeds & Liverpool Canal, 34-5, 43, 46-8, 57, 86, 88-9, 92, 94, 159, 161, 180, 185, 207, 229, 247-8, 252, 269, 302, 304-6, 308, 317
Leeds & Selby Canal project, 88
Leek, 31, 230-1, 324
Legging through tunnels, 60-1
Leicester, 34, 108, 118, 126-7, 160, 167, 207, 218, 279, 292, 297-8
Leicester Navigation, 36, 109, 118, 126, 128, 218, 267, 298
Leicester & Swannington Rly, 218
Leics & Northants Union Canal, 126, 207, 267, 298
Leigh branches, 89, 161
Leighton Buzzard, 124
Leitrim, 178, 213
Leominster Canal, 109, 111-12, 194, 210, 233
Leven Canal, 163
Lever, Charles, author, 188
Lichfield, 82
Lifts, canal, 46, 67-8, 102, 141-2, 165, 169, 205, 260, 278-9, 324, 333
Lighters (Fenland), 58
Lime, carried by packhorse, 101; on canals, etc, 101, 103, 123
Limehouse basin, see Regent's Canal Dock
Limehouse, and cut, 126-7, 326
Limekilns, limeworks, 69, 72, 101, 103, 115
Limerick, 213, 215, 261, 299
Limestone, carried on canals, etc, 69, 72, 101, 103, 123, 164, 167

Lincoln, 21, 28, 167, 312
Linton Lock Navigation, 163, 304
Lisburn, 29, 92-3
Liskeard & Looe Union Canal, 43, 228
Littlehampton, 127, 174, 255
Liverpool, 23, 28-30, 32, 35, 57, 81, 86, 88-9, 120, 161, 171, 180, 192, 197, 223, 236, 248, 250, 262, 282-3, 285-6, 288, 290, 296, 304, 306, 334
Liverpool & Manchester Rly, 191, 218, 223, 225, 282
Llanfoist, 322
Llangollen, 103, 105, 303
Llangollen Canal, *see* Ellesmere Canal
Llanymynech, 103, 106, 322
Loch Fyne, 132, 136
Loch Lochy, 133-5
Loch Lomond, 138
Loch Ness, 133, 135
Loch Oich, 133
Lock & Quay, 307
Lock-keepers, 51, 55, 75, 78, 80, 188, 264
Lock, pound, 22-3, 39, 46, 57-9, 63-5, 100, 146, 164, 178, 204-5, 208-9, 212-13, 215, 224, 245, 269-70, 278, 288, 293, 298-9, 311, 325, 333; mechanisation of, 278, 311, 326, 333; Banavie, 136; Devizes, 91-2, 147, 322; Falkirk, 172; Foxton, 127, 279; Laggan, 323; Parkhead, 320-1; Runcorn, 46-7, 82; Smethwick, 98; Tardebigge, 100; Tinsley, 65; Union (Sprucefield), 93; Watford, 127; Wolverhampton, 66; Wordsley, 318, 320. *See also* Flash-locks
Locomotive towage, 193-4
London, *passim*
London & Birmingham Rly, 176, 223, 235-6, 271
London & Cambridge Junct Canal project, 128, 131
London, Midland & Scottish Rly, 306
London & North Western Rly, 193, 229, 235-6, 238, 248, 253
London and Portsmouth canal schemes, 119, 175
London & Western Canal project, 57-8
Long Sandall, 311, 333
Longbothom, John, engineer, 86, 88, 107, 140
Longdon-on-Tern, 102
Longford, 85, 243
Lough Allen, 213, 215
Lough Derg, 213, 215
Lough Erne, 178, 213, 325
Lough Neagh, 29, 92-3, 171, 178, 213, 261, 315, 325
Lough Ree, 213, 215
Loughborough, 77, 118, 207
Loughborough Navigation, 126, 167, 194, 207, 218, 267, 298. *See also* Soar River

Louth Canal, 299
Lower Avon Navigation, Trust, 307, 315
Lowestoft, 205
Lugg River, 26-7
Lune River, 159-60

Macclesfield Canal, 160, 163, 194, 249, 310
McIntosh, Hugh, contractor, 43
Mackell, Robert, surveyor, 138
Maigue River, 29
Maisemore, 212
Mance, Brig Sir Osborne, 301
Manchester, 23, 28, 30, 32, 57, 81-2, 89, 109, 159-61, 163, 175, 180, 207, 223, 225, 241, 248-9, 255, 282ff, 291, 302, 322
Manchester, Bolton & Bury Canal, 112, 161, 193, 227-8, 282, 302, 313
Manchester & Dee Ship Canal project, 175, 282-3
Manchester & Leeds Rly, 225, 227
Manchester & Salford Junct Canal, 163, 207, 243, 282
Manchester, Sheffield & Lincolnshire Rly, 228, 248, 268
Manchester Ship Canal, 57, 139, 157, 175, 238, 258, 261, 269, 278-9, 282-90, 304, 311-12, 327, 330
Manpower Services Commission, 322-3
Manure, carried by road transport, 100; on canals, etc, 33, 70, 100-1, 103
Marine Transport Centre, 334-5
Market Harborough, 126, 128, 308
Market Weighton Navigation, 304
Marple, 49, 117, 160, 162-3
Medway River, 26, 52, 58, 60, 72, 223
Mells, 68, 142
Melton Mowbray Navigation, 109, 128, 247
Mercantile Lighterage, carriers, 330, 336
Mersey & Irwell Navigation, 23, 27-9, 32, 72, 81, 161, 185, 194, 198-9, 207, 243, 252, 282
Mersey River, 23, 28, 30-1, 58-9, 81-2, 85-6, 89, 92, 95, 103, 105-7, 139, 178, 190, 204-5, 238, 255, 262, 278, 282-3, 286, 292-3, 297, 301, 328, 330, 334
Merthyr Tydfil, 164
Mexborough, 268, 306
Middlewich, 103, 106; branch, 106, 193
Midland Rly, 230, 236, 248, 271-2
Mid-Scotland Ship Canal project, 139
Mills, on canals, navigable rivers, etc, 17-20, 22, 36-7, 64, 89, 208, 220, 246, 251, 274
Mistley, 327
Moira, 70, 115, 230
Monk Meadow wharf, 326, 335

Monkland Canal, 66, 86, 138, 148, 163, 172, 279, 309
Monmouthshire Canal, 37, 109, 112, 115, 117-18, 167, 228, 309, 314
Montgomeryshire Canal, 103, 111, 238, 320, 322-3
Morgan, James, engineer, 65
Morwellham, 121, 124
Muirtown, 135
Munk, Capt Lionel, 313, 318
Mylne, Robert, engineer, 151-2, 209

Nantwich, 94, 103-4, 106, 178, 312
Napton, 126, 244-5
National Inland Navigation League, 300
National Trust, 315-16, 318, 323
National Water Authority (proposed), 331-2
National Waterways Restoration & Development Fund, 320
National Waterways Transport Association, 329-31, 334
Nationalisation of waterways, 136, 197, 234, 241, 260, 293-5, 301, 303ff
Navan, 94, 220
Navigation levels (mine canals), 31-2, 58, 82, 102
Navvies, 39-43, 74, 112, 151, 153, 258
Neath, 51, 164
Neath Canal, 112, 164, 304
Neath & Swansea Junct Canal, see Tennant Canal
Nene, River, 21, 25, 28, 64, 126-8, 144, 304
Netherton, 61, 98, 236, 243, 324
New Junction Canal, 183, 243, 270, 319, 333
Newark, 297, 305
Newburgh, 86, 88-9
Newbury, 23, 37, 90-1, 100, 200, 203
Newcastle & Carlisle Rly, 138
Newcastle under Lyme, 57
Newcastle upon Tyne, 20, 26-7
Newport (Gwent), 109, 156, 164
Newport (Salop), 169
Newport Pagnell Canal, 126, 171
Newry, 29, 178, 213, 261, 296
Newry Canal, 29-30, 92, 171, 178, 326; Ship Canal, 92, 222, 315
Newtown, 103, 322-3
North Eastern Rly, 248
North Staffordshire Rly, 262
North Wilts Canal, 92, 198, 210
Northampton, 126-8
Northwich, 184, 304
Norton Junct, 126, 279
Norwich, 205, 245, 327
Norwich & Lowestoft Navigation, 59, 129, 175, 204-5, 228
Nottingham, 23, 35, 121, 167, 292, 296-8, 302, 305, 311-12, 319

Nottingham Canal, 35, 46, 112, 167, 309
Nutbrook Canal, 167, 267

Oakham Canal, 128, 233
Oil, carried on canals, etc, 77, 277, 288, 301-2, 305-6, 314-15, 326, 334
Oldham, 159, 286
Omer, Thomas, engineer, 29, 46, 92-4, 213
Oulton Broad, 205
Ouse (Great) River, 21, 23, 25-6, 60, 131, 144, 246, 322
Ouse (Yorkshire) River, 22, 26-7, 59, 88, 107, 163, 185, 200, 251, 270, 304, 333
Outram, Benjamin, engineer, 44, 102, 114-15, 117, 124, 162
Owen, Richard, engineer, 92-3
Oxford 21, 55, 70, 85, 92, 108, 124, 126, 146, 171, 208-9, 243, 245, 271, 273, 308
Oxford-Burcot Commission, 208
Oxford Canal, 45-7, 57, 61, 71, 85-6, 109, 124, 126, 171, 177, 193-7, 209, 211, 225, 230, 243-6, 248-9, 253, 279, 298, 300, 310, 312, 324
Oxford, Worcester & Wolverhampton Rly, 155, 233, 248, 250, 277

Packhorses, 19-21, 30, 81
Paddington, 54, 55n, 120, 124, 126-7, 166, 201, 249, 263, 292
Page family, 203-4, 207
Paisley, 182, 185, 191
Parham, Adm Sir Frederick, 313, 316
Parkhead locks, 320-1
Parrett River, 140, 206
Passenger carrying on canals, etc, 21, 59, 103, 113, 127, 154, 166, 180-2, 185-94, 215, 223, 282, 300
Peak Forrest Canal, 43, 49, 55, 65, 72, 112, 115, 117, 160, 162-3, 194, 249, 257, 310, 319, 322-3
Pearce, E. L., surveyor-general, 29
Pearse, Rev G. M., author, 265
Peat, carried on canals, etc., 101, 203, 220
Peckham, 157-8
Perth, 138, 182
Peterborough, 21, 28
Phillips, John, author, 109, 150
Pick, Frank, 301
Pickering, Exuperius, inventor, 67
Pickfords, carriers, 59, 73-4, 120, 224
Pilotage, Act, Commission, 328-9
Pinkertons, contractors, 43-4
Pleasure boating, craft, trips, 17, 91, 136-7, 142, 180, 191, 219, 221, 239, 254-6, 267, 275, 299-300, 303, 307-10, 312, 317ff
Pontcysyllte, 102, 104-5, 134, 324
Pontypool, 109, 164
Poor Employment Act (1817), 51, 153

Port of London Authority, 158, 295, 335-6
Port Tennant, 164
Portsmouth, 102, 119, 174-5
Portsmouth & Arundel Canal, 51, 172, 174
Portumna, 213, 215
Potter, Richard, promoter, 271-2
Praed, William, promoter, 124
Pratt, E. A., author, 294
Preston, 86, 159, 185
Preston Brook, 82, 249, 333
Price, Sir Frank, 316, 329
Priestley, Joseph sen 86; jun author, 86,
    269
Public houses, 17, 53, 55-6, 61, 63, 75, 78,
    320, 325
Push-towing, 269, 326-7, 333

Quarter Sessions, powers of, 70, 207

Railway Amalgamation, Committee on
    (1872), 267
Railway & Canal Commission, 280
Railway & Canal Historical Society, 308
Railway & Canal Traffic Act (1854), 247,
    251n
Railway & Canal Traffic Act (1888), 251n,
    254, 261, 280, 305
Railway Commission, 226, 259, 280
Railway Executive Committee (1914), 295
Railway mania, 111, 223, 225, 228, 233,
    238, 241, 247-8, 250
Railway Rates & Fares, Committee on
    (1882), 267
Railways, competition from, 63, 69-70,
    73-5, 91, 102, 149, 154-6, 158, 175-8,
    185, 191, 197-8, 205, 217-54, 259-60,
    267-8, 270-3, 277, 282-3, 285, 288, 291,
    314-15, 326, 331, 334, 336
Railways, horse, see Tramroads
Ramsden's, Sir John, Canal, 57, 160
Reading, 21, 23, 37, 100, 171, 179, 200,
    203, 209
Regent's Canal, 51, 59, 63, 65, 68, 77, 80,
    126, 128, 194, 201, 227, 248, 254, 292,
    298, 306; dock, 298, 308, 310-11, 325-6
Regent's Park explosion, 77-8, 240, 254
Regional Water Authorities, 331
Regulation of Railways Act (1873), 247,
    259, 272
Remainder waterways, 319-20, 322-4
Rennie, John, engineer, 44, 46, 68, 91, 136,
    140, 142, 159-60
Reservoirs, see Water supplies
Reynolds family, promoters, etc, 49, 66,
    108, 169
Rhodes, Thomas, engineer, 215
Ribble River, 86, 88, 117, 159
Rievaulx Abbey Canals, 28
Ripon Canal, 163, 239
Roads and road transport, 18-21, 23, 26-7

30, 33, 36-7, 54, 62, 69-70, 72-3, 100,
    104, 118, 144, 172, 182, 185, 187, 189,
    203, 223, 241, 258, 296, 299, 305, 309,
    315-16, 326, 331, 333, 336. See also
    Turnpike trustees
Rochdale Canal, 46, 57, 89, 109, 112,
    159-61, 166, 194, 207, 225, 241, 243,
    248, 252, 282, 299, 304, 323
Rochester, 52-3, 127, 327
Rolt, L. T. C., author, 300, 303, 307, 313
Roman canals, 28
Roosky, 213, 215
Rother (Eastern) River, 204
Rother (Western) River, 299
Rotherham, 163, 268, 311, 326, 333
Rowland, Edward, inventor, 67
Royal Canal, 79, 113-14, 171, 188, 213,
    229, 303, 326
Royal Commission on Canals (1907-11),
    236, 260-2, 268, 291-5, 305, 330
Royal Commission on Canals, etc (Ireland)
    (1880), 261
Royal Commission on Transport (1930),
    296
Royal Military Canal, 119
Ruabon, 67, 103, 105
Rugby, 57, 245
Rufford branch, 88
Runcorn, 28, 46-7, 81-2, 107, 161, 205,
    207, 265, 282, 290, 312, 327
Runcorn & Weston Canal, 205, 243
Rushall Canal, 243
Rusholme Board of Survey, 309-10, 312-13

St Helens, 30
St Helens Canal, 309, 316. See also Sankey
    Brook
St Mullins, 94, 171
Salford, 30, 32, 285-6, 288
Salisbury, 100, 203
Salisbury & Southampton Canal, 51, 112,
    194
Salt, carried on canals, etc, 21, 59, 81-2,
    165, 204-5, 278, 288
Salwarpe River, 26, 207
Sankey Brook Navigation, 30. See also St
    Helens Canal
Sapperton, 48, 61, 90
Sea-going barges, 327-9, 335
Sea-sand, carried on canals, etc, 101, 174-5
Selby, 27, 88, 163, 327, 333
Selby Canal, 43, 88, 107, 163, 200, 251
Select Ctte on Nationalised Industries,
    331-3
Selly Oak, 96, 98
Semington, 91-2, 273
Severn bridge (rail), 155, 272
Severn & Canal Carrying Co, 277, 304
Severn Corridor scheme, 335
Severn River, 21, 26, 28, 58-60, 64, 81-2,

85-6, 89-90, 92, 95-6, 98, 103, 105, 109,
113, 126, 144, 146, 150, 152, 155-6,
169-71, 175, 191, 197, 200, 208-9, 211-13,
217, 250, 255, 261-2, 271, 274, 277-8,
292-3, 296, 301-3, 305-8, 311, 317, 319,
323, 334-5
Sewers, Commissioners of, 22
Shannon Harbour, 93, 213
Shannon River, 29, 93, 113, 171, 178-9,
187, 213-16, 221, 261, 299, 315, 325
Shardlow, 224, 297, 325
Sharpness and docks, 63, 152-3, 155-6, 293,
310, 312, 326-7
Sharpness New Docks Co, 299. See also
Gloucester & Berkeley Canal
Sheasby, Thomas, sen, engineer, 44
Sheffield Canal, 65, 163, 200, 228, 268
Sheffield & South Yorkshire Navigation,
60, 183, 268-70, 306, 308, 311, 316-17,
319, 326, 329, 331-3
Shrewsbury, 21, 49, 60, 103, 106, 169, 211,
323
Shrewsbury Canal, 33, 61, 66, 102, 112,
148, 169, 194, 238, 309
Shropshire Canal, 49, 66, 108, 169, 174,
194, 238, 325
Shropshire Union Canals, 46, 96n, 102,
144, 177, 193, 198, 228, 234, 238, 250,
255, 262, 270, 275, 288, 299, 302-3, 308,
310
Silkstone, 113, 163
Simcock, Samuel, engineer, 46
Simpson, John, engineer, 134
Skipton, 88
Skipwith, Thomas, promoter, 22, 199
Slateford aqueduct, 219
Slates, carried on canals, etc, 103, 123, 157
Sleaford Navigation, 247, 323
Slough branch, 243, 324
Smeaton, John engineer, 44, 46, 86, 93,
138
Smethwick, 98
Smith, Emma, author, 302
Smith, George, reformer, 75, 261, 264-5,
267
Soar River, 22, 199, 207, 292. See also
Loughborough Navigation
Somersetshire Coal Canal, 67, 71, 92, 117,
163, 247, 255
South Yorkshire County Council, 331, 333
South Yorks Rly & River Don Navigation,
228, 268
Southampton, 102, 111, 119, 143, 271
Sowerby Bridge, 89, 160, 323
Spalding, 202
Stafford, 82, 238, 262
Staffs & Worcs Canal, 35, 45, 54, 61, 65-6,
75, 78, 82, 85-6, 95-6, 98, 106, 108-9, 126,
155, 178, 194, 197, 211-12, 227, 235,
250, 261, 264, 274, 277, 306, 309, 318

Staffs & Worcs Canal Society, 318
Staines, 208-9, 211
Stainforth & Keadby Canal, 163, 199-200,
228, 268
Stamford Junction Canal project, 128
Standedge, 89, 102, 160-1
Stanley Ferry, 200, 330, 333
Stanlow, 288, 290
'Starvationers', 31, 58
Statistics, waterway, 330, 332, 334
Staunches, see Flash-locks
Steam boats, ships, tugs, 59-60, 63-4, 77,
134-5, 139, 143-4, 149, 151, 154, 156,
183-4, 191, 246, 251, 257, 260, 262,
269-70, 277-80
Steers, Thomas, engineer, 29-30, 46, 92
Stevens, Harry, canal owner, 316
Stirling, 182, 191
Stockton & Darlington Canal project, 175,
217
Stockton & Darlington Rly, 175-6, 217,
223, 225
Stockwith, 94, 163
Stoke Bruerne, 71, 312, 325
Stoke-on-Trent, 262
Stone, carried on canals, etc, 21, 28, 91,
113, 118, 123, 140-1, 167, 233, 299. See
also Slates
Stony Stratford, 126
Stop-locks, gates, 65, 163
Stoppages, on canals, 63
Stort River, 128, 309
Stour (Dorset) River, 142
Stour (Kent) River, 22
Stour (Suffolk) River, 60, 62, 245-6
Stour (Worcs) River, 26-7
Stourbridge, 27, 95
Stourbridge Canal, 36, 74, 95-6, 98, 109,
250, 309, 318
Stourbridge Extension Canal, 229, 233,
250, 309
Stourport, 54, 75, 82, 98, 109, 155, 211-12,
224, 250, 274, 293, 302, 323
Strabane Canal, 172, 296
Stratford-upon-Avon Canal, 35, 61, 92,
98, 112, 175, 178, 194, 199, 229, 233,
300, 315-16, 318, 323
Stratford-upon-Avon Canal Society, 315
Strood, 52
Stroud, 89-90, 217, 270-3
Stroudwater Navigation, 57, 60, 63, 89-90,
95, 126, 146, 152-3, 212, 217-18, 271,
273, 320, 323
Subsidence, affecting canals, 268, 311
Sudbury, 245-6
Suir River, 29
Sunday working, on canals, 224-5, 262
Surrey Iron Rly, 117, 127, 217
Sutherland's, Duke of, Canal, see
Donnington Wood Canal

Swale River, 28
Swansea, 35, 156, 164
Swansea Canal, 33-5, 49, 55, 73, 78, 112, 117, 164, 194, 255, 309
Swindon, 91-2, 270-1, 274
Swinton, 163, 311
Symington, William, inventor, 139

Tadcaster, 27, 163
Tamar River, 121, 123
Tame Valley Canal, 243
Tardebigge, 68, 100
Taunton, 57-8, 67, 111, 140-1, 206-7, 232-3
Tavistock Canal, 33, 121-4, 247
Teddington, 80, 295, 335
Tees River, 21, 144, 204
Telford, Thomas, engineer, 33, 44, 46, 60, 66, 102, 115, 133-4, 142, 153, 177-8, 211, 243
Tennant, George, promoter, 52, 164
Tennant Canal, 35, 51-2, 63, 164, 304
Tewkesbury, 21, 274, 307
Thames Conservancy, 211, 273, 304
Thames Head 64, 271
Thames & Medway Canal, 52-3, 127, 228
Thames River, 17, 20-3, 26, 37, 52, 57-9, 76, 80-2, 85-6, 89-92, 95, 100, 116, 124, 126-9, 131, 144, 155-7, 171-2, 191, 199-200, 203-4, 208-12, 217, 245, 252, 255, 262, 271, 273, 292, 295-6, 311, 323, 325, 328, 330-1, 334-5
Thames & Severn Canal, 26, 37, 46, 48-9, 51, 57, 61, 64, 71, 81, 90-2, 95, 108, 126, 146, 152, 155-6, 171, 209-12, 217, 255, 270-3, 299-300, 323
Thurlwood, 311
Thurston, E. Temple, author, 300
Timber, carried on canals, etc, 28, 91, 113, 157, 203; sold by canal, etc, companies, 72
Tinsley, 65, 163, 200, 319
Tipton, 96
Tiverton, 140-1, 232
Toll-keepers, 51, 55, 71, 75, 78, 80
Tolls, compensation, 36-7, 70-1, 126, 198, 243-4
Tone River, 26, 140, 199, 206-7
Topsham, 140-1, 146
Torksey, 28, 163, 167, 312, 330
Torrington Canal, 35, 66, 141
Towing, 59-63, 135, 154, 193-4, 226, 236, 306
Town & Country Planning Acts, 324
Towpaths, 18, 52, 60-2, 69, 102, 108, 135, 203, 211-12, 245, 319-20, 323, 325
Trail, John, 93
Tramroads, horse, 113-15, 117-18, 167, 175-6, 180, 223: Ashby Canal, 115;

Blisworth, 117, 124, 126; Brecknock & Abergavenny Canal, 115, 117; Caldon, 117; Coalbrookdale area, 115; Cromford & High Peak, 160, 175; Croydon, Merstham & Godstone, 127; Derby Canal 115: Gloucester & Cheltenham, 155; Hay, 34, 111, 117, Llanvihangel, etc, 34, 111, 115,; Marple, 49, 117; Monkland & Kirkintilloch, 117; Monmouthshire Canal, 115, 118; North-east 115; Northampton, 127-8; Oystermouth, 117; Peak Forest Canal, 115, 161; Preston, 117, 159; Ruabon, 105; Sirhowy, 175; Somersetshire Coal Canal, 117; Stratford & Moreton, 175; Stroud & Severn project, 217; Surrey Iron, 117, 127, 217
Transhipment centres, 236, 330
Transport, Dept, of, 136-7, 295-296, 300-2, 304-5, 313, 319, 328-9, 332, 335
Transport Act (1944) (Eire), 303
Transport Acts, (1947) 204, 303, 319; (1955) 309; (1968) 318-9, 326, 332; (1978) 332; (1981) 335
Transport on Water (TOW), 329
Trench incline, 148, 169
Trent & Mersey Canal, 31, 33, 38, 45, 57, 60-1, 68, 72, 81-2, 85-6, 103, 106-8, 117, 160, 163, 165, 177, 194, 199, 204-205, 224-5, 230-1, 249-51, 262, 270, 278, 292, 297, 308, 311
Trent River and Navigation, 21, 23, 26, 28, 31, 46, 57, 59, 71, 81-2, 92, 94-5, 113, 126-7, 160, 163, 167, 200. 207, 262, 270, 295-8, 302, 305-6, 308, 311, 319, 329-30, 335
Trent (Upper) Navigation, see Burton Navigation
Trevithick, Richard, engineer, 63, 217
Trew, John, engineer, 23, 146
Tring, 64, 124, 271
Trows, 21, 58, 89, 90, 211-12, 224
Tub-boats, 58-9, 115, 148, 169, 171, 174-5
Tullamore, 189, 220
Tunnels, canal, 39, 45-6, 60-1, 63, 224, 279; Armitage, 61; Berwick, 61; Blisworth, 124, 324; Braunston, 124, 324, 333; Butterley, 268; Cookley, 61; Crick, 333; Dudley, 96, 98, 320-1; Falkirk, 165; Fenny Compton, 279; Foulridge, 89, 333; Harecastle, 46, 61, 82, 84, 163, 177, 324; Hincaster, 159; Islington, 59, 61; King's Norton, 333; Lappal, 98; Morwelldown, 123-4; Newbold, 61; Preston Brook, 333; Sapperton, 48, 61, 90, 270-1; Standedge, 89, 102, 160-1; Strood, 52; Wast Hill, 333. See also Navigation levels
Turnpike trustees, attitude to canals, 36-7, 72, 118, 203

Tyne River, 20-1, 27, 30, 58, 113, 115, 117-19, 139, 144, 158, 175, 204, 217, 328
Tyrone Canal, 66, 171

UK Waterway Holidays Ltd., 325
Ulster Canal, 58, 178-9, 213, 261, 296
Ulverston Canal, 43, 146, 157
Upper Avon Navigation, Trust, 316
Upton, John, engineer, 153
Ure River, 163, 199, 309
Utoxeter, 57, 230-1

Vernon-Harcourt, L. F., engineer, 67, 291

Waggon-boats, 117, 173, 180
Wain, G. F., hirer, 300
Wakefield, 23, 27, 36, 163, 200, 225, 251, 269, 319, 328, 330
Walker, James, engineer, 135
Walker, T. A., contractor, 286
Walsall, 100, 235
Wantage, 91
Warrington, 28, 180, 282
Warwick, 178
Warwick & Birmingham Canal, 98, 126, 178, 227, 243, 249, 268, 298
Warwick & Napton Canal, 126, 227, 249, 268, 298
Water, sale or supply by canal, etc, companies, 69, 93, 175, 247, 309-10, 317
Water Act (1973), 331
Water Space Amenity Commission, 331
Water supplies, reservoirs, etc, 19, 22-3, 26, 37-8, 58, 63-8, 90, 96, 105, 108, 135, 140, 151, 154, 164, 174-5, 197, 207, 212, 236, 273, 279, 322, 324
Waterways, 325
Waterways museums, 71, 312, 325
Waterways News, 325
Waterway Recovery Group, 320
Waterways World, 325
Watford (Herts), 304
Watford (Northants), 127
Watt, James, engineer, 138
Waveney River, 205
Wear River, 115, 118, 144
Weaver Navigation, 27, 30, 58, 60, 68, 81-82, 103, 165, 184, 198-9, 204-5, 243, 262, 270, 274, 278, 293, 302, 308, 317, 319, 326, 333
Wednesbury, 85, 95-6, 98, 235
Wedgwood, Josiah, promoter, 32-3, 38-9, 46, 81, 108, 180
Weedon, 121, 126
Weighing machines, for boats, 71
Weldon, Robert, engineer, 67-8
Welland River, 21, 25, 28, 128, 202, 327
Wellington (Salop), 49, 238
Welsh Development Agency, 322
Welshpool, 103, 111, 320, 322, 325

Wendover, 126
Westall, George, author, 299-300
Weston (Salop), 103, 105
Weston Canal, 205
Weston Point, 63, 204, 205; docks, 205, 278, 310, 312, 326-7
Wey & Arun Junction Canal, 50, 127, 172, 174, 211, 247, 254-5, 320, 323
Wey River, 23, 28, 100, 172, 180, 247, 304, 316
Weybridge, 100, 172
Whaley Bridge, 160
Wharfe River, 27, 163
Wharves, public, 54-5, 59
Wherries, 58
Whitaker's, carriers, 327-8, 330
Whitchurch (Salop), 104
Whitworth, Robert, engineer, 44, 46, 86, 88, 90, 92, 128, 138, 140
Wigan, 86, 88-9, 159, 171, 180, 229
Wilden Ferry, 81-2, 297
Wilkinson, John, ironmaster, 59
Williams, Edward Leader, sen, engineer, 277-8
Williams, Sir Edward Leader, engineer, 258, 278–9, 284
Willow Wren Carrying Co, 306, 317, 326
Wilts & Berks Canal, 91-2, 155-6, 171, 198, 210-11, 241, 247, 270, 272-4, 323
Windsor, 21, 209
Winsford, 81, 262
Wirral canal line, 103, 288
Wisbech, 144, 327
Wisbech Canal, 64, 299
Witham River, 21, 28, 41, 128, 163, 233, 274
Woking, 247
Wolverhampton, 36, 66, 100, 235, 262, 277, 293, 306
Wolverton, 121, 124
Woodhouse, John, engineer, 153
Woodfitt, Susan, author, 302
Worcester, 21, 96, 150, 155, 211-13, 274, 277, 293, 302, 305, 335
Worcester Bar, 65, 96
Worcester & Birmingham Canal, 36, 64-5, 68, 96, 98, 100, 109, 112, 155-6, 178, 197, 210-12, 224, 243, 248, 250, 261-2, 267, 302, 309
Wordsley, 318, 320
Worsbrough, 163
Worsley, 28, 30-2, 58, 81-2, 161, 282
Wrexham, 103-4
Wye River, 26-7, 60, 108
Wyrley & Essington Canal, 66, 112, 198, 235

Yare River, 205, 304
Yarmouth, 205, 245
York, 22-3, 27, 163